THE WAY OF THE (MODERN) WORLD

The Way of the (Modern) World

Or, Why It's Tempting to Live As If God Doesn't Exist

CRAIG M. GAY

William B. Eerdmans Publishing Company • Grand Rapids

Paternoster Press • Carlisle, Cumbria

Regent College Publishing • Vancouver

© 1998 Wm. B. Eerdmans Publishing Co.

Published jointly 1998 by
Wm. B. Eerdmans Publishing Co.
255 Jefferson Ave. S.E., Grand Rapids, Michigan 49503
and by
Paternoster Press
P.O. Box 300, Carlisle, Cumbria CA3 0QS U.K.
and by
Regent College Publishing
an imprint of Regent College Bookstore
5800 University Boulevard, Vancouver, B.C. V6T 2E4

Printed in the United States of America

03 02 01 00 99 98   7 6 5 4 3 2 1

Library of Congress Cataloging-in-Publication Data

Gay, Craig M.
        The way of the (modern) world: Or, why it's tempting to live
as if God doesn't exist / Craig M. Gay.
            p.   cm.
        Includes bibliographical references and index.
        ISBN 0-8028-4362-X (pbk.: alk. paper)
            1. Christianity and Culture.   2. Secularism.   I. Title.
        BR115.C8G335   1998
        261 — dc21   98-11275
                                                             CIP

British Library Cataloguing-in-Publication Data

A catalogue record for this book is available from the British Library

ISBN 0-85364-890-5

Regent College Publishing ISBN 1-57383-122-0

Contents

Foreword

Once upon a time in the West worldliness and separation were code words among gospel people. Worldliness meant smoking, drinking, ballroom dancing, novel reading, theatre- and movie-going, makeup for women, deodorant for men, mixed bathing for adults, and late nights for children. Separation meant eschewing all the above, being frugal at home, ignoring fashion, fleeing from luxury, being in church several times on Sunday, and building life around Bible study, personal evangelism, missionary support, and perhaps some local philanthropy. Most exponents of this form of pietism worked hard, looked after their families, and were warm-hearted and generous to those they helped, but their interests were narrow. As those in the world but not of it, they tried to have as little to do with it as possible. They spoke of a coming apostasy and breakdown of community life, and watched fatalistically to see if it was yet happening, while debating whether taking out insurance would be an act of faith or of unbelief. What I describe must sound light years away to the modern reader, but in my youth it was all going strong; I remember how it bemused me when I became a Christian at age 18.

The past half-century, however, has seen swift social change in the West, due to the burgeoning technology of transportation and communication, the computer revolution and the knowledge explosion, the rocketing development of the advertising and entertainment industries, the coming of the multinational industrial juggernauts and the international money market and much else, plus the abandoning of national

Christian commitments in favor of materialistic atheism masquerading as religious relativism and inclusivism. Where Marxism is execrated no less than where it is embraced, secular collectivism has taken over, and the children of Western pietism are realizing that they are victims of this process, in that post-Christian assumptions about the value and significance of people and things, as mediated by the media, the press, the school system and the arts, and as modeled by politicians, entertainers, and other public figures, keep pulling their thinking out of Christian shape. Analyzing the antitheses between the historic Christian and the modern Western mindsets, and articulating a countercultural rather than a conformist way for gospel people to take their place in today's world, is thus badly needed: without it, deep-level worldliness cannot be avoided. There is far more to worldliness today than was dreamed of at the fag-end of the Christendom culture of the West fifty years ago, and a far more radical view of separation from the world has now to be thought out.

In this urgent task Craig Gay's learned, lucid, wide-ranging, deep-diving chapters impressively lead the way. I for one am very grateful for them, and I predict that others will be too.

J. I. Packer

Acknowledgments

"Of the making of books," the writer of Ecclesiastes observed (Eccl. 12:12), "there is no end. . . ." Still, I have to confess that I am glad that the study you have in hand has come to something of an end, and I would like to thank many of the people who made this possible. I have taken the study's foundational insight, that the pervasive secularity of modern social life is most tellingly interpreted in terms of "practical atheism," from Klaus Bockmuehl, late Professor of Theology and Ethics at Regent College (Vancouver), with whom I had the privilege to study between 1981 and 1983. There are a great many of us, I know, who are deeply indebted to Dr. Bockmuehl both for the substance of his instruction and for the spirit in which he taught. Klaus managed to convey the tremendous urgency and importance of theology in the life of the Church — and in the life of the world — while at the same time reminding us that evangelical theology must always be *modest*, wholly dependent upon the God who speaks. I learned a great deal about the joy of being called to the work of theology during my brief association with Dr. Bockmuehl, and I can only hope that the present study communicates something of this same spirit.

The insight that modern secular culture discloses a kind of "practical atheism" complements that of another one of my teachers, Peter L. Berger (University Professor, Boston University), who emphasized the "methodological atheism" built into modern institutions and habits of thought. It was my privilege to study with Professor Berger between 1985 and 1989 at Boston University's Institute for the Study of

Economic Culture, and Peter's name and ideas will appear frequently in the following study.

Several of my colleagues at Regent College read an early draft of this study and offered a number of helpful suggestions for its revision. I am particular grateful to Eugene Peterson, Jim Packer, and Ross Douglas for their substantive input, as well as to Jim Houston, Edwin Hui, and Walter Wright for their encouragement. I also want to thank Jonathan Dent, Doug Farrow, Stan Biggs, Ron Rittgers, and Jonathan Mills for their willingness to wade through the early draft, as well as all of the students I've conscripted to read and comment on the study over the last several years in a Regent College course called "Secularization and Christian Faith in Modern Society." I am also very grateful to my friends David Stewart, Bill Reimer, and Harvey Guest, who encouraged me to persevere with the manuscript at one crucial juncture. My sincere thanks also go out to Mary Manson-Hennig for carefully proofing the manuscript, to my teaching and research assistants of the last several years — Dave Benedict, Kevin Reimer, Sean Gallagher, George Sweetman, Calvin Townsend, Jonathan Reilly, and Sam Keator — as well as to all those at Wm. B. Eerdmans who have labored so hard to bring this study to press.

Finally, I want to thank my wife, Julie, for her patience and tireless support on this and many other projects, but more importantly for her friendship and unmitigated commitment to making a home for the six of us. I am, in truth, *very* thankful for her.

Craig M. Gay

Introduction

The fear of the LORD is a fountain of life,
　　turning a [person] from the snares of death.

(Proverbs 14:27 NIV)

The kings of the earth take their stand and the rulers gather together
　　against the LORD and against his Anointed One.
"Let us break their chains," they say, "and throw off their fetters."

(Psalm 2:2-3 NIV)

It is said that ideas have consequences, and this is undoubtedly true. Still, it seems that the ideas with the most profound consequences are frequently taken for granted. They are the ideas that lie just behind conscious thought, providing a kind of foundation for the deliberations of everyday life. They are the ideas that define "the way things are" and demarcate the possibilities of life. Indeed, the more consequential an idea is, the more likely that it is deeply embedded in institutions and traditions and habits of thought. This is why the most important ideas are often the most difficult to weigh and to reflect upon. To say that ideas have consequences, then, should not be taken to mean that it is ever very easy to identify the ideas that lie behind the consequences that define our own social and cultural circumstances.

The difficulty of distinguishing the ideas behind our social and cultural circumstances is, it seems to me, particularly perplexing in the modern — and now purportedly "postmodern" — context. On the one hand, contemporary society and culture are quite obviously animated by a number of uniquely successful and powerful ideas, ideas which have given rise to an explosion of scientific knowledge, to marvelous techniques and technologies, to huge transnational corporations and global markets, to the expansive social and political aspirations of sovereign nation-states, and to a seemingly invincible faith in the possibilities of self-fulfilling individuality. And yet it is probably also true that most of us are only dimly aware of the suppositions that lie beneath the surface of these remarkable achievements. Beyond our familiarity with terms like "freedom," "democracy," "progress," "science," and "nature," it is easy to lose sight of the deep ideas and assumptions that underlie these concepts and that animate contemporary society and culture at a basic level. Yet to the extent that the ideational basis of our society and culture has become obscure to us, we probably have also become somewhat obscure to ourselves. For our own individual biographies are, after all, the most important consequences of the ideas and assumptions that underlie contemporary society and culture.

One of the principal aims of this study is to try — in spite of the difficulty — to disclose some of the basic ideas and assumptions that animate contemporary society and culture. The thesis we will advance in the following chapters is that one of the most consequential ideas embedded in modern institutions and traditions and habits of thought is theological. Stated bluntly, it is the assumption that even if God exists he is largely irrelevant to the real business of life. To put this somewhat more tactfully, contemporary society and culture so emphasize human potential and human agency and the immediate practical exigencies of the here and now, that we are for the most part tempted to go about our daily business in this world without giving God much thought. Indeed, we are tempted to live as though God did not exist, or at least as if his existence did not practically matter. In short, one of the most insidious temptations fostered within contemporary secular society and culture, a temptation rendered uniquely plausible by the ideas and assumptions embedded within modern institutional life, is the temptation to *practical atheism*.

Succumbing to this temptation is obviously of rather dire consequence to the Church as well as to other expressly religious institutions. Yet it is also, we will contend, of very far-reaching consequence to truly human existence. For when we lose sight of God, we also lose sight of ourselves. It is the thought of God, after all, that gives substance to words like "truth," "freedom," "justice," and "persons": words which lend substance and meaning to human life. Without the thought of God such notions are empty or, at best, only convenient fictions. A completely secular society is, therefore, not simply "godless," but impersonal and inhumane as well.

Yet because practical atheism is so deeply embedded in the central institutional realities of our society and culture — in political life, in science and technology, in the economy, and in the production and transmission of culture — the threat that it poses to the Church and to truly human existence in general is not always immediately evident. Indeed, practical atheism has become so disarmingly attractive in the contemporary situation that we have actually embraced it within our churches, and not only in the so-called "secular theologies" of the last generation, but more significantly in the ordinary practice of Christian ministry. The contemporary mental climate is such that faith and prayer are rather routinely eclipsed by the practical efficacy of expertise and technique. As a result of this, we find ourselves in the difficult position of needing now to evict certain modern — and now "postmodern" — ideas and assumptions from our churches, and, indeed, to dislodge them from our hearts. Yet evict them we must if we are to be truly related to the God of the gospel and if we are to act as "salt and light" within an increasingly impersonal and inhumane culture.

In But Not of Which World?

Considering the threat that distinctively modern ideas and assumptions pose to our churches involves us in the paradoxical problem of trying to determine just what Jesus meant when he prayed (in John 17:13ff.) that his disciples should remain *in* the world but that they should not be *of* it. Concerning the first preposition "in," Jesus draws a parallel (v. 18) between his having been sent *in* to the world by the Father and his own sending of his disciples *in* to the world. From this we might conclude that Christians are called to exhibit, following Jesus's example, God's redemptive love *in* the world. And yet we are also strictly warned (as, for example, in 1 John 2:15ff.) *not* to "love the world or anything in the world" and that "if anyone loves the world, the love of the Father is not in him." And so, in saying that we are to be *in* the world but not *of* it, Jesus seems to have called us both to love the world and yet not to love the world at the same time. Resolving this peculiar paradox has never been easy. More than a few Christians have surrendered the attempt altogether and have opted instead for one or the other of the apparently contradictory prepositions, either losing themselves in worldly affairs or remaining so aloof from the world that they render the gospel of little actual import to life in the world. Some of the most bitter and divisive theological battles of this last century have been waged over this issue. The protracted "fundamentalist-modernist" controversy, for example, often saw Christians on either side of the conservative/liberal divide castigating each other either for being *of* the world as well as being *in* it or for not really being *in* the world at all. "Liberals" have thus been regularly accused by "conservatives" of collapsing the gospel into a merely social and political agenda; and "conservatives" have been routinely ridiculed by "liberals" for being obscurantists, completely out of touch with social and political reality. And yet perhaps the crux of the problem lies in how easy it is to lose sight of the *object* that makes sense of the prepositions "in" and "of," namely, *the world*.

If we are "conservative," we have probably tended to think of "the world" — and hence "worldliness" — in terms of temptations to various kinds of dissipation and to personal, and particularly sexual, immorality. If we are "liberal" in disposition, we have perhaps conceived of "the world" in terms of socio-structural evils such as racism or oppressive political-economic systems, and of "worldliness" as complicity in these evils. Both views are certainly correct. Personal immorality and socio-political injustices are indeed worldly evils to be condemned and avoided. But what if it can be shown that both the "conservative" and the "liberal" positions, while partly correct, actually miss the heart of the matter? What if the essence of "the world" — and hence of "worldliness" — is not personal immorality and/or social injustice as such, but is instead an *interpretation of reality* that essentially excludes the reality of God from the business of life? One of the purposes of our study is to argue just this point, and to contend that "the world" that Christians are called to be *in* but not *of* is, in effect, an interpretation of the realm of human affairs that places far too much emphasis upon human agency and far too little (if any) upon God's. As we will see, such an interpretation is *very* deeply embedded in contemporary political, technological, economic, and cultural institutions. Indeed, a kind of atheism has been literally *built into* the central institutional realities of modern societies. While the reasons for this will be explored in some detail in subsequent chapters, the point to make here at the outset is simply that the most insidious temptations to "worldliness" today do not necessarily come in the form of enticements to sexual dissipation, or even to complicity in socio-political oppression, but rather in the form of the suggestion that it is possible — and indeed "normal" and expedient — to go about our daily business in the world without giving much thought to God. Under modern, and now "postmodern" conditions, in other words, "the world" is an interpretation of human life that is largely void of the *living* God, and "worldliness" is characterized by practical atheism.

"The World" in the New Testament

The suggestion that "the world" is an *interpretation* of human affairs that excludes the reality of God may seem to support the notion — voiced most recently by the theorists of "postmodernity" — that all social worlds are always only interpretations of changing human circumstances, and that "reality" is always, in effect, "socially constructed." But this is not what is meant. Rather, the point is simply that it is possible for us to *imagine* our world in such a way that we ignore the *real* reality of God's gracious presence within it. The New Testament's use of the term "world" makes this quite clear.

The New Testament Greek term for "world" is *cosmos* (κόσμος). In classical usage *cosmos* originally denoted "building" and "construction," but it eventually came to mean the "order of things" in the largest possible sense, a meaning readily recognizable in the English terms "cosmic" and "cosmology." *Cosmos* has a number of related meanings in the New Testament.[1] Consistent with classical usage, *cosmos* can mean heaven and earth in their entirety, as in Acts 17:24, where Paul speaks of the "God who made *the world* and everything in it." *Cosmos* can also mean the

---

1. See the entry "Earth" in *New International Dictionary of New Testament Theology*, vol. 1, ed. Colin Brown (Grand Rapids, MI: Zondervan, 1975), 524ff.; see also Rudolf Bultmann, *Theology of the New Testament*, vol. 2, trans. Kendrick Grobel (New York: Charles Scribner's Sons, 1955), particularly the section entitled "The World and Man" in chapter 2, 15ff.

specific place or sphere of human life, as in Matt. 4:8, where Jesus is offered "all the kingdoms of *the world* and their splendor." Even more specifically, *cosmos* occasionally denotes the sphere of fallen humanity at enmity with God. This is particularly true in the writings of the apostle John, where *cosmos* is often used to describe the world of humanity in rebellion against the Father and utterly opposed to the work of the Son. "If *the world* hates you," Jesus is said to have told his disciples in John 15:18ff., "keep in mind that it hated me first. If you belonged to *the world,* it would love you as its own. As it is, you do not belong to *the world,* but I have chosen you out of *the world.* That is why *the world* hates you." Evangelical theologian Oliver O'Donovan has described "the world" in this latter sense as a falsely structured reality exhibiting an unreal continuity and coherence. "'The world' . . . ," O'Donovan writes, "is not the real and good world that God has made, nor any other real world, but a fantasy world of sinful imagination, a nothingness which will destroy us if we love it simply because it is nothingness and offers nothing on which we may nourish ourselves."[2]

As O'Donovan's comments indicate, "the world" is a human construction. It represents a kind of false order that we construct for ourselves in the place of God's good creation. Indeed, the *cosmos* is something we must continually reconstruct and maintain for ourselves in the face of threats posed to its unreal continuities and coherences by the *real* reality of created order and particularly by the reality of creation's Creator. But how is this possible? How is it possible for us to create and then to maintain a falsely structured reality with continuities and coherences that are unreal? Although the answers to these questions are ultimately shrouded in the mystery of freedom, suffice it here to say that our construction and maintenance of the *cosmos* require us to lower our sights, metaphysically speaking, and to pretend that the causal continuities of space and time interpret reality without remainder — that is, that the sorts of things we are able to observe in the ordinary course of events circumscribe the boundaries of the possible. Our construction of "the world," in other words, is often premised upon the assumption that we are capable of comprehending reality in its totality, that we are capable of rendering it stable and predictable, and that we are capable — at least in principle — of making reality work for us. This comes more or less naturally for us, for

2. Oliver O'Donovan, *Resurrection and Moral Order: An Outline for Evangelical Ethics* (Grand Rapids, MI: Eerdmans, 1986), 227.

when it is viewed from within, "the world" appears to be all that there is: the *cosmos*, the sum-total of reality. Indeed, it is the very nature of "the world" to prevent us from recognizing the existence of anything beyond sensible and temporal regularities.[3] Although the plausibility of this narrowing of our field of vision owes in part to the operations of human reason, it is also a matter of selfish convenience. For once we have reduced reality to a "world" of things and objects, which is the end-product of this convenient fiction, we can begin to exert our will over reality, and we can begin to act "as gods" within it.

The New Testament asserts that our construction and maintenance of "the world" is impelled ultimately by fallen human pride, by our rebellious struggle for autonomy, and by our grasping after a kind of godlike mastery over the world and over each other. To the extent that the creation can be rendered a world of "things" to be exhaustively comprehended by human reason, the desired mastery appears — at least from the perspective of "the world" — to be both possible and plausible. This is why the apostle describes "the world" in terms of "darkness," but then goes on to suggest that fallen humanity *loves* this darkness and *hates* the light of the Gospel (John 3:16ff.). For the "darkness" does not refer to blindness as such, but instead to a blindness that is *willed*, that is, to a kind of blindness that does not understand itself to be blind, but on the contrary believes that it sees and that it comprehends reality in its entirety.

It is important to stress that our sinful construction of "the world" does not preclude religious understanding. On the contrary, it simply requires that the object of religious understanding be subject to more or less "natural" regularities. The Pharisees' use of the Law in Jesus' day provides a salient example of this. By rendering *Torah* perfunctorily, and in terms of more or less predictable causes and effects, the Pharisees sought to establish control over the religious life of Israel. In seeking to maintain this control, however, they neutralized the possibility of having any real encounter with the living God, and it was the deliberate constriction of their understanding for the sake of control that prevented the Pharisees from recognizing the Christ when he came. Needless to say, the deliberate constriction of understanding for the sake of

3. This point is made quite assiduously by Glenn Tinder in his recent work, *The Political Meaning of Christianity: The Prophetic Stance, An Interpretation* (San Francisco: HarperSanFrancisco, 1991), 39-40.

control still prevents many of our contemporaries — "religious" though they may well be — from recognizing Jesus as the Christ.

Because our humanly constructed "world" is ultimately illusory, however, it is exceedingly fragile and must continually be protected from the light of divine intervention. For the light of the Scriptures and of the Incarnation exposes the narrowness and unreality of the continuities and coherences of our humanly constructed darkness for what they really are — that is, as simply *fake* — thereby exploding our sinful bid for autonomy and mastery. It is not at all surprising, then, that "the world" acted to kill Jesus as quickly as it did; nor that the gospel of Jesus Christ continues to look foolish from the perspective of the "wisdom of this world" (1 Cor. 1:20ff.). Finally, it is hardly surprising that the authors of the New Testament refrain from using the term *cosmos* to describe the future redeemed creation, describing it instead in terms of the "kingdom" of God. For the term *cosmos*, or order *as such*, carries the insidious connotation of a conception of order that excludes the Creator of order, a ploy which is the very essence of "worldliness" and of human rebellion (cf. Rom. 1:18ff.). When, in the future, the world is redeemed, it will not be known as *cosmos* but as the *Kingdom* of God under the Lordship of Christ.[4]

In speaking of the New Testament's understanding of "the world" as a human construction we collide, as indicated above, with one of the central insights of modern secular social theory, namely, that "reality" is socially constructed.[5] What passes for "reality" in society, in other words, is something that we determine and construct together with others. We decide, more or less deliberately, how our world is to be understood and interpreted, who we are and how we fit into the world, what is important and why, and, conversely, what is safe to ignore and neglect. This socially constructed "reality" is held together, furthermore, by way of a whole host of assumptions which we take largely for granted, assumptions which

---

4. We note that the agency and sovereignty implied in the phrase "the Kingdom of God" illustrates a rather striking difference between early Christian and classical Greek thought. For while Greek thought aspired — and continues to aspire — to a rational understanding of cosmic *order*, Christian thought aspires instead to the reconciliation of the *creation*, including humanity, to its *Creator* and its Lord. See H. Sasse, "κοσμέω, κόσμος, κόσμιος, κοσμικός," in G. Kittel (ed.), *Theological Dictionary of the New Testament*, vol. 3 (Grand Rapids, MI: Eerdmans, 1965), 867ff.

5. See, for example, Peter L. Berger and Thomas Luckmann, *The Social Construction of Reality: A Treatise in the Sociology of Knowledge* (New York: Penguin, 1967).

provide a framework for "making sense" of our social environment. Taken together these assumptions form the stock of knowledge that enables us to know and to tell each other who we are and what in the world is "real."

As we mentioned at the outset, we do not often reflect on the validity of our socially constructed "reality." Indeed, we go to great lengths to avoid this kind of reflection because it is difficult and only raises disturbing questions about matters which are much more comfortably left unexamined. The truth that one's life does not consist in the abundance of possessions, for example, is not easily digested in the context of modern consumer culture. That it is impossible to lengthen our lives by worrying about them is another truth best left unmentioned in the context of the contemporary fascination with modern medical technology. And yet the importance — at least for Christians — of periodically subjecting our social "reality" to critical examination should by now be clear given our discussion of "the world" and of "worldliness." For if "the world" tends, finally, to be an interpretation of order, or *cosmos*, that essentially excludes the reality of the living God, then "worldliness" will consist in basic assumptions about our lives that either explicitly or implicitly neglect God's agency in them, assumptions which we probably take largely for granted. If recent sociological studies of the process called "secularization" are at all correct, this kind of neglect of God is one of the more striking characteristics of modern society and culture.

The Modern World

While modern societies and the processes by which they have become modern have been characterized in any number of ways, American sociologist Peter Berger formulated a very concise definition of "modernity" a number of years ago with which it may be helpful to begin. Berger defined modernity in terms of "the institutional and cultural concomitants of economic growth under the conditions of sophisticated technology."[6] The institutional features of modernity to which Berger and others commonly refer include the modern nation-state, the modern scientific and technological establishments, capitalism and/or so-

6. Peter L. Berger, *Pyramids of Sacrifice: Political Ethics and Social Change* (Garden City, NY: Anchor, 1976), 34.

cialism, the mass media, and modern higher education, all of which operate within the enormously complex environment of the modern city. The "cultural concomitants" most often discussed under the heading of modernity, furthermore, include the characteristically modern fascination with technique and with technical domination, the pervasive bureaucratization of modern institutional life, the modern preoccupation with planning for the future combined with antipathy toward the "traditional" past, the modern proclivity toward individualism, and the curiously modern penchant for introspection and narcissism.[7]

While we will have occasion to discuss these various features of modern society and culture in greater detail in the following chapters, we need only note here that the crucial theme that runs through the list of the institutional and cultural concomitants of economic growth under the conditions of sophisticated technology is that of a particular kind of *control*. While striving for control over the world characterizes worldliness *as such*, the desire to maintain autonomous *control* over reality by rational-technical means is particularly central to the modern world. Put somewhat differently, we might say that a modern society is one in which the prevailing conception of the human task in the world is that of mastery by way of systematic manipulation. As Berger has noted:

> Modernity means (in intention if not in fact) that men take control over the world and over themselves. *What previously was experienced as fate now becomes an arena of choices.* In principle, there is the assumption that all human problems can be converted into technical problems, and if the techniques to solve certain problems do not as yet exist, then they will have to be invented. The world becomes ever more "makeable."[8]

Following closely upon this emphasis on control, a second characteristically modern theme is *secularity*. For once the range of human

7. See, for example, Peter L. Berger, *Facing Up to Modernity: Excursions into Society, Politics, and Religion* (New York: Basic Books, 1977); James Davison Hunter has also provided a nice survey of sociological analysis and criticism of modernity in an essay entitled "The Modern Malaise," in James Davison Hunter and Stephen C. Ainlay (eds.), *Making Sense of Modern Times: Peter L. Berger and the Vision of Interpretive Sociology* (New York: Routledge & Kegan Paul, 1986), 76-100.

8. Berger, *Pyramids of Sacrifice*, 20.

responsibilities for controlling the world has been fully delimited, there turns out to be very little room — and indeed very little need — left for God. As Martin Buber suggested in an essay entitled "The Eclipse of God," the reality of God has essentially been overshadowed for many modern people by their hugely inflated estimation of human potential.[9] The most significant consequence of modernity's inflated stress upon human agency and rational-technical control, then, is that many aspects of modern social life have been quite thoroughly secularized. This secularization is evident in modern political life, in scientific and technological work, in modern economic systems, and even in the production and transmission of modern culture. All of the central spheres of modern social and cultural life are, for the most part, both theoretically and practically atheistic.

A third characteristically modern theme, not surprising given the largely secular stress upon taking control of the world, is *anxiety*. The vast expansion of human responsibility in and for the world, while liberating us from the purportedly suffocating weight of such things as tradition and religion, has turned out to be a heavy burden. Trembling beneath the weight of this burden, we have together become, as Peter Berger captured it so aptly a number of years ago, "a very nervous Prometheus."[10] Indeed, modernity's secularization of the world for the sake of human control has made us ever more acutely aware of how much we have yet to learn about how the world works and, at the same time, of how desperately and urgently we need this knowledge to prevent our world from spinning out of our control.

Modernity's secularization of social life has also left us peculiarly vulnerable to what religious historian Mircea Eliade called the "terror of history,"[11] that is, to the terrifying necessity of having to create our own meanings and purposes in the world in the absence of revelation and without the aid of any kind of religious understanding. Now that Nature, the gods, and even the God of the Bible are not permitted to tell us who we are any more, we are left to try to make sense of who we are only on the basis of our own accomplishments and in the light

9. Buber cited in Thomas F. Torrance, *God and Rationality* (Oxford: Oxford University Press, 1971), 29.

10. Peter L. Berger, *The Heretical Imperative: Contemporary Possibilities of Religious Affirmation* (Garden City, NY: Anchor, 1979), 20ff.

11. See Mircea Eliade, *Cosmos and History: The Myth of the Eternal Return*, trans. Willard R. Trask (New York: Harper Torchbooks, 1959), 139ff.

of our own historical striving. Eliade observed that, unlike archaic humans, "modern man can be creative only insofar as he is historical; in other words, all creation is forbidden him except that which has its source in his own freedom; and, consequently, everything is denied him except the freedom to make history by making himself."[12] While the modern freedom to make history by making ourselves is exhilarating, it is also profoundly frightening and disturbing, especially in light of the awesome power of modern technology. Like Cain, it seems that we have been condemned to be itinerant wanderers in the world, always seeking but never really able to find rest, always learning but never really able to understand who we are. Unlike Cain, however, we possess portentous technical "know-how," including the ability to construct and employ weapons of mass destruction.[13]

Modern Worldliness

Of course, it is not difficult to trace a connection between the New Testament's understanding of "worldliness" and our modern obsession with taking technical-rational control over the natural and social worlds. Indeed, "modernity" may actually be defined in terms of its worldliness. For although the temptation to worldliness is obviously not new, the extent to which modern societies provide structural and institutional support for a practically atheistic view of life is quite remarkable. Perhaps at no other time in history has the structural coherence of a social order depended less upon religious and/or theological understanding than it does today in modern societies. The secularity of modern institutional life helps to explain the unprecedented number of self-consciously atheistic social movements — positivism, social Darwinism, various kinds of secular humanism, Marxism, etc. — that have arisen over the course of the last several centuries. More importantly, however, the secularity of modern institutional life helps to explain why a kind of *tacit* or *practical* atheism has become increasingly plausible even for those of us who are not

12. Ibid., 156.

13. See Romano Guardini, *The End of the Modern World: A Search for Orientation*, trans. Joseph Theman and Herbert Burke (1956; Chicago: Henry Regnery Company, 1968), 100ff.

self-consciously atheistic. Under the banner of human abilities and human potential, modernity appears to render a uniquely potent form of worldliness plausible and even attractive, one in which the temptation to practical atheism is so subtle as to be all but irresistible.

As indicated earlier, the great attraction of modern worldliness has caused even Christian churches to become so infatuated with "this-worldly" existence that they have actually sought, on a number of occasions, to reinterpret the Christian religion to suggest that the whole point of the gospel is to facilitate human control over the world. The themes of human autonomy and of taking rational control over the world, for example, were pivotal within the "liberal" Protestant theology of the last century. Conservative evangelicals have taken up these themes most recently as they have become increasingly fascinated with the possibility of taking rational-technical control over the growth and management of conservative churches.

And there is every reason to believe that modern "worldliness" will continue to present itself — with the full force and backing of modernity's central institutions — as the only responsible way forward into the future, and as the only reasonable way to understand the human situation. Thus, while the Church traditionally posited a distinction between the "sacred" and the "secular" in order to relativize the importance of this world over and against the paramount importance of *the world to come*, the conditions of modern social life tempt us to reverse this order, and encourage us to locate all of our aspirations in *this world*. Indeed, from the perspective of modernity, the traditional Christian concern for otherworldliness is seen to be escapist and irresponsible.

The Way of the (Modern) World

The coincidence of the New Testament's understanding of "the world" and "worldliness" and the sorts of issues commonly discussed in sociological circles under the heading of "secularization" is the reason the following essay on the secularity of modern society and culture is entitled "the way of the modern world." "The world" here refers to a particular construction of a reality which occasionally is explicitly hostile, but more commonly simply *indifferent*, to the existence and reality of God. "Secularization" refers to the process in which various sectors of modern social life have been emptied of theological substance and have ceased to need even the concept of God to function reasonably smoothly and "normally."

The following chapters represent attempts to connect these ideas by looking at the ways in which secularity has become deeply entrenched in modern institutional life. We are concerned to discover how and why it is that the practically atheistic outlook has become so uniquely plausible even for Christians in the modern context. Along this line, our focus will not be on traditions of explicit philosophical secularity as such, but rather upon the secularity that is carried on implicitly — one is tempted to say innocently — in institutional arrangements that we probably take largely for granted. That liberal pluralism requires modern political discourse to be secular and to rely upon nontheistic moral sources of authority and legitimacy is one example of this apparently innocent secularization. That modern science and technology require the mental habit of "methodological agnosticism" to function properly is another. That the efficiency of modern economic life does not really require, and may actually be hindered by, substantive religious considerations is still another indication that secularity may be more deeply embedded in our society than many Christians commonly recognize. Yet it is precisely the implicit secularity of many of modernity's central institutions that shapes our culture's pervasive indifference to serious religion. By examining the tacit secularity of some of these institutions, then, we will hopefully develop an aptitude for recognizing the specific contours of the particular "world" that we are called to be in but not of.

Our equation of the process of secularization with "worldliness" is not particularly novel; nor it is new to suggest that secularity and practical atheism are built into modernity's central institutions. After all, the secularization of modern society and culture has been a central theme within modern social theory for well over a century. Yet there are several very good reasons to call the reader's attention back to the matter of secularization. The first is that the New Testament links "worldliness" with unfruitfulness (cf. Jesus' Parable of the Sower, Matt. 13:3ff.). If we find ourselves distressed by the unfruitfulness of Christian witness in contemporary culture, then this may well signal that our churches have themselves succumbed to modern worldliness. In this connection, identifying the specific ways in which secularity and practical atheism have been built into modern social life cannot help but clarify the nature of the temptations our churches are currently facing and the places at which they may already have given ground to modern and "postmodern" ideas and assumptions.

Even more importantly, if it is true that secularity and practical atheism have become uniquely attractive and plausible in modern society, then the threat of apostasy and spiritual death must also be uniquely grave in the contemporary context. This threat obviously calls for as detailed an understanding of the specific dynamics of the process of secularization as Christians can muster. As evangelical theologian Klaus Bockmuehl observed in an insightful article entitled "Secularism and Theology":

> In my opinion the questions concerning the relationship between theology and secularism [secularization] are about the most fundamental and decisive issues of our age. At stake, basically, is the question of the world's final authority. We are in the midst of a historic struggle for world dominion: will it be man's rule or God's rule, human autonomy or the Kingdom of God.[14]

It is also extremely important to recognize that there is a very close connection between the secularity of modern social life and its *impersonality*, both of which have been observed and lamented — but for the most part separately — by Christians and non-Christians alike. Just as God's existence has become increasingly irrelevant within modern social life and therefore implausible to modern people, so it seems that we have lost sight of what constitutes truly human existence. This is not a coincidence. Indeed, one of the central contentions of our study is that the removal of God's personal agency from the world necessarily has the effect — however ironic and unintended — of removing *all* personal agency from the world. As Henri de Lubac observed: "Man cannot organize the world for himself without God; without God he can only organize the world against man. Exclusive humanism is inhuman humanism."[15] The history of our own century certainly bears this insight out. Modern worldliness is every bit as hard on the belief in humanity

14. Klaus Bockmuehl, "Secularism and Theology," *Crux* 19 (June 1983): 6.
15. Henri de Lubac, *The Drama of Atheist Humanism*, trans. Edith M. Riley (1950; New York: World Publishing Company, 1963), ix.

as it is on the belief in God. Where there is no God, it has truly been said, there is no *human being* either. Indeed, the importance of establishing the connection between the secularization of modern society and culture and the impersonal quality of modern social and cultural life can perhaps not be overemphasized today. Among other things, it means that Christian witness in face of the threat of secularization must not simply be understood in terms of defending the right of the Church to exist in modern society and culture, though this is obviously important. Rather, Christian witness today must be understood in terms of defending the possibility of personal and truly human existence *as such*.

Finally, it is crucial for Christians to make a detailed inventory of the specific mechanisms of secularization in modern society and culture because the Christian religion is itself partly to blame for many of them. This is the thrust of the so-called "gravedigger hypothesis," in which it is maintained that in contributing so substantially to the rise of modern culture, Christianity — and Protestant Christianity in particular — has essentially created its own secular gravediggers.[16] From this perspective, modern secular "worldliness" may be understood as a kind of ironical realization of certain Christian ideals (such as, say, the commitment to try to improve the conditions of material life for the sake of our neighbor) at the expense of the Christian religion itself. This, after all, was the gist of Max Weber's celebrated Protestant Ethic thesis, a thesis elaborated more recently by theorists like Talcott Parsons, who suggested (following Hegel) that modern secular society, with its emphasis upon the rights of individual conscience, is actually more consistently "Christian" than its medieval antecedent.[17] And it does appear to be the case that Protestant Christianity swept early modern society clean of pagan religiosity only to see premodern superstitions replaced by modern rationalism and by secular and often decidedly anti-Christian sensibilities.

16. See, for example, Os Guinness, *The Gravedigger File: Papers on the Subversion of the Modern Church* (Downers Grove, IL: InterVarsity Press, 1983). Guinness attributes the gravedigger hypothesis to Peter Berger (cf. *The Sacred Canopy*, 110ff.), who, in turn, takes it from Max Weber; but the idea originally emerges out of nineteenth-century German Idealism. It is implicit, for example, in Hegel's suggestion that secular modernity represents the highest realization of the Christian spirit.

17. Talcott Parsons, "Christianity and Modern Industrial Society," in *Secularization and the Protestant Prospect*, ed. James F. Childress and David B. Harned (Philadelphia: Westminster, 1970), 43-70.

Although the validity of the gravedigger hypothesis continues to be debated, the historical linkages between Protestantism and the process of secularization are certainly ones that Christians, and perhaps especially evangelical Christians, need to ponder very seriously. The gravedigger hypothesis helps to explain why thinking Christianly about modern society and culture is so difficult, and why it is not always entirely clear where Christianity ends and modern secular culture begins. In addition, the gravedigger hypothesis suggests that resisting the distinctively modern form of worldliness may require more than simply the recovery of six-teenth- or seventeenth-century Protestant spirituality. It may well require reforming certain aspects of the Reformation tradition itself.

"Modernity" or "Postmodernity"

I must also explain why I believe it is still important to dwell on the topic of modernity, in spite of the fact that it is widely asserted that Western society and culture have now moved beyond modernism and are more accurately described under the caption of "postmodernity." Of course, in light of widespread disillusionment with scientific positivism and with the modernist project of trying to construct a completely rational social order by means of technology there is considerable warrant for substituting "postmodern" for modern in describing contemporary intellectual culture. We also note increasingly widespread disaffection with the modern as-sumption that all human cultures are explicable in terms of the single and presumably normative metanarrative of "progress." Still, I have chosen to keep the focus of the present study on modernity for several reasons. The first is simply that there is very little agreement as yet as to what "post-modernity" means. While the term occasionally simply denotes dissatis-faction with modernity, it is increasingly used to suggest that we have entered into an entirely new cultural situation in which none of the old "modern" rules and habits of mind need be taken seriously anymore. All such suggestions are mistaken and misleading. As I hope to show in the following chapters, the ideals of the modern project are still very firmly embedded in the central institutional realities of contemporary society. Although modernity may well be *passé* in certain intellectual circles, typically modern ideas and assumptions are still quite effectively com-municated within contemporary culture by many of the institutional realities that surround us and by many of the ways we do things today. A number of these institutional realities and ways of doing things continue to underwrite the plausibility of practical atheism, in spite of "postmodernity's" purported openness to "spirituality."

One other reason for keeping the discussion focused on "modernity" rather than "postmodernity" is that the essential features of "postmodernism" — however this term is defined — are demonstrably modern in origin. Indeed, I would contend that "postmodernity" represents only a kind of *extension* of modernity, a kind of "hyper-modernity." As British sociologist Anthony Giddens suggested recently: "Rather than entering a period of post-modernity, we are moving into one in which the consequences of modernity are becoming more radicalised and universalised than before. Beyond modernity, I shall claim, we can perceive the contours of a new and different order, which is 'postmodern'; but this is quite distinct from what is at the moment called by many 'post-modernity'."[18] In this connection, it may help to recall that the patron saint of "postmodernity" theory, Martin Heidegger, did not himself believe that we had arrived at anything like the end of modernity. "[T]he 'modern age'," Heidegger commented not so very long ago, "is not at all at an end. Rather it is just entering the beginning of its presumably long-drawn-out consummation."[19]

An Excursus on the Problem of Secularization

There is also, admittedly, very little agreement among scholars as to what exactly "secularization" means. The word "secular" comes from the Latin *saeculum*, which meant "age" or "century" and connoted the temporal over and against the eternal. The word "secularization" was apparently first used in Europe during the seventeenth century in negotiating the Peace of Westphalia to denote the transfer of properties from ecclesiastical to "secular" political authorities. The term has subsequently been used in Roman Catholic canon law to describe the return

18. Anthony Giddens, *The Consequences of Modernity* (Stanford, CA: Stanford University Press, 1990): 3.

19. Martin Heidegger, *What is Called Thinking?*, trans. J. Glenn Gray (New York: Harper & Row, 1968): 54.

to "the world" of a person formerly under monastic or clerical orders.[20] In a sociological sense the concept of "secularization" does not refer to the explicit promotion of secularity over and against religion so much as it describes a subtle and largely inadvertent process in which religion — at least as it has traditionally been understood — forfeits its place in society. Secularization describes a process in which religious ideas, values, and institutions lose their public status and influence and eventually even their plausibility in modern societies.

Although the decline of religion in modern societies is practically indisputable, the subject of secularization has generated a vast literature characterized by considerable disagreement.[21] As Canadian political

20. See Peter L. Berger, *The Sacred Canopy: Elements of a Sociological Theory of Religion* (Garden City, NY: Anchor, 1967), 106ff.

21. Useful surveys of this literature include the following (listed alphabetically): Karel Dobbelaere, "Secularization Theories and Sociological Paradigms: Convergences and Divergences," *Social Compass* 31 (1984): 199-219; Peter E. Glasner, *The Sociology of Secularization: A Critique of the Concept* (London: Routledge & Kegan Paul, 1977); David Lyon, "Secularization and Sociology: The History of an Idea," *Fides et Historia* 13 (Spring 1981): 38-52; David Lyon, "Secularization: The Fate of Faith in Modern Society," *Themelios* 10 (September 1984): 14-22; Larry Shiner, "The Concept of Secularization in Empirical Research," *Journal for the Scientific Study of Religion* 6 (1967): 207-20; and Roy Wallis and Steve Bruce, "Secularization: The Orthodox Model," in *Religion and Modernization: Sociologists and Historians Debate the Secularization Thesis*, ed. Steve Bruce (Oxford: Clarendon Press, 1992), 8-30. Although a number of studies have been devoted to discussing the various historical and sociological disagreements about the concept of secularization — most recently Steve Bruce (ed.), *Religion and Modernization* — the scholarly debate tends to focus on the following problems: 1) *On the nature of religion.* Should religion be defined *functionally,* that is, as a kind of epiphenomenon reflecting certain more basic requirements of social life, and in terms of how religious beliefs function socially and/or psychologically? Or should religion be defined *substantively,* as a *sui generis* human phenomenon, and in terms of its actual beliefs? The decision one makes with respect to this definition determines the limits and possibilities of secularization. While it would not be difficult to show, for example, that certain substantive beliefs — say, in "eternal life" Christianly understood — have dropped out of modern discourse, it is not possible to envision a society — even a modern one — without a functional equivalent to religious worship. From a purely functionalist point of view, then, secularization is an impossibility *by definition.* This is why the use of the term "secularization" usually rests upon a substantive definition of religion. 2) *On the nature of the relation between religion and society.* Did, for example, the secularization of religious thought (say, during the seventeenth and eighteenth centuries in Europe) eventually give rise to the secularization of European society at large? Or, as Alasdair MacIntyre maintained in a study entitled *Secularization and*

philosopher Charles Taylor has commented, secularization is more "a locus of questions than a source of explanations." Yet in spite of his reservations, Taylor went on to suggest the following "undeniable" features of modern life:

> The regression of belief in God, and even more, the decline in the practice of religion, to the point where from being central to the whole life of Western societies, public and private, this has become sub-cultural, one of many private forms of involvement which some people indulge in.[22]

Taylor's observations accurately reflect the state of the ongoing debate over the problem of secularization, for the decline of traditional religious

Moral Change (London: Oxford University Press, 1967), did social change (class divisions) actually give rise to the secularization of thought? 3) *On the problem of dating the beginning of the process of secularization in Western history.* Estimates range from roughly the eleventh to the nineteenth century depending upon how the process is understood. 4) *On the problem of measuring "secularity,"* which, in turn, raises the problem of measuring "religiosity." So-called "classical" secularization theory often contrasts modern secularity with premodern religiosity. But was the average person-on-the-street really any more "religious" in the twelfth century than he or she is now? This sort of question turns out to be quite difficult to answer conclusively. 5) *On the problem of explanation.* A number of explanations for the process of secularization have been forwarded. It has been suggested that secularization is an inevitable expression of the maturation of the human race and/or a reflection of the evolution of human freedom. Along this line, it has been argued that secularization is due to the withering away of the illusion of religion in light of enlightened scientific understanding. On the other hand, it has been suggested that secularization is a kind of accidental and largely unintended consequence of the progressive differentiation of institutions in modern societies — that is, that religious interpretation has simply not been able to keep up with a rapidly changing modern society. But a great many questions remain. Is not modern science itself a kind of religion? Have religious meanings really been excised out of modern social institutions? Or are modern institutions secular simply because they developed in such a way as not to need religion? Here again, these turn out to be very difficult questions to answer in any conclusive way. Indeed, the disagreement over the concept of secularization was so intense during the early 1960s that British sociologist of religion David Martin suggested dropping the term from the field of sociology altogether. That Martin went on to publish *A General Theory of Secularization* in 1978 (New York: Harper Colophon) was, however, a telling indication of the tenacity and usefulness of the concept in interpreting modern Western social history.

22. Charles Taylor, *Sources of the Self: The Making of the Modern Identity* (Cambridge, MA: Harvard University Press, 1989), 309.

observance in modern society is at once undeniable and yet very difficult to explain. The "classical" explanation of secularization, developed perhaps most insightfully by Max Weber, is that in modern society religion — and in particular Christianity — has suffered under the twin processes of "disenchantment" and "rationalization."

"Disenchantment" refers to the criticism, emerging initially out of the Protestant Reformation, of magic and of the belief that the world is somehow infused with supernatural spirits.[23] This criticism, which was originally theologically motivated, was subsequently developed and disseminated within modern society and culture by science and technology. "New age" religiosity notwithstanding, most of us no longer believe the world to be animated and "enchanted" by spiritual forces. Rather, we ordinarily view the world "naturalistically" as a closed, interlocking system of natural and material causes and effects. That such a view has become the norm within modern society and culture, Weber contended, is the result of the process of "disenchantment."

"Rationalization" refers to the process in which social actions have come more and more to depend upon purely calculable and controllable (i.e., "rational") criteria. Steven Seidman helpfully summarizes Weber's argument as follows:

> As the secular-scientific ethos permeates the culture and psychology of modernity, religion is pushed into the realm of the irrational. Religion is viewed as an emotive and expressive act of the private individual. . . . Weber contends, moreover, that the irreligious nature of the scientific and intellectualized culture of modernity compels religious belief and practice to empty itself of worldly content. Religion in the modern world assumes an other-worldly and mystical form. [This] mystical turn of religion further sustains its status as irrational and a private concern of the individual. Furthermore, even mystical striving and the creation of intimate religious circles [are] unable to withstand the overwhelming power of secular culture. . . .[24]

23. Cf. Keith Thomas, *Religion and the Decline of Magic* (New York: Charles Scribner's Sons, 1971).

24. Steven Seidman, "Modernity, Meaning, and Cultural Pessimism in Max Weber," *Sociological Analysis* 44 (1983): 269.

Of the exponents of the Weberian interpretation of secularization, Peter Berger has undoubtedly been most prominent in North America. In his most important work on the subject of secularization, *The Sacred Canopy: Elements of a Sociological Theory of Religion* (1967), Berger defines secularization as a "process by which sectors of society and culture are removed from the domination of religious institutions and symbols."[25] Of the sectors to be removed from religion's domination, Berger (like Weber) understands the economic to have been the first and most crucial, but he suggests that a number of other areas, such as modern politics, the mass media, and modern educational institutions, have been equally subject to the process of secularization. One after another, the central institutional sectors of modern social life have, for a variety of reasons, ceased to appeal to religion either for direction or legitimacy.

The evacuation of religion from the institutional core of modernity has, Berger contends, led to the secularization and "pluralization" of modern consciousness. Whereas religious understanding once provided a kind of overarching system of explanations — or "sacred canopy" — over the entire social order, modern society has become so institutionally complicated that individuals are now left largely to their own devices to choose whichever explanation and interpretation of the social order makes the most sense of their own individual circumstances and experience. Religion has thus forfeited its role as the interpreter of social order and has become instead a matter of personal preference and choice, something to be adopted and/or discarded privately as each one of us sees fit.

The remarkable irony in this process of secularization, Berger contends (again following Weber), is that Christianity, and in particular Protestant Christianity, had so much to do with setting the historical stage for it. In criticizing Roman Catholicism's over-emphasis upon mystery, miracle, and magic, the Protestant Reformers effectively focused the possibility of our relationship to God to the single channel of God's sovereign grace. Thus natural and supernatural realities were no longer conceived to exist along a hierarchically arranged continuum. Instead, the creator God was held to *transcend* his creation quite radically and to act in and upon it, not necessarily, but intentionally, surprisingly, and graciously. Protestantism thus focused the issue of Chris-

25. Berger, *Sacred Canopy*, 107.

tian faith somewhat more narrowly than did Roman Catholicism. "If compared to the 'fullness' of the Catholic universe," Berger observed:

> Protestantism appears as a radical truncation, a reduction to "essen-tials" at the expense of the vast wealth of religious contents. . . . Protestantism may be described in terms of an immense shrinkage in the scope of the sacred in reality, as compared with its Catholic adversary. The sacramental apparatus is reduced to a minimum and, even there, divested of its more numinous qualities. The miracle of the mass disappears altogether. Less routine miracles, if not denied altogether, lose all real significance for the religious life. . . . At the risk of some simplification, it can be said that Protestantism divested itself as much as possible from the three most ancient and most powerful concomitants of the sacred — mystery, miracle, and magic.[26]

Of course, the Protestant divestment of "mystery, miracle, and magic" was not intended to narrow the scope of human existence. Rather, it was intended only to render the believer all the more dependent upon, and thus all the more receptive to, God's sovereign grace; and as long as the plausibility of this conception of grace was maintained, the process of secularization was effectively arrested. Still, Berger continues:

> It needed only the cutting of this one narrow channel of mediation [grace], though, to open the floodgates of secularization. . . . A sky empty of angels becomes open to the intervention of the astronomer and, eventually, of the astronaut. It may be maintained, then, that Protestantism served as a historically decisive prelude to seculariza-tion, whatever may have been the importance of other factors.[27]

Berger does not suggest that the "disenchantment" of the world was a Protestant invention — for he recognizes (again following Weber) that the possibility of radical disenchantment was latent already in the religion of ancient Israel — but he does suggest that the Reformers extended the logic of disenchantment a good deal further than either Hebrew religion or Roman Catholicism, and that it was this extension

26. Ibid., 111.
27. Ibid., 112-13.

of the principle of disenchantment that eventually led to the secularization of modern society and culture.

Many theologically concerned scholars have sought to render
Berger's (Weber's) interpretive material useful to the contemporary
Church. British historian Alan Gilbert rehearsed much of it in *The Making
of Post-Christian Britain* (1980), concluding that secularization "is a much
deadlier foe than any previous counter-religious force in human history."[28]
A number of North American evangelical authors have addressed the issue
of secularization in recent years as well. As its title already implies, Os
Guinness's *The Gravedigger File: Papers on the Subversion of the Modern
Church* (1983) discusses modern Christianity's ironic subversion of itself
and follows Berger's analysis quite closely. In *Evangelicalism: The Coming
Generation* (1987), James Davison Hunter makes use of extensive survey
research to document the corrosive toll modern social forces have been
taking upon evangelical college and seminary students, that is, the "coming
generation" of evangelical leadership. On a more theoretical note, sociologist David Lyon discusses various problems with Berger's and others'
renderings of "the secularization story" from a Christian point of view in
The Steeple's Shadow: On the Myths and Realities of Secularization (1985).
Berger's interpretive material on secularization also surfaces in Lesslie
Newbigin's attempt to reconceptualize Western culture as a cross-cultural
missionary problem in *Foolishness to the Greeks: The Gospel and Western
Culture* (1986). Most recently, David Wells has made use of Berger's
theoretical framework to examine and criticize the evangelical theological
establishment in *No Place for Truth: or, Whatever Happened to Evangelical
Theology?* (1993) and *God in the Wasteland: The Reality of Truth in a World
of Fading Dreams* (1994). The present study generally reflects Berger's (and
Weber's) line of reasoning, though interpreting the secular quality of
modern society and culture theologically and not simply historically.

Significance and Outline of the Study

Søren Kierkegaard once insisted that if scholarship is to qualify for
the name *Christian* it must somehow edify and encourage Christian

---

28. Alan D. Gilbert, *The Making of Post-Christian Britain: A History of the Secularization of Modern Society* (London: Longman, 1980), 153.

faith. In this connection, it is hoped that reorganizing the analytical material on the process of secularization around the New Testament themes of "the world" and "worldliness" will prove genuinely helpful to Christian readers and to the contemporary Church. In this connection, the reader will notice that I cite a mélange of Christian authors over the course of the study, from Søren Kierkegaard to Helmut Thielicke, from G. K. Chesterton to Karl Barth. In an effort to avoid any confusion that might be caused by this eclecticism, I should say here at the outset that this study's theological presuppositions are broadly evangelical and conservative. If there are solutions to the perplexing problem of the secularization of (post)modern society and culture, I will conclude, they are to be found in historic trinitarian orthodoxy.

Kierkegaard was also among the first to perceive the nature of the relation between modern society's practical godlessness and its impersonality and, although we will have occasion to treat Kierkegaard's understanding of personhood in some detail in our fourth chapter, it will be helpful to launch our study with one of Kierkegaard's characteristically penetrating observations:

> Each age has its own characteristic depravity. Ours is perhaps not pleasure or indulgence or sensuality, but rather a dissolute pantheistic contempt for the individual man. In the midst of all of our exultation over the achievements of the age . . . , there sounds a note of poorly conceived contempt for the individual man; in the midst of the self-importance of the contemporary generation there is revealed a sense of despair over being human. Everything must attach itself so as to be a part of some movement; men are determined to lose themselves in the totality of things, in world-history, fascinated and deceived by a magic witchery; no one wants to be an individual human being. . . .[29]

G. K. Chesterton made a similar observation when he said that the "huge modern heresy" is that of "altering the human soul to fit its [social] conditions, instead of altering human [social] conditions to fit the human

29. Søren Kierkegaard, *Concluding Unscientific Postscript*, trans. David F. Swenson and Walter Lowrie (Princeton: Princeton University Press, 1941), 317.

soul."[30] And what appears to have been the "characteristic depravity" of mid-nineteenth-century Denmark and the "huge heresy" of early twentieth-century London appears to be equally, if not even more, true of contemporary North American society and culture. There is perhaps a bit more ambivalence today about the achievements of modern technological society, and perhaps less optimism about the future, but "contempt for the individual man" and a "sense of despair over being human" continue to bedevil us, and appear to be even more of a problem today than they were a hundred years ago. This is profoundly ironic; for it was within our own Western tradition — and due almost entirely to the impact of the Christian religion within it — that the concerns for authentic individuality and for the infinite value of the human person developed. Yet it is precisely this legacy that the process of secularization has almost completely eroded. Again, it may be observed that where there is no God, there are no human persons either. It is for this reason that the path toward arresting the insidious process of secularization must pass through theology, and specifically through the recovery of a Christian theology of personhood. After all, as Chesterton noted, "you cannot possibly know what is wrong with the world unless you have some idea of what is right."[31]

This study's style is largely descriptive and analytic. Each of the following chapters seeks to describe and analyze the internal logic and development of one of modernity's central institutional spheres. The underlying assumptions of the analytical sections are those of what might be termed a *modest* sociology of knowledge, a perspective that simply expects thought and action — including Christian thought and action — to reflect the contours of its social context. This is a particularly useful perspective in the case of secularization because it suggests that the interrelationship of thought, action, and society may well be ironic, and it refuses to simply reduce thought and action to its social context or vice versa.[32]

30. G. K. Chesterton, *What's Wrong with the World?* (New York: Sheed & Ward, 1910), 104.

31. Ibid., 17.

32. It should be noted that the sociology of knowledge perspective is potentially quite deadly to Christian faith; for if it is construed radically the sociology of knowledge suggests that all thought — and particularly religious thought — is simply reducible to social-structural factors. The temptation to reduce theology to material factors is rather easily resisted, however, and I believe that the benefits of the perspective outweigh the

Our differentiation of the terms "society" and "culture," as well as our division of chapter topics — on modern political life, on science and technology, on the rationalization of modern economic life, and on the characteristics of modern culture — reflects an observation made by American sociologist Daniel Bell a number of years ago with respect to the makeup of modern societies and concerning the future of religion within them. In opposition to what he termed "holistic" or reductionistic views of modern social order, Bell contended that modern society actually consists of a number of relatively autonomous spheres or realms. "If I look at contemporary society," Bell noted:

> I would say that there is a radical antagonism between the norms and structures of the techno-economic realm (whose axial principle is functional rationality and efficiency, and whose structure is bureaucratic); the polity (whose axial principle, in Western democratic societies, is equality, and whose structures are those of representation or participation); and the culture (whose ruling principle is that of self-realization, and, in its extremes, self-gratification). It is the tensions between the norms of these three realms — efficiency and bureaucracy, equality and rights, self-fulfillment and the desire for novelty — that form the contradictions of the modern world. . . .[33]

Bell went on to suggest that religion has fared somewhat differently in each of these distinct spheres and, although his predictions concerning the future of religion were not entirely convincing, his division of modern society into different spheres is quite useful. For while the political, the "techno-economic," and cultural spheres have all obviously evolved together over the course of the last several centuries, each has its own peculiar history and internal logic and none is simply reducible to any of the others. The sequence of the chapters, furthermore, attempts to represent Western experience historically, in that distinctively modern ideas appear to have surfaced in political life somewhat earlier than in the

---

potential dangers in approaching the matter of secularization, especially given the multiple ironies that continue to characterize the relationship between Christianity and modern society and culture.

33. Daniel Bell, "The Return of the Sacred?: The Argument on the Future of Religion," *British Journal of Sociology* 28, no. 4 (1977): 424.

scientific, economic, and cultural spheres. The fifth chapter, "Taking Stock of 'The Huge Modern Heresy,'" summarizes our findings up to that point and looks at the damaging consequences of several mistaken attempts to accommodate certain modern ideas and assumption within modern Protestant theology; and the last chapter offers a constructive alternative to modernity's secularity and impersonality on the basis of a Christian theology of personhood. Finally, I have concluded each chapter with a short meditation on that Christian doctrine or virtue which, I believe, most clearly exposes the vanity and inhumanity of the worldly assumptions rendered plausible by each of the institutional spheres of modern life under discussion. Just as the first temptation to sin appealed to Eve's imagination and encouraged her to envision a plausible alternative to the divine command — "Did God *really* say . . . ?" — so the temptation to live godlessly today still begins in subtle yet plausible reinterpretations of what God has said. For this reason, the short meditations appended to the end of each chapter are intended to direct our attention away from analysis per se and back to the Holy Scriptures.

It bears repeating here at the outset that the temptation to worldliness in modern society and culture is very grave, for practical atheism is very deeply embedded in modernity's central institutions. The temptation to worldliness is also quite subtle — emanating from seemingly innocent sources — and very attractive. After all, the world *wants* to be deceived, and does not want to know the truth about itself. And so the temptation to worldliness must, finally, be understood to be a *spiritual* temptation with our opposition consisting, not simply of flesh and blood, but, as the Apostle writes (Eph. 6:12), "of the rulers, authorities, and powers of this dark world, and ultimately of the spiritual forces of evil in the heavenly realms." This being the case, our struggle against worldliness in the modern situation and against the secularization of modern society and culture must never be construed as simply one of description, analysis, and calculated resolution. Rather, our labor calls for prayer, supplication, and obedience. The purpose of this study, then, is only to try to identify the features of our society and culture which make it plausible, and indeed even attractive, for so many people to live their lives as though the Author of life did not exist. Sadly, the blasphemous assertion that "God has died" appears to be quite literally true for many of our contemporaries and, indeed, even for many Christians. We must try to discover why this is.

CHAPTER ONE

The Worldliness of
Modern Political Aspirations

As the traveler on serious business may be tempted to linger, while
he gazes on the beauty of the prospect which opens on his way, so
this well-ordered and divinely governed world, with all its blessings
of sense and knowledge, may lead us to neglect those interests which
will endure when itself has passed away. In truth, it promises more
than it can fulfill. . . . And hence it is that many pursuits, in themselves honest and right, are nevertheless to be engaged in with caution, lest they seduce us; and those perhaps with special caution,
which tend to the well-being of men in this life. The sciences, for
instance, of good government, acquiring wealth, of preventing and
relieving want, and the like, are for this reason especially dangerous;
for fixing, as they do, our exertions on this world as an end, they go
far to persuade us that they have no other end.

John Henry Newman[1]

The state is the realized moral life of a people, and a political constitution is the expression of a people's substance, or spirit; it is a reflection

---

1. Newman cited in William Oddie, "Introduction," in William Oddie (ed.), *After
the Deluge: Essays Towards the Desecularization of the Church* (London: S.P.C.K., 1987),
13-14.

of the quality of their culture generally.[2] So G. W. F. Hegel asserted at the introduction of a remarkable series of lectures on the philosophy of world history in 1830. The form of a people's religion, Hegel continued, determines the form of the state and the character of its constitution.[3] Put somewhat differently, political life provides a kind of window into the soul of a people, revealing their most basic assumptions about the nature of the world and their most cherished aspirations for life within it. It is for this reason that we begin our analysis of the secularization of modern society and culture by considering modern political aspirations. In spite of the fact that the process of secularization is more frequently associated with economic developments, or with modern science and technology, modern political life discloses the specific character of modern worldliness quite strikingly. Worldly assumptions also appear historically to have surfaced first in the early modern political ethos.

To say that modern political life is worldly and a great source of temptations to worldliness does not come as much of a surprise. Is not "politics," as we so often say pejoratively, worldly by definition? Indeed, exposing the worldliness of modern political life is one of the principal preoccupations of the mass media, and we are virtually assaulted with political worldliness every time we read a newspaper or turn on a television set. The political soil seems to yield such a consistent harvest of intrigue and scandal that it would appear to be unnecessary to mention the worldliness of modern political life. But what if the kind of worldliness so often bared and debated *ad nauseam* by contemporary commentators and pundits — the blind ambition, the ruthlessness, the deceit, the abuse of power for personal gain — actually acts to distract our attention away from a far more serious form of worldliness inhering in modern political life? What if the real worldliness in modern political life is something that is rarely commented upon or discussed in the media because it is at once more subtle and more commonplace? What if worldliness in modern political life is a function, not simply of the actions of individual political figures, but of the *character* of a people that seems to demand ever more from the political process?

2. G. W. F. Hegel, *The Philosophy of History*, trans. J. Sibree (1830-31; New York: Dover, 1956), 38, 45-46.

3. Ibid., 51.

Such questions are meant to tease out the difficulty of discussing the problem of worldliness in modern political life today, for although we may think that we already know all about the worldly character of this most visible of spheres, it is far from clear, given the increasing number of things we seem to expect to accomplish by political means, that we really do. Although we have learned to apply the art of suspicion with respect to the personal ambitions of individual politicians, we seem to be largely oblivious to the Promethean ambitions inhering in the modern political project as a whole. Yet this is where its worldliness lies. *The worldliness of modern political life lies precisely in the modern tendency to relativize all human aspirations over and against those of immanent political-social change.* Or, put somewhat differently, it has become increasingly *plausible* for us to focus essentially religious aspirations on the possibilities of political action and organization. While we may lose faith in this or that politician and/or party from time to time, our belief in the *potential* of the political process tends to be largely unshakable. The confidence that we place in the possibilities of political-social change, furthermore, rests upon a vastly exaggerated sense of human responsibility in and for the world and has given rise to a tremendous expansion of the political apparatus in modern times. Indeed, faith in the political process has produced a veritable apotheosis of the modern state.

The modern tendency to relativize all concerns over and against those of political-social action and the bloated estimation of human potential have a great deal to do with the secular quality of modern life. For again, once our responsibilities in and for the world have been fully delimited — responsibilities which inevitably call for political expression — there is very little need left for God. Our instinctive reaction to natural disasters today — to what used to be called "acts of God" — is instructive in this connection. The focus of contemporary concern is typically either upon holding individuals or agencies responsible for the events or upon allocating the moneys necessary for preventing them from reoccurring in the future. While these reactions are not necessarily bad, they do tend to preclude any kind of collective reflection as to the ultimate significance of these mercifully infrequent indications of human powerlessness. It is probably also true that the plausibility of the modern secular outlook is only strengthened by the obsessive attention the modern mass media give to political theater, for such attention simply reinforces the impression that there is nothing else in the world that really matters, indeed that all other concerns are either illusory or are eventually reducible to the political will-to-power. As Newman's wise comments cited at the outset of the chapter suggest, the "sciences of good government" do indeed have an insidious way of persuading us that our exertions in this world have no other end than in the here and now.

Of course, it would be nice to be able to say that Christians have held out against this secular modern drift, but unfortunately many have not. The politicization of Christian theology — among "liberals" and "conservatives" and on both the "left" and the "right" — has been one of the more striking features of recent church history. The Social Gospel movement, Christian socialism, various and sundry "liberation theologies," Christian feminism, the Moral Majority, and Christian Reconstructionism are simply the most visible manifestations of this trend, which appears to have begun, as we will see in a moment, at least as early as the eighteenth century. Modern political worldliness, it seems, is highly compelling. It presents itself as the only responsible reading of the human situation. As Jacques Ellul observed concerning contemporary culture:

> Everything is political. Politics is the only serious activity. The fate of humanity depends on politics, and classic philosophical or religious truth takes on meaning only as it is incarnated in political action. Christians are typical in this connection. They rush to the defense of political religion, and assert that Christianity is meaningful only in terms of political commitment. In truth, it is their religious mentality which plays this trick on them. As Christianity collapses as a religion, they look about them in bewilderment, unconsciously of course, hoping to recover where the religious is to be incarnated in their time. Since they are religious, they are drawn automatically into the political sphere like iron filings to a magnet.[4]

Of course, whether or not "political Christianity" is only a final stage in the collapse of Christianity as a religion or a more faithful reading of the gospel texts is debatable, but Ellul's observation that modern life has become increasingly politicized is indisputable and calls for interpretation.

---

4. Jacques Ellul, *The New Demons*, trans. C. Edward Hopkin (New York: Seabury Press, 1975), 199.

Interpreting the Secularity of Modern Political Life

The plausibility of modern political worldliness stems from a number of disparate sources. One of the crucial problems appears to be the intrinsically secular logic of modern political ideologies, a defining characteristic of which is the promise of autonomous human control over the world. This preoccupation with control effectively precludes religious humility and openness to the possibility of revelation. Yet before discussing modern political ideologies in any detail, it will be helpful to review a few of the structural features of modern societies which point political discourse — accidentally, as it were — in a secular and impersonal direction. Along this line, we will survey observations that have been made concerning the growth of the modern state, the bureaucratization of political administration, the complexity of modern social life, and the characteristics of "mass" democracy. It is also true that secularity lies very close to the heart of the modern political project historically and philosophically, and so we will want to explore — even if only briefly — some of the theoretical roots of this project. Finally, we want to broach the matter of Christianity's role in fostering modern political worldliness, and the extent to which the Church may have contributed — unintentionally or otherwise — to the rise of secular political theory and practice. Reviewing the Church's contribution(s) to this development may help to explain why contemporary Christians find it so difficult to speak effectively *as Christians* in the modern political arena. It may also help to explain why the temptation to politicize Christian theology is so acute under modern conditions.

It bears repeating here at the outset of this chapter that the character of modern politics contributes quite substantially to the *plausibility* of practical atheism in modern society and culture. Secular politics also contributes quite substantially to the impersonality of modern life. The purpose of this first chapter is to clarify how these contributions are made with an eye toward encouraging contemporary Christians to take political affairs seriously, but not nearly as seriously as they increasingly demand to be taken.

a. Crisis and Leviathan

"The modern state," Peter Berger commented several years ago, "even in its democratic form, represents the greatest agglomeration of power in human history."[5] This is not, Berger opined, necessarily because of any malign totalitarian ideology somehow inherent in modernity, but simply because of the immense technological resources available to governments for the purposes of social control.[6] Much of the expansion of the modern political apparatus has occurred in the last several generations, since the turn of this century and particularly since mid-century, and has been due to a dramatic expansion of the breadth of perceived governmental responsibilities. In addition to the tasks of defining and maintaining law and social order, of minting and underwriting a supply of money, and of defending its borders, the reach of the modern state now extends rather deeply into cultural territory as well, and even increasingly into the family and the most intimate areas of interpersonal relations. Indeed, the seemingly inexorable politicization of various aspects of modern life suggests that our political destiny may well be to simply suffocate under the sheer weight of the political apparatus. And yet the larger modern governments become, the more immediately we are inclined to turn to them for assistance and the more we are predisposed to demand of them. We have apparently acquired quite a taste for the political manipulation of our circumstances.

In this century, the periods of the most rapid growth of government correspond to social crises of various kinds, and particularly to wars and

5. Peter L. Berger, *The Capitalist Revolution: Fifty Propositions about Prosperity, Equality, & Liberty* (New York: Basic Books, 1986), 212.

6. Interestingly, the computer is probably the most significant of the technological resources to which Berger refers. In a study entitled *Computer Power and Human Reason: From Judgment to Calculation* (San Francisco: W. H. Freeman, 1976), Joseph Weizenbaum commented on the largely conservative impact the computer has had on the modern welfare-state. Weizenbaum suggests that, while the welfare state was close to collapsing under its own weight at mid-century, computer technology not only enabled it to survive, but to actually thrive and to continue to expand its vast reach. "Yes, the computer did arrive 'just in time,'" Weizenbaum writes (pp. 31-32). "But in time for what? In time to save — and save very nearly intact, indeed, to entrench and stabilize — social and political structures that otherwise might have been either radically renovated or allowed to totter under the demands that were sure to be made on them. The computer, then, was used to conserve America's social and political institutions. It buttressed them and immunized them, at least temporarily, against enormous pressures for change. . . . [Hence] of the many paths to social innovation it opened to man, the most fateful was to make it possible for him to eschew all deliberate thought of substantive change."

economic downturns. While these crises inevitably passed, however, in each instance the political growth they spawned became permanent. This one-way development has aptly been termed the "ratchet effect" of modern political life.[7] Crises create a kind of generalized demand for governments to "do something," and political action in response to such demand — *regardless of its efficacy* — has the effect of expanding the range of things we come to expect of government. As political scientist Robert Higgs has noted:

> Crises lead to permanent shifts in the *tolerable limits* [emphasis added] of the true size of government. Crises break down the ideological resistance to Big Government by (1) providing occasions for the improvement of command-and-control mechanisms, which renders them less obnoxious; (2) discrediting the conservative domino theory, with its implications that all civil and political liberties will be lost in a mixed economy; and (3) creating opportunities for many people both within and without the government to do well for themselves and hence to look more favorably on the new order.[8]

7. See Robert Higgs, *Crisis and Leviathan: Critical Episodes in the Growth of American Government* (New York: Oxford University Press, 1987). Higgs is by no means the first to have noticed the inexorable growth of the modern state. Max Weber, for example, made the following observations a number of years ago: "Whereas in early times even actions which were openly recognized as felonious were not proceeded against by the organized community except upon pressure on the part of religious or military interests, now the prosecution of an ever-widening sphere of injuries to persons and property is being placed under the guaranty of the political coercive apparatus. Thus the political community monopolizes the legitimate application of violence for its coercive apparatus and is gradually transformed into an institution for the protection of rights." See Max Weber, *Economy and Society*, vol. 2, ed. Guenther Roth and Claus Wittich (Berkeley, CA: University of California Press, 1978), 980.

8. Higgs, *Crisis and Leviathan*, 73. In a recent essay, Higgs suggests that the implementation of a military draft was perhaps the principal factor in the legitimation of state expansion in the United States in the twentieth century. Once the concept of drafting men into the service of the state became acceptable, Higgs argues, other — and, by definition, less significant — forms of governmental coercion seemed more or less automatically legitimate, especially if they could be said to be necessary to protect the lives of those drafted. Higgs concludes: "The government's organization of the economy for war, more than anything else, determined how the central government would grow in the United States in the twentieth century. And conscription, more than anything else, determined how the government would organize the economy for

Strikingly similar observations have been made in recent years by German social theorist Jürgen Habermas. In attempting to alleviate the social problems associated with cyclical economic downturns, the modern welfare state maneuvers itself into a "legitimation crisis."[9] As it expands into areas traditionally reserved for private discretion and action, the state draws attention to itself and to the possibilities of ostensibly rational planning and control. Even if the actual planning and control of previously private matters proves to be ineffective or even harmful, it turns out to be quite difficult politically to restore them to the private sphere. "The 'hand of the state,'" one author has commented describing Habermas's position, "is more visible and intelligible than 'the invisible hand' of liberal capitalism,"[10] and the growth of modern government may be interpreted in terms of this visibility and intelligibility.

Of course, it is not difficult to trace the connection between the growth of the modern state and the secular political worldliness we are presently concerned to identify. If political worldliness entails the relativization of all aspirations over and against those of immanent political-social action, then the dramatic growth of the political apparatus in recent decades seems a fairly clear indication that many of us have indeed become quite enthusiastic about the possibilities of political organization. What is perhaps not quite so obvious is that this preoccupation with political-social organization often seems to preclude the concern for personal integrity and for the development of moral character.[11] Politically

---

war. Thus in a multitude of ways, the military draft has shaped not only the contours of the nation at war but the course of its politico-economic development throughout the past eighty years." Robert Higgs, "War and Leviathan in Twentieth Century America," *Transaction* 33, no. 6 (September/October 1996): 57.

9. See Jürgen Habermas, *Legitimation Crisis*, trans. Thomas McCarthy (Boston: Beacon Press, 1975).

10. David Held, "Crisis Tendencies, Legitimation, and the State," in John B. Thompson and David Held (eds.), *Habermas: Critical Debate* (Cambridge, MA: M.I.T. Press, 1982), 184.

11. See Nicholas Berdyaev, *The Fate of Man in the Modern World* (Ann Arbor, MI: University of Michigan Press, 1935), 25ff. "We are witnessing," Berdyaev observed, "the process of dehumanization in all phases of culture and social life. Above all, moral consciousness is being dehumanized . . . democratized and generalized humanism has ceased to be attentive to man: it is interested in the structure of society, but not in man's inner life. This is a fatal and inevitable process. Hence humanism can never be a force capable of withstanding the process of dehumanization."

speaking, we do indeed appear to be committed to the project of, in the words of T. S. Eliot, "dreaming of systems so perfect, that no one will need to be good."[12]

b. Bureaucracy

The worldliness of modern political life also stems from its distinctive *style* of administration, a style most commonly analyzed and discussed under the heading of "bureaucracy." Without going too deeply into this, bureaucratic administration may be defined as a method of protecting an organization from changing personnel and from unwelcome innovation. This protection is achieved by the formalization of rules and procedures and by the strict hierarchical delineation of authority. Of course, the stability of bureaucratic administration is famous, and bureaucracy has enabled us to undertake enormously complicated tasks and projects in recent centuries. In addition to the modern welfare state, neither science, nor technology, nor business corporations, nor modern economic systems could exist either on the scale or at the level of complexity that they do today were it not for the administrative genius of bureaucracy.

The stability of bureaucratic administration exacts a high social price, however. In the first instance, bureaucracy is relentlessly impersonal. It deliberately abstracts away from individual personalities for the sake of organizational continuity. Bureaucracy also shows a seemingly ineluctable tendency to substitute the pragmatic means of efficiency and effectiveness for the original ends of the organization, whatever they may happen to have been. Taken together, this bias toward impersonality and the pragmatic concern for efficiency and effectiveness tend to narrow bureaucracy's focus, as Parkinson's celebrated law suggests, to simple organizational survival. These inbuilt tendencies also render bureaucracies almost completely immune to traditional moral and/or religious comment and criticism. Bureaucracies are thus almost inevitably worldly, for their entire frame-of-reference is secular and pragmatic *by definition*. This is why the chief theorist of bureaucracy, Max Weber, so lamented the diffusion of bureaucratic administration in modern

12. T. S. Eliot, "Choruses from 'The Rock,'" in *Collected Poems* (London: Faber and Faber, 1963), 174.

times, for this diffusion seemed to him to portend the end of genuinely moral and/or philosophical reasoning in modern political life. "It is horrible to think," Weber wrote:

> that the world could one day be filled with nothing but those little cogs, little men clinging to little jobs and striving towards the bigger ones — a state of affairs which is to be seen once more, as in the Egyptian records, playing an ever increasing part in the spirit of our present administrative system, and especially of its offspring, the students. This passion for bureaucracy . . . is enough to drive one to despair. It is as if in politics . . . we were deliberately to become men who need 'order' and nothing but order, become nervous and cowardly if for one moment this order wavers, and helpless if they are torn away from their total incorporation in it. That the world should know no men but these: it is in such an evolution that we are already caught up, and the great question is, therefore, not how we can promote and hasten it, but what can we oppose to this machinery in order to keep a portion of mankind free from this parceling-out of the soul, from this supreme mastery of the bureaucratic way of life.[13]

While Weber's comments are perhaps somewhat extreme, and although it has apparently become possible to soften bureaucratic administration by means of the so-called "behavioral sciences," one wonders if this "humanization" is not also, finally, impersonal. And it is undoubtedly still true that bureaucratic administration tends to keep institutions — political and otherwise — rather narrowly focused on this-worldly concerns, insulating them from substantive moral and/or religious reflection. "The modern industrial and social state," Tage Lindbom observes in a provocative essay entitled *The Myth of Democracy* (1996), "is quantitative in nature and, as centralized bureaucracy, it has no moral norms. The aim of the modern state is to intervene continuously and to regulate the secular order wherein sensate interests are increasingly dominant."[14]

---

13. Weber, cited in Wolfgang Mommsen, *Max Weber and German Politics: 1890-1920*, trans. Michael S. Steinberg (Chicago: University of Chicago Press, 1984), 127-28.

14. Tage Lindbom, *The Myth of Democracy* (Grand Rapids, MI: Eerdmans, 1996), 54.

c. The Ordeal of Civility

Additional light is shed on the intrinsic secularity of modern political discourse if we view it as a reflection of a process John Murray Cuddihy termed "the ordeal of civility."[15] Developing one of the principal insights of Emile Durkheim and Talcott Parsons, Cuddihy contends that the process of modernization is one of progressive "differentiation," that is, of the separation of any number of things that have traditionally been unified in human cultures. A typically modern society, for example, is one which exhibits the separation of nuclear from extended families, of home from job, of economics from politics, of politics from religion, of religion from culture, of public from private, of fact from value, of theory from praxis, of means from ends, of culture from personality, and, finally, of individuals themselves from the ideas they hold.[16] The celebrated "separation of church and state" provides an interesting example of this process. Although the original intent of this separation was not to secularize political discourse, this is commonly what the so-called "wall of separation" between Church and state is taken to imply. A great many people today seem to simply take it for granted that religion and politics have virtually nothing to do with each other.[17]

Although we will discuss the reasons for this process of "differentiation" more thoroughly in a subsequent chapter, it appears to have to do with the rationalization, and particularly with the specialization, fostered by the modern technological economy. Modern specialization has apparently overwhelmed the ability of religion to interpret and to make sense of an increasingly complicated social order, with the result that modern societies increasingly tend to be held together "technically"

15. John Murray Cuddihy, *The Ordeal of Civility: Freud, Marx, Lévi-Strauss, and the Jewish Struggle with Modernity* (New York: Basic Books, 1974).

16. Ibid., 98.

17. This is perhaps due to the psychological difficulties presented by the separation of Church and state. As Walter Lippmann observed in *A Preface to Morals* (New York: Macmillan, 1929), 75: "The separation of church and state involves more than a mere logical difficulty for the churchman. It involves a deep psychological difficulty for the members of the congregation. As communicants they expected to believe without reservation that their church is the only true means of salvation. . . . But as citizens they are expected to maintain a neutral indifference to the claims of all the sects, and to resist encroachments by any one sect upon the religious practices of the others." Under modern conditions, the balance appears to be tipped in this latter direction.

and by contractual arrangement rather than by religious understanding. Along this line, Cuddihy suggests that, while this process of relentless differentiation does enable us to live and work "with unknown others without transforming them into either brothers or enemies,"[18] it also dissolves, and eventually destroys, traditional religious cultures. Under modern conditions, he asserts, religion is civilized, privatized, trivialized, and finally reduced to the status of a mere private preference. In short, religion must be kept under wraps for the sake of civil political discourse. Needless to say, this is profoundly traumatizing for the serious adherents of religion. To the extent that religious understanding is integral to truly human existence, furthermore, the "ordeal of civility" is also fundamentally dehumanizing. Ironically, the final result of this process of differentiation is a kind of secularized cultural homogeneity. "Public faith," as British sociologist David Martin wryly observed, "becomes the standard deviation of religious idiosyncrasy."[19]

The civility of modern political discourse also requires the state to become a kind of neutral and impartial entity standing over and above competing religious and/or other "special interest" groups. While different groups of people may well have different ideas about what constitutes the good life, so the modern argument runs, we can at least agree to treat each other fairly and equally in spite of these differences. The political task, therefore, is not to adopt and enforce some particular view of the good life, but simply to unite around a strong procedural commitment to treat all people with due respect.[20] It is the task of the state to police this commitment from a position of neutrality. Not surprisingly, this modern commitment to impartiality has resulted in largely secularized political discourse or, as it has aptly been termed, the uniquely modern phenomenon of the "naked public square."[21] As

18. Cuddihy, *The Ordeal of Civility*, 12.

19. David Martin, "General Tendencies and Historical Filters," *The Annual Review of the Social Sciences of Religion* 3 (1979): 3-4.

20. See Charles Taylor, "The Politics of Recognition," in *Multiculturalism and "The Politics of Recognition,"* ed. Amy Gutman (Princeton: Princeton University Press, 1992): 56. Taylor suggests that American scholar Ronald Dworkin is perhaps the most able representative of this position.

21. See Richard John Neuhaus, *The Naked Public Square: Religion and Democracy in America* (Grand Rapids, MI: Eerdmans, 1984).

Richard John Neuhaus observes, however, this "naked public square" is probably only a transitional phenomenon:

> It is a vacuum begging to be filled. When the democratically affirmed institutions that generate and transmit values are excluded, the vacuum will be filled by the agent left in control of the public square, the state. In this manner, a perverse notion of the disestablishment of religion leads to the establishment of the state as church. Not without reason, religion is viewed by some as a repressive imposition upon the public square. They would cast out the devil of particularist religion and thus put the public square in the proper secular order. Having cast out the one devil, they unavoidably invite the entrance of seven devils worse than the first.[22]

Whether or not the modern secular political apparatus merits being labeled "demonic" is doubtless debatable, but Neuhaus is certainly correct to suggest that when modern political life ceases to be understood in terms of traditional religion, the subsequent vacuum is often quickly filled by secular alternatives that have shown a tendency to become at least as repressive as the worst of traditional religions. Thus while the concern for righteousness *before God* in political affairs has undoubtedly led to peremptory political practices, the modern commitment to secular, rational political control, especially as enhanced by modern technology, has also repeatedly proven to be profoundly oppressive.

d. The Revolt of the Masses

The worldliness of modern political life also owes to the political consequences of what has been called "mass society." Understood positively, a mass society is one in which the broad mass of the population is more thoroughly incorporated into the central institutions and value systems of society than they were previously in either traditional contexts or

22. Ibid., 86; see also Phillip E. Johnson, "Nihilism and the End of Law," *First Things* (March 1993): 19-25; and Phillip E. Johnson, *Reason in the Balance: The Case against Naturalism in Science, Law & Education* (Downers Grove, IL: InterVarsity Press, 1995).

even in earlier phases of modernity.[23] Yet "mass society" has also been held responsible for the denigration of personal character and for the collapse of genuine individuality into mass conformism. The advent of mass society and culture has thus been rather routinely decried as a threat to human personality. Reflecting on the impoverished quality of mass culture, for example, Romano Guardini observed:

> Mass man has no desire for independence or originality in either the management or the conduct of his life. . . . [T]he new man of the masses has no desire to live his life according to principles which are uniquely his own. Neither liberty of external action nor freedom of internal judgement seems for him to have unique value. . . . Mass man acts almost as if he felt that to be one's self was both the source of all injustice and even a sign of peril. . . . With the loss of personality, comes the steady fading away of that sense of uniqueness with which man had once viewed his own existence, which had once been the source of social intercourse. It is increasingly taken for granted that man ought to be treated as an object.[24]

Alexis de Tocqueville was among the first to reflect seriously upon the correlation between mass participation in modern political life and the secular and impersonal quality of modern democratic culture. Indeed, one of Tocqueville's principal concerns in his remarkable study *Democracy in America* (1848) was that the increasingly trivial and mundane quality of nineteenth-century American culture might actually be a kind of unintended by-product of democracy.[25] Because the democratic institutionalization of liberty and equality has the effect of liberating individuals from all traditional sources of authority, Tocqueville reasoned, it also leaves the matters of goodness and justice up to each individual to decide for him- or herself. Democracy declares all individuals to be equal, but in the process disconnects them from divine rev-

23. Edward Shils, *The Intellectuals and the Powers* (Chicago: University of Chicago Press, 1972), 229.

24. Romano Guardini, *The End of the Modern World: A Search for Orientation*, trans. Joseph Theman and Herbert Burke (1956; Chicago: Henry Regnery Company, 1968), 78-79.

25. Alexis de Tocqueville, *Democracy in America*, trans. George Lawrence (1848; Garden City, NY: Doubleday & Co./Anchor, 1969).

elation as well as from one another. Along this line, Tocqueville suggested that Americans were actually — albeit unwittingly — the world's most faithful disciples of Descartes.[26] They were skeptical, largely secular in outlook, materialistic, pragmatic, activistic, and egoistic.

Tocqueville went on to suggest that the democratic habit of relying only upon oneself creates a character that is extremely practical and inventive, but also profoundly restless and ultimately quite narrow. "Most of the people in these [democratic] nations," Tocqueville wrote:

> are extremely eager in the pursuit of immediate material pleasures and are always discontented with the position they occupy and always free to leave it. They think about nothing but ways of changing their lot and bettering it. For people in this frame of mind every new way of getting wealth more quickly, every machine which lessens work, every means of diminishing the costs of production, every invention which makes pleasures easier or greater, seems the most magnificent accomplishment of the human mind.[27]

Success in the realm of practical achievement, Tocqueville maintained, however, encouraged Americans to imagine that everything in the world was explicable in largely technical-rational terms. "Hence," Tocqueville wrote, "they have little faith in anything extraordinary and an almost invincible distaste for the supernatural."[28]

Tocqueville's greatest fear for American democracy was that this "almost invincible distaste for the supernatural" and the pursuit of immediate material pleasures might eventually extinguish the American spirit. "The prospect really does frighten me," he lamented, "that they may finally become so engrossed in a cowardly love of immediate pleasures that their interest in their own future and in that of their descendants may vanish, and that they will prefer tamely to follow the course of their destiny rather than make a sudden energetic effort necessary to set things right. . . ."[29]

A number of Tocqueville's concerns were restated earlier in this

26. Ibid., 429.
27. Ibid., 462.
28. Ibid., 430.
29. Ibid., 645.

century by Spanish philosopher José Ortega y Gasset in a study provocatively entitled *The Revolt of the Masses* (1932).[30] Ortega y Gasset contended that "hyperdemocracy" and the fabulous expansion of consumer goods by means of modern industrial technology have together created a "mass" society in which cultural and political aspirations have, in effect, been surrendered to the lowest common denominators of comfort, convenience, and safety. "[We] live at a time," Ortega y Gasset opined:

> when man believes himself fabulously capable of creation, but he does not know what to create. Lord of all things, he is not lord of himself. He feels lost amid his own abundance. With more means at its disposal, more knowledge, more technique than ever, it turns out that the world today goes the same way as the worst of worlds that have been; it simply drifts.[31]

Ortega y Gasset thus decried the "mass" appropriation of political power as a kind of "revolt" that threatens the very survival of Western civilization. For while it is true that the masses have replaced the repressive *ancien regime*, they possess no clear philosophical vision for political life and are far too easily fascinated by the unprecedented power of the modern political apparatus. Indeed, he argued that it is the facile fascination with power that produces the increasing politicization of modern life. The gravest danger threatening civilization today, Ortega y Gasset concluded:

> [is] State intervention. . . . When the mass suffers any ill-fortune or simply feels some strong appetite, its great temptation is that permanent, sure possibility of obtaining everything — without effort, struggle, doubt, or risk — merely by touching a button and setting the mighty machine in motion. . . . The result of this tendency will

30. José Ortega y Gasset, *The Revolt of the Masses* (New York: Mentor, 1932). Toqueville's concerns about unintended consequences of the democratic insitutionalization of equality and liberty have also been voiced recently by Tage Lindbom in *The Myth of Democracy*. "Unbridled liberty . . . ," Lindbom observes, for example (p. 71), "dissolves all ideas of value, it relativizes and atomizes. In the life of secularized man as well as in secularized society, strivings for liberty always open up new and growing sectors of pluralism and relativism at the expense of stability and continuity of values. Endless dialogue, debate, and scientific investigation fill the vacuum. . . ."

31. Ortega y Gassett, *Revolt of the Masses*, 31-32.

be fatal. . . . Society will have to live for the State, man for the governmental machine. . . .[32]

While his comments are perhaps somewhat elitist, Ortega y Gasset was surely correct to sense the incipient danger in abandoning the political process to mass sentiment; for this has the effect of reducing political aspirations to greed, immediacy, resentment, and other least common denominators of "public opinion."

The mention of "public opinion" reminds us that mass society owes its existence not simply to modern democracy, but even more basically to the possibilities of communication opened up by modern media; and it is therefore not surprising to find that "mass media" and political discourse have become very tightly interwoven in contemporary society. In this connection, although there is obviously much that could be said about the intransigent secularity of contemporary political journalism, it is perhaps more significant that mass media, because they expose us to so many points of view and to so many possible avenues of action, make it increasingly difficult for us to take traditional religious certainties and assumptions for granted. Put somewhat differently, mass media tend to foster — by and large accidentally — rationalized and predominantly secular sensibilities. As sociologist Daniel Lerner observed in an interesting study called *The Passing of Traditional Society* (1958):

> A mobile [modern] society has to encourage rationality, for the calculus of choice shapes individual behavior and conditions its rewards. People come to see the social future as manipulable rather than ordained and their personal prospects in terms of achievement rather than heritage. Rationality is purposive: ways of thinking and acting are instruments of intention (not articles of faith); men succeed or fail by the test of what they accomplish (not what they worship). So, whereas traditional man tended to reject innovation by saying "It has never been thus," the contemporary Westerner is more likely to ask "Does it work?" and try the new way without further ado. The psychic gap between these two postures is vast.[33]

32. Ibid., 88.
33. Daniel Lerner, *The Passing of Traditional Society: Modernizing the Middle East* (New York: The Free Press, 1958), 48-49.

Finally, we note that the mass-mediation of modern political discourse, combined with the phenomenal growth of government since mid-century, has contributed to the rise of what has been called a "new class" or "knowledge class" in contemporary Western societies.[34] This is the class of persons — consisting of intellectuals and educators, media personnel, artists, and producers of "high culture," those employed in public welfare and regulatory activities, and others employed in the so-called "knowledge industry" — who have benefited most materially from the recent expansion of governmental expenditures and services. The emergence of this "knowledge class" bears on the discussion of political worldliness for at least two reasons. The first is that this "class" has a vested interest in the continued expansion of the welfare state, and particularly in the expansion of state-subsidized "human services" and entitlements of various kinds. This interest stems not simply from the fact that "knowledge class" specialties and services are themselves often state-subsidized, but also because support for such specialties and services is not, for a variety of reasons, likely ever to come entirely from the private sector.[35] The second reason is simply that this class is so

34. Discussions of the "new class" thesis have gone on in a variety of contexts since mid-century. See, for example, Alvin Gouldner, *The Future of Intellectuals and the Rise of the New Class* (New York: Seabury Press, 1979); C. Everett Ladd Jr. and Charles D. Hadley, *Transformations of the American Party System: Political Coalitions from the New Deal to the 1970s* (New York: W. W. Norton, 1978); B. Bruce-Briggs, *The New Class?* (New Brunswick, NJ: Transaction Books, 1979); Peter L. Berger, "Ethics and the Present Class Struggle," *Worldview* (April 1978): 6-11; Peter L. Berger, *The Capitalist Revolution: Fifty Propositions about Prosperity, Equality, and Liberty* (New York: Basic Books, 1986); and Hansfried Kellner and Frank W. Heuberger (eds.), *Hidden Technocrats: The New Class and the New Capitalism* (New Brunswick, NJ: Transaction, 1992). A thorough bibliographic essay on the topic is given in an appendix to Gouldner's work, and the Introduction to Bruce-Briggs's volume provides a good overview of the recent debate about the "new class." See also my *With Liberty and Justice for Whom?: The Recent Evangelical Debate over Capitalism* (Grand Rapids, MI: Eerdmans, 1991), 177ff.

35. It should perhaps be noted that private sector support for "new class" services and specialties is apparently growing as many of these services and specialties become increasingly "mainstream." While once largely hostile to private enterprise, "new class" entrepreneurs have become increasingly successful at marketing their particular products, services, and outlook. As Hansfried Kellner and Peter L. Berger have noted recently: "The old industrial order is being modified, to some extent 'softened' by the cultural trends of which the new professionals are the principal carriers. The latter, however, are themselves being changed as they enter into this bargain. At the end of

much more thoroughly secularized than other social groups.[36] Indeed, to the extent that we understand secularization to be a process in which sectors of society and culture are withdrawn from the interpretive power of religion, the "knowledge class" is made up of those persons within modern society for whom religion has the least meaning. The reasons for this are not particularly mysterious. Modern higher education, which is perhaps the single most crucial qualification for membership in the "knowledge class," is inherently secularizing. We will have occasion to discuss the specific reasons for this in a later chapter, but suffice it here simply to note that there are any number of structural features of modern higher education which effectively discourage both faculty and students from maintaining religious faith.[37] In addition, as many "knowledge class" occupational specialties are *therapeutic* and focus entirely on this-worldly well-being, this class may be said to have something of a professional interest in secularity.[38] We will also discuss this issue at some length in a later chapter. Here we simply note that the therapeutic ideal of the present experience of well-being tends to be at odds with the Christian view of the impermanence of this world. Instead of relativizing this world over and against the world to come, the therapeutic ideal tends to devalue all other concerns in favor of the more or less immediate experience of well-being here and now.

---

the day, it is not clear *who* is coopting *whom* in this somewhat surprising symbiosis!" Hansfried Kellner and Peter L. Berger, "Lifestyle Engineering: Some Theoretical Reflections," in *Hidden Technocrats: The New Class and the New Capitalism*, ed. Hansfried Kellner and Frank W. Heuberger (New Brunswick, NJ: Transaction Books, 1992), 19.

36. Compare, for example, Peter Berger's comments in *The Capitalist Revolution*, 199, with those of Alvin Gouldner in *The Future of Intellectuals and the Rise of the New Class*, 1, 47.

37. "With few exceptions," Howard R. Bowen has noted in *Investment in Learning: The Individual and Social Value of American Higher Education* (San Francisco: Jossey-Bass, 1980), 125-26, "[attitudinal studies] indicate that [college] students become less favorable to the church, less convinced of the reality of God, less favorable to the observance of the sabbath, less accepting of religious dogma, less fundamentalistic, less orthodox, and more religiously liberal." Bowen also suggested that this heightened secularity tends to stay with students after college as well; Robert Wuthnow has made similar observations in *The Restructuring of American Religion: Society and Faith Since World War II* (Princeton: Princeton University Press, 1988), 156ff. We will return to this problem in Chapter 4.

38. Peter L. Berger, "The Worldview of the New Class: Secularity and Its Discontents," in *The New Class?* ed. B. Bruce-Briggs, 53.

Significantly, the secularity of the "knowledge class" also renders its members more vulnerable to the alienating effects of modernization than other segments of the population. As Peter Berger has commented:

> There are good grounds for saying that in most countries intellectuals have become more estranged from religion and religiously based morality than any other significant population group. Consequently, more than other groups, intellectuals suffer from the "alienation" and the *anomie* of modernity. They are *ipso facto* more susceptible to any secular messages of redemption from these ills.[39]

Not surprisingly, many of these "secular messages of redemption" are political in nature. Thus not only do members of this "knowledge class" benefit more or less directly from the expansion of the modern political apparatus, but they are uniquely prepared spiritually, as it were, to relativize all aspirations over and against those of political social change. A great many of our contemporaries are thus, in effect, occupationally predisposed to political worldliness.

Summarizing the above considerations, it is not difficult to see that worldliness has been literally *built into* the modern political process for any number of reasons. In the first instance, the democratization of equality and liberty has apparently had the effect of lowering the focus of modern political concerns to those of safety, creature comfort, and convenience. The vast expansion of the modern political apparatus, furthermore, both reflects and provides the perfect ongoing locus for mass aspirations to power. The conditions for "civil" political discourse in a highly differentiated society also apparently require the public square to be stripped of religion and other potentially divisive sources of input. Add to these considerations the facts that the "mass mediation" of political discourse has a way of relativizing religious certainties, that the "knowledge elite" in modern society is both highly secularized and therapeutically predisposed, and that the style of bureaucratic administration is inherently secular and impersonal, and there are obviously a number of powerful structural undercurrents pointing contemporary political discourse in a secular and worldly

---

39. Berger, *Capitalist Revolution*, 199.

direction. The burden of proof has thus increasingly fallen on those who would refuse to place secular political concerns above all others in the list of priorities.

Worldly Ideologies

We began by saying that a modern society is one in which it is typically assumed that all problems must lend themselves, at least in principle, to humanly calculable solutions. Given our discussion above, we might modify this assertion slightly here to say that a modern society is one in which it is assumed that all problems lend themselves to *politically* calculable solutions, for the assumption underlying so much of modern political life is that it is the responsibility of governments to distribute the material, and even spiritual benefits of modernity to their citizens.[40] The state has thus become the focus of a great deal of attention in modern times. Indeed, something very much like religious faith has often been placed in the state and in the possibilities of political-social change. In the context of mass society and culture, furthermore, this faith in the possibilities of political-social action is almost always communicated by way of *ideology*.

"When a particular definition of reality comes to be attached to a concrete power interest," Peter Berger and Thomas Luckmann suggested in *The Social Construction of Reality* (1966), "it may be called an ideology."[41] This sociological definition corresponds quite closely to the Marxist understanding of ideology as a body of knowledge that benefits some at the expense of others in society. I want to use a somewhat broader definition of ideology in the following, however, one that corresponds more closely to the common usage of the term as a synonym for worldview. From this perspective an ideology is not simply a definition of reality that "attaches to concrete power interests"; rather, it is a definition of reality that, precisely because it purports to comprehend and explain the world, promises power over the world and legitimates the use of this power. Indeed, the single most important characteristic

40. See Berger, *Pyramids of Sacrifice.*
41. Peter L. Berger and Thomas Luckmann, *The Social Construction of Reality: A Treatise in the Sociology of Knowledge* (New York: Penguin, 1966), 141.

of an ideology is its promise of *control*.[42] This is not to deny the fact that ideologies do inevitably benefit some at the expense of others in society, for they do indeed; but the attraction of ideology in the modern context far transcends the promotion of vested interest. Ideology's real attraction lies in its promise of collective mastery over the world, and in its capacity to mobilize mass support for political action.[43] This explains why ideologies are commonly both comprehensive and yet simple, for even as they purport to address all of the problems of the human condition, they must be relatively easy to understand in order to be communicable to the modern mass audience.

The worldliness of modern political ideologies stems from their promise of control over the social world, which requires this world to be reduced to a closed system amenable in principle to calculation and planning. This is why ideologies tend to be rationalistic and why they tend to rule such things as mystery, transcendence, and wisdom out of their definitions of reality *a priori*. It is also why those who continue to insist upon the importance of mystery, transcendence, and wisdom often become targets of ideological reproach for standing in the way of "progress" and for obstructing the practical task at hand. The modern ideological temper is both manipulative and impatient. It is confident of its own ability to grasp and manipulate the social world, and deeply distrustful of tradition — and especially of religious tradition — for its humility and hesitancy.[44] As political philosopher Michael Oakeshott noted a number of years ago, manipulative secular rationalism has, in effect, become "the stylistic criterion of all respectable politics" in the modern age.[45] The rationalistic temper of modern ideological politics has had the effect, furthermore, of greatly expanding the range of things for which we now feel responsible. In the absence of grace and mystery, the task of seeing that history develops reasonably has fallen to us; and it is held to be politically unsophisticated to suggest that we may not, in the end, be up to this task.

Of course, it may be asserted that the secularity of contemporary

42. See Glenn Tinder, *The Political Meaning of Christianity: The Prophetic Stance, An Introduction* (San Francisco: HarperSanFrancisco, 1989), 222-23.

43. Ibid., 222.

44. Ibid., 222-23.

45. Michael Oakeshott, *Rationalism in Politics and Other Essays* (Indianapolis, IN: Liberty Press, 1962), 5ff.

political discourse is mitigated to some extent by the sets of beliefs, symbols, and rituals — "civil religion," as it has been called — that frequently accord political events with a kind of religious dignity.[46] Yet however "religious" these civil creeds and ceremonies may appear, they are more or less obviously socially constructed with instrumental ends in view. The recent emergence of "new age" and/or "green" politics is instructive in this connection. At one level, the movement appears to be highly critical of modern rationalism and purports to represent a clear protest against technological artificiality in favor of a more natural and humble existence. Yet it would be mistaken to imagine that the proponents of the return to nature necessarily envision the renunciation of rational control over nature. Even as they reprove modern science and technology, "new age" critics still assume *a priori* that the problems of the human condition are up to us to solve, and that we must be prepared to use practically any means at our disposal in seeking to solve them. It is only in this light, then, that religion is of interest to advocates of "new age" ideology. Their concern is not so much with religious truth as it is with determining the instrumental value of various religious traditions with respect to various cultural and ecological problems. Indeed, we are told that the urgency of the practical task at hand is such that we must dispense with the knotty problems of truth and error altogether and focus instead upon constructing a new religious outlook that will enable us to cope with our universal responsibilities more effectively than traditional religion was able to do. As the authors of the *Millennium Whole Earth Catalogue* put it recently: "Now that we know we are gods, we might as well get good at it."[47]

Of course, "green" ideology is neither the only ideological alternative available today, nor is it the most important. While it is attractive to certain segments of the population in recent years, the "new age" is itself a kind of amalgamation of a number of older and more common ideological varieties. "Liberalism," or "classical liberalism" as it is sometimes called to distinguish it from the "liberal" wing of the Democratic party in the United States, is undoubtedly the most important of these varieties. As it

46. See Robert N. Bellah, "Civil Religion in America," *Daedalus* 96 (Winter 1967): 1-21.

47. Howard Rheingold (ed.), *The Millennium Whole Earth Catalogue: Access to Tools and Ideas for the Twenty-first Century* (San Francisco: HarperSanFrancisco, 1994), 1.

emerged out of the eighteenth century, modern liberal ideology suggested that the mastery of the world would be achieved a) by scientific advancement and b) by the liberation of individuals from the repressive constraints of religion and tradition, two commitments which together comprise the modern notion of "progress." While there have been a number of conflicting and, at times, competing schools within the liberal camp, the touchstone of liberal ideology has always been individual liberty. The ideological center of modern liberalism, Robert Bellah et al. noted, for example, in their influential study *Habits of the Heart*, "is the autonomous individual, presumed to be able to choose the roles he will play and the commitments he will make, not on the basis of higher truths but according to the criterion of life-effectiveness as the individual judges it."[48] As the word itself implies, then, liberalism focuses primarily on individual freedom. It is rationalist and secular in spirit, suspicious of tradition, opposed to privilege based upon ancestry, ethnicity, or religion, defensive of individual "rights," and largely respectful of conscience and private property.[49] Given the near-global commitment to the market economy today, liberalism is also likely to continue to be the predominant ideological alternative into the foreseeable future.

Modern times have also witnessed the emergence of a number of "radical" ideologies, however, that have customarily advertised themselves as more moral alternatives to liberal bourgeois decadence. Radical ideology also places a great deal of faith in our ability to progressively comprehend and fashion our world by way of science and technology. It is also typically secular in spirit, if not explicitly atheistic. Radicals have tended to part company with liberals, however, over the use of political power in the process of social reconstruction. "If there is any one element that gives distinction to the radicalism of the nineteenth and twentieth centuries," Robert Nisbet has noted in a discussion of modern ideologies, "it is . . . the sense of the redemptive possibilities which lie in political power: its capture, its purification, and its unlimited, even terroristic, use in the rehabilitation of man and institu-

48. Robert N. Bellah, Richard Madsen, William M. Sullivan, Ann Swidler, and Steven M. Tipton, *Habits of the Heart: Individualism and Commitment in American Life* (Berkeley: University of California Press, 1985), 47.

49. An excellent description of modern liberalism is provided in Harold J. Laski, *The Rise of European Liberalism: An Essay in Interpretation* (1936; London: Unwin Books, 1962), 13ff.

tions."[50] To the extent that modern political worldliness entails the relativization of all aspirations over and against those of political-social change, radical ideologies are the most explicitly worldly.

Modern political life has also been animated by the rise of a number of self-consciously "conservative" ideologies envisioned in opposition to both liberalism and radicalism. "If the central ethos of liberalism is individual emancipation, and that of radicalism the expansion of political power in the service of social and moral zeal," Nisbet observes:

> [then] the ethos of conservatism is tradition, essentially medieval tradition. From conservatism's defense of social tradition sprang its emphasis on the values of community, kinship, hierarchy, authority, and religion, and also its premonitions of social chaos surmounted by absolute power once individuals had become wrenched from the contexts of these values by the forces of liberalism and radicalism.[51]

Yet in speaking of conservatism's defense of the medieval tradition, it is important to stress that community, kinship, hierarchy, authority, and religion are not really valued for their own sakes, but only for the contribution they are potentially able to make in recovering whichever particular vision of the past conservatives happen to revere. Thus conservatism's focus is still altogether worldly and entirely trained on the maintenance of worldly social order. This is why it is just as necessary to speak of conservatism as an ideology as it is of liberalism and radicalism. For while the conservative bid for social mastery is often hidden behind its apparent reverence for the religious past, the conservative vision still tends to be premised upon a simplified understanding of social order, and it promises to recover the past by means of a kind of rational and controlled resurrection of traditional values and relationships. Contemporary advocacy on behalf of the need to return to "family values" is instructive in this connection. Although the values in question are largely biblical in origin, it is not entirely clear that all of the advocates of the "return to family values" would really be willing to submit to the obedience of Christian faith. Indeed, even the use of the term "values" in the contemporary discussion suggests a fundamentally modern, secu-

50. Robert A. Nisbet, *The Sociological Tradition* (New York: Basic Books, 1966), 10.
51. Ibid., 11.

lar, and ideological approach to social order which — albeit often unintentionally and unwittingly — is very much at odds with Christian faith. After all, doesn't the very use of the term imply that it is really up to *us* to choose whatever "values" *we* deem appropriate to whichever vision of social order *we* are seeking to construct?

While there is obviously a great deal more that could be said in describing and contrasting the liberal, radical, and conservative ideological alternatives, suffice it here to say that they all promise control over the social world by means of a comprehensively rational understanding of what the world is and how things work. In short, they [ideologies] are all profoundly worldly. As Glenn Tinder has recently suggested, ideologies are intolerant of all realities that surpass human control. "If they [ideologies] acknowledged realities such as [human] destiny and God — mysteries," Tinder writes:

> they would have to be far more circumspect. They would have to be humble, hesitant, and open. Were they in these ways circumspect, however, they would not be ideologies. Essential to their appeal is the claim to assured knowledge and powers of confident action. Ideologies promise dominion over history. . . . History cannot be brought under human dominion unless it is exhaustively accessible to human understanding. This is the source of ideological naturalism. . . . Ideologies must be not only naturalistic, but also, at least tacitly, atheistic. Within a universe that in all of its depths and distances is nothing more than a vast conflux of comprehensible and controllable realities, there can be no God.[52]

But perhaps Tinder overstates this last point, for ideologies do not necessarily rule out the existence of God altogether. Rather, they simply deny the possibility that God could speak or act in the world in any meaningful way. This is why Christianity has historically posed and continues to pose problems for modern ideologies. For the Christian religion insists, not simply upon a living and acting God, but also upon the absolute incapacity of human beings to solve their most pressing problems by themselves. Christianity thus denies the central tenet of modern political ideologies, namely faith in the possibility of autono-

---

52. Tinder, *Political Meaning of Christianity*, 223.

mous human control over the world. This, again, is why liberal and radical political ideologies have tended to be explicitly atheistic, or at least agnostic, with respect to the Christian religion. Recall, for example, Marx's celebrated assertion that the debunking of religion must precede all constructive social action.[53] Yet even conservative ideologies tend to have problems with God to the extent that his presence poses a threat to the stability of social order and to the traditions that people have constructed to honor him.

Given the impossibility of the promise of establishing autonomous human control over the world, however, it is not surprising to find that any number of ironies and internal contradictions float close to the surface in all of the major ideological paradigms. How is it that modern liberalism can promise unconstrained personal autonomy, for example, and yet also pledge an unwavering allegiance to modern science that, as we will see in the next chapter, debunks the notion of personhood altogether? And just how plausible is the radical claim that we can only be truly liberated by intentionally destroying — by means of political coercion — the very traditions and institutions that have provided people with meaning and purpose, not to mention sustenance and protection, throughout all of human history? Even conservative ideologies reveal a number of fateful contradictions. How is it possible, for example, to choose to reconstitute traditional society while at the same time refusing to submit to the original source of authority for the tradition? How, in other words, could conservatives recreate medieval — that is, by and large, *Christian* — social order without also creating the possibility — the *inevitability*, really — that the radical spirituality which lies at the very heart of the Christian faith would subvert this order?

Yet the most fateful contradiction inherent in all of the various ideological alternatives is that trying to establish autonomous human control over the world is, ironically, profoundly dehumanizing. This is because, if the ideological project is to be rational and controlled, it must eventually dispose of the possibility of human freedom. Persons must themselves be reduced to objects within the ideological equation

53. Karl Marx, "Contribution to the Critique of Hegel's Elements of the Philosophy of Right," in *The Marx-Engels Reader*, ed. Robert C. Tucker, 2nd edition (New York: Norton, 1978), 33-34, 59-60.

if political-social outcomes are to be predicted and managed. As Tinder has noted: "The effort to dominate nature brings about an incidental effort to dominate humanity. . . . The two motives of control of nature and control of humanity often are so fused as to be indistinguishable."[54] Of course, looking back over the course of the last century, one does not find it difficult to see that this is indeed the case. The actual expressions of the ideological pursuit of control have been enormously costly in human terms. Admittedly, some of these expressions have been far worse than others. Liberal ideology, for example, given its commitment to individual liberty, has not been anything like as repressive of political and religious freedoms as National Socialism, Marxist-Leninism, and/or the various versions of fascism and nationalism. Still, in seeking to establish political control over the world even liberal ideology has given rise to political mechanisms so gigantic and so thoroughly impersonal that they have, in effect, assumed a kind of fate-like character over and against us. And what is even worse is that, in the context of our increasingly secularized culture, the anxiety produced by the impersonality of social life seems only to intensify the attraction of ideology. It is a vicious and altogether worldly cycle.

Grounding Modern Political Aspirations

Yet beyond the structural secularity of contemporary political discourse, and even beyond the intrinsically secular logic of political ideologies, it is important to recognize that modern political aspirations were *intended* to be "this-worldly" from the very beginning. Early modern political theorists *began* by rejecting the traditional notion that political behavior needed to be legitimated and/or disciplined by religious understanding. Instead, they contended that rational political-social organization is its own justification, and that the political goal is therefore an end in itself. Put somewhat differently, early modern political theorists shifted the whole focus of the discussion away from the question of how we *ought* to live together in society, toward the pragmatic consideration of how

54. Glenn Tinder, *Against Fate: An Essay on Personal Dignity*, Loyola Lecture Series in Political Analysis, ed. Richard Shelley Hartigan (Notre Dame, IN: University of Notre Dame Press, 1981), 90.

human beings actually do live together, and on how this behavior can be effectively managed. From an originally religious frame-of-reference, then, modern political theory was intentionally grounded in this world. More specifically, it was grounded in *what can be made to work* in this world.[55] Worldliness and the express rejection of a religious view of life thus lie at the very root of the modern political project theoretically.

Although the traditional Christian understanding of political life — which was, by and large, Augustinian — began to come under pressure as early as the tenth and eleventh centuries with the rediscovery of Aristotle and the classical rationalists, the thinker most often associated with the distinctively modern turn is Niccolo Machiavelli (1469-1527). Machiavelli was the first to contend openly that the political craft ought to be guided exclusively by considerations of expediency, and that those in positions of authority could use whatever means were necessary in achieving their purposes so long as these purposes, and the means used to achieve them, were socially and politically cohesive.[56] In this connection, it is important to stress that the Machiavellian proposal did not simply call for a modification of the traditional Christian position, but rejected it altogether because of the Church's deep-seated pessimism concerning the possibilities of this-worldly political achievements. Machiavelli sought instead to rehabilitate ancient pagan political virtues which had stressed that "justice" and "morality" are really only social conventions that rest, finally, upon the often unjust and immoral exercise of power. From this point of view, the foundation of freedom is, in effect, tyranny.[57] Machiavelli's revisioning of political

55. Leo Strauss, "The Three Waves of Modernity," in *Introduction to Political Philosophy: Ten Essays*, ed. Hilail Gildin (Detroit: Wayne State University Press, 1989), 88.

56. See Leo Strauss, "Niccolo Machiavelli," in *History of Political Philosophy*, ed. Leo Strauss and Joseph Cropsey, 3rd edition (Chicago: University of Chicago Press, 1987), 296ff.

57. It is perhaps important to note that apologies for the Machiavellian project were made much more gently and persuasively than perhaps Machiavelli himself made them. For example, in his study entitled *The Making of Post-Christian Britain: A History of the Secularization of Modern Society* (London: Longman, 1980), Alan Gilbert includes the following quotation from Coluccio Salutati, a Florentine humanist, at the close of the fourteenth century (p. 21). "Do not believe, my friend," Salutati wrote, "that to flee the crowd, to avoid the sight of beautiful things, to shut oneself up in a cloister, is the way to perfection. In fleeing from the world you may topple down from heaven to earth, whereas I, remaining among earthly things, shall be able to lift my heart securely

life, which conjoined the renunciation of Christian otherworldliness
with an ostensibly more realistic view of human nature and society,
initiated a theoretical development in which pragmatic calculation and
coercion were to become the preeminently modern political principles.
"Be it known," Machiavelli asserted in *The Prince* (1513):

> that there are two ways of contending, one in accordance with laws, the
> other by force; the first of which is proper to men, the second to beasts.
> But since the first method is often ineffectual, it becomes necessary to
> resort to the second. A Prince should, therefore, understand how to use
> well both the man and the beast . . . to know how to use both natures,
> and that the one without the other has no stability.[58]

Yet in spite of its having come to expression in the work of Machiavelli at the end of the fifteenth century, the distinctively modern political
project does not really get off the ground philosophically until the seventeenth century in the work of Thomas Hobbes (1588-1679) and John
Locke (1632-1704). According to Hobbes, the basis for social and political
order must not be construed to be "justice" or any other fundamentally
religious notion, but is instead simply the common fear of anarchy and of
violent death. "For there is no such *finis ultimus*, (utmost ayme), nor
summum bonum, (greatest good), as is spoken of in the Books of the old
Morall Philosophers," Hobbes argued in *Leviathan* (1651), but only that
"felicity" which consists in the satisfaction of this-worldly desires.[59] We
consent to being governed simply because we recognize that, in the
absence of government, the pursuit of this-worldly desires results in a
dangerous war of "every man, against every man."[60] Locke subsequently

---

to heaven. In striving and working, in caring for your family, your friends, your city
which comprises all, you cannot but follow the right way to please God." Of course, it
is in the "you cannot but follow" that the crucial assumption is embedded, which is
that it is possible simply to equate "remaining among earthly things" with pleasing God.
One would be hard-pressed to find a more representative apology for modern political
worldliness.

58. Niccolo Machiavelli, *The Prince*, trans. N. H. Thompson (1513; New York:
Dover, 1992), 45.

59. Thomas Hobbes, *Leviathan*, ed. C. B. Macpherson (1651; New York: Penguin,
1983), 160.

60. Ibid., 185.

enlarged this calculation of self-interest to include the rational and supposedly God-given desire for comfort as well as the fear of death. "The great and chief end . . . of men's uniting into commonwealths, and putting themselves under government," Locke insisted, "is the preservation of their property, to which in the state of nature there are many things wanting."[61] Both thinkers thus contended for a new, and purportedly more rational, basis for moral and political order than the Church had been able to provide, in effect shifting the political focus from the *ought* to the *is* of human life. This new basis, it was felt, while admittedly more sordid than the traditional Christian view, had the advantage of being readily observable and — sadly — more reliable. "Against the traditional view, according to which a just society is a society in which just men rule," Leo Strauss commented concerning this distinctively modern shift, "Kant [eventually] asserted: 'Hard as it may sound, the problem of establishing the state [i.e. the social order] is soluble even for a nation of devils, provided they have sense,' that is, provided they are shrewd calculators."[62] In addition, to the extent that religion interfered with such shrewd calculation, it was held to be a hindrance to political and social order. Indeed, the modern scheme called for an intentional weakening of religion's hold on the public imagination. The secularization of political discourse was thus deemed necessary to the "enlightened" modern solution to the age-old problem of political and social order.[63]

Yet we note that the openly subversive and secular quality of modern political aspirations was mitigated during the eighteenth century by Jean-Jacques Rousseau's inventive contention that what had once been understood to be *meta*-physical sources of social and political authority — such as Holy Scripture — were really only primitive expressions of human longing for liberty and equality. Thus classical philosophical concerns for goodness and virtue as well as Christian concerns for the Kingdom of God did not have to be repudiated within modern political life, as Machiavelli had asserted. Rather, they simply needed to be reinterpreted in terms of "progress" and historical "development." This clever contention was

---

61. John Locke, "The Second Treatise of Government," in *The Political Writings of John Locke*, ed. David Wootton (1681; New York: Mentor, 1993), 325.

62. Strauss, "Niccolo Machiavelli," 298; see also his *Natural Right and History* (Chicago: University of Chicago Press, 1950), 165ff.

63. Strauss, *Natural Right and History*, 198.

advanced within German Idealism as well and was eventually systema-
tized by G. W. F. Hegel in the nineteenth century. The repressive and
often totalitarian quality of political developments since the middle of the
nineteenth century owes a great deal to this historicist interpretation of
social and political "progress," for within such an interpretive system there
can be no higher court of appeal than that staffed by representatives of
the so-called "Popular Will." As Tage Lindbom observes:

> In the final analysis, what is it that we call popular, democratic power?
> Beyond the expressed will of the people, as it is supposedly formulated,
> there is no appeal; here we meet the absolute, the universal, the
> indivisible, and the immovable. There is nothing *a priori*, nothing
> anterior to democratic power; no ideas of truth, no notions of good
> or bad, can bind the Popular Will. This "will" is free in the sense that
> it stands above all notions of value. It is egalitarian because it is reared
> on arithmetic equality. . . . It is not open to any appeal, it listens to
> no demand for grace, no plea for compassion. Like the Sphinx, the
> Popular Will is immovable in its enigmatic silence.[64]

Yet in spite of its explicit commitment to practical atheism, the
enlightened political theory of the seventeenth, eighteenth and
nineteenth centuries bore a striking resemblance to the Christian theory
it claimed to supplant. Along this line, Christopher Dawson contended
in *Progress and Religion* (1931) that, while the enlightened political
philosophy was decidedly secular, it really only amounted to a kind of
heretical variation on a fundamentally Christian theme:

> When the philosophers of the eighteenth century attempted to substi-
> tute their new rationalist doctrines for the ancient faith of Christendom,
> they were in reality simply abstracting from it those elements which had
> entered so deeply into their own thought that they no longer recognized
> their origin. Eighteenth-century Deism was but the ghost or shadow of
> Christianity, a mental abstraction from the reality of a historical religion,
> which possessed no independent life of its own. It retained certain
> fundamental Christian conceptions — the belief in a beneficent Cre-
> ator, the idea of an overruling Providence which ordered all things for

64. Lindbom, *The Myth of Democracy*, 85.

the best, and the chief precepts of the Christian moral law, but all these were desupernaturalized and fitted into the utilitarian rational scheme of contemporary philosophy. Thus the moral law was divested of all ascetic and other-worldly elements and assimilated to practical philanthropy, and the order of Providence was transformed into a mechanistic natural law. Above all this was the case with the idea of Progress, for while the new philosophy had no place for the supernaturalism of the Christian eschatology, it could not divest itself of the Christian teleological conception of life. Thus the belief in the moral perfectibility and the indefinite progress of the human race took the place of the Christian faith in the life of the world to come, as the final goal of human effort.[65]

"For the love of God," Carl Becker commented similarly in a provocative essay entitled *The Heavenly City of the Eighteenth Century Philosophers* (1932), "they [the eighteenth-century philosophers] substituted the love of humanity; for the vicarious atonement the perfectibility of man through his own efforts; and for the hope of immortality in another world the hope of living in the memory of future generations."[66] The similarities between modern political theory and Christian theology were also underlined in Eric Voegelin's *The New Science of Politics* (1952).[67] The distinguishing characteristic of the modern political project, Voegelin argued, is not its commitment to the perfection of social order — for this is also the Christian hope — but rather its insistence that this perfection is immanently achievable by means of human effort. "Modern civilization, especially as manifested in its most uncompromising form in the ideological mass movements . . . ," David Walsh recently commented summarizing Voegelin's insights, "is primarily a deformation of the Christian experience that redirects the eschatological

65. Christopher Dawson, *Progress and Religion: An Historical Inquiry* (1931; Peru, IL: Sherwood Sugden & Co., 1991), 190-91.
66. Carl L. Becker, *The Heavenly City of the Eighteenth Century Philosophers* (New Haven, CT: Yale University Press, 1932), 130.
67. Eric Voegelin, *The New Science of Politics: An Introduction* (Chicago: University of Chicago Press, 1952). Voegelin labeled this deformation of Christianity and its consequent "re-divinization" of this-worldly political life "gnosticism," and he traced the problem back to the heretical theology of a twelfth-century monk named Joachim of Flora. Joachim was the first to predict the sort of immanent fulfillment of history that has become the trademark of modern political ideology.

transformation toward an innerworldly fulfillment within time."[68] Along this line, we note that this secularization of Christian eschatology betrays the human expropriation of divine prerogatives in which human creativity is all but substituted for God's providential direction of history.[69]

Beyond its ambivalent relation to Christianity, however, the modern political project has tended to have problems with *any* understanding of social and political order that implies *any* limits to human freedom. Thus modern liberalism also rejected the classical understanding of the political task, and even went so far as to reject the classical philosophical notion of "nature" because it implied the existence of an objective standard to which human life must be made to conform. The modern view puts quotation marks around words like "nature" to indicate that whatever passes for "nature" is really only a social convention. Because society is socially constructed, so the modern argument runs, "nature" is only meaningful insofar as we deem it to be in our free construction of social and political order.[70] Besides depreciating nature, this glorifies the political task, for it suggests that we are the creators — in effect, *ex nihilo* — of our own meanings and purposes.[71] Thus did eighteenth- and nineteenth-century social and political theory wage a war, not simply against Christian understanding, but against any kind of religious understanding of the order of the world.[72] Prometheus, just as Marx asserted, is indeed the patron saint of modern political aspirations.[73]

68. David Walsh, *After Ideology: Recovering the Spiritual Foundations of Freedom* (San Francisco: HarperCollins, 1990), 103.

69. See, for example, Karl Löwith, *Meaning in History: The Theological Implications of the Philosophy of History* (Chicago: University of Chicago Press, 1949).

70. See John Milbank, *Theology and Social Theory: Beyond Secular Reason* (Oxford: Basil Blackwell, 1990), 148.

71. See Strauss, *Natural Right and History,* 201.

72. See Steven Seidman, *Liberalism and the Origins of European Social Theory* (Berkeley: University of California Press, 1983). Seidman writes (p. 39): "Implicit in the structure of Enlightenment criticism [of religion and philosophy] of closed systems is an attack upon cosmological presuppositions. . . . In contrast to cosmological presuppositions, a secular order projects a universe that places all entities on the same level of being, and is changing, infinite, and governed by efficient, nonteleological causality. Translated into sociocultural terms, secularism reveals a pronounced drift toward liberal values and orientations: progress, tolerance, egalitarianism, and empiricism."

73. Karl Marx, from the preface to his doctoral dissertation of 1841, *Karl Marx, Friedrich Engels: Collected Works,* vol. 1 (New York: International Publishers, 1975), 31.

Christian Contributions to
Modern Political Worldliness

It is important to stress, however, that the Church has not simply been a victim in this process of secularization. On the contrary, Christianity — and in particular Protestant Christianity — appears to have contributed quite significantly to the secularization of modern political life both accidentally and, to a certain extent, intentionally. The religious wars that followed the Reformation, for example, so splintered European moral and political authority as to suggest that religion might, after all, be detrimental to settled society, and so encouraged disaffected intellectuals to search for a more rational basis for social and political order.[74] The wars of religion also created a political vacuum which was rather quickly filled by early modern nation-states equipped with new notions of state-sovereignty vis-à-vis the authority of the Church. Along a somewhat similar line, British historian John Sommerville has recently suggested that the process of secularization in England was initiated by Henry VIII's confiscation of church property in 1530.[75] Not only did this "profanation" of monastic holdings have the effect of secularizing ordinary "space" within English consciousness, but it rather dramatically demonstrated the relative power of Church and state. "In 1486," Sommerville notes, "the English government was glad to have the support of a papal bull which announced the Holy Father's 'great curse' on those who did not acknowledge Henry VII. . . . Two centuries later the English government refused to allow its emasculated church even to define blasphemy for legal purposes."[76] The disconnection of theology and politics inaugurated at the English Reformation thus seems to have portended the eventual emergence of completely *a*-theistic sources of moral and political legitimacy.[77]

---

74. See Wolfhart Pannenberg, *Christianity in a Secularized World* (New York: Crossroad, 1989); see also Stephen Toulmin, *Cosmopolis: The Hidden Agenda of Modernity* (Chicago: University of Chicago Press, 1990), 45ff.

75. C. John Sommerville, *The Secularization of Early Modern England: From Religious Culture to Religious Faith* (New York: Oxford University Press, 1992).

76. Ibid., 111.

77. In *Sources of the Self: The Making of the Modern Identity* (Cambridge, MA: Harvard University Press, 1989), Charles Taylor suggests that contemporary political discourse is chiefly informed by "non-theistic sources" of moral authority such as "rea-

Protestant theological innovations also appear to have contributed to the secularity of modern political discourse. By curtailing the number of things deemed essential to salvation, and by distinguishing them from mere ceremonies, superstitions, and other matters considered to be "indifferent" *(adiaphora)* or merely secular, the Reformers opened up social *space* for secularity in a way that medieval Catholicism had not. Protestantism's renewed emphasis upon conversion, furthermore, and the great stress that Luther and others placed upon the operations of individual conscience implied that the larger social order was not, and indeed would not ever be, entirely Christian. This inevitably led to a situation in which unbelief would become more of a social and political problem in Protestant societies than it had been within medieval Christendom, for from the Protestant point of view, the interests of true faith could never be served by compulsion. In this connection, Talcott Parsons has gone so far as to suggest (following Hegel) that the Protestant "enfranchisement of the individual" all but necessitated the emergence of modern secular culture.[78] While Christianity had traditionally separated the "sacred" and "secular" realms, and had conceded a kind

---

son" and/or "nature." These sources are held up as purely self-contained goods capable of providing a surer foundation for social and moral order than older theistic sources which still relied upon grace and mystery. Interestingly, Taylor notes that most of these secular substitutes emerge out of the Christian tradition. "In each case," he notes (p. 315), "the stimulus existed within Christian culture itself to generate these views which stand on the threshold [of modernity]. . . . What arises in each case is a conception which stands ready for a mutation, which will carry it outside the Christian faith altogether." Also in this connection, in an article entitled "Autonomy and the Rationalization of Moral Discourse," *Sociological Analysis* 35 (Summer 1974): 95-101, E. Leites contends that the reliance upon nontheistic moral sources helps to account for the tremendous emphasis upon individual autonomy in modern culture. It is, Leites argues, the individual rational agent who must finally draw out the implications of these sources for social and moral order. "A reliance on what are believed to be universally valid modes of ascertaining truth and the demand for autonomy may seem to be only contingently linked," Leites concludes (p. 101), "but perhaps there is more to their connection. It could be that this 'rationalization' of moral and religious thought sustains the demand for individual autonomy. Were this so, one form of the often condemned 'objective' consciousness is a basis for one of the profound freedoms that mankind can achieve."

78. Talcott Parsons, "Christianity and Modern Industrial Society," in James F. Childress and David B. Harned (eds.), *Secularization and the Protestant Prospect* (Philadelphia: Westminster, 1970), 43-70.

of relative autonomy to secular affairs, Protestantism extended the principle so far that it eventually released individuals from the tutelage of religion altogether. At present, Parsons observed:

> The individual is responsible not only for managing his own relation to God through faith within the ascribed framework of an established church, which is the Reformation position, but for choosing that framework itself, for deciding as a mature individual what to believe, and with whom to associate himself in the organizational expression and reinforcement of his commitments. This is essentially the removal of the last vestige of coercive control over the individual in the religious sphere; he is endowed with full responsible autonomy.[79]

Contemporary denominational pluralism, Parsons continued, represents a kind of logical conclusion to this process, with religious toleration now extended even to those who choose, in good conscience, not to believe anything at all.[80]

In defense of the Reformers, it should be noted that late medieval Scholasticism's conception of "natural law" had already effectively conceded a kind of *relative* autonomy of the secular state by suggesting that the state belonged to a *natural* community endowed by God with laws available to the unaided human intellect. Within this view, the political authorities did not have to appeal to supernatural revelation, but needed only to perform their tasks reasonably and in accordance with nature.[81] In one of the signal ironies of modern intellectual history, however, it was the Reformers' rejection of "natural law" doctrine with

79. Ibid., 61.

80. It should be noted that Parsons falsely equates the Reformers' protest against Roman Catholicism's abuse of religious authority and the modern rejection of religious authority *per se*. This is how it is possible for him to trace a continuity between the Reformation and modern secular culture. Yet, as Klaus Bockmuehl noted in an article entitled "Secularism and Theology," in *Crux* 19 (June 1983): 12: "The Reformation refuses to set the sacred apart; it moves into the profane world, declaring all of it sacred, because of its quality of being God's creation. Today's ideologists depart from the world as creation into atheism, making the world the field of human autonomy. That is a new concept of secularism, a second secularism, as different from the first as human autonomy is from the hallowing of this world for God."

81. See Edward Schillebeeckx, "Silence and Speaking about God," in *Theology* 71 (1968): 256-67.

its confidence in human reason that seems eventually to have resulted in such typically modern notions as the separation of Church and state. Why this happened becomes clear if we recall that the medieval conception of "nature" was still entirely *theological*, that is, it was understood in terms of final, and ultimately religious causes. Rational political activity was thus still embedded in a thoroughly theological — if not entirely biblical — framework. The Reformers subsequently rejected the "natural law" framework — which, after all, was a synthesis of biblical and Aristotelian categories — out of their concern for the sole authority of Scripture and for the sole efficacy of grace. But this rejection was full of paradoxical possibilities. Indeed, it defined a kind of watershed between medieval and modern conceptions of social order. In his classic study *Religion and the Rise of Capitalism* (1926), R. H. Tawney contended that the rejection of Roman Catholic "canon law," based as it was upon natural law theory, was Luther's signal contribution to the modern world:

> Since salvation is bestowed by the operation of grace in the heart and by that alone, the whole fabric of organized religion, which had mediated between the individual soul and its Maker — divinely commissioned hierarchy, systematized activities, corporate institutions — drops away, as the blasphemous trivialities of a religion of works. The medieval conception of the social order, which had regarded it as a highly articulated organism of members contributing in their different degrees to a spiritual purpose, was shattered, and differences which had been distinctions within a larger unity were now set in irreconcilable antagonism to each other. Grace no longer completed nature: it was the antithesis of it. Man's actions as a member of society were no longer the extension of his life as a child of God: they were its negation. Secular interests ceased to possess, even remotely, a religious significance: they might compete with religion, but they could not enrich it. Detailed rules of conduct — a Christian casuistry — are needless or objectionable: the Christian has a sufficient guide in the Bible and in his own conscience.[82]

---

82. Tawney, *Religion and the Rise of Capitalism: A Historical Study* (1926; New York: Harcourt, Brace & Company, 1952), 97-98.

Of course, the point of Luther's rejection of canon law was to *resacralize* the social order and to eliminate the false divisions between sacred and secular that Roman Catholicism had introduced into social life. The thrust of his protest, furthermore, was to insist that *all* Christians and *all* vocations are honoring to God. Yet Luther's protest created the possibility that, once elevated in this way, secular vocations might cease to be understood in faith and might come instead to be valued in and of themselves. Along this line, Klaus Bockmuehl has observed that in his concern to defend the religious value of ordinary secular work over and against monasticism's distortion of the biblical theology of vocation, Luther overemphasized the importance of the civil vocation for Christian faith and life.[83] This overreaction appears also to have stemmed from Luther's concern that the Anabaptists had placed far too much emphasis upon the individual guidance of the Holy Spirit in the matter of calling or vocation. "The real 'saint,'" Bockmuehl observes concerning Luther's position, "is now the 'secular saint' — not the one who withdraws from society. . . . Moreover, one gets the impression that Luther secularized the New Testament doctrine of the Spirit's gifts and tasks in the church . . . in applying it to the interplay of vocations in civil society which for him, of course, was identical with the church."[84] The legacy of this largely unintentional secularization of the notion of vocation, Bockmuehl laments, is still evident in European Protestantism in its suspicion of spirituality and in its disinterest in cross-cultural Christian missions.

Of course, Luther's understanding of the "two kingdoms" and "two governments" is also instructive in this regard, for, while his intention was to reassert the mutual interdependence of the secular and spiritual governments, later Lutheran theologians — under the influence of Enlightenment rationalism — began to interpret the "two kingdoms" in terms of mutually exclusive spheres of influence and began to view political life as subject only to "scientific" consideration. In his study of eighteenth- and nineteenth-century Protestant theology, Karl Barth laid much of the blame for the devolution of the Lutheran understanding of the two governments at the feet of German Pietism. With

83. Klaus Bockhmuehl, "Recovering Vocation Today," *Crux* 24 (Summer 1988): 25-35.

84. Ibid., 30-31.

their characteristic stress upon private religious experience, the Pietists appear to have surrendered all too easily to enlightened rationalism in the public realm and thereby unwittingly allowed the Church to be absorbed into the secular state.[85] In part, this unfortunate development had to do with Pietism's concern to prevent the official state churches from interfering with the pursuit of *true* Christianity. But preventing the state church from interfering with true religion suggested a tolerant and religiously-indifferent state.[86]

Perhaps the most important reason for eighteenth-century Pietism's tractable surrender to rationalism in public life, however, was that the Pietists themselves began to understand the Christian religion as principally a matter of improving this-worldly social conditions, and rational science seemed to promote this improvement more immediately than religious dogma. "It is important to note," Barth observed,

> that despite the great differences in the structure of the preaching of Pietists and rationalists . . . [they] were not in the last resort [of] two minds about the direction that had been taken. . . . The attention of both was focused on the practical life that was to be changed, on the Christian works that came from faith, but the Pietists were more concerned with inner works (though not without all kinds of very outward regulation and determination) and the rationalists more with outward works (though this did not prevent them from speaking most earnestly about the renewal of the heart, the conscience and the

85. Karl Barth, *Protestant Theology in the Nineteenth Century: Its Background and History* (London: S.C.M. Press, 1972), 85. Barth may be accused of a somewhat *ad hominem* reading of Pietism here, for the likes of Spener and Francke cannot be charged with surrendering public political life to rationalism; and, to the extent that subsequent generations of Pietists did withdraw from public political life, it is not clear that this surrender was theologically motivated.

86. This appears to have been true of English nonconformism as well. Guenther Roth argued, for example, that the freedom of conscience, which arose out of the nonconformist demand to be tolerated by the state churches, is really the oldest of the modern "Rights of Man." See Guenther Roth, "Religion and Revolutionary Beliefs: Sociological and Historical Dimensions in Max Weber's Work — In Memory of Ivan Vallier (1927-1974)," in *Social Forces* 2 (December 1976): 257-72. "The other Rights of Man or civil rights," Roth writes (p. 260), "were joined to this basic right, especially the right to pursue one's own economic interests, which includes the inviolability of individual property, the freedom of contract, and vocational choice."

disposition, and from laying weight on the appropriate feelings) . . . both Pietists and rationalists were modern men and, more particularly, modern citizens, who applied to traditional Christianity a particular presupposition, namely the presupposition, the idea, the systematic principle that in all circumstances Christianity must serve to improve life.[87]

Of course, the religious stress upon the improvement of this life was not a Pietist invention, but is implicit in the Christian understanding of creation and of humanity's place within it. Still, it was the Reformers' reemphasis of the creation mandate and their stress upon serving one's neighbor by improving the material conditions of life that had the effect of focusing a potentially unbalanced amount of interest in this world. This is particularly evident in the Protestant redefinition of the notion of "calling."

In contrast to medieval Catholicism's insistence that the only truly Christian "calling" entailed a retreat from the world, the Reformers reinterpreted the notion of calling to affirm the religious value of work in this world. Not only were Protestants thereby enabled to feel much more comfortable doing worldly work, but ordinary work would become increasingly significant religiously from the Protestant point of view. This religious value of worldly work was perhaps most evident among the English Puritans, who deliberately sought to bring all work under the discipline of the Christian religion. The intensity of the Puritan effort had the effect of unleashing an extraordinary amount of creative energy into English society. Indeed, two recent students of English Puritanism have gone so far as to suggest that "in this doctrine of calling . . . we find as in no other single concept perhaps the ideological wa-

87. Barth, *Protestant Theology in the Nineteenth Century*, 97-99. Barth's sentiments were echoed by Samuel H. Miller in a series of lectures he delivered at Yale University in 1963 and subsequently published as *The Dilemma of Modern Belief* (New York: Harper & Row, 1963). "The iconoclasts [i.e. rationalists]," Miller argued (p. 46), "cleared out the rubbish of superstition, but they prepared the way for empty abstractions to take the place of a real God. The pietists wanted nothing more than to know God inwardly, to feel Him spiritually, sensationally; yet they ended by seeing Him no longer in the creation He had made, but only in their self-manipulated emotions. The liberals wanted to understand God intelligently, rationally, but before they were through they had reduced Him to a harmless and impotent set of principles. God was killed by his friends."

tershed between the ancient, medieval and the modern mind. . . ."[88] Tawney, for example, contended that it was the Puritan rejection of the natural law tradition and their radicalization of the notion of "calling" which ultimately gave way to the modern utilitarian understanding of social order. Tawney attributed this development to the fact that, while the Puritans deemed nature and natural human society to be aspects of God's good creation, they nevertheless did not expect to find truly human meanings inhering in either. Rather, nature and natural society only became Christianly significant to the extent that they could be made to conform to the will of God as revealed in Scripture. This meant that Puritans were at once less contemplative and more manipulative than their late-medieval forbears. True, it would take several generations for this manipulative bent to devolve into secular utilitarianism, and it would only transpire as the religious fervor of Puritanism was quenched by brutal political repression toward the end of the seventeenth century, but devolve it did. After all, Locke's suggestion that we most please God by living rationally — that is, scientifically — in this world is a kind of secularized variation on the typically Puritan theme of employing practical reason in the service of God and the common good. And so, although the early Puritan conception of social order was decisively theological and stressed the importance of integrating one's vocation into the larger religious framework of service to God and neighbor, later Puritans increasingly tended to segregate religion from everyday life in the world and to place the accent on the latter.[89] With the emergence of early modern science, the problems of everyday life in this world appear to have become relatively much more interesting and engaging than those of theology anyway.

The subtle reinterpretation of Christian faith such that it was seen to be principally a matter of improving life in this world is obviously relevant to the concerns of our study. It not only heralded the secularization of Protestantism from within, but it also left Protestant churches

---

88. Charles and Katherine George, "Protestantism and Capitalism in Pre-Revolutionary England," in *The Protestant Ethic and Modernization: A Comparative View*, ed. S. N. Eisenstadt (New York: Basic Books, 1968), 174.

89. This point was made very convincingly by Robert S. Michaelson in "Changes in the Puritan Concept of Calling or Vocation," in *New England Quarterly* 26 (1953): 315-36; see also Robert Shenk, "Robert Frost and the Early Puritan Idea of Vocation," *Christian Scholar's Review* 10, no. 3 (1981): 229-37.

vulnerable to the rationalist suggestion that the Christian religion is an impediment to social and political progress. While this objection was met with apologetic attempts to demonstrate the social and political usefulness of Christian faith, this only had the effect of making Christianity seem to the intellectual classes to be even more alien to the paramount concerns of social and political order. As Peter Berger has noted, the strategy of apologizing for Christian faith by trying to demonstrate its social utility is always eventually self-liquidating. Sooner or later people realize that a great many of the supposedly practical and secular benefits of the Christian religion can be had more easily without the religion.[90] The consequences of this odd dynamic of self-liquidation have been felt most acutely in "liberal" Protestant circles in recent decades, but the fact that this tendency first surfaced in the late seventeenth and early eighteenth centuries, and in precisely those movements which would eventually give rise to modern evangelicalism, should give even conservatives pause. The logic of practical atheism may well be more deeply ingrained in the evangelical tradition than conservatives perhaps have realized.

Summary

There has been and will undoubtedly continue to be considerable disagreement over which of the theological and/or philosophical innovations discussed above was most crucial to the development of the modern political project, not to mention over the question of whether the distinctively modern view is better or worse than its antecedents. Yet however these questions are eventually resolved, it is important to stress that the most crucial presumptions informing modern political life — that nothing is more important than social and political order; that social and political order is something that we are responsible for constructing, and that we are, furthermore, free to construct and reconstruct this order more or less as we see fit — have deep structural and intellectual roots in modern Western culture. Stated this bluntly, the audacity of these presumptions appear almost ludicrous, but they are clearly no laughing matter. The enormous growth in the power and

90. Peter L. Berger, *The Heretical Imperative: Contemporary Possibilities of Religious Affirmation* (Garden City, NY: Anchor, 1980), 106.

pretensions of modern governments is a direct reflection of the vast number of things we currently expect to be able to accomplish by political means, and the extent to which we are not alarmed by this growth may be an indication of just how worldly we have become. We have apparently become so enticed by the ideological promises of political-social control that we simply have not noticed the degree to which modern life has become politicized. And yet, perhaps because some aspects of the modern outlook are Christian in origin helps to explain why the pretentiousness of modern political aspirations does not stand out in as much relief for contemporary Christians, and particularly for modern Protestants, as it probably should. The fact that the modern political project already represents a secularized form of Christianity also explains why it has proven so difficult for Christians to speak distinctively *as Christians* in the modern political arena.

It is vital to stress at the conclusion of our discussion of modern political worldliness that the Promethean pretensions of modern political life pose a dire threat, not simply to religious understanding, but ultimately to human freedom. For the pursuit of rationalized political mastery inevitably has the effect of reducing reality — including human persons — to mere "objects" and "things" which are relatively easily, and potentially carelessly, manipulated and controlled. In the absence of any countervailing religious understanding, furthermore, there is little to prevent political ends from justifying whatever means are necessary for achieving them. As Romano Guardini noted: "As long as men are unable to control themselves from within . . . they will inevitably be 'organized' by force from without. . . ."[91]

And so the initial exhilaration that came from realizing that we could, in God's absence, do whatever we wanted, has by now given way to the sobering awareness that, because we can no longer appeal to God, we have no way of preventing others from doing what *they* want to do to *us*.[92] Put somewhat differently, the promise of control always boils down to the control of some at the expense of others and, what is more likely, the control of the few at the expense of the many. Modern political algebra thus states that the price of freedom is freedom itself. This is

91. Guardini, *The End of the Modern World*, 119n.
92. Phillip E. Johnson, "Nihilism and the End of Law," *First Things* (March 1993): 19-20.

the ironical cost of modern political worldliness. "The project of bringing heaven down to earth," Lesslie Newbigin wisely noted in this connection, "always results in bringing hell up from below."[93]

Christian Hope as a Political Virtue

As we have noted, Søren Kierkegaard insisted that the characteristic depravity of the nineteenth century lay in its theoretical contempt for individual human beings and in the elevation of abstract humanistic ideals over real human existence. Looking back on our own century, it is evident that this theoretical contempt rather quickly gave way to practical contempt and to an actual disdain for real people. Over the course of the last one hundred years or so at least one hundred million human lives have been sacrificed on the altars of "progress," "development," "social justice," "brotherhood," "national identity," and other abstract "humanistic" ideals. This is almost unbearably sad. It is also bewildering. How can there have been — and, indeed, how can there continue to be — such a vast discrepancy between the exalted ideals of modern political life and the depravity of modern political practice? Why has the modern world so consistently elevated political-social aspirations over and above the lives of real people?

One possible answer to these questions is that modern — and by now presumably postmodern — social and political theory has encouraged us to imagine that things like human freedom and dignity are ultimately *social* in origin, that is, that these are values which exist *only* to the extent that we decide to realize them by constructing them socially and politically. Such a view, after all, carries a certain self-evident plausibility, for it seems to interpret what we imagine to be true about our own history and about the histories of other cultures. It appears more or less obvious that values such as "freedom," "equality," and "justice" are historically situated and arise out of local custom and certain social and political conventions. This is why the current intellectual assault on "Western" civilization and on "Eurocentric" values has left us somewhat dumbfounded. For however uneasy we may be

93. Lesslie Newbigin, *Foolishness to the Greeks: The Gospel and Western Culture* (Grand Rapids, MI: Eerdmans, 1986), 117.

with the notion of "political correctness," the advocates of such things as multiculturalism are simply extending the logic of a typically modern proposition that we already take largely for granted, namely, that we create our own meanings, purposes, and values for ourselves.

But what if this modern view is fundamentally mistaken? What if such things as freedom, dignity, and justice are *not* social in origin and *not* simply "values" that have been socially constructed under certain local and historical circumstances? What if freedom, dignity, and justice are actually part and parcel of created moral order? And what if these things do *not* ultimately depend upon our political acumen and our ability to guarantee them? What if, on the contrary, social and political organization actually pose a profound threat to freedom, dignity, and justice precisely because of the tendency of power to corrupt and of political and social aspirations to eclipse all other human purposes? What if, instead, freedom, dignity, and justice are actually the consequences, as the Scriptures suggest that they ought to be, of each of us determining, before God, to love our neighbor as ourselves? This possibility — that modern social and political theory is fundamentally mistaken about the natures of freedom and dignity and, indeed, about the nature of human existence — is what we want to consider briefly in the light of a Christian understanding of *hope.* Indeed, because it reverses typically modern assumptions and relativizes social and political aspirations over and against the infinite significance of real individual people, Christian hope turns out to be a profoundly important political resource.

To be a human being is to be "on the way."[94] From the moment our lives begin we are in motion, moving either toward or away from certain possibilities, constantly being thrust forward into unfamiliar territory. Although our lives are grounded in the past and present, we are always advancing toward an unknown and largely unknowable future. This accounts for the restless quality of our lives. This restless quality, while occasionally fulfilling and energizing, is also quite disturbing and unnerving. To be perpetually "on the way" is a source of considerable anxiety, for it means always to be at risk of losing those things we have managed to grasp hold of along the way, and the ultimate trajectory of our lives is always occluded by the inevitability of death. We are, in short, creatures

---

94. I have taken much of the following material from Josef Pieper's excellent booklet *On Hope* (San Francisco: Ignatius, 1986).

of *destiny*, and the crucial questions about our existence have always had to do with destiny. What controls it? Is it meaningful? To what extent can we influence or take control of it? Is it, finally, an illusion?

Christian hope answers the question of destiny. Indeed, it anwers it quite decisively, and this is why the gospel is such profoundly good news. It is the Christian hope that prevents us, as the apostle Paul wrote to the Thessalonians, from grieving over death "like the rest of men, who have no hope" (1 Thess. 4:13).

From a Christian standpoint the restless quality of our lives in this world is not lamented. Rather, it is celebrated as a gracious reminder that we are currently on the way to a lasting rest and that our destiny — at least if we do not refuse it — is to stand forever before the face of the living God. This destiny has already been guaranteed by the resurrection of Jesus Christ from the dead, and by his glorious ascension into heaven, where he sits enthroned at the right hand of the Father, vested with all power and authority (Phil. 2:9-11). This is why, in sharp contrast to the common usage of the word as a synonym simply for "wish" or "desire," the Christian use of the word *hope* denotes certain knowledge and utter reliability. It is synonymous with confidence. We remind ourselves of this when we confess: "And He *shall* come again with glory to judge both the living and the dead, and His kingdom *will* have no end." The triadic formula: "Christ has come; Christ is risen; Christ will come again" conveys real knowledge and forms the basis of real hope. It settles the question of destiny.

Humility, patience, and magnanimity are virtues that attend the Christian hope. In humility we recognize that the future, though secure, is not under our control, and hence that we are not finally responsible even for the "success" of our own lives here and now. Patience enables us to endure our present sufferings and to wait for our revelation as sons and daughters of the living God (Rom. 8:18-19). Magnanimity, further- more, means taking courage in the sure knowledge of our final end and that we *will*, as the Westminster Confession of Faith puts it, know the living God and enjoy him forever.

There are two kinds of hopelessness from a Christian point of view, both of which the Church has traditionally discussed under the heading of *spiritual sloth*, and both of which are linked, finally, by human pride. The first kind of hopelessness lies in the *presumption* that we are actually the masters of our own fate and that the matter of destiny is therefore under our control. Presumption is a form of hopelessness because its aspirations have no surer foundation than those of human decision and human effort. It is also slothful because it more or less willfully neglects spiritual reflection. Presumption does not want to risk discovering the inadequacy of its answers to the question of destiny. Instead, presumption attempts to take matters into its own hands and impatiently tries to secure its own guarantees for the future.

The second kind of hopelessness, Christianly understood, is either to neglect the question of destiny altogether and to live in immediacy, or to *despair* over the excellence of human destiny, or at least to doubt the possibility of actually being able to achieve it. Despair commonly appears as diffidence and resignation, but it also gives rise to hedonism and to that restless activism which seeks to drown anxiety in the waters of activity and busyness. This is why despair is not necessarily overcome by work and exertion, but only, as Josef Pieper has noted, "by that clear-sighted magnanimity that courageously expects and has confidence in the greatness of its own nature and by the grace-filled impetus of the hope of eternal life."[95]

From the Christian perspective, then, it is not difficult to see that the exalted aspirations of modern political life are really only indications of deep-seated *hopelessness*, for they betray an abundance of both presumption and despair. It is on account of this deep-seated hopelessness, furthermore, that modern states have been so careless with real people. After all, modern political aspirations presume the occasional necessity of sacrificing individuals in the interests of guaranteeing social and political outcomes; and the despairing quality of modern political life assures us that this sacrifice is not really that great, for we all die sooner or later anyway. In spite of its glorious pretensions, then, modern political life is really quite hopeless. As Glenn Tinder noted in a study entitled *Against Fate: An Essay on Personal Dignity* (1981):

> With all of our self-confidence . . . we do not have great hope. What we have instead is assurance — a different thing. Assurance is the feeling that all is under our control or at least that it can be. All problems, consequently, are soluble. Hope, on the other hand, is the feeling that all will turn out well, although not necessarily due to human foresight and action. . . . Summarily, assurance rests on the

95. Ibid., 60.

belief that the universe is rationally comprehensible, hope on the sense that the universe is mysteriously in accord with humanity.[96]

This absence of hope, Tinder continues, explains why the modern age is so proud and yet so desperately anxious at the same time, for assurance is easily challenged and debunked. When assurance is challenged, however, it does not give rise to hope, but only to an even more desperate search for newer and greater assurances, often by way of totalitarianism and/or authoritarianism.[97]

It is in this context of hopelessness that we can begin to see the political implications of Christian hope. In the first instance, hope exposes the hollowness and precariousness of modern political ideologies and encourages us to be skeptical of all assurances of future control. Hope also recognizes the threat that political pretensions pose to freedom and dignity and how closely modern "humanistic" presumptions are linked to despairing indifference. Hope thus relativizes the importance of large-scale political-social aspirations over and against the concerns of protecting and preserving the lives of real individual people here and now. Indeed, from the Christian point of view, as Nicholas Berdyaev noted, "every single human soul has more meaning and value than the whole of history with its empires, its wars and revolutions, its blossoming and fading civilizations."[98]

Finally, Christian hope frees us up to act hopefully in the world. It enables us to act humbly and patiently, tackling visible injustices in the world around us without needing to be assured that our skill and our effort will somehow rid the world of injustice altogether.[99] Christian hope, after all, does not need to *see* what it hopes for (Heb. 11:1); and neither does it require us to *comprehend* the end of history. Rather, it simply requires us to trust that even the most outwardly insignificant of faithful actions — the cup of cold water given to the child, the widow's mite offered at the temple, the act of hospitality shown to the

96. Glenn Tinder, *Against Fate: An Essay on Personal Dignity*, Loyola Lecture Series in Political Analysis, ed. Richard Shelley Hartigan (Notre Dame, IN: University of Notre Dame Press, 1981), 26.

97. Ibid., 27.

98. Berdyaev, *The Fate of Man in the Modern World*, 12.

99. Tinder, *The Political Meaning of Christianity*, 66.

stranger, none of which has any overall strategic socio-political significance so far as we can now see — will nevertheless be made to contribute in some significant way to the construction of God's Kingdom by the action of God's creative and sovereign grace. As Oliver O'Donovan comments at the end of his study of evangelical ethics, *Resurrection and Moral Order* (1986): "However much our moral decisions strive for clarity, they are never unambiguous or translucent, even to ourselves. But — and is this not the gospel at the heart of evangelical ethics? — it is given to them by God's grace in Christ to add up to a final and unambiguous Yes, a work of love which will abide for eternity."[100]

Far from being quietistic, then, humble Christian hopefulness actually frees us to act magnanimously in whatever circumstances we happen to find ourselves, confident of the glorious destiny to which we have been called. As Emil Brunner once commented:

> The New Testament says we are living in a wicked world. Therefore to live as a Christian in the State means above all to hope for the new world which lies beyond history — beyond history which was and will be the history of states — for that world where death and killing, force, coercion, and even law will cease, where the only "power" which will then be valid is the power of love. It is the *meditatio vitae futurae* which makes it possible for the Christian to do his difficult duty in this political world without becoming hard; and it is this which prevents him from lapsing into irresponsibility out of the fear of becoming hard. Both his joyful readiness for service and his sanity in service spring from this hope.[101]

In the midst of modern political worldliness, then, we can — and, indeed, we *must* — take hope. By disclosing the hopeless inhumanity of political presumption and despair and so preserving the life of our neighbor, acting hopefully embraces much of what it means to be salt and light in the present age.

100. Oliver O'Donovan, *Resurrection and Moral Order: An Outline for Evangelical Ethics* (Grand Rapids, MI: Eerdmans, 1986), 264.

101. Emil Brunner, *The Divine Imperative: A Study in Christian Ethics,* trans. Olive Wyon (Philadephia: Westminster, 1957), 482.

CHAPTER TWO

The Irrelevance of God
in the Technological Society

> An architect built many houses, cities, and squares, but no one could learn his art or match his skill until several people persuaded him to teach them. When they had learned it they quarreled with him and set up as architects themselves at lower prices. Then the people stopped admiring the original architect and gave their commission to the apprentices. In the same way God has created you in his own image and likeness. But now that you, like him, have created marvelous things, it will be said: There is no God in the world apart from you.[1]

Just as nature abhors a vacuum, so too society and culture. For the Christian view of social and political life to be replaced, then, as early modern political theorists such as Machiavelli had advocated, its replacement needed to fill completely the void left behind by Christian theology. This was not easily accomplished, for Christian theology provided a kind of interpretive canopy over the natural world as well as

---

1. Adapted from a cabalistic pseudepigraphon cited in Helmut Thielicke, *The Evangelical Faith*, vol. 1, trans. Geoffrey W. Bromiley (Grand Rapids, MI: Eerdmans, 1974), 234.

the social and political worlds, and it had already incorporated and "Christianized" a great deal of classical wisdom. The Renaissance rediscovery of pagan political virtue and the subsequent bid to secularize early modern political life was not, by itself, comprehensive enough to displace the Christian worldview from European society and culture. It remained for this bid to be fit into a larger account of nature that could make the call for human autonomy seem "natural" and normal. This did eventually happen. Toward the end of the seventeenth century, a new "scientific" paradigm for understanding the natural world began to replace what seemed to many to be a repressive and outmoded medieval Christian paradigm. From the seventeenth century onward it thus became legitimate to shift the political and social focus away from the question of how we *ought* to live, understood Christianly, and toward the question of how social and political order can be rationally reconstructed in the light of the positive knowledge revealed by the methods of modern science. "The victory of the new [political] philosophy," Leo Strauss suggested in this connection, "was decided by the victory of its decisive part, namely, the new physics."[2]

Of course, modern science and technology are routinely blamed for the problem of secularization in its entirety, and this is not surprising. Although the distinctively modern form of worldliness first surfaced in early modern political life, it is certainly the case that the plausibility — and indeed the attraction — of practical atheism in contemporary culture owes much to the impact that science and technology have had upon the modern imagination. Science has provided us with a kind of interpretive grid within which the temptation to focus our attention solely on the material exigencies of *this world* makes a great deal of sense and, indeed, seems only reasonable and responsible. Science assures us that life's real purposes do not transcend nature, but are embedded within nature in such a way as to be scientifically discoverable. Technology, on the other hand, lends credence to the Promethean worldliness of modern aspirations. Indeed, technology has made it possible to manage the natural world and even — apparently — to effect changes in *human nature* such that we imagine that we can direct individuals and society as a whole toward ends

---

2. Leo Strauss, *Natural Right and History* (Chicago: University of Chicago Press, 1950), 78.

of our own choosing. Recent scientific and technological achievements have been so impressive that science and technology have acquired a kind of intellectual hegemony over our understanding of the world. As Martin Heidegger observed so insightfully, technology has become the metaphysic of the modern age.[3]

From a scientific and technological point of view, God's existence is largely irrelevant. He has been left to inhabit only that space defined by our ever-diminishing scientific ignorance, and so has become the doubtful "god-of-the-gaps." And what little need we may still have for this god-of-the-gaps should, at some point in our technological future, diminish practically to the vanishing point. As one recent M.C.I. Communications advertisement for fiber-optic technology put it: "The space-time continuum is being challenged. The notion of communication is changed forever. All the information in the universe will soon be accessible to everyone at every moment."[4] Granting, for a second, the validity of the contemporary equation of information with control,[5] what choice have we but to conclude that there will no longer be any real need to pray once this remarkable technological feat has been accomplished?

3. Heidegger, cited in George Grant, *Lament for a Nation: The Defeat of Canadian Nationalism* (1965; Ottawa: Carleton University Press, 1989), ix. In an introduction to Heidegger's essay, "The Question Concerning Technology," William Lovitt notes: "Heidegger sees every aspect of contemporary life, not only machine technology and science but also art, religion, and culture understood as the pursuit of the highest goods, as exhibiting clear marks of the ruling essence of technology that holds sway in the dominion of man as self-conscious, representing subject. Everywhere is to be found the juxtaposing of subject and object and the reliance on the experience and evaluating judgment of the subject as decisive. The presencing of everything that is has been cut at its roots. Men speak, significantly enough, of a 'world picture' or 'world view.' Only in the modern age could they speak so. For the phrase 'world picture' means just this: that what is, in its entirety — i.e., the real in its every aspect and element — now is 'taken in such a way that it first is in being and only is in being to the extent that it is set up by man, who represents and sets forth.' Were contemporary man seriously to become aware of this character of his life and of his thinking, he might, with the modern physicist, well say, 'It seems as though man everywhere and always encounters only himself.'" See Martin Heidegger, *The Question Concerning Technology and Other Essays*, ed. William Lovitt (New York: Harper & Row), xxxiii.

4. *New York Times*, January 5, 1994.

5. See, for example, James R. Beniger, *The Control Revolution: Technological and Economic Origins of the Information Society* (Cambridge, MA: Harvard University Press, 1986).

If the technological society has rendered God's existence irrelevant, however, it is important to stress that it has also rendered truly human existence increasingly problematic. In part, this is because scientific and technological means and procedures have an insidious way of becoming ends in and of themselves. Mary Shelley captured this irony quite chillingly at the beginning of the nineteenth century in her classic novel *Frankenstein* (1818), and the most convincing science fiction still tends to depict the future in dystopian terms. Admittedly, it is rather easy to exaggerate the potential of science and technology for ill, but there appear to be good reasons to suspect that the technological future may not be entirely hospitable to human beings. As Christopher Dawson commented, "It would be a strange fatality if the great revolution by which Western man has subdued nature to his purposes should end in the loss of his own spiritual freedom."[6] Strange as this fatality may well be, it is not at all implausible in light of such things as genetic engineering and nuclear weaponry.

We should not, however, let concerns for the future distract our attention away from the subtle secularity that science and technology have *already* instilled in the popular imagination. In fact, the crucial point to make in connection with our discussion of modern worldliness is not that we are on the road to a technological dystopia, but simply that our reliance upon science and technology may hinder our ability to depend upon, and hence to pray to, God. The purpose of this second chapter is therefore neither to predict an Huxleyan future nor to abet Luddite sensibilities, but only to suggest that science and technology have substantially reinforced the *plausibility* of practical atheism in modern society and culture. They have made it easier for us to go about our daily business and even to live out our entire lives without giving God much thought. We will explore the specific reasons for this below, but suffice it here at the outset to say that this is largely because science and technology define the world in such a way as to render God *practically* irrelevant. Science and technology also encourage us to become so preoccupied with our own knowing and making that we tend to forget that we are ourselves creatures within a larger Creation. That Christianity appears to have had quite a lot to do with the development of

6. Christopher Dawson, *Religion and the Rise of Western Culture* (1950; New York: Image Books, 1991), 14.

modern science and technology, then, and that the Church has largely condoned the advancement of both in recent centuries, is something we will want to examine quite closely. Once again, this may help to explain why the distinctively modern form of worldliness has proven so difficult for our churches to recognize and resist. Of course, our churches are not alone in this difficulty. The hegemony of technical rationality has proven stubbornly resistant to all substantive criticism. As Canadian philosopher George Grant insightfully commented: "We live then in the most realised technological society which has yet been. . . . Yet the very substance of our existing which has made us the leaders in technique, stands as a barrier to any thinking which might be able to comprehend technique from beyond its own dynamic."[7] Let us see if we can overcome this barrier.

Science, Technology, and Technopoly

At one level, the word "science" simply signifies a methodical investigation into the nature of things. *Webster's*, for example, defines science as knowledge of the physical world attained through systematic study or practice.[8] In pursuing science, then, we are simply concerned to know the truth of things, how they really are in and of themselves as opposed to how we might imagine that they ought to be. Two of the principal concerns of the scientific endeavor, then, are for *certainty* and *accuracy*, with regard to arriving at knowledge of the world. Although science is committed in principle to remaining open to new evidence, it strives nevertheless to achieve the clearest possible point of view, and employs only those methods that promise to yield the highest degree of probability. This is why mathematics is the preferred language of science. Indeed, only mathematics is capable of the degree of precision that science deems appropriate to the positive description of things.[9] Num-

7. George Grant, "In Defense of North America," in *Technology and Empire: Perspectives on North America* (Toronto: Anansi, 1969), 40.

8. *Webster's New Collegiate Dictionary* (Springfield, MA: G. & C. Merriam & Co., 1977): 1034.

9. Of interest in this connection are Patricia Cline Cohen's recent observations in *A Calculating People: The Spread of Numeracy in Early America* (Chicago: University

bers, it is felt, carry a degree of accuracy and certainty surpassing that of words.

In addition to accuracy and certainty, science is also concerned with *control*. This is evident at two levels. In the first instance, science is concerned to control how we know and describe things. Appropriately scientific knowing requires examining things and putting questions to them in a certain way.[10] Practically speaking, this means that we must construe the world as a field of neutral "objects" from which we must separate ourselves mentally if these objects are to be known accurately and "objectively." In rendering the world objectively, science also insists upon rendering it algebraically. The various objects under investigation must be conceived as standing in a mathematical relation to each other. The continua of time and space, for example, are envisioned quantitatively and not qualitatively within the scientific enterprise, for this enables us to describe objects and events with numerical accuracy and therefore, presumably, in an objective fashion.

Galileo, Bacon, Descartes, and Newton are the thinkers commonly credited with formulating modern science's peculiar habit of "objectification." Galileo Galilei (1564-1642), for example, asserted that only the physically measurable properties of things are appropriately deemed

---

of Chicago Press, 1982). Cohen suggests that it was not actually the rise of science or commercial activity that led to the increase in numeracy in seventeenth-century England, but rather it was the political and social uncertainty of the period that led to the increased interest in the precision of mathematics. "Numbers brought satisfaction," Cline contends (p. 18), "because they signified certainty, quite apart from any practical application. What was measured in the seventeenth century, then, was not only what was thought to be necessary but also what most urgently needed to be made certain." "Quantification," she continues (p. 45), "emerged in the seventeenth century as an alternative way to make sense of the world, a way that would account for activities newly perceived in the interstices of the classical categories. A vast, undifferentiated sea could not easily be thought about in terms of qualitative units, but a grid of numbered vertical and horizontal divisions, like Mercator's, reduced it to manageable proportions. Overseas trade and human traffic to the colonies were somehow disrupting the economy at home, but no one could quite explain why. Economic quantification made it possible to impose control and order on tobacco, linen, indentured servants; longitudes, latitudes, and navigation methods facilitated control of the ocean. Censuses pinned people down to a time, place, and class; life tables suggested a numerical idea about the stages of life one could expect to live through."

10. See George Grant's discussion of the "modern paradigm" in *Technology and Justice* (Toronto: Anansi, 1986), 36.

"objective" from a scientific standpoint.[11] Francis Bacon (1561-1626) insisted that painstaking inductive analysis is the only way to achieve truly useful knowledge of objects. René Descartes (1596-1650) posited the scientific ideal of the absolute detachment of the knowing subject from the world of objects. Descartes also insisted that the world of objects is explicable without remainder in terms of limitless extension (space) and duration (time). Finally, Isaac Newton (1642-1727) demonstrated how the world of objects could indeed be described and predicted with mathematical precision. Taken together, these foundational insights comprehend the manner in which science seeks to control our knowledge of the world. As social historian Lewis Mumford noted in his classic study *Technics and Civilization* (1934):

> The method of the physical sciences rested fundamentally upon a few simple principles. First: the elimination of qualities, and the reduction of the complex to the simple by paying attention only to those aspects of events which could be weighed, measured, or counted, and to the particular kind of space-time sequence that could be controlled and repeated — or, as in astronomy, whose repetition could be predicted. Second: concentration upon the outer world, and the elimination or neutralization of the observer as respects the data with which he works. Third: isolation: limitation of the field: specialization of interest and subdivision of labor. In short, what the physical sciences call the world is not the total object of common human experience: it is just those aspects of this experience that lend themselves to accurate factual observation and to generalized statements.[12]

Of course, science is also concerned to control our use of the knowledge acquired by means of objectification. After all, the whole point of the early modern scientific endeavor was to gain positive knowledge of the world so as to be better able to manage the material

---

11. Galileo's distinction between "primary" and "secondary" qualities illustrates this assertion nicely. Galileo held that the "primary," or truly objective, aspects of a thing were only those that could be precisely measured. All other predicates — including such things as color, odor, "feel," etc. — were held to be merely "secondary," in effect in the eyes of the beholding "subject."

12. Lewis Mumford, *Technics and Civilization* (London: Routledge & Sons, 1934), 46-47.

conditions of life. Descartes, for example, viewed science as a *practical* philosophy by means of which we might "render ourselves the masters and possessors of nature."[13] Similarly, Bacon understood empirical science as the only effective means by which to produce desirable *practical* effects. "Nature," he asserted, "to be commanded must be obeyed, and that which in contemplation is as the cause is in operation as the rule."[14] Science has thus never been envisioned passively. From its inception it was closely associated with practical human activity and with the provision of technique.[15] Science, in short, is thoroughly instrumental.

To assert that science is thoroughly instrumental is not to deny that "pure science" may perhaps be distinguished from "applied science," nor is it meant to impugn the research motives of individual scientists; rather, it is simply to recognize that the cultural context within which modern science first emerged, and the context in which it continues to flourish, is wholly *technological*. For the last several centuries, it seems, our culture has focused a great deal of energy upon effecting *practical* purposes by means of the application of scientific knowledge.[16] Our culture has been principally concerned with *making* things, and has exhibited far more interest in *using* the world than in philosophizing about it or admiring it. Thus, while pure science may still be pursued for its own sake, the culture that subsidizes this activity has much more *practical* matters at heart. Indeed, the technological milieu is one in which admiration is reserved, for the most part, only for those things that bear the imprint of human creativity.[17] Although certain scientists may well still be amazed at the beauty of the natural order, many of the

13. Descartes, cited in John Passmore, *Man's Responsibility for Nature: Ecological Problems and Western Traditions* (New York: Charles Scribner's Sons, 1974), 20.

14. Francis Bacon, "Novum Organum," in *Classics of Western Thought, Vol. 3: The Modern World,* ed. Charles Hirschfeld (New York: Harcourt, Brace & World, 1964), 2.

15. John Macmurray, *The Boundaries of Science: A Study in the Philosophy of Psychology* (London: Faber & Faber, 1939), 97-98.

16. Ian Barbour defines technology as "the application of organized knowledge to practical tasks by ordered systems of people and machines." See Ian Barbour, *Ethics in an Age of Technology: The Gifford Lectures, Volume Two* (San Francisco: HarperSanFrancisco, 1993), 3.

17. Thomas F. Torrance, *God and Rationality* (Oxford: Oxford University Press, 1971), 44.

rest of us are more impressed by the genius of the scientists themselves and by the *practical* potential of their discoveries.

In a recent polemic entitled *Technopoly: The Surrender of Culture to Technology* (1993), educator and social critic Neil Postman argues that technology has actually displaced the heart of modern Western culture.[18] As the book's subtitle suggests, Postman is concerned that in the process of using technology to enhance the quality of our lives, we have actually allowed it to empty our culture of substance and wisdom. Our fascination with modern technology, it seems, has invited us to substitute quantitative calculation for qualitative judgment, to replace genuinely human ends with technical means, and ultimately to evacuate our world of all but technical meanings. The problem is thus not simply that we have surrendered certain sectors of social life to the logic of technology, but that increasingly everything that passes for culture in our society is determined solely by technical logic. Postman labels this sorry condition "technopoly":

> Technopoly is a state of culture. It is also a state of mind. It consists in the deification of technology, which means that the culture seeks its authorization in technology, finds its satisfaction in technology, and takes its orders from technology. This requires the development of a new kind of social order, and of necessity leads to the rapid dissolution of much that is associated with traditional beliefs.[19]

Postman's criticism of modern technological society is instructive because it assumes that there is a dialectical relationship between the tools we use, our conception of the nature of the world, and our own self-consciousness. Along this line, he cites Marx's celebrated observation that modern technology discloses our mode of dealing with nature and creates the conditions of intercourse by which we relate to the world, to each other, and indeed to ourselves. "To a man with a hammer," Postman observes, "everything looks like a nail."[20] Technological change is thus not simply additive to or subtractive from a given culture;

18. Neil Postman, *Technopoly: The Surrender of Culture to Technology* (New York: Vintage, 1993).
19. Ibid., 71.
20. Ibid., 14

rather, it is *ecological*.[21] It changes the culture altogether. Modern technology has altered the structure of our interests and the things we think about. It has altered the character of our symbols and the things we think with. And it has altered the nature of community and the arena in which our thoughts develop.[22] In connection with all of these cognitive alterations, our concern in this chapter is simply to demonstrate how technology buttresses the *plausibility* of practical atheism in modern society and culture. Indeed, to the extent that we understand modern worldliness to entail an overemphasis of human agency at God's expense, the culture of "technopoly" may be said to be worldly by definition.

Technological Habits of Mind

Science and technology foster certain habits of mind. As Peter Berger et al. suggested a number years ago in a provocative study entitled *The Homeless Mind: Modernization and Consciousness* (1973), the technological society tends to foster a style of cognition that is at once highly pragmatic and deeply skeptical.[23] The pragmatic cast of this style of mind owes to the matter-of-factness with which science and technology confront the world of objects. Its skeptical bent betrays the assumption that the scientific way of knowing the world is superior to all others. This peculiar "cognitive style," as Berger et al. put it, is not simply characteristic of scientists and engineers, but tends to some extent to characterize the attitudes of all those who use technological products. Taken to extremes, technological pragmatism and scientific skepticism give rise to what is sometimes labeled "scientism," or the view that refrains from believing anything that has not been "scientifically" proven and, conversely, refuses to doubt anything that carries the *imprimata* of modern science and technology.[24] "Scientism" ob-

---

21. Ibid., 18.

22. Ibid., 20.

23. Peter Berger, Brigitte Berger, and Hansfried Kellner, *The Homeless Mind: Modernization and Consciousness* (New York: Vintage, 1973).

24. See Alan D. Gilbert, *The Making of Post-Christian Britain: A History of the Secularization of Modern Society* (London: Longman, 1980), 56. See also Neil Postman's interesting discussion of "scientism" in *Technopoly*, 144ff. Postman writes (p. 160):

scures the moral ambiguity of scientific and technological development and impedes our ability to reflect ethically about it because it assumes the unequivocally positive value of science and technology.[25] Scientific and technological development is, from the scientistic point of view, good *by definition*.

Albert Borgmann coined the term "device paradigm" to describe the contemporary scientistic preoccupation with pragmatic instrumentality.[26] The "device paradigm," Borgmann argues, biases our attention toward purely technical activities and away from activities whose meaning and significance cannot be derived instrumentally and are not readily quantifiable. Distinguishing between these two kinds of activities, Borgmann reflects on the difference between giving a child a stereo set and giving her a violin and lessons. Both gifts have to do with making music, but the second kind of "making" is very different from the first and, Borgmann contends, it is more humanly valuable. Our preoccupation with the utilization of devices, however, all but insures that this second, more valuable, kind of making will be neglected in contemporary culture. And indeed it is. We have become so fascinated with technical possibility — perhaps especially with the possibilities of computer technology — that we have lost sight of human actuality and the contours of real human need.

Of course, we have not intended to impoverish ourselves. Rather our lack of concern for substantive and qualitative reasoning and our neglect of humanly valuable making are the accidental by-products of our becoming so preoccupied with instrumentality. As Karl Mannheim observed a number of years ago:

"When the new technologies and techniques and spirit of men like Galileo, Newton, and Bacon laid the foundations of natural science, they also discredited the authority of earlier accounts of the physical world, as found, for example, in the great tale of Genesis. By calling into question the truth of such accounts in one realm, science undermined the whole edifice of belief in sacred stories and ultimately swept away with it the source to which most humans had looked for moral authority. It is not too much to say, I think, that the desacrilized world has been searching for an alternative source of moral authority ever since."

25. Stanley L. Jaki, *The Road of Science and the Ways to God* (Chicago: University of Chicago Press, 1978), 303.

26. Albert Borgmann, *Technology and the Character of Contemporary Life: A Philosophical Inquiry* (Chicago: University of Chicago Press, 1984).

When the analytical procedure [i.e., science] was first used, the end or goal prescribed by the activity was still in existence (often composed of fragments of an earlier, religiously understood world). Men strove to know the world so that they could mold it to conform to this ultimate goal; society was analyzed so as to arrive at a form of social life more just or otherwise more pleasing to God; men were concerned with the soul in order to control the path to salvation. But the further men advanced in analysis, the more the goal disappeared from their field of vision, so that today a research worker might say with Nietzsche "I have forgotten why I ever began."[27]

Jacques Ellul's lifetime concern with the hegemony of technical rationality should be mentioned in this connection as well. Ellul felt that the principal intellectual tragedy of the modern world lay in the fact that our obsession with technology has completely eclipsed our ability to reflect about *what* we are doing with technology and *why*.[28] We have become so fascinated by our technical capabilities, Ellul argued, that we have essentially allowed ourselves to be absorbed into the technological apparatus.[29]

Our preoccupation with technique explains the profound restlessness of modern culture. As Hannah Arendt observed: "The shift away from the 'why' and 'what' to the 'how' implies that the actual objects of knowledge can no longer be things or eternal motions but must be processes, and that the object of science therefore is no longer nature or the universe but the history, the story of coming into being, of nature of life or the universe."[30] For modern technological humanity, the important thing is thus not to discern how we might fit into a fixed order of nature, but instead how natural processes might be made to serve human interests. We do not understand the human task in terms of

27. Karl Mannheim, *Ideology and Utopia: An Introduction to the Sociology of Knowledge,* trans. Louis Wirth and Edward Shils (New York: Harcourt, Brace & World, 1968), 20.

28. See, for example, Jacques Ellul, *The Technological Society,* trans. John Wilkinson (New York: Vintage Books, 1964); most recently, *The Technological Bluff,* trans. Geoffrey W. Bromiley (Grand Rapids, MI: Eerdmans, 1990).

29. Ellul, *The Technological Bluff,* 145.

30. Hannah Arendt, *The Human Condition* (Chicago: University of Chicago Press, 1958), 296.

"knowing" (*homo sapiens*), but instead primarily in terms of "making" (*homo faber*). Indeed, we tend to understand ourselves as the beings who must continually construct, build, and fabricate by means of science and technology. This self-understanding naturally gives rise to a kind of restless activism in which, finally, we imagine ourselves to be the only creative agents in the universe.

It is perhaps important to stress, however, that the modern preoccupation with technological making need not appear arrogant. While the Promethean possibilities of modern technology do occasionally surface in such things as modern warfare,[31] they are more commonly obscured by the concerns for creature comforts and convenience. Democracy and the operations of the market system tend to ensure that consumer-electronic gadgetry and the production of action-adventure films outweigh storming the gates of heaven on the list of contemporary technological priorities. Although there is nothing inherent in the logic of technology to suggest this relatively benign outcome, it appears to reflect the popular "leveling" of democratic populism and consumer capitalism. Put somewhat differently, modern technological aspirations are still thoroughly *bourgeois*, and the possibilities of technological development are limited, for the time being at least, by the fact that it is under the supervision of, as Max Weber put it, "specialists without spirit and sensualists without heart."[32]

At an even more basic level, the Promethean character of modern technological aspirations are hidden behind the fact that, individually speaking, our knowledge of the technological system is rather limited. Yet while each of us obviously cannot possess all the knowledge necessary to control our own circumstances, we tend to assume that this knowledge is at least *potentially available* to us by way of a hierarchy of professions, specializations, and expertise. The critical assumption here is that technical knowledge is *componential* and that, taken together, the specialized skills of all of the various experts can solve practically any problem we might encounter. This assumption goes some distance toward explaining our confusion of technical means and ends. As Berger et al. remark:

31. The recent series of novels by Tom Clancy might be cited in this connection.
32. Max Weber, *The Protestant Ethic and the Spirit of Capitalism*, trans. Talcott Parsons (New York: Charles Scribner's Sons, 1958), 182.

Since reality is apprehended in terms of components which can be assembled in different ways, there is no necessary relationship between a particular sequence of componential actions and the ultimate end of these actions. To take an obvious example, a particular assemblage of cogs produced in a highly specific production sequence may eventually go into a passenger automobile or a nuclear weapon. Regardless of whether the worker involved in this particular production process approves or even knows about its intended end, he is able to perform the actions that are technologically necessary to bring it about.[33]

The separation of means and ends also suggests the curious bifurcation of "fact" and "value" in modern technological society. "Facts" are those bits of knowledge that are objectively given and scientifically verifiable and are therefore presumably incontrovertible, solid, and dependable. Facts are technically useful. "Values," on the other hand, precisely because they cannot be tested by the methods of science, have become increasingly problematic in modern society. Even our use of the word "values" suggests that, whatever these commitments are taken to be, they are somewhat less than objectively real. And so, while almost no one today would deny their importance, values cannot be made to bear any real weight in public life. Because they are simply impossible to quantify, values are difficult to link with empirically testable goals and practical strategies. Another way of making this point is simply to say that the technological habit of mind is *anti-teleological*. It is largely uninterested, and indeed incapable, of appreciating the notions of final causality or ultimate purpose. Indeed, to the extent that values do point us in the direction of ultimate purposes, they are commonly ruled out-of-bounds in modern public discourse. As evangelical missiologist Lesslie Newbigin observed:

A missionary encounter with our culture must bring us face to face with the central citadel of our culture, which is the belief that is based on the immense achievements of the scientific method and, to a limited but increasing extent, embodied in our political, economic and social practice — the belief that the real world, the reality with which we have to do, is a world that is to be understood in terms of

33. Berger et al., *The Homeless Mind*, 27-28.

efficient [i.e. mechanical] causes and not of final causes, a world that is not governed by an intelligible purpose, and thus a world in which the answer to the question of what is good has to be left to the private opinion of each individual and cannot be included in any body of accepted facts that control public life.[34]

From a technological point of view, then, religious values are not understood to convey truth about the world so much as they are simply "processed," as it were, as reflections of the strength of public opinion. In this connection, it has been suggested that contemporary democracy is really only a kind of enacted political technology in which the issues of political and social order are increasingly construed as technical problems to be solved by technical means.[35] Even the questions of justice and of the nature of goodness are discussed today as though they were simply problems of technical procurement. As Joseph Weizenbaum recently commented concerning the modern transition "from judgment to calculation":

> Our time prides itself on having finally achieved the freedom from censorship for which libertarians in all ages have struggled. . . . The credit for these great achievements is claimed by the new spirit of rationalism, a rationalism that, it is argued, has finally been able to tear from man's eyes the shrouds imposed by mystical thought, religion, and such powerful illusions as freedom and dignity. Science has given to us this great victory over ignorance. But, on closer examination, this victory too can be seen as an Orwellian triumph of an even higher ignorance: what we have gained is a new conformism, which permits us to say anything that can be said in the functional languages of instrumental reason, but forbids us to allude to . . . the

34. Lesslie Newbigin, *Foolishness to the Greeks: The Gospel and Western Culture* (Grand Rapids, MI: Eerdmans, 1986), 79.

35. Borgmann, *Technology and the Character of Contemporary Life,* 92. The crafting of "public image" on the basis of sophisticated polling techniques and by means of "testing" possible opinions on so-called "focus groups" might be mentioned in this connection. Although these procedures may be said to reflect a commitment to democracy, they tend to completely ignore substantive considerations. Indeed, one is led to suspect that these techniques really disclose only a fundamentally manipulative spirit in which the only real "value," finally, is the possession and exercise of power.

living truth . . . so we may discuss the very manufacture of life and its "objective" manipulation, but we may not mention God, grace, or morality.[36]

Of course, for the most part, this "Orwellian triumph" and the exclusion of God, grace, and morality from contemporary public discourse have been unintentional. We have imagined that science and technology were just useful tools to be put in the service of improving the material conditions of life. Yet the explanatory success of modern science and the material improvements wrought by modern technology have inevitably led us to adopt a kind of technical attitude toward life in general.

The Technological Self-Understanding

In addition to fostering certain habits of mind, modern technology also encourages us to adopt a self-consciously anthropocentric point of view. This self-understanding is unwilling, and by now largely incapable, of appreciating any meaning or significance in the world save that of our own making. Put somewhat differently, what is at stake in modern "technopoly" is not simply the continued existence of traditional or non-technical culture *as such*, but the possibility of a certain kind of relation to the world. Such a relation may be loosely termed "religious" both because it is commonly expressed in religious terms and, more importantly, because it recognizes — often in nature — the existence of an Intelligence and Will superior to and encompassing the human will. Modern technology has rendered us increasingly incapable of this simple recognition. We have, in effect, become religiously tone-deaf. As Gabriel Marcel observed a number of years ago:

A technique is a specialized and rationally elaborated practical knowledge, a procedural *savoir-faire* which is at once perfectible and transmissible . . . to say that man is led to think of himself and of the world in technical terms means first of all that he sees the world as capable of being transformed methodically, by industrious human activity,

36. Joseph Weizenbaum, *Computer Power and Human Reason: From Judgment to Calculation* (San Francisco: W. H. Freeman, 1976), 261.

until it should more and more completely satisfy human needs . . . this kind of thinking develops into a practical anthropocentrism — which is to say that man tends more and more to think of himself as the only principle which can give meaning to a world which in itself seems to him completely meaningless.[37]

But perhaps Marcel's assessment is too harsh. Could it not be argued, after all, that modern technology is simply an extension of tool-using, and therefore essential to human existence? Perhaps modern technology is even justifiable theologically under the heading of humankind's "cultural mandate" to have dominion over creation. From this perspective, the problem is not really technology as such, but the uses to which modern technology has been put. In his recent Gifford Lectures, *Ethics in an Age of Technology* (1993), Ian Barbour, for example, concludes: "The challenge for our generation is to redirect technology toward realizing human and environmental values on planet earth."[38] Yet while this concern for human and environmental values is to be commended, the assumption that modern technology is simply an extension of tool-making is one that must be carefully unpacked. For though modern technology does entail the use of tools, our commitment to modern technology may also betray a uniquely manipulative relationship to the world and a peculiarly autonomous self-understanding that is quite different from that of traditional tool-using cultures. As George Grant observed: ". . . modern technology is not simply an extension of human making through the power of a perfected science, but it is a new account of what it is to know and to make in which both activities are changed by their co-penetration."[39]

This "new account of what it is to know and make" is the subject of a small book written a number of years ago by Roman Catholic theologian Romano Guardini and recently republished as *Letters from Lake Como: Reflections on Technology and the Human Race*. In a manner similar to Postman, Guardini begins by observing the odd impoverish-

37. Gabriel Marcel, "The Sacred in the Technological Age," in *Theology Today* 19 (1962): 28-29.
38. Ian Barbour, *Ethics in an Age of Technology: The Gifford Lectures*, Volume Two (San Francisco: HarperSanFrancisco, 1993), xix.
39. Grant, *Technology and Justice*, 13.

ment of modern industrial culture. "How can I put this to you?" he queries:

> Look, what has already taken place up in the North I saw beginning here. I saw machines invading the land that had previously been the home of culture. I saw death overtaking a life of infinite beauty, and I felt that this was not just an external loss that we could accept and remain who we were. Instead, a life, a life of supreme value that can arise only in the world that we have long since lost, was beginning to perish here, as well as in the North.[40]

In an attempt to interpret this disturbing development, Guardini wrestles with the makeup of human culture and with the quality of the relation between culture and nature. He concludes that, while the construction of authentic human culture necessarily entails a measure of distance and abstraction away from the "immediate vitality" of nature, still it must remain vitally connected *to*, and in a sense in conversation *with*, nature. It is this vital link with nature that is broken in modern technological culture. To illustrate this point, Guardini contrasts a sailing ship, which cooperates with the forces of nature and in some mysterious way completes them, to a modern steam vessel:

> Go even further [from nature] and the sailing vessel becomes a steamer, a great ocean liner — culture indeed, a brilliant technological achievement! And yet a colossus of this type presses on through the sea regardless of wind and waves. It is so large that nature no longer has power over it; we can no longer see nature on it. People on board eat and drink and sleep and dance. They live as if in houses and on city streets. Mark you, something has been lost here. Not only has there been step-by-step development, improvement, and increase in size; a fluid line has been crossed that we cannot fix precisely but can only detect when we have long since passed over it — a line on the far side of which living closeness to nature has been lost.[41]

40. Romano Guardini, *Letters from Lake Como: Explorations in Technology and the Human Race*, trans. Geoffrey W. Bromiley (1923; Grand Rapids, MI: Eerdmans, 1994), 5.

41. Ibid., 13.

This line past which a "living closeness to nature" is lost may also be illustrated by the difference between manual work and industrial labor. In traditional manual work, Guardini contends, we were still listening to and working with nature. We stood, Guardini writes, "breast to breast with the things and forces of nature" and were therefore "human in the deepest sense of the term."[42] Modern industrial labor, on the other hand, appreciates nature only as an object and as a source of raw materials and energy, and thus discloses a fundamental breach in the relation between culture and nature.

This breach, Guardini continues, has been precipitated by modern machine technology. To make this point he posits a very useful distinction between "tools," what he terms "contrivances," and "machines." A "tool" represents an extension of human nature. Tools enhance what the organs and members of our bodies do naturally. A "contrivance," on the other hand — say, a handmill or waterwheel — lies outside the realm of natural bodily functions, but still relies on immediate natural forces. In using tools and/or contrivances, then, we are still forced to work *with* nature, and we still encounter a kind of natural resistance to the imposition of our will upon nature. To be sure, tools and contrivances make for truly creative human activity; but this creative activity is constrained by a natural order which is not of our own making and which must, in a sense, be respected. In contrast to tools and contrivances, a "machine" functions more or less completely in accordance with our own predetermined purposes, and in constructing machines, we are no longer working with immediate nature so much as we are *utilizing* the abstracted forces of nature to accomplish our own purposes.[43] We do so largely without respect and without regard to natural constraints, even to those of time and place.

Guardini's subtle distinction between the use of tools and contrivances and the development of machines is quite significant; for the former implies a kind of natural restraint upon human willing, while the latter does not. Machine technology may thus be said to represent — in conception as well as in actual practice — a liberation of the human will from the forces of nature. Along this line, Guardini comments on the close connection between machine technology and

42. Ibid., 16.
43. Ibid., 100-101.

the scientific emphasis upon achieving conceptual mastery over the world:

> What the concept is for knowledge of things, mechanisms, instruments, and machines are for practical action. What concepts do for knowledge — i.e., grasp many things, not in their vitality, but only by means of posited signs that rightly indicate common features — machines do for action. Machines are steel concepts. They lay hold of many things in such a way as to disregard their individual features and to treat them as though they were all the same. Mechanical processes have the same character as conceptual thinking. Both control things by taking them out of a special living relation to what is individual and creating an artificial order into which they are, more or less, fit.[44]

This modern emphasis upon knowledge for the sake of "laying hold" of things is fundamentally different from, and indeed is largely at odds with, traditional religious understanding. It betrays a fundamentally new kind of relation to the world. While traditional wisdom tended to stress knowing a thing for the sake of living with it and ultimately *loving* it, the modern view, as Guardini notes, "unpacks, tears apart, arranges in compartments, takes over and rules. . . ."[45] The modern interest is not in the thing itself, but in what kind of work a thing can be made to do.

> This [manipulative] knowledge does not inspect; it analyzes. It does not construct a picture of the world, but a formula. Its desire is to achieve power so as to bring force to bear on things, a law that can be formulated rationally. Here we have the basis and character of its dominion: compulsion, arbitrary compulsion devoid of all respect. . . . The new desire for mastery does not in any sense follow natural courses or observe natural proportions. Indeed, it treats these with complete indifference. The new mastery posits its aims arbitrarily on rational grounds. . . .[46]

44. Ibid., 23-24.
45. Ibid., 43.
46. Ibid., 44-45.

While Guardini's reverence for traditional culture is perhaps some-what romantic, his suggestion that the *spirit* of modern technology is fundamentally anthropocentric and manipulative is surely correct. Think, for example, of *plastic*, a characteristically modern product. Al-though it is possible to speak of working with plastic, this is somewhat misleading; for we do not work *with* plastic so much as we *develop* it. We engineer it at the molecular level to satisfy predetermined perfor-mance characteristics. Plastic thus represents an almost completely ra-tionalized product. Its development and manufacture require us to abstract away from given nature so completely that most of us probably don't have any idea what the original "raw material" for plastic produc-tion even is. Digital technology represents a similar abstraction away from given nature. Indeed, it suggests the absolute elimination, or ab-sorption, of nature into an absolutely rational construct. By converting sound, speech, and light into binary notation, digital technology frees us from having to rely even upon the *analogy* of nature as we transmit and manipulate "information." The trajectory of this kind of technical rationality is indicated by current enthusiasm about the possibilities of "virtual reality." While it is difficult to say what will actually come of cybernetic technology, there is apparently a great demand for the con-struction of a completely abstract and purely rational — which is to say *absolutely humanly willed* — "reality."

Modern machine technology has thus disconnected us from na-ture. As technology advances, furthermore, we seem to recognize fewer and fewer (if any) limits to our own technical-rational will to power. This must not be understood romantically or sentimentally. The point is not simply that we have lost a kind of natural simplicity or innocence. Rather, what has been lost, in abstracting away from immediate nature, is the possibility of encountering something outside of ourselves which might discipline — and thus give order to — human making and willing. In the absence of such discipline, modern machine technology appears destined to be destructive of nature, of living human cultures, and indeed of living human beings.

It is important to recognize, however, that the actual disconnec-tion of modern industrial labor from immediate nature was rendered almost inevitable by Descartes's *theoretical* separation of the human subject from the world of objects. Discussing the *spirit* of early modern science in a book called *The Human Condition* (1958), Hannah Arendt described this separation in terms of "Archimedean freedom." Early modern scientists encouraged us to imagine ourselves as standing at a point wholly outside of nature for the sake of achieving a kind of leverage over the world:

> The Cartesian solution was to move the Archimedean point into man himself, to choose as ultimate point of reference the pattern of the human mind itself, which assures itself of reality and certainty within a framework of mathematical formulas which are its own products. Here the famous *reductio scientae ad mathematicam* permits replacement of what is sensuously given by a system of mathematical equations where all real relationships are dissolved into logical relations between man-made symbols. It is this replacement which permits modern science to fulfill its "task of *producing*" the phenomena and objects it wishes to observe. And this assumption is that neither God nor an evil spirit can change the fact that two and two equal four.[47]

Here, then, is the theoretical substructure of modern technological development. Descartes's bifurcation of the knowing subject from the world of objects set into motion an apparently inexorable progression from objectification, through mathematization, to technological manipulation.[48] The explanatory successes of modern science, furthermore, and the practical achievements of modern technology have made it all but impossible to challenge the validity of this progression.

In sum, the impact of science and technology upon the modern imagination is such that it has effectively stripped us of the ability to apprehend the reality of any other meaning and any other purpose in the world save those which we have managed to "engineer" for ourselves. This technical-rational spirit pervades much of modern — and now "postmodern" — life. In the first instance, it is evident in the tremendous emphasis we place upon *planning*. Far transcending simple prudence, the contemporary preoccupation with planning discloses an obsession with control and a kind of religious commitment to the

47. Arendt, *The Human Condition*, 284.

48. Robert Doede, "The Decline of Anthropomorphic Explanation: From Animism to Deconstructionism," an unpublished paper delivered to the Regent College Faculty (1992).

validity of technical rationality.[49] The modern predilection for "intellectuality" might be mentioned in this connection as well; for it suggests our concern for achieving conceptual mastery over the world. As Arnold Gehlen observed in assessing the impact of modern technology upon consciousness, "One is at first struck by the thorough intellectualization of the cultural fields of the arts and sciences, with a consequent loss of intuitiveness, immediacy, and unproblematical accessibility. The frontiers of the arts and sciences are ever more abstract and disembodied."[50] As abstract and unreal as modern intellectual life may appear to be, beneath the surface it has the practical control of the world at heart.

Yet perhaps the most telling indicator of the radically anthropocentric drift of modern technological self-understanding is the disconnection of language itself from nature. Language is no longer held to correspond to nature, but is instead believed to be constitutive of it. Indeed, an increasing number of contemporary theorists suggest that we can actually change the nature of reality simply by *speaking* it differently. The emphasis upon the absolutely creative use of words has been extended to the point that it has all but shattered the connection between language and the world. As George Steiner has suggested in his provocative study *Real Presences* (1989): "*It is this break of the covenant between word and world which constitutes one of the very few genuine revolutions of spirit in Western history and which defines modernity itself*" [emphasis in original].[51] Although Steiner contends that this revolution of spirit may be traced back to intellectual developments in Europe and Russia toward the end of the nineteenth century, the distinctively modern disruption of "word and world" was clearly anticipated in the relation to nature disclosed by early modern scientific theory and eventually by modern technological practice. The plausibility of contemporary theories which stress our ability to construct and/or deconstruct ourselves through the use of language may thus be said to rest upon the foundation of modern science and technology.

49. Arnold Gehlen, *Man in the Age of Technology*, trans. Patricia Lipscomb (New York: Columbia University Press, 1980), 103-4.

50. Ibid., 26-27.

51. George Steiner, *Real Presences* (Chicago: University of Chicago Press, 1989), 93.

The Cost of Technological Affluence

Even if it is possible to find fault with modern technological society for a number of reasons, we should not gainsay the level of material and technological affluence modern science and technology have generated, and we should not underestimate the *control* over our environment that we have been able to purchase with this affluence. Most of us would simply not be here were it not for the remarkable achievements of modern science and technology. These material benefits have obviously come at a price, however. In the first instance, technological solutions to certain material problems have unintentionally created additional problems to which further technological solutions must be found and so forth. The enormously complicated technical problems associated with the disposal of nuclear waste is one of the more obvious examples of this problem, as are the ecological problems associated with our intensive use of chemical fertilizers and refrigerants.

Yet as serious as the material problems associated with scientific and technological development have been, perhaps the most serious costs of this development have been incurred at the level of consciousness. As we have discussed above, science and technology encourage us to substitute quantitative calculation for qualitative judgment; to replace truly human ends with impersonal technical means; to cleanse the world of religious meaning; and to exaggerate the importance of a certain kind of manipulative making. All of these tendencies are rather directly linked to the secularity and impersonality of modern life.

Of course, it is not difficult to see why science and technology have had a secularizing effect upon modern culture. Scientific explanations of the world have eliminated the instrumental value of their religious alternatives. We no longer need religion to explain such things as disease or natural calamities. Rudolf Bultmann's celebrated observation about the use of radios and light bulbs cuts to the heart of this problem. We cannot use such devices, Bultmann asserted, "and at the same time believe in the spirit and wonder world of the New Testament. And if we suppose that we can do so ourselves, we must be clear that we can represent this as the attitude of Christian faith only by making the Christian proclamation unintelligible and impossible for our contemporaries."[52] While Bultmann appears to have overstated this case, he was certainly correct to stress the logical incompatibility of science — or at least of "scientism" — and religion. Scientism does not render religious explanations of such things as disease improbable, after all. It rules them out *by definition*. It simply does not admit the possibility of the interpenetration of the natural and supernatural or of matter and spirit. Even if science proper does not necessarily rule out the existence of God, he must remain largely invisible and irrelevant from within the scientific frame of reference.

If God is largely hidden from view in modern technological society, however, his attributes have resurfaced as the prerogatives of humanity. As we have seen, the human subject has essentially eclipsed God and has emerged as the sole creator of meaning, value, and historical development. An additional indication of this deification of humanity is given in how modern science encourages us to understand our place in the universe. It is no accident that the names of Galileo, Kepler, Copernicus, and other astronomers are commonly associated with the scientific revolution, for the emergence of early modern science comprehended a cosmological revolution in which the geocentric astronomy of the ancient Greeks and the anthropomorphic view of medieval astronomers were replaced, first by the heliocentric, and subsequently by the centerless universe of modern astrophysics.[53] Yet although this revolution is often interpreted as a rebuke to the apparent anthropocentrism of the medieval view, it actually heralded a far more radically human-centered cosmology than either the Greeks or the medievals had dared imagine. This is simply because the revolutionary new cosmology — while superficially threatening human significance in a universe of infinite extension and duration — was itself a human discovery. The new knowledge had not been revealed to us; it had not been the gift of the gods; rather, it was the product of our own determined and disciplined

52. Rudolf Bultmann, "New Testament and Mythology: The Problem of Demythologizing the New Testament Proclamation," in Rudolf Bultmann, *New Testament and Mythology and Other Basic Writings*, trans. and ed. Schubert M. Ogden (1941; Philadelphia: Fortress Press, 1984), 4-5.

53. Alexandre Koyré summarized this revolution as a shift from a closed and hierarchically ordered universe to one of infinite extension and duration. See Alexandre Koyré, *From the Classical World to the Infinite Universe* (New York: Harper Torchbooks, 1957).

reasoning. In this connection, Barth noted how paradoxical it was that the new scientific cosmology, within which human existence seemed so precarious and marginal, appears to have encouraged the rapid development of supremely self-confident philosophical systems like rationalism, empiricism, and skepticism during the eighteenth century.[54] From the perspective of early modern science, the reasoning human mind had become the axis around which the world was believed to turn.

If the technological milieu has not been entirely hospitable to belief in God, it is also important to stress that it has not been conducive to a particularly high view of real individual human beings. This is not simply because people are often treated like machines, and are occasionally even replaced by machines in the modern technological workplace.[55] Rather, it is also because, as we mentioned in the last chapter, the typically modern quest for technical-rational control over the world inevitably boils down to control of *some* at the expense of others. As C. S. Lewis observed so trenchantly a number of years ago: ". . . the power of Man to make himself what he pleases means . . . the power of some men to make other men what *they* please."[56] Along this line, British philosopher John Macmurray provided a useful schematic history of this peculiar problem.[57] It was first recognized toward the end of the Middle Ages that social progress was going to require the control of nature, and it was not long thereafter that the "novum organum" of the early modern scientific method emerged as the solution to this problem. Yet it became apparent over the course of several successive generations that rational social progress could not really be achieved unless society was itself rationally organized for the sake of this progress. And so it was that the scientific method began to be applied to human behavior, individually by way of modern psychology, and collectively by means of

54. Karl Barth, *Protestant Theology in the Nineteenth Century: Its Background and History* (London: S.C.M. Press, 1972), 38.

55. In this connection, it may help to recall the warning issued by Norbert Wiener at the conclusion of his study *The Human Use of Human Beings: Cybernetics and Society*, second edition (1950; London: Free Association Books, 1954), 162: "Let us remember that the automatic machine, whatever we think of any feelings it may or may not have, is the precise economic equivalent of slave labor. Any labor which competes with slave labor must accept the economic conditions of slave labor."

56. C. S. Lewis, *The Abolition of Man* (1943; Glasgow: Collins, 1978), 37.

57. See Macmurray, *The Boundaries of Science*, 163-64.

sociology. Yet this incursion of the methods of science into human affairs gave rise to a number of perplexing questions which modern society has yet to answer:

> To control his environment man must control himself, and to control himself he must know how he is made and how, in fact, he does behave. But if he knows how he behaves, how can that help him to behave differently? If he can behave differently, the psychology which enables him to do so cannot be a true and complete account of how he behaves. If he cannot behave differently, what use is his psychology to him, and how indeed could he behave so differently as to produce it? So far from solving the problem with which science began, 'How can we control the world?', its completion in psychology merely sets the question, 'Who is to control whom?', and introduces a universal struggle to control one another which, if it develops, must make all effort to control the environment impossible and make the work of science itself equally impossible.[58]

Macmurray's mention of the "universal struggle to control one another" goes some distance toward explaining why so many modern — and now purportedly postmodern — philosophers have been tempted to describe human existence solely in terms of the will to power.[59] For while struggle and bloody conflict have characterized the human condition since Cain murdered Abel, a ceaseless struggle for control is quite literally *built into* modern societies by reason of the modern quest for technological mastery over nature.

Yet in addition to raising the troubling question of "Who is to control whom?" modern technological development raises even more perplexing questions about the very nature of human beings. This is simply because, from a scientific and technological perspective, humans aren't simply useful as machines — or *as* ciphers in the so-called "information age" — but rather we *are* machines. We are explicable

---

58. Ibid., 164.

59. Philosophical systems premised upon a kind of "ontology of violence" may be understood to reflect the intrinsic violence of the technological quest for mastery over nature. See, for example, John Milbank's discussion of this in *Theology and Social Theory: Beyond Secular Reason* (Oxford: Basil Blackwell, 1990), 278ff.

without remainder in terms of functionality. This depressingly reductionist view of human beings accounts for what philosopher William Barrett has termed the "death of the soul" in modern scientific culture:

> We note the extraordinary power and constructivity of the human mind in constructing the great edifice of modern science. And yet, precisely here occurs one of the supreme ironies of modern history: the structure that most emphatically exhibits the power of mind nevertheless leads to the denigration of the human mind. The success of the physical sciences leads to the attitude of scientific materialism, according to which the mind becomes, in one way or another, merely the passive plaything of material forces. The offspring turns against its parent.[60]

C. S. Lewis termed this reversal the "abolition of man": that breathtakingly ironic development in which humanity's conquest of nature has turned out to be nature's conquest of humanity.[61] "We who have personified all other things," Lewis commented, "turn out to be ourselves mere personification. Man is indeed akin to the gods: that is, he is no less phantasmal then they."[62]

The "death of the soul" has made a whole host of human questions difficult to frame, much less to answer, in the modern technological context. In the first instance, we cannot seem to decide how to define "goodness" with respect to specific practices and endeavors. Technical rationality can only approach such questions by means of concepts like feasibility, effectiveness, and/or efficiency. But these concepts miss the whole point of the question; for what if the goodness of certain practices — say, of motherhood or of friendship — turns out to have very little to do with efficiency or effectiveness understood technically? And if technical rationality has difficulty evaluating specific practices, it has even more trouble trying to make sense of life as a whole. Indeed, the technological paradigm is wholly incapable of addressing basic human

---

60. William Barrrett, *Death of the Soul: From Descartes to the Computer* (New York: Anchor, 1986), 75.

61. Lewis, *The Abolition of Man*.

62. C. S. Lewis, "The Empty Universe," in *Present Concerns: Essays by C. S. Lewis* (New York: Harcourt, Brace, Jovanovich, 1986), 81-82.

questions like: Who are we? Why are we here? What ought we to do with our lives? This curious incapacity explains why, in spite of its provision of technological affluence, modernity weighs so very heavily upon us. As Berger et al. comment at the conclusion of *The Homeless Mind* (1973): "Modernity has accomplished many far reaching transformations, but it has not fundamentally changed the finitude, fragility, and mortality of the human condition. What it has accomplished is to seriously weaken those definitions of reality that previously made that human condition easier to bear."[63] That the Christian religion appears to have contributed quite substantially to the rise of modern science and to the development of modern technology, then, is curious and calls for careful examination.

Christianity and the Rise of Modern Science

Modern science emerged in Europe during the sixteenth and seventeenth centuries; on this point there is little disagreement. But social historians have long debated how and why this happened.[64] A number of other cultures apparently possessed sophisticated mathematics, technological acumen, detailed observations of nature, and other logical prerequisites for scientific understanding long before Western Europe. What prevented these cultures from developing a genuinely modern science? Even more to the point, why, given Europe's relative lack of technological sophistication at the end of the Middle Ages, did science emerge in Europe shortly thereafter? Although we may never possess conclusive answers to these questions, most historians agree that Christianity — and perhaps particularly Protestant Christianity — played a significant, even decisive role in the development of early modern science. There are a number of reasons for this. On the one hand, the Christian understanding of created nature seems to have rendered scientific investigation of it both possible and desirable. Yet the relationship between science and Christianity also seems to have been somewhat

63. Berger et al., *The Homeless Mind*, 185.

64. An excellent and comprehensive review of the historiographical debate over the rise of modern science is provided by H. Floris Cohen, *The Scientific Revolution: A Historiographical Inquiry* (Chicago: University of Chicago Press, 1994).

accidental. Indeed, the gist of the "gravedigger hypothesis" mentioned in the Introduction suggests that Christianity may accidentally have given rise to the very scientific understanding which has proven so corrosive of Christian faith in recent centuries. The relationship between the Christian religion and modern science, it appears, is rich in irony.

Modern science's debt to Christianity is, in the first instance, cosmological. The scientific presupposition that the world is rationally ordered according to regular laws and thus amenable to a rational science follows from the Christian belief that God is a rational Creator and that he has subjected his creation to a single code of law.[65] In this connection, A. N. Whitehead observed that modern science required the "inexpungable belief that every detailed occurrence can be correlated with its antecedents in a perfectly definite manner, exemplifying general [rational] principles. . . . It is this instinctive conviction, vividly poised before the imagination, which is the motive power of research; that there is a secret, a secret which can be unveiled. . . ."[66] From the Christian perspective, furthermore, this secret is *worth* discovering; for it will reflect, even if only in some small way, the glorious character of its Creator. Put somewhat differently, the scientific willingness to take pains to investigate the natural order stems from the Christian conviction that the creation bears the gracious stamp of its Maker. In addition, the Christian religion emphasizes the importance of human agency in healing and restoring created relationships. Love, Christianly understood, requires us to try to improve the material conditions of our neighbor's life and so to assume an active, and not simply a passive, stance vis-à-vis nature.[67]

While Christian belief in the inherent rationality of the created order and the emphasis upon the ministry of healing and reconciliation are as old as the Church, these commitments apparently only began to find fruitful practical and technical expression in late medieval monasti-

65. See Christopher Kaiser, *Creation and the History of Science* (Grand Rapids, MI: Eerdmans, 1991). Kaiser contends that this belief that God has subjected his creation to a single set of laws is the fundamental tenet of the Christian "creationist tradition," out of which modern science eventually emerges.

66. Alfred N. Whitehead, *Science and the Modern World* (London: Pelican, 1926), 23-4.

67. Kaiser, *Creation and the History of Science*, 7ff.

cism. In this connection, it has been suggested that this was the result of the impact of the restless "Germanic spirit" upon classical Latin Christianity.[68] It was probably also due to late-medieval monasticism's reverence for manual labor and to its fascination with natural processes.[69] Whatever the reasons, it appears that late medieval monasticism laid the *practical* foundations for the development of early modern science and technology. Indeed, along this line it has been suggested that it was the monastic invention of the mechanical clock that eventually enabled modern science to apply its quantitative methods to the study of nature.[70]

Yet monasticism's fascination with nature was apparently prevented from developing into a genuinely empirical science by late-medieval scholasticism's reverence for Aristotle and by its fondness for extravagant deductive reasoning. The development of modern scientific understanding was probably also impeded by the Roman church's inconsistent stance on the matter of magic. Although magical practices were officially condemned by the Church, the magisterium unofficially condoned belief in magic to the extent that it seemed in the Church's interest to do so. The medieval Church was thus made to appear to the average person-on-the-street as a kind of reservoir of magical power which could, at the discretion of the priests, be made available for secular purposes.[71] This was not particularly conducive to the development of a disciplined and wholly "disenchanted" scientific outlook.

68. Romano Guardini, *The End of the Modern World: A Search for Orientation*, trans. Joseph Theman and Herbert Burke (1956; Chicago: Henry Regnery Co., 1968), 25. Guardini follows Hegel in this interpretation.

69. Ibid., 53ff. Kaiser underlines the significance of the medieval antecedent to modern science. In addition to monasticism's reverence for nature, he stresses the value the medievals placed upon mathematics and their encouragement of observation and experimentation.

70. See Mumford, *Technics and Civilization*. "Was it by reason of the collective Christian desire to provide for the welfare of souls in eternity by regular prayers and devotions," Mumford queries (pp. 14-15), "that time-keeping and the habits of temporal order took hold of men's minds . . . ? One must perhaps accept the irony of this paradox. . . . The clock . . . is a piece of power-machinery whose "product" is seconds and minutes: by its essential nature it dissociated time from human events and helped create the belief in an independent world of mathematically measurable sequences; the special world of science."

71. Keith Thomas, *Religion and the Decline of Magic* (New York: Charles Scribner's Sons, 1971), 47.

The effect of the Protestant Reformation was to remove, or at least to mitigate, many of these medieval impediments to the emergence of empirical science. Indeed, this clearing of the decks may well have been Protestantism's chief contribution to the rise of early modern science. The Reformers' vigorous criticism of magic and superstition might be mentioned in this regard, as well as their repudiation of Scholastic (Aristotelian) rationalism. Somewhat more incidentally, the warfare that followed the Reformation appears also to have engendered a deep distrust of *all* religious dogma among the educated classes.[72] But before examining these matters in detail, it should be noted that any number of other factors appear to have contributed to the emergence of the empirical and experimental frame of reference. The discovery of and increasing contact with other non-Christian cultures was one of these factors, as were the following: the decline of population pressures in Europe, practical agricultural improvements, a respite from outbreaks of the plague, improvements in travel and communications, more effective fire-fighting techniques, deposit banking, and the invention of insurance against risk. All of these late-medieval developments, which had very little to do with religion per se, tended to undermine belief in the instrumental value of magic, and contributed to an upsurge of confidence in disciplined human reasoning and technological innovation during the seventeenth century.[73]

In considering the specifically Protestant contribution to the rise of early modern science, one of the more interesting accounts appeared in 1938 in an essay entitled "Motive Forces of the New Science" by American sociologist Robert K. Merton.[74] Taking his cue from Weber's

72. As mentioned in the last chapter, British historian John Sommerville has recently argued that it was Henry VIII's confiscation of ecclesiastical property in 1530 that had the effect of preparing the English mind to accept Newton's radical secularization of time and space. Sommerville also suggests that the Protestant translation of the Bible into the vernacular and the great stress the Reformers placed upon print literacy fostered the critical and inquiring habits of mind necessary for the rise of science. Indeed, Sommerville's thesis in *The Secularization of Early Modern England: From Religious Culture to Religious Faith* (New York: Oxford University Press, 1992) is that far from being the cause of secularization in early-modern England, the "new science" was itself simply a kind of logical extension of the English Reformation's radical disenchantment of social order.

73. Thomas, *Religion and the Decline of Magic*, 650ff.

74. See Robert K. Merton, "Motive Forces of the New Science," in *Puritanism and the Rise of Modern Science: The Merton Thesis*, ed. I. Bernard Cohen (1938; New Brunswick, NJ: Rutgers University Press, 1990), 112-31.

unsubstantiated suggestion that the practical Protestant ethic had been just as crucial to the *spirit* of modern science as it had been to the rise of the capitalist economy, Merton observed that Puritanism and the new science did indeed share a "community of assumptions," and that this may well explain how rapidly scientific understanding was diffused and popularized within seventeenth-century England. Crucial within this community of shared assumptions were the importance of improving material living conditions, the value of disciplined and rigorous reasoning, and a willingness to subject all assertions to empirical verification. The significance of these shared assumptions, Merton contended:

> is profound though it could hardly have been consciously recognized by those whom it influenced: religion had, for whatever reasons, adopted a cast of thought which was essentially that of science so that there was a reinforcement of the typically scientific attitude of the period. This society was permeated with attitudes toward natural phenomena which were derived from both science and religion and which unwittingly enhanced the continued prevalence of conceptions characteristic of the new science.[75]

Of course, a number of qualifications have been offered to Merton's original thesis.[76] R. Hooykaas, for example, took issue with Merton's suggestion that the affinities between Puritanism and science were largely coincidental, and argued, to the contrary, that they must have been quite consciously recognized by both sides.[77] The similarity, for example, between the Puritan suspicion of ecclesiastical authority and science's suspicion of medieval and classical authorities was not simply a coincidence. Rather, Hooykaas contended that both were quite intentionally derived from Protestantism's insistence upon the priesthood of all believers before God. The Puritans, for their part, appear to have been quite convinced that the liberation of science and theology from scholastic rationalism could not help but benefit the religious reformation of English society. Defenders of the new science, on the other hand,

---

75. Ibid., 131.

76. Cohen discusses Merton's thesis at some length in *The Scientific Revolution*, 314ff.

77. R. Hooykaas, *Religion and the Rise of Modern Science* (Grand Rapids: Eerdmans, 1972).

"were perfectly conscious of the analogy between the liberation from ecclesiastical and philosophical tradition by the Reformation and the liberation of science from ancient authority by the new learning."[78]

Several additional qualifications to Merton's thesis were put forward by Charles Webster in an historical study entitled *The Great Instauration: Science, Medicine, and Reform 1626-1670* (1976).[79] Agreeing with Merton, Hooykaas, and others who stressed the scientific relevance of Puritanism's practical and utilitarian bent, Webster also developed the importance of Puritanism's commitment to education, and especially to specialized vocational education. Along this line, he calls attention to the Puritan penchant for forming organizations or "societies" dedicated to specific practical purposes. Webster concludes that this activistic practicality accounted for the ready acceptance of experimental science in seventeenth-century England:

> The Puritans were dedicated to unremitting exertion, and increasingly they were sympathetic to the virtues of manual labor; successful accomplishment of works provided one of the major means whereby some intimation of election might be obtained, and the sciences, particularly the utilitarian sciences, were one of the avenues whereby substantial works could be performed. The Calvinist God was distant and inscrutable, but the patient and accurate methods of experimental science, penetrating slowly towards the understanding of the secondary causes of things in the search for a gradual conquest of nature, represented the form of intellectual and practical endeavor most suited to the puritan mentality. Immediate goals were conceived with proper humility, and progress was necessarily slow, but every step brought further insight into the providence of God, so constantly reaffirming the correctness of the procedure.[80]

As Webster's comments indicate, Puritan eschatology also appears to have legitimated the early modern scientific endeavor. The Puritans

---

78. Ibid., 113.

79. Charles Webster, *The Great Instauration: Science, Medicine, and Reform 1626-1670* (New York: Holmes & Meier, 1976).

80. Charles Webster, "'Conclusions' to *The Great Instauration*," in I. Bernard Cohen (ed.), *Puritanism and the Rise of Modern Science* (New Brunswick: Rutgers, 1990), 282.

believed that the practical conquest of nature contributed to the immanent recovery of the dominion over creation that had been lost at the Fall. Each step in this practical conquest was thus held to be a step in the direction of the New Jerusalem.[81]

Moving beyond the significance of seventeenth-century Puritanism's popularization of early modern science, however, it has been suggested that the most consequential *theological* contributions to the rise of empirical science may well have been John Calvin's. As T. F. Torrance has observed, it was Calvin's understanding of Scripture, and in particular his understanding of the appropriate manner of *interpreting* Scripture, that initiated the move toward a truly inductive science.[82] Instead of beginning with theological abstractions and then working back to the text, Calvin's hermeneutic insisted that the Scriptures must be allowed to interpret themselves. The critical question was not "What can be said about the text on the basis of what we already know, say, on the basis of what the Church has already authoritatively established?" but rather "What does the text disclose to us?" Calvin's position was thus at once more humble and more searching than the medieval rationalist (deductive) alternative. While prohibiting us from reading our own meanings into the text, it also requires us to examine the text very closely; for only in this way can texts be coaxed into disclosing their meaning to us. Torrance suggests that Calvin's careful and inductive approach to Scripture provided a model for early modern empirical science.

> We know God by looking at God, by attending to the steps He has taken in manifesting Himself to us and thinking of Him in accordance with His divine nature. But we know the world by looking at the world, by attending to the ways in which it becomes disclosed to us out of itself, and thinking of it in accordance with its creaturely nature. Thus scientific method began to take shape both in the field of natural science and in the field of divine science.[83]

81. Ibid., 283.
82. See Thomas F. Torrance, *God and Rationality* (Oxford: Oxford University Press, 1971).
83. Ibid., 39.

Science's purely empirical investigation of nature appears also to have been aided by the Reformers' reassertion of the importance of the doctrine of creation *ex nihilo*, and thus that the creation bore no *necessary* relation to the divine nature. By contrast, Scholastic theology had been hampered by Augustine's neo-Platonic suggestion that nature had existed eternally in the mind of God. This, in turn, recommended the amalgamation of theology and natural science, and had therefore encumbered empirical inquiry with all sorts of unnecessary and unhelpful theological presuppositions.

If the logic of certain Christian doctrines contributed to the rise of early modern science, however, so the emergence of scientific understanding may also be traced to a number of distortions of Christian belief. Dutch Reformed philosopher Herman Dooyeweerd, for example, contended that modern science emerged out of a theologically mistaken understanding of "nature."[84] Modern science understands nature as a completely *autonomous* realm exhibiting its own internal regularities and principles of development, which are wholly divorced from those of theology. But this, Dooyeweerd contends, is profoundly unbiblical. It suggests a false dichotomy between nature and grace, and introduces a false tension between natural determinism, and divine and human freedom. Dooyeweerd believed that this problem could be traced to the fact that both Roman Catholic and Protestant Scholasticism had misunderstood the notion of contingency and had therefore ceded so much autonomy to the natural order that they had effectively exempted it from the fallen condition in sin. Exempting nature from sin, however, had suggested the possibility that the path to salvation might lie in a return to nature, and an alien religious "motive" had thus been introduced into early modern culture. The typically modern faith in the redemptive possibilities of science, Dooyeweerd felt, must therefore be traced to theological confusion; for modern scientism simply relocates the Christian eschatological hope to belief in the possibility of an immanent restoration of natural order by means of science and technology. Dooyeweerd's mentor, Abraham Kuyper, formulated the alternatives in the following manner in a lecture entitled "Calvinism and Science" (1931):

84. Herman Dooyeweerd, *The Secularization of Science*, trans. Robert D. Knudsen (Memphis, TN: Christian Studies Center, 1954).

The conflict [today] is not between faith and science, but between the assertion that the cosmos as it exists today, is either in a *normal* or *abnormal* condition. If it is *normal*, then it moves by means of an eternal evolution from its potencies to its ideal. But if the cosmos in its present condition is *abnormal*, then a *disturbance* has taken place in the past, and only a *regenerating* power can warrant it the final attainment of its goal. This, and no other is the principal antithesis, which separates the thinking minds in the domain of Science into two opposite battle-arrays.[85]

Nature, in other words, may either be conceived as self-contained and self-regulating, or it may be conceived as embedded in the larger drama of cosmic redemption. The former suggests the possibility that human happiness might lie in the restoration of an original "state of nature," while the latter looks to the Creator of nature for the resolution of the human condition. "For us there are only two ways open," Dooyeweerd concludes after a Kuyperian fashion in *The Secularization of Science* (1954), "that of Scholastic accommodation, which by reason of its dialectical unfolding results in secularization, or that of the spirit of the Reformation, which requires the inward, radical reformation of scientific thought by the driving power of the biblical motive."[86]

Dooyeweerd's analysis sheds helpful light on the question of Puritanism's contribution to the rise of science; for it substantiates Merton's suggestion that Puritan enthusiasm for the "new science" may have unintentionally introduced a secular impulse into early modern thought which would eventually prove very much at odds with Christian faith.[87]

85. Abraham Kuyper, *Lectures on Calvinism* (Grand Rapids, MI: Eerdmans, 1931), 131-32.

86. Dooyeweerd, *The Secularization of Science*, 24.

87. Political philosopher Leo Strauss suggested that this was really the tragedy of Puritanism. While the Puritans would not have wanted to have had anything to do with the likes of Machiavelli and Hobbes, they actually served to "carry" the new secular-scientific outlook to the extent that they used it to repudiate medieval Scholasticism. In *Natural Right and History* (Chicago: University of Chicago, 1950), Strauss observes (note p. 61): "Puritanism, having broken more radically with the 'pagan' philosophic tradition (i.e. chiefly with Aristotelianism) than Roman Catholicism and Lutheranism had done, was more open to the new philosophy than were the latter. Puritanism thus could become a very important, and perhaps the most important, 'carrier' of the new philosophy both natural and moral — of a philosophy which had been created by men of an entirely non-Puritan stamp."

Viewing nature "naturalistically," as it were, rather quickly tempted many to view nature as a source of redemption, and to view the scientific recovery of natural order as a direct route back to Eden. This temptation apparently surfaced first in the suggestion that disciplined scientific advance might begin to repair the damage that had been done to the creation by sin.[88] The references to sin became more and more infrequent, however, and by the end of the seventeenth century the invocation of "nature" and "natural right" had itself become sufficient to legitimate social and political policy initiatives. As we have seen, modern social and political theory eventually abandoned theology altogether in favor of purely scientific legitimation.[89]

Puritanism was not the only Protestant movement to have unintentionally contributed to the rise of scientific secularity, however. Barth made similar observations with respect to continental Pietism's accidental slide into liberal rationalism. Just as in England, the crucial period appears to have been the seventeenth century, and the critical theological mistake appears to have been to concede epistemological autonomy to science for the sake of preserving the integrity of both science and theology. Pietists assumed that there was little risk in this concession as science and theology must inevitably complement each other, but it eventually resulted in the subordination of the latter to the former:

88. See Passmore, *Man's Responsibility for Nature*, 19.

89. See R. H. Tawney, *Religion and the Rise of Capitalism: A Historical Study* (1926; New York: Harcourt, Brace & Company, 1952), 191. Kaiser stresses this point as well in *Creation and the History of Science*, but argues that the problem did not stem so much from science itself as from popular misconceptions about the nature and efficacy of science. The apprehension of the relevance of God did not disappear from the culture because of some kind of tension between science and religion, but because ordinary people began to believe that scientific and technological progress might eventually solve the problems of the human condition. Along this line, Kaiser contends that the temptation to deny the *relative* autonomy of natural order and to assert its *absolute* autonomy (as in "scientism") has been present in the West since at least the twelfth century. Yet this decisive shift does not actually occur until the eighteenth and nineteenth centuries. The reason for this historical gap is that it is not until the eighteenth, and probably not really until the nineteenth century, that the average person became tempted to direct essentially religious aspirations to scientific and technological progress. Kaiser thus suggests that it was not until scientism became part of the popular imagination that the creationist tradition was eclipsed; and that the fruitlessness of "scientism" for science is only just now becoming apparent to the popular imagination.

Good Protestant theology had prescribed for itself a doctor whose treatment could prove impossible in the long run. . . . It had thought . . . that it could combine these two absolute claims [of science and theology] with one another by means of the usual trivial misunderstanding of the words of the Gospel: Render unto Caesar that which is Caesar's and to God that which is God's. But the question had to be put, and was in fact put, whether the choice that had to be made was not to understand one of these claims as absolute and the other as relative.[90]

The subsequent emergence of science as the chief criterion for evaluating public truth left eighteenth- and nineteenth-century Protestant theologians the choice of either rendering theology scientifically acceptable, or reinterpreting the Christian religion in terms of a "private" religious experience exempt from rational scientific scrutiny.[91]

It is important to stress that Protestant theology has continued to suffer from a crippling inability to evaluate the claims of science *theologically*. Indeed, the same displacement of theology by scientific understanding that first surfaced in the seventeenth century still plagues North American evangelicalism. Commenting on the astonishingly rapid secularization of American higher education at the turn of this century, for example, George Marsden has argued that it was their confusion over the relation between science and theology that prevented evangelical scholars and college administrators from recognizing the secular scientific threat until it was too late to repulse it.[92] On the basis of their conviction that scientific and theological truth must ultimately converge, evangelical scholars had, by the last third of the nineteenth century, already conceded a methodological agnosticism to the scientific disciplines. As Marsden has noted:

90. Barth, *Protestant Theology in the Nineteenth Century*, 162-63.

91. Kaiser, *Creation and the History of Science*, 273.

92. George M. Marsden, "Evangelicals and the Scientific Culture: An Overview," in *Religion and Twentieth-Century American Intellectual Life*, ed. Michael J. Lacey (New York: Cambridge University Press, 1989), 23-48. For a detailed study of the history of this problem within nineteenth-century American Protestantism, see Theodore Dwight Bozeman, *Protestants in an Age of Science: The Baconian Ideal and Antebellum American Religious Thought* (Chapel Hill, NC: University of North Carolina Press, 1977).

Science and Protestant religion went hand in hand, since both stood for free inquiry versus prejudice and arbitrary authority. Francis Bacon . . . was high among the saints in the American Protestant hierarchy. Praise for Bacon's nonspeculative, nonmetaphysical down-to-earth methods knew few bounds. Neither the natural order nor the moral order was a matter of sectarian doctrine; rather, both were of divine creation, open for all to see. The candid inquirer had nothing to fear from a disciplined search for the truth.[93]

Yet this commitment to "nonmetaphysical" Baconian science left North American evangelicals almost completely unprepared to cope with the intellectual drift toward an understanding of science that affirmed the ongoing and ultimately purposeless development and evolution of all things, an understanding which denied the permanence of created nature and undermined the traditional argument for God's existence from design in nature. Committed as they were to free inquiry and scientific progress, then, turn-of-the-century evangelicals were largely confounded by the Darwinian, and eventually Freudian, challenges to traditional Christian understanding, challenges purporting to be genuinely scientific. The remarkably rapid "disestablishment" of theological reasoning from within North American intellectual culture between roughly 1890 and 1930 may thus be said to stem in large part from the failure of evangelicals to develop an adequate theology of science. That insights from completely secularized social-scientific disciplines have recently been reintroduced into evangelical churches in the name of scientific efficiency and effectiveness only consummates the irony of this development.

It is important to stress, however, that Protestant confusion about the nature of "nature" may simply reflect a rather long-standing confusion about the nature of creation in the Western theological tradition. Along this line, British theologian Colin Gunton has recently gone so far as to suggest that the Western theological tradition has been plagued by a kind of disconnection of creation from the larger economy of salvation for centuries, perhaps even since the time of Augustine.[94] The implications

---

93. George M. Marsden, The Soul of the American University: From Protestant Establishment to Established Nonbelief (New York: Oxford University Press, 1994), 85.

94. Colin E. Gunton, The One, the Three and the Many: God, Creation and the Culture of Modernity (Cambridge: Cambridge University Press, 1993).

of Gunton's provocative thesis are quite profound: for if the larger creation is separated from the economy of salvation, this implies that the natural world does not need to be brought under theological discipline, and yet if nature does not need to be envisioned theologically, then why does "human nature" or "natural" human existence need to be? Here again, the disconnection of created nature from grace suggests the "naturalness" of pursuing scientific progress without reference to religion or theology.

According to Gunton, the distinctively modern disjunction between nature (science) and the larger economy of salvation (theology) began to take shape during the late thirteenth and fourteenth centuries in a philosophical movement loosely termed "nominalism" or, as it was then called, the *via moderna* ("modern way").[95] Over and against the Scholastic rationalists, or *"via antiqua,"* who insisted that they could infer all sorts of things about the meaning and purpose of the creation on the basis of theological principles, advocates of the "modern way," such as William of Ockham (d. 1349), contended that the meaning of the created order was entirely immanent within it and thus discernible only by observation and experience. To be sure, the purpose of the nominalist contention was ultimately to preserve the freedom of God and the graciousness of the gospel by insisting that God was not *bound* to create in the way that he actually has, and that he did not *have* to act to redeem his creation in the way that he has.[96] Yet the nominalist

---

95. See also Heiko Oberman's discussions of the *via moderna* in *The Harvest of Medieval Theology: Gabriel Biel and Late Medieval Nominalism* (1963; Grand Rapids, MI: Eerdmans, 1967), and *Masters of the Reformation: The Emergence of a New Intellectual Climate in Europe* (Cambridge: Cambridge University Press, 1981); see also Alister McGrath, *The Intellectual Origins of the European Reformation* (Oxford: Blackwell, 1987).

96. In this connection, we note that late medieval "nominalists" appear to have become dissatisfied with the *via antiqua's* answer to the basic question of just how it is that a Holy God is able to save sinful creatures. The *via antiqua* (following Aristotle) suggested that God saves us because we are *intrinsically worth saving* due to the grace God has infused in us. The "realist" focus, therefore, was ontological, that is, upon how our being is actually changed to merit salvation. The *via moderna*, by way of contrast, suggested that God saves us simply because he has determined — in grace and by way of covenant — to save us *in spite of* our intrinsic unworthiness. The nominalist focus was thus covenantal, that is, upon God's sovereign decision to declare us worthy of salvation. It is this shift from ontological to covenantal causality that lay at the root of Martin Luther's conception of justification by grace through faith. See Alister McGrath, *Luther's Theology of the Cross* (Oxford: Basil Blackwell, 1985).

view also implied that the scope of natural theology ought to be limited to the simple observation of nature, and that natural causation ought to be understood solely in terms of efficient causality. The nominalists thus ruled extravagant speculation about nature's final causes out of their system *a priori*; and they would not permit the creation and its Creator to be linked by an analogy of being. In preserving God's freedom, therefore, the nominalist critique had the effect — at least we can say so in retrospect — of overemphasizing the relative autonomy of the creation. It also had the effect of reversing the traditional relation between theology and experience. Instead of preceding and interpreting the human experience of the world, natural theology was forced to follow behind observation and experience, making sense of both as best it could. As Tage Lindbom has noted concerning Ockham's contribution to secular modernity:

> For traditional [religious] man . . . reality is a translucent objectivity, perceptible through the world of sensory experience; natural things are lamps through which shines the light of their heavenly — ultimately Divine — prototypes. But Ockham replaces this with a misplaced subjectivity, the consciousness that we gain through our sensory and mental faculties. The real is the evidence of the senses. Ockhamism informs "truth" or reality with a new content: it is thisworldly, subjective, [and] gained by mental processes, especially rational and logical processes that depend upon sense data.[97]

Ockhamism's "modern way," Lindbom contends, represented a fundamental revolution in medieval thinking and set the stage for what was to become an increasingly profane conception of human existence within modern society and culture.

As it happened, the nominalist view was adopted by the Protestant Reformers in their defense of Scripture and in their attack upon Scholastic rationalism; and from Protestantism the *via moderna* passed into modern humanism and early modern science. The *via moderna* was a position inherently vulnerable to secularization, however, for it was possible to interpret the assertion that nature should not be envisioned

97. Tage Lindbom, *The Myth of Democracy* (Grand Rapids, MI: Eerdmans, 1996), 20.

theologically and teleologically to suggest that even belief in a Creator is redundant and irrelevant to life in this world. The contemporary preponderance of the notion that it is up to *us* to ascribe meaning and significance *to* the natural world is a good indication that this was, in fact, the way many of the heirs of the Reformation interpreted the *via moderna*. As Gunton notes:

> God was no longer needed to account for the coherence and meaning of the world, so that the seat of rationality and meaning became not the world, but the human reason and will, which thus *displace* God or the world. When the unifying will of God becomes redundant, or is rejected for a variety of moral, rational and scientific reasons, the focus of the unity of things becomes the unifying rational mind.[98]

A mistaken theological conception of the nature of creation may thus lie behind the activistic, manipulative, and thoroughly anthropocentric bent of modern scientific culture. Science's understanding of nature, after all, does not simply expose the fact that nature has been disenchanted, but also that nature is theologically mute. Indeed, understood scientifically, nature does not bespeak anything beyond the possibility that God — if he exists at all — is apparently creative and powerful. This narrowing of creation's theological significance has granted a great deal of freedom to scientific inquiry and to the technological manipulation of nature; but it has also contributed quite substantially to the sterility, barrenness, and impersonality of modern technological society and culture.

Finally, it appears that the modern scientific endeavor may also have benefited from a distorted understanding of Christian *conviction*. Such was the thesis of Ernst Troeltsch's provocative essay *Protestantism and Progress* (1912).[99] In short, Troeltsch contended that Protestantism's most significant contribution to the rise of secular science may well have been made through a mistaken reading of the Reformers' emphasis upon conscience and upon the importance of conviction. While the stress on conviction had originally been juxtaposed to formal religiosity, it appears to have been reinterpreted within the early modern

---

98. Gunton, *The One, the Three and the Many*, 28.
99. Ernst Troeltsch, *Protestantism and Progress: The Significance of Protestantism for the Rise of the Modern World* (1912; Philadelphia: Fortress, 1986).

scientific enterprise to suggest that scientific and technological truth must, in addition to theological truth, be pursued as a matter of con-science. This subtle reinterpretation, Troeltsch felt, formed the crucial link between Protestantism and the modern notion of progress:

> Once the point was reached in the development of Protestantism at which the "way" of personal conviction became more important than the goal of supernatural salvation, religious convictions could not remain wholly unrelated to scientific conviction. The former had to take on the experimental character of the latter, while the latter assumed the character of a sacred religious duty which belongs to the former.[100]

Troeltsch's insights have been confirmed more recently in Amos Funkenstein's detailed historical study *Theology and the Scientific Imagination from the Middle Ages to the Seventeenth Century* (1986).[101] Funken-stein contends that there was indeed a curious convergence of theolog-ical, philosophical, and scientific concerns during the seventeenth century and that this resulted in the conviction that science was to supersede traditional Christian theology. The amalgamation of theology, philosophy, and science has tended to characterize modern intellectual life ever since. This is evident in the essentially religious devotion that secular scientific progress still elicits.[102] It may also be seen in the recurrent suggestion that Christian theology must be scientifically "de-mythologized" for the sake of conscience and as a logical extension of the Reformation's criticism of formal religiosity.

100. Ibid., 99. Sommerville makes a similar point in *The Secularization of Early Modern England* by suggesting that the effect of the Reformers' criticism of Roman Catholic religiosity in England was to leave Protestant Christianity without any real social function except that of protecting the freedom of individual conscience.

101. Amos Funkenstein, *Theology and the Scientific Imagination from the Middle Ages to the Seventeenth Century* (Princeton, NJ: Princeton University Press, 1986); see also Richard S. Westfall, "Isaac Newton's *Theologiae Gentilis Origines Philosophicae*," in *The Secular Mind: Transformations of Faith in Modern Europe*, ed. W. Warren Wager (New York: Holmes & Meier, 1982), 15-34.

102. See, for example, David A. Hollinger, "Justification by Verification: The Scientific Challenge to the Moral Authority of Christianity in Modern America," in *Religion and Twentieth-Century American Intellectual Life*, ed. Michael J. Lacey (New York: Cambridge University Press, 1989), 116-35.

While our survey has obviously revealed a number of differences of opinion as to the nature of Christianity's contribution to the rise of modern science, *that* Christianity did contribute to this development, however, and *that* this contribution was quite important, is practically beyond dispute. On the one hand, the modern scientific enterprise appears to have been founded upon a fundamentally Christian understanding of created order, and received its initial impetus from the Christian convictions that we ought to glorify God by exploring and celebrating this order, and that we ought to love and serve our neighbor by using our knowledge of the created order, where possible, to improve the material conditions of human life. The vast improvements in material living conditions wrought by modern science and technology in recent centuries, then, owes much to the Christian religion.

Yet the modern scientific enterprise also appears to have derived its distinctively autonomous logic on the basis of a *mis*understanding of the Christian doctrine of creation. While Christian theology had traditionally stressed only the *relative* autonomy of the created order, early modern scientists interpreted this to mean that nature, and eventually even human nature, could be understood wholly without reference to the gospel or theology. A great many Protestant theologians gave their blessing to this modern interpretation. Christian theology must therefore shoulder a good deal of the responsibility for the fact that modern science and technology have, by now, largely emptied the world of religious meaning.[103]

To conclude, modern science and technology substantially buttress the plausibility of practical atheism in contemporary society and culture. The secular and closed quality of "natural" existence is one of science's foundational assumptions; and the spectacular technological achievements of recent centuries have encouraged us to imagine either that we are capable of mastering the world, or that we have no choice but to try to do so. Science and technology have also contributed quite substantially to the impersonality of modern technological society. After

103. It is not terribly surprising in this connection that many of the "new age" critics of modern science and technology have concluded that any solution to the problems of scientific and technological culture must begin with the repudiation of Christianity. Yet it is perhaps an indication of the depth of our predicament that the spirit of the "new age" is itself profoundly technological.

all, if natural order is at once explicable and manipulable solely in terms of mechanical causality, then what sense can be made of freedom, love, justice, and all of the other things we value in connection with truly personal existence? Does not the objectification of the world by means of scientific and technological understanding inevitably result in the death of the soul? Yet because the Western Church contributed so significantly to the rise of modern science, and because Christianity, science, and technology have been so closely intertwined over the course of the last several centuries, it is often quite difficult to tell where one begins and the others leave off. Perhaps the most important thing to be said in this regard is that any adequate critique of modern technological society must carefully rethink the nature of "nature" and must itself be grounded in a theology which is able to bear the full weight of personal existence.

On the Contingency of the Created Order

Describing the ironic progression of the modern dismissal of the medieval view of nature, C. S. Lewis observed:

> At the outset the universe appears packed with will, intelligence, life and positive qualities. . . . [Yet] [t]he advance of knowledge gradually empties this rich and genial universe: first of its gods, then of its colours, smells, sounds and tastes, finally of solidity itself as solidity was originally imagined. . . . The same method which has emptied the world now proceeds to empty ourselves. The masters of the method soon announce that we were just as mistaken (and mistaken in much the same way) when we attributed "souls," or "selves" or "minds" to human organisms, as when we attributed Dryads to the trees. . . .[104]

As we have seen, then, the peculiar intellectual plight of modernity is not simply that the larger world has been emptied of transcendent meaning and significance, but that we have even dissolved ourselves in the acids of our own scientific and technological methods.

104. C. S. Lewis, "The Empty Universe," 81-82.

Christians — and in particular Protestants — appear to have unintentionally contributed to this modern plight by assuming a) that early modern scientific criticism of classical and medieval authorities was a logical extension of the Reformers' repudiation of papal authority and of their criticism of the quasi-magical quality of medieval religiosity; and b) that the findings of the various modern sciences would inevitably prove to be consistent with biblical truth in spite of the fact that these sciences required an attitude of methodological atheism, or at least agnosticism. Both assumptions proved to be highly problematic. The latter resulted in the secularization of much of modern intellectual discourse, and the former ended in the "demythologization" of Christianity itself.

Admittedly, Protestants had no intention of emptying the universe of "will, intelligence, life and positive qualities," as Lewis put it, but only to criticize a mistaken theological understanding of creation which had implied that the meaning and significance of the world — its *telos* — was somehow ontologically embedded within it in such a way as to be discernible merely by rational speculation. And they were right. Aristotelian science was not adequate to the reality of the natural world, nor can nature's ultimate purpose be determined by way of a merely "natural theology." Yet the impact of the Protestant (nominalist) criticism of the Scholastic (Aristotelian) view of nature was to endorse a position which would quickly supplant the Christian view altogether. Contemporary reflections about the emptiness of modern scientific understanding notwithstanding, we have obviously managed, over the course of the last several centuries, to repack the universe with *human* will, *human* intelligence, and with the supposed requisites for *human* life. If there was a void created by scientific disenchantment, in other words, it was rather quickly filled by *homo faber* and his technological *re*-enchantment of the world.

Of course, to the extent that modern technological society has *intentionally* displaced God from the realm of nature it is, from a Christian point of view, damnable. It recalls the Psalmist's warning that, although the rulers of the earth vainly conspire together against the LORD and against his Anointed One to "break their chains" and "throw off their fetters," they will ultimately be dashed to pieces like pottery (Psalm 2). Yet because the modern secular view developed so unintentionally and accidentally, perhaps it is still possible to reform it with biblical understanding. We ought to try to do so in any event. The challenge is to give an account of nature that does not deny the validity of scientific inquiry, and yet does not so stress the autonomy of the created order that it tempts us to believe that science can reveal the meaning of nature and of our own lives. Our account of *human* nature, furthermore, must leave room for real creativity, and yet must reject the modern — and "postmodern" — notion that we create our own meanings and values *ex nihilo*. In developing such an alternative account of nature, one of the crucial concepts would surely be that of *contingence*.

The Bible suggests that God created the world freely, graciously, and out of nothing *(ex nihilo)*. God did not *have* to create the world, therefore, and the world is not an extension of his being; but neither could the world continue to exist, even for an instant, apart from his gracious permission. Indeed, it is only by God's providential grace that the creation is kept from lapsing back into nothingness. The creation is therefore both *independent* of and yet utterly *dependent* upon its Creator. This is the crucial paradox captured in the term "contingence." As T. F. Torrance recently noted:

> It is this elusive interlocking of dependence and independence that makes contingence so difficult to grasp and express. The universe is not self-supporting or self-explaining as though it had an interior principle of its own, but neither is it mere appearance, for it is ontologically grounded beyond itself on God who has given it authentic reality and lawfulness of its own which he unceasingly sustains through the presence of his Creator Word and Spirit. If he were to withdraw that presence from the creation it would vanish into nothing. Thus in the last resort the inherent meaning and truth of the universe lie beyond its own limits in God who loves it, sustains it, and undergirds it by his own divine reality.[105]

That the paradox of contingence has indeed been difficult to grasp and express is indicated by how frequently theologians have tipped the balance toward one or the other of its two aspects. Along this line, Western theology has tended either to overemphasize the *dependence* of the created order, thus minimizing human creativity and discouraging

---

105. T. F. Torrance, *The Trinitarian Faith: The Evangelical Theology of the Ancient Catholic Church* (Edinburgh: T. & T. Clark, 1993), 100-101.

a genuinely empirical science, or to stress the independence of the created order in such a way as to suggest that it is *self*-supporting and *self*-interpreting, and thus entirely comprehensible by means of humanly devised sciences. As we have seen, modern "positivism" and "scientism" push this latter position toward its logical conclusion by suggesting that there is no truth beyond that disclosed by the methods of modern empirical sciences. Recent proponents of so-called "postmodernism" finish this job by insisting that even the notion of "truth" itself is a human construction. Everything that appears to be ultimately meaningful or significant in the world, so the contemporary argument runs, is really only a reflection of the collective hunger for security against a backdrop of nothingness.

The incoherence of the postmodern position, however, combined with the abject failure of modern science to discover — by means of its various and sundry methods — genuinely satisfying meaning, suggests the importance of steering the contemporary discussion of nature back in the direction of *dependence*. Today, perhaps as no other time in history, it needs to be stressed that the meaning and truth of the world lie *beyond* its own limits in God who created it and who loves it, sustains it, and undergirds it by his own divine reality. The meaning and truth of the world are not therefore discoverable, even by determined human effort. Neither is it simply given to us to create our own "meanings" and "truths" for ourselves. The former only leads to frustration, and the latter to decadence and death. Rather, if the truth of our existence is to be known it must be spoken into the world from *outside* the world. It must be *revealed*.

In trying to steer the contemporary discussion of nature back in the direction of dependence, however, we must be very careful not to forget the paradoxical contingency of created order and accidentally deny the possibility of authentic human making and human creativity. We must be careful, in other words, not to collapse the genuine independence of the created order into some sort of rigid conception of revealed order. In this connection, we recall that the Scriptures affirm that the creation is mysteriously *open* to human direction, and that the meaning of nature must ultimately be unfolded and disclosed by human agency. This is why the apostle Paul writes that "the creation waits in eager expectation for the sons of God to be revealed" (Rom. 8:19). As astonishing as it may sound, the *telos* of the entire world depends upon free human decision as moved by the Spirit of God in Christ. It has been given to *us* — in Christ — to direct the world to its Creator in love. Indeed, that which is not God — the created world — is to be made to participate in the fullness of the divine life by being freely taken up into our spiritual expression of love and adoration for our Maker. This defines the mystery of the Church inherent in creation:

> Throughout all the vicissitudes which followed upon the fall of humanity and the destruction of the first Church — the Church of paradise — the creation preserved the idea of its vocation and with it the idea of the Church, which was at length to be fully realized after Golgotha and after Pentecost, as the Church properly so-called, the indestructible Church of Christ. From that time on, the created and contingent universe has borne within itself a new body, possessing an uncreated and limitless plenitude which the world cannot contain. This new body is the Church; the plenitude which it contains is grace, the profusion of the divine energies by which and for which the world was created. . . . The entire universe is called to enter within the Church, to become the Church of Christ, that it may be transformed after the consummation of the ages, into the eternal Kingdom of God. Created from nothing, the world finds its fulfillment in the Church, where the creation acquires an unshakable foundation in the accomplishment of its vocation.[106]

That it is, in fact, the Church's divinely ordained task to enable the creation to participate in the divine life by being taken up in our conscious and freely willed love of God is given — ironically — in the evidence so often cited for the thesis that reality is, after all, socially constructed. Such observations point to the impossibility of separating human willing from morality and culture and, indeed, suggest that there is a genuine element of human freedom even in the affirmation of natural law. While secular modern critics take this to mean that there is no such thing as a divinely willed order in the world, the real point is that it was divinely willed that created order would be taken up into the created *human* will and *re*-presented to its Creator in love. The

106. Vladimir Lossky, *The Mystical Theology of the Eastern Church* (1944; London: James Clarke & Co., 1957), 113.

drama of history is thus defined by the fact that we have been granted the freedom to turn the creation either toward or — for a time — against its Creator. It is our awareness of these two alternatives that ought to inform our assessment of modern science and technology. As James Schall commented in an essay entitled "Technology and Spirituality":

> If technology or science in fact take on an anti-God or humanly destructive hue, as they sometimes have, it is not because of themselves but because of a will that stands behind them. The question is never properly posed as: science or faith, religion or technology. The only way for a created thing to be diverted from its goodness or potential is by being caught up in a choice, a movement originating in, or at least passing through, the human will.[107]

We do not need to renounce human creativity, therefore; nor do we need completely to forgo technological making; rather, we need only insist that this creative activity be informed by the love of Christ, by the love of neighbor, and by the love of the world for the sake of both.

---

107. James V. Schall, "Technology and Spirituality," in *The Distinctiveness of Christianity* (San Francisco: Ignatius, 1982), 147.

CHAPTER THREE

The Intrinsic Secularity
of Modern Economic Life

"Be careful that you do not forget the LORD your God, failing to
observe his commands, his laws and decrees that I am giving you this
day. Otherwise, when you eat and are satisfied, when you build fine
houses and settle down, and when your herds and flocks grow large
and your silver and gold increase and all you have is multiplied, then
your heart will become proud and you will forget the LORD your God,
who brought you out of Egypt, out of the land of slavery."

Deuteronomy 8:11-14

The fallen human proclivity to forget God is obviously nothing new, but
it has become particularly tempting for us today because practical atheism
and secularity are so deeply embedded in the central institutions of
modern society and culture. This is one of the central theses of our study.
In support of this thesis we have reviewed the secular quality of modern
political theory and practice, the methodological atheism presupposed by
modern science, and the practical anthropocentrism fostered by our
development and use of modern technology. Indeed, given our previous
discussions, it might seem that we had already substantially interpreted
the secularity of modern society and culture. Unfortunately, there is more
to say. Recalling our initial definition of modernization as a process driven

by technologically induced *economic* growth, our analysis of modern worldliness would not be complete without giving careful consideration to the character of contemporary economic life. Far from being incidental to the process of secularization, the modern economy is one of its chief institutional culprits. Indeed, the economy underwrites much of the plausibility of practical atheism in the contemporary situation. In light of the apparent triumph of capitalism over socialism in recent years, we might further qualify this assertion by suggesting that the *market economy* is one of the most significant "carriers" of secularity and practical atheism in contemporary society and culture. After all, it is the near-global market that provides the institutional context within which science, technology, and even political life operate today. As Nicholas Berdyaev observed a number of years ago, "The power of economics was never so strong as in our time. Now nothing can escape its influence. . . . The life of the whole world moves beneath the sign of economism, and economic interests have put all things under their feet."[1]

Putting the matter this bluntly will probably offend conservative sensibilities; for theological conservatives have tended to be very protective of the market economy in recent decades, and have voiced far more concern over the threat that secular *political* ideologies pose to contemporary Christian faith and life than they have about secular economic practices. Indeed, their preoccupation with political culture has largely blinded theological conservatives to the temptations to practical atheism which emanate quite powerfully and pervasively from the contemporary marketplace. To say this is not to preface an apology for some alternative to the market economy, however, for there do not appear to be any very desirable alternatives. All the proposed substitutes have not only proven economically unattractive, but they have also shown an insidious tendency to exacerbate the kind of political worldliness we discussed in our first chapter. In spite of the market economy's extraordinary productivity, however, and even in spite of its close affinities with religious freedom and liberal democracy, it is still necessary to raise the question of capitalism's contribution to modern worldliness. The logic of the market pervades so much of contemporary life that if secularity and practical atheism have become increasingly plausible

---

1. Nicholas Berdyaev, *The Fate of Man in the Modern World* (Ann Arbor, MI: University of Michigan Press, 1935), 77-78.

within our culture, it is only reasonable to assume that the operations of the economy have had something to do with this.

Of course, to the extent that rising standards of living tempt us to locate more and more of our aspirations in this world, capitalism's contribution to the secularization of modern culture may be said to be somewhat accidental. After all, the market economy can hardly be blamed for the fact that affluent people have the tendency to put all of their eggs into temporal baskets; for surely this has always been the case. In this connection, we might recall Jesus' parable of the rich fool (Luke 12:16ff.). Still, modern economic life exhibits a certain pattern that appears to exacerbate this age-old problem. The desire to improve the material conditions of life, it seems, gives rise to the application of industrial technologies which, in turn, leads to mass production, marketing, and consumption, which seem inevitably to issue in cultural decadence and secularity.[2] This peculiar pattern has been observed and lamented at least as far back as the mid-eighteenth century. John Wesley, for example, made the following comments circa 1740:

> I fear wherever riches have increased, the essence of religion has decreased in the same proportion. Therefore, I do not see how it is possible in the nature of things for any period of revival of religion to continue long. For religion must necessarily produce both industry and frugality, and these cannot but produce riches. But, as riches increase, so will pride, anger, and love of the world in all its branches. How, then, is it possible that Methodism, that is a religion of the heart, though it flourishes now as the green bay trees, should continue in this state? For the Methodists in every place grow diligent and frugal; consequently, they increase in goods. Hence they proportionately increase in pride, in anger, in the desire of the flesh, the desire of the eyes, and the pride of life. So, although the form of religion remains, the spirit is swiftly vanishing away. Is there no way to prevent this — the continual decay of pure religion?[3]

2. See Bernard Eugene Meland, *The Secularization of Modern Cultures* (New York: Oxford University Press, 1966), 25-26.

3. Wesley, cited in Max Weber, *The Protestant Ethic and the Spirit of Capitalism* (New York: Charles Scribner's Sons, 1958), 175; see also Robert Southey, *Life of Wesley and the Rise and Progress of Methodism*, 2nd American edition (New York: Harper, 1847), 308.

Although Wesley suggests that this pattern is true of any period of religious revival, we note that the modern market economy has rendered the relationship between industry, frugality, and the increase in goods particularly predictable. Under market conditions, diligence and frugality almost invariably result in upward mobility, and so also in the spiritual temptations that accompany the increase in wealth. The fact that most of us would simply not survive for very long in the absence of the material benefits produced and distributed by the modern industrial economy makes Wesley's anguished question even more germane today than it was at the beginning of the eighteenth century. Just how *do* we prevent the decay of pure religion in the context of a modern growth economy?

The secularization of modern society and culture also appears to stem indirectly from the relations of production that the market economy seems to engender. Along this line, in a study entitled *Secularization and Moral Change* (1967), Alasdair MacIntyre contended that the secularization of English culture was an inevitable consequence of the increasingly sharp class-divisions induced by industrial capitalism.[4] As the Christian religion began to be used by different classes to legitimate different, and largely conflicting, interests, it simply lost its overall plausibility. Because it failed to hold the various class factions of the modern industrial society together, in other words, Christianity became unbelievable. MacIntyre wrote:

> [I]t is not the case that men first stopped believing in God and in the authority of the Church, and then subsequently started behaving differently. It seems clear that [in the modern industrial context] men first of all lost any over-all social agreement as to the right ways to live together, and so ceased to be able to make sense of any claims to moral authority. Consequently they could not find intelligible the claims to such authority which were advanced on the part of the Church. . . . Social change and with it moral change is chronologically prior to the loss of belief effected by intellectual argument.[5]

4. Alasdair MacIntyre, *Secularization and Moral Change* (London: Oxford University Press, 1967).
5. Ibid., 54-55.

Of course, the assumption that the Christian religion must immediately lose its plausibility once it ceases to unite an entire culture is debatable. Yet in the case of nineteenth-century England, class divisions do appear to have had a significantly negative effect upon the plausibility, and indeed upon the credibility, of the Church of England.[6]

It is important to stress, however, that secularity is not simply accidental to the operations of the capitalist economy, but it appears to be intrinsic to the functioning of the market itself. In this connection, Nathan Rosenberg and L. E. Birdzell Jr. recently argued in a study entitled *How the West Grew Rich: The Economic Transformation of the Industrial World* (1986), that it has been the *relative autonomy* of the economic sphere in the capitalist political economy — that is, the economy's freedom *from* religion and politics — that has, among other things, accounted for the remarkable growth in productivity that the West has experienced in recent centuries. The key elements of the West's "growth system," as Rosenberg and Birdzell term it, "were the wide diffusion of the authority and resources necessary to experiment; *an absence of more than rudimentary political and religious restrictions on experiment* [emphasis added]; and incentives which combined ample rewards for success . . . with a risk of severe penalties for failing to experiment."[7] To the extent that secularization is defined as a process in which different sectors of society and culture cease to be informed by religion, then, the market system may not only be said to be secularized, but it actually appears to function effectively for precisely this reason. Those who grow used to the "absence of religious restriction on experiment" in the marketplace, furthermore, tend to exhibit resistance to this restriction in other areas of their lives as well. It is for just this reason that Peter Berger has gone so far as to suggest that "economic data on industrial productivity or capital expansion can predict the religious crisis of credibility in a particular society more easily than data derived from the 'history of ideas' of that society."[8] The intrinsic secu-

6. See Alan D. Gilbert, *The Making of Post-Christian Britain: A History of the Secularization of Modern Society* (London: Longman, 1980), 69ff.

7. Nathan Rosenberg and L. E. Birdzell Jr., *How the West Grew Rich: The Economic Transformation of the Industrial World* (New York: Basic Books, 1986), 33.

8. Peter L. Berger, *The Sacred Canopy: Elements of a Sociological Theory of Religion* (Garden City, NY: Anchor, 1969), 151.

larity of economic activity, it seems, has shown an insidious tendency to spill out of the economy and into other not-necessarily-economic parts of our lives.

The observation that secularity has spilled out of the marketplace and into the rest of modern culture lies at the heart of Max Weber's seminal essay *The Protestant Ethic and the Spirit of Capitalism* (1904-5). Indeed, it was for this very reason that Weber submitted at the conclusion of his essay that the modern economic order, linked as it is to technology and the conditions of machine production, had become a kind of "iron cage" from which there was very little hope of escape. Capitalism, Weber felt, had become a most fateful and irresistible force in modern social life, a force that might possibly continue to determine the shape of modern existence until, as he put it, "the last ton of fossilized coal is burnt."[9] Although Weber's argument has already spawned a vast literature,[10] I want to spend most of the rest of this chapter focusing on his analysis of the modern economic order. Weber's suggestion that the modern economy had become an "iron cage" is grounded in an insightful analytical framework that goes some distance toward explaining how and why secularity and practical atheism have become so characteristic of modern society and culture.

The conceptual key within Weber's analysis, and indeed the conceptual key to his understanding of the larger process of modernization, lay in his understanding of *rationality* and, in particular, in his understanding of the process of *rationalization*. Rationalization denotes a process in which social action ceases to be determined by traditional wisdom and/or custom and comes instead to be determined by abstract, calculable, and often impersonal, "rational" criteria. It entails the elimination of all decisions that cannot be shown to contribute to planned outcomes, outcomes that have themselves been rationally defined and determined according to generally valid empirical laws.[11] Rationalization thus systematizes social action. As Thomas Luckmann observed with respect to Weberian analysis:

9. Weber, *The Protestant Ethic*, 181.

10. For a short history of the debate over Weber's Protestant Ethic thesis, see Ephraim Fischoff, "The Protestant Ethic and the Spirit of Capitalism: The History of a Controversy," in *The Protestant Ethic and Modernization: A Comparative View*, ed. S. N. Eisenstadt (New York: Basic Books, 1968), 67-86.

11. Eduard Shils, *Tradition* (Chicago: University of Chicago Press, 1981), 291.

In Weber's view the outstanding characteristic of modern society is its 'rationality'. . . . In modern society he discerned the prevalence of a highly systematic, anonymous and calculable form of law, he found an economy guided by its own principles of calculability and means ends rationality, he observed a trend to an anonymous, calculable and bureaucratic system of political administration and, last but not least, he of course noted the social significance of an objective science that made nature technically calculable. . . . The 'rationality' [rationalization] of modern society was perceived by Weber as the result of a unique line of historical development which — as soon as it became welded into the structure of society — became divorced from the conditions of its origin and either overwhelmed all other lines of historical development or came to serve as a model for them.[12]

Of the other lines of historical development overwhelmed by the process of rationalization, the most significant in our own Western context has been the Christian. Whereas Christianity had provided *the* interpretive grid for Western European society and culture for many hundreds of years, with the onset of modernity aspects of European social and cultural life began to be surrendered to purely pragmatic, calculable, scientific, "rational" judgment. At present, the central institutions in modern Western societies no longer function, either theoretically or practically, with religious ends in view. Instead they operate only on the basis of such penultimate considerations as efficiency, effectiveness, and viability.

Of course, the repeated mention of *anonymity* in Luckmann's summary suggests that, in addition to being intrinsically secular, the logic of modern institutional life is also intrinsically *impersonal*. We have explored the reasons for this impersonality with respect to modern political life and in connection with modern science and technology, but it remains to be seen why this is also profoundly true of modern economic life. Suffice it here at the outset of the chapter to say that modern economic activity *has* to be envisioned more or less impersonally and in a largely secular fashion to qualify for "rational" legitimacy.

12. Thomas Luckmann, "Theories of Religion and Social Change," *The Annual Review of the Social Science of Religion* 4 (1980): 13-14.

Types of Rationality

"Rational" conduct, according to Weber, entails the intentional orientation of one's actions with respect to predetermined and freely chosen
purposes.[13] One may be said to act "rationally," in other words, if one uses
the appropriate means — or at least tries to use such means — to achieve
ends which have been deemed in advance to be desirable. Along this line,
Weber distinguished rational action from that prescribed more or less
unthinkingly by tradition and/or custom, as well as from actions that result
from merely affective or emotional states. Rational action may also be
distinguished from that suggested by traditional wisdom, which commonly
subjects means-end calculation to larger teleological considerations.
Traditional action, for example, does not analyze means and ends very
closely, and tends to respond to questions about why certain actions are
performed either by simply stating that they have always been done in such
a fashion or by asserting that harmony requires adherence to the tried and
true, even if we cannot exactly say why. Passionate action, on the other
hand, may well have consequences, but they are hardly predictable.
Rational action may therefore be said to be action that strives, however
successfully, to master and/or shape reality in some predetermined way. It
requires the careful coordination of means and ends, and, as far as possible,
the elimination of uncertainties and contingencies.

Weber also understood rationality to be of significant rhetorical
significance in the sense that the term "rational" is often attached to
actions to justify them after the fact. Rationality is thus to be understood
as an expression *of* desire itself, and not simply as a kind of instrument

---

13. See, for example, Max Weber, *Economy and Society: Volume Two*, eds.
Guenther Roth and Claus Wittich (Berkeley: University of California Press, 1978),
1375ff. It is perhaps important to stress here that Weber's various discussions and
definitions of "rationality" and "rationalization" are somewhat confused (or at least
confusing). As Stephen Kalberg has noted in his excellent survey article entitled "Max
Weber's Types of Rationality: Cornerstones for the Analysis of Rationalization Processes
in History," *American Journal of Sociology* 85 (1980): 1146: "Weber himself is largely
responsible for the lack of clarity that surrounds his analyses of 'rationality' and the
interplay of multifaceted historical rationalization processes. His scattered and fragmented discussions of this theme are more likely to mystify than to illuminate." For an
additional discussion of this problem, see Donald N. Levine, "Rationality and Freedom:
Weber and Beyond," *Sociological Inquiry* 51 (1981): 5-25.

to be put in the service of our desires. As the late Jacques Ellul noted after a Weberian fashion:

> And what is so reassuring as the rational? It is reassuring because it is both understandable and certain. Implying the development of a series of linked operations, it can be fully grasped. If, then, the world is to be grasped (i.e., understood and mastered), it must be rational. All that we ask of people in this society must be rational. It is rational to consume more, to change immediately what is worn out, to acquire more information, to satisfy an increasing number of desires. Constant growth is rational for our economic system. We can take the ordinary actions of 99 percent of the population in a so-called advanced country and we shall find that the key to them is always rationality.[14]

Of course, Ellul's purpose here is to point out how utterly unreasonable many of the activities that presently qualify for "rational" legitimacy really are, and although we will need to unpack Ellul's comments below, we simply note here that the term "rationality" always presupposes a prior decision as to what it is appropriate to seek by acting rationally. "A thing is never irrational in itself," Weber observed, "but only from a particular point of view. For the unbeliever, every religious way of life is irrational, for the hedonist, every ascetic standard. . . ."[15] Rationality, in other words, is in the eye of the beholder. It is inevitably perspectival.

Weber went on to develop the insight that rationality is perspectival by delineating several different types of rationality, all of which become curiously amalgamated in modern economic activity in such a way as to promote secularity and impersonality. The four kinds he identified (though these are not the exact words he used) are: practical, theoretical, formal, and substantive.[16] Each type is oriented toward a fundamentally different kind of end or goal, and so gives rise to a different perspective on social action. It is precisely for this reason that there has been a great deal of tension between the different types historically, as well as between rational conduct generally and traditional

14. Jacques Ellul, *The Technological Bluff*, trans. Geoffrey W. Bromiley (Grand Rapids, MI: Eerdmans, 1990), 161.
15. Weber, *The Protestant Ethic*, 194 n. 9.
16. See Kalberg's discussion here in "Max Weber's Types of Rationality," 1148ff.

and/or affective action. Indeed, Weber held that many of the most characteristic and ironic features of modernity stem from conflicts between different types of rationality, and hence between different kinds of rationalization.

Of the four kinds Weber identified, *practical* rationality is perhaps most familiar as it simply entails trying to employ practical means for the sake of realizing subjectively and egoistically determined ends. It aims, in other words, at the practical satisfaction of individual self-interest. Not surprisingly, the practical and self-interested cast of mind has historically been most characteristic of merchants and businessmen. Those engaged in commercial activity do not, as a rule, tend to be philosophically inclined and tend instead to be concerned with practical results, with the proverbial "bottom line." Indeed, merchants and businessmen are often those most critical of the *im*practicality of other, and particularly of religious, ways of assessing the legitimacy of social action.[17] "Let's dispense with arcane philosophical and/or theological debate," practical rationality says in effect, "and get down to business."

Yet it is important to stress that, however normal the simple pursuit of self-interest may seem, it has historically almost always been subject to some kind of religious discipline, for practical rationality has almost always tended to be subversive of social order in the absence of such discipline. In this connection, Weber stressed that the disposition toward purely practical rationality has only become predominant historically during periods of religious "disenchantment," that is, during those odd times when religious understanding has lost its ability to police the pragmatic pursuit of individual self-interest. The fact that much of modern social life — and particularly contemporary economic life — is dominated by practical rationality, then, appears to be an indication that something is shielding it from substantive religious criticism. There appear to be two possible explanations of the contemporary situation: either practical rationality has somehow received the sanction of modern religious understanding, so that what appears to be purely pragmatic and egoistic behavior is actually religiously motivated in some way, or religious understanding has somehow been debunked and disenchanted within contemporary culture in such a way as to give free rein to pragmatism and egoism. Weber observed that both are true of modern

17. Ibid., 1152.

society and culture, and that the former is what has given rise to the latter. We will return to this point in a moment.

In contrast to practical rationality, *theoretical* rationality transcends the simple pursuit of self-interest and entails trying to understand and make sense of the world by means of theoretical abstraction. Theoretical rationality may be applied to specific problems, or to the construction of entire worldviews. It may depend upon or develop religious doctrines as, for example, in the case of Aristotelian science, or it may generate purely secular understandings, as in the case of modern empirical science. Ultimately, theoretical rationality receives its impetus in humanity's irrepressible quest for *meaning*. "The ultimate question in all metaphysics has always been something like this," Weber noted, "if the world as a whole and life in particular were to have a meaning, what might it be, and how would the world have to look in order to correspond to it?"[18] The plausibility and apparent rationality of particular actions and assertions in any given situation, then, always have to do with how well or poorly they fit within the reigning theoretical paradigm. In the Middle Ages, the reduction of moral behavior to purely physical causation would have been viewed as a kind of madness. Today one is often considered mad if one refuses to do so.

Formal rationality, according to Weber, is oriented toward formally established rules, principles, and procedures. It is an orientation largely (though not entirely) unique to the modern situation. Similar in many respects to practical rationality, formal rationality employs simple means-ends calculation, but instead of applying this logic to the problems of pragmatic self-interest, it applies it instead to maintaining the coherence of a formally established order.[19] Formal rationality, in other words, goes by the book. It works by the rule. Indeed, the only *irrational* action, from a formally rational point of view, is to break the rules, no matter how irrational these rules might appear from a larger perspective. Needless to say, the logic of bureaucracy is formally rational. Bureaucratic administration is charged with the preservation of formally established institutions and organizations. Yet because rules, laws, procedures, and/or regulations define only specific and relatively limited spheres of activity — civil service, jurisprudence, administration, etc. — and because it is only con-

18. Weber, *Economy and Society: Volume One*, 451.
19. Kalberg, "Max Weber's Types of Rationality," 1158.

cerned with the letter of the law, formal rationality tends to be only of limited use in restraining the purely practical and pragmatic pursuit of self-interest. Bureaucracy is of little use, for example, in the formation of moral character. Nevertheless, because it is so crucial to modern institutional life, the formally rational — which is to say bureaucratic — orientation pervades much of modern society and culture.

The fourth and final kind of rationality Weber identified may be termed *value* or *substantive* rationality. Substantive rationality holds *ultimate* ends in view and requires the active reformation of life — both practically and theoretically, externally and internally — such that life may be brought into line with these, often explicitly religious, values and purposes. As substantive rationality entails far more than simply reflecting about existence and calls instead for the active reshaping of the world, Weber considered it to be a crucial catalyst of historical social change. In this connection, Weber suggested that only substantive rationality possesses the strength to effectively restrain the practical pursuit of self-interest and to challenge the formal *status quo*. With respect to the former, Weber observed that the substantive restraint of practical self-interest has historically been particularly effective when the ends deemed substantively valuable also serve to make sense of the world from a theoretically rational point of view. If the world is understood in terms of divine law, for example, then the substantive concern for righteousness and ethical behavior will be a particularly potent social force.[20] As Kalberg comments describing Weber's view:

> Only ethical [substantive] rationalities are capable of permanently suppressing practical rational regularities of action or, just as important, intensifying them by transforming them into practical ethical action. In addition, only ethical rationalities possess the analytical vigor to subdue formal rationalization processes fully. Finally, only ethical rationalities provide a value content for theoretical rationalization processes, set them in motion in specific directions as value-rationalization processes, and give rise to comprehensive, internally unified value configurations.... [A]ccording to Weber, *action motivated by values* and resistant to and counterpoised against environmental molding by interests has been of the greatest historical consequence.[21]

20. Ibid., 1165.
21. Ibid., 1170.

Specifically with respect to economic activity, Weber's analysis suggests that only substantive — that is, essentially religious — rationality is finally able to restrain practical and formal rationality. Only the concerns for justice and righteousness, in other words, are capable of disciplining the inevitable tendencies toward self-interest, on the one hand, and toward formal ossification, on the other.[22] Again, the predominance of practical rationality in modern economic life is an indication either of the absence of substantive discipline or that practical rationality has somehow become substantively legitimate.

Episodes of Rationalization

Weber observed that each of the four different kinds of rationality have given rise to episodes of *rationalization*. Rationalization refers not simply to the evacuation of purely traditional and/or affective behavior from different spheres of social life, but to the surrender of these spheres to rational methods, practices, and — one is tempted to say somewhat anachronistically — "techniques." The formal rationalization of law in ancient Rome was one of the examples Weber discussed and, following from this episode, the formal (bureaucratic) rationalization of canon law within Roman Catholicism. Weber also observed that a number of religions had given rise to highly theoretically rational views of the world. Hinduism, for example, manifests an almost perfectly rational theodicy by means of its doctrine of reincarnation. Each individual will receive *exactly* what his or her actions deserve in the next incarnation, and so on.

Weber also observed that the rationalization of different spheres of social life has historically tended to occur independently of each other. Indeed, one of the things that makes the modern period so unusual is the fact that so many of modernity's central social institutions have been rationalized simultaneously and in a largely synergistic manner. In this connection, we note that all of the institutions that commonly come to mind when we think of modernity — science, technology, modern higher education, the bureaucratic state, capitalism, socialism, etc. — appear to have become characteristic of the modern situation precisely

22. Weber, *Economy and Society: Volume One*, 85-86.

because they have been so successfully rationalized. The continuing achievements of modern science and technology, for example, owe to the hegemony of a particular kind of theoretical and formal rationality; the modern state could not continue to exist in its present form were it not for the formal (bureaucratic) rationalization of political administration; the modern economy, furthermore, requires the actions of self-interested producers and consumers to be consistently practical and pragmatic and hence (practically) rational; and, as we will discuss at some length below, *all* of these crucial institutions and endeavors have their origins in, and to some extent still depend upon, a substantively rational worldview that was initially provided by the Christian religion.

In spite of the linkages that can be traced between them, however, the various kinds of rationalization that characterize modern social existence did not develop at exactly the same times, nor at exactly the same rates; and they did not develop in a particularly harmonious fashion. Indeed, the rationalization of modern life has been marked by sharp tensions and by a number of curious ironies. Recalling Ellul's caustic remarks above, one of these ironies is reflected in the observation that, for all of their claims to rationality and to having enhanced human freedom and mastery, many ostensibly "rational" social institutions actually appear, from the perspective of those involved in them, to function quite *irrationally* and to permit very little freedom. Indeed, the supposedly "rational" means we have employed to try to enhance our freedom have not only frequently failed to deliver this freedom, but these means have shown an insidious tendency to become ends themselves, even to the extent that their continued use has become a kind of fateful necessity in modern times. As Glenn Tinder observed in a study entitled *Against Fate: An Essay on Personal Dignity* (1981): "In its totality it [modern industrial society] is irrational, bearing little relationship to genuine human needs and largely exempt from reasoned control. In its inner structure, however, it exhibits an extreme of rationality. The irony of fate takes the form of comprehensive irrationality characterized by highly developed but circumscribed rationality."[23] Social historian Karl Löwith has noted similarly:

23. Glenn Tinder, *Against Fate: An Essay on Personal Dignity* (Notre Dame, IN: University of Notre Dame Press, 1981), 68.

As that which was originally merely a means (to an otherwise valuable end) becomes an end or an end-in-itself, actions intended as a means become independent rather than goal-oriented and precisely thereby lose their original "meaning" or end, i.e., their goal-oriented rationality based on man and his needs. This reversal, however, marks all of modern culture: its establishments, institutions, and enterprises are rationalized in such a way that it is these structures, originally set up by man, which now, in their turn, encompass and determine him like an "iron cage."[24]

Of course, the most striking irony that the modern situation confronts us with — particularly if we are Christians — is that the theoretical, formal, and especially practical rationalization of such things as science and technology, politics, and the economy have by now almost completely undermined the originally substantive — and largely Christian — understanding of the world that legitimated these developments in the first place. We are thus reminded yet again of the "gravedigger hypothesis," and of the fact that Christianity appears to be largely responsible for its own demise in the modern period. Summarizing Weber's assessment of this irony, Kalberg notes:

> Practical, theoretical, and formal rationalization processes strongly dominate substantive rationalization processes in modern Western societies. The Judeo-Christian world view, which once provided the point of reference for major groupings of substantive and ethical rationalities as well as for the theoretical rationalization of their values, has been largely replaced by the scientific world view. . . .

24. Karl Löwith, "Weber's Interpretation of the Bourgeois-Capitalistic World in terms of the Guiding Principle of 'Rationalization,'" in Dennis Wrong (ed.), *Max Weber* (Englewood Cliffs, NJ: Prentice Hall, 1970), 114. Of course, self-described "postmodern" critics have become particularly sensitive to such ironies and have suggested, following Nietzsche, that every use of the term "rationality" must always be placed in quotation marks because it simply masks an ultimately irrational will to power on the part of particular social interests. Yet because this analysis cannot, by definition, point beyond itself to any kind of substantively rational view of life, it possesses, ironically, no socially constructive energy. It thus becomes a kind of self-fulfilling prophecy. By debunking all religious views of life, it insures that social life will be dominated by whoever's self-interest happens to be the strongest.

With the eclipse of substantive rationality's power to order comprehensively all aspects of life in behalf of values, *a resurgence of the practical rational way of life could take place* [emphasis added]. . . .[25]

This resurgence of "the practical rational way of life" is most evident in the area of modern economic activity. Modern economic life is dominated by the calculation of self-interest; its horizons are wholly temporal; and it is increasingly impervious, or at least resistant to, substantive religious reasoning. Indeed, the modern economy has become a bastion of modern worldliness.

Elements in the Practical Rationalization of Modern Economic Life

Weber defined capitalistic economic action as that "which rests on the expectation of profit by the utilization of opportunities for exchange, that is, on (formally) peaceful chances for profit."[26] The concept of "profit," he insisted furthermore, and the conditions of exchange are formally regulated within the modern capitalistic economy by accounting procedures and laws which have, in turn, been shaped by theories about how markets should function, and by substantive convictions of how best to achieve the common good. The formal, theoretical, and even substantive legitimation of practical rationality, Weber felt, explained capitalism's uniquely productive power. It also explains why capitalism has proven so resilient to traditional religious criticism. The rationalization of modern economic life, in other words, has not simply eliminated tradition, custom, and substantive reflection from exchange relationships, but — and this is very important — *it has virtually guaranteed that the character of these relationships will be practical and pragmatic.* This practical orientation lies at the heart of the modern theory of enterprise. It is also crucial to the formal legitimation of business activity. Indeed, modern economic activity is both theoretically conceived and formally required to be practically rational. It is thus explicitly geared — both in theory and practice — toward this-worldly self-interest.

25. Kalberg, "Max Weber's Types of Rationality," 1173-74.
26. Weber, *Protestant Ethic*, 17.

The burden of proof today thus falls upon anyone who would dare suggest that there ought to be some other basis *besides* that of rational self-interest on which to make business decisions. After all, individuals and firms *must* pursue their own self-interest in a rational fashion for the market system to function efficiently and for the economy to continue to grow. The economy *must* continue to grow, furthermore, if it is to attract the capital of rational and self-interested investors, and thus if it is to support the material aspirations of those who participate in the larger system. Not only do the theory and the formal requirements for enterprise buttress the practical pursuit of self-interest, but self-interest is substantively sanctioned under the banners of "growth" and "progress." We are thus committed to perpetual growth by means of practical-rational production and consumption. This goes some distance toward explaining the peculiar worldliness of contemporary culture; for our culture is indeed one in which self-interest is pursued unapologetically and often with a kind of religious intensity.

Yet it would be mistaken to equate our culture's preoccupation with self-interest with selfishness *as such*, for the modern pursuit of self-interest discloses a type of discipline which is substantially at odds with mere self-indulgence. Thus, although the practical rationalization of modern economic life may well give rise to social conditions in which "dog eats dog," it is important to stress that the dogs in question are expected to adhere to and, for the most part, do adhere to certain standards of conduct. Under modern conditions, then, the practical rationalization of economic life does not result in an economic free-for-all, but instead in a kind of contest in which players are expected and encouraged to pursue their own self-interest according to rules and within definite boundaries.[27]

27. In this connection, it is often noted that the increasing globalization of the market economy raises serious questions about the abilities of nation-states to implement and police adequate boundaries for global economic behavior. What is not commonly noted, however, is that some such boundaries *must* somehow be implemented and policed, and not simply in the interests of social justice, but for the sake of the modern rationalized market economy itself. Black markets, protection rings, corrupt governments, and uncontrolled currencies all have the effect of rendering the realization of profit by way of peaceful and predictable exchange impossible. The exchange relationships involved in these sorts of practices are not only not *capitalist* in the modern sense, but will most definitely not produce the economic, social and political benefits — that

Weber understood the requirements for this peculiar rationalization of modern economic life to be as follows: the existence of a market in which real competition is possible and in which monopoly interests are not allowed to dominate; the individual ownership of property; a method of rational accounting based upon a money economy; and formally (legally) free labor dependent largely upon wage-labor for survival.[28] What this list of requirements suggests is that the emergence of the modern economic system depended, at least initially, upon social conditions which encouraged self-interested economic exchange within peaceful and formally predictable boundaries. Given the historical importance of substantive rationality in catalyzing social change, furthermore, the emergence of this modern system based upon self-interested exchange must at one time have been substantively, even religiously, legitimated. Yet the ongoing rationalization of modern economic life has, by now, landed us in a situation in which we have little choice *but* to pursue self-interested exchange within the confines of the formally rational requirement of "growth" legitimated only by theoretically rational notions of "progress." Substantive considerations appear to have dropped out of the equation entirely. Why has this happened? Important clues appear to lie in the ways in which modern enterprise is organized and administered, in the rhetorical aspects of rational accounting, in the types of action the market is able to reward, in the peculiar habits of mind fostered by the use of money, and in the increased degree of specialization that rational economic exchange naturally produces.

a. The Incorporation of Self-Interest

As noted above, practical rationality seeks to coordinate means and ends as precisely as possible and so seeks to eliminate uncertainties and contingencies. One obvious source of uncertainty and contingency in economic life has to do with the intrinsic unpredictability and frailty of human life and the extent to which economic enterprises are either

---

is, long-term sustained economic growth, rising standards of living, increased political participation, etc. — of the modern market economy.

28. Wolfgang Mommsen, *The Age of Bureaucracy: Perspectives on the Political Sociology of Max Weber*, trans. Michael S. Steinberg (Oxford: Basil Blackwell, 1974), 66.

disrupted by the death of those responsible for them or, conversely, by the entry of new personnel into them. A number of institutional arrangements have been developed historically to shield organizations from this kind of uncertainty. The guild was one of these, as were the joint-stock corporation and the politically franchised corporation.[29] The development of bureaucratic administration must obviously be mentioned in this connection, for, as we have seen, bureaucracy may be defined as an administrative technique designed to minimize the threat that individual personalities pose to an organization. In addition, it appears that professional societies and programs of certification serve to rationalize the entry of new personnel into various fields.[30] The organizational structure that has most effectively mitigated the uncertainties and contingencies that attach to the so-called "human factor," however, is the modern publicly owned and limited-liability corporation. This is why the modern corporation has proven so conducive to enterprise, and why it has become such a dominant actor on the contemporary world stage. Not only does incorporation enable an enterprise to transcend the limitations of the lives of those involved in it, but this organizational form has also proven to be very effective at spreading, and hence for minimizing, the risk of enterprise to rational investors.

The modern corporation received its formal legal definition toward the end of the nineteenth century, and while the development of the business corporation has a long and interesting history, we need only note here that its development has contributed quite substantially to the practical rationalization of modern life for at least two reasons. First, the logic of the modern publicly owned and traded corporation is such that practical, formal, and theoretical rationality are essentially fused within it. The modern firm is formally required to pursue its own self-interest in a practical-rational fashion and in the context of a market which, in theory, needs its participants to act in just such a fashion in order to function properly. The second reason the modern corporation has contributed so substantially to the practical rationalization of mod-

---

29. See Nathan Rosenberg and L. E. Birdzell, Jr., *How the West Grew Rich: The Economic Transformation of the Industrial World* (New York: Basic Books, 1986), 189ff.

30. See Paul J. DiMaggio and Walter W. Powell, "The Iron Cage Revisited: Institutional Isomorphism and Collective Rationality in Organizational Fields," *American Sociological Review* 48 (April 1983): 147-60.

ern life is that the logic of the firm is anonymous and, in effect, "eternal." This has rendered the modern corporation largely immune to traditional substantive considerations which, as we have seen, hold ultimate ends in view but only for real persons. What would it mean, for example, to threaten a modern business corporation with eternal damnation? While the individuals responsible for modern firms may well want to consider this possibility, their ability to reflect substantively about the firm itself will be complicated by the fact that they are formally required to manage it in a demonstrably rational — which is to say self-interested — fashion. As the phrase "going concern" suggests, the only eternity envisioned within modern business enterprise is thoroughly this-worldly, and the only real "end" to which the modern firm may be held substantively accountable is that of continued growth defined largely in terms of practical rationality.[31]

b. Accounting for Self-Interest

In considering the contribution that rational accounting has made to the practical rationalization of modern economic life, we may begin by recalling that the terms "rational" and "irrational" are used to justify or condemn alternative courses of action. Given the fact that the use of these terms is always perspectival, however, the question arises as to how it is possible for them to carry any real rhetorical weight. The answer to this question, at least as far as economic activity is concerned, has to do with the specific conventions we have adopted to *account* for economic activity. In this connection, we note that Weber insisted that the development of rational accounting, and in particular of double-entry bookkeeping, was crucial to the development of early capitalism, for it enabled early managers to assess the effectiveness of their actions. It is very important to stress, however, that rational accounting continues to be crucial to capitalism, and not simply because it enables us

31. Ironically, one of the most significant sources of pressure to rationalize corporate operations at present is the modern state in its desire to shield citizens from the practical rationalization of business activity. As DiMaggio and Powell note in "The Iron Cage Revisited" (p. 147), the rationalization of today's organizations is driven less by competition and/or efficiency (as Weber had predicted) and more by state regulation and professionalization, which have become, in effect, "the great rationalizers of the second half of the twentieth century."

to measure the relative effects of economic actions accurately, but also because it enables us to "give account" for these actions and to defend them publicly. As Bruce G. Caruthers and Wendy Nelson Espeland note:

> As a classification scheme, double-entry bookkeeping edits and frames information. The complexity of economic reality is reduced, and decision makers are presented with a simple "bottom line," one that does not reflect all possible interpretations and judgments. Since it is not confined to a single organization, the uncertainty absorption resulting from the double-entry method takes on an almost hegemonic quality. . . . Abstraction and the reduction of quality to quantity are particularly significant in accounting. Formerly noncomparable objects are made commensurable: apples and oranges find a common denominator in monetary price. Commensurability makes it feasible to compare and evaluate alternatives. Trade-offs can be made, satisfying a precondition of rational choice.[32]

The "rationality" or appropriateness of economic activity is thus linked to a formal procedure which abstracts away from the complexity of real life in order to render the criteria for decision making — including the so-called "bottom line" — relatively easy to assess and interpret. Although there are indications that the relentless pressure to show quarterly profits may actually produce *ir*rational results in the longer run, the point to make here is simply that the modern business firm is frequently obliged to demonstrate that it has successfully pursued its own self-interests in the marketplace and in the interests of its shareholders. While it is to be assumed that this realization of self-interest has been accomplished legally and therefore that it has satisfied certain social requirements, and although firms often do demonstrate substantive concerns for such things as the environment, practical self-interest is still necessarily the "bottom line." Substantive considerations — at least beyond those useful in public relations campaigns — are simply too contentious, too difficult to quantify, and too difficult to account

32. Bruce G. Caruthers and Wendy Nelson Espeland, "Accounting for Rationality: Double-Entry Bookkeeping and the Rhetoric of Economic Rationality," *American Journal of Sociology* 97, no. 1 (July 1991): 57, 58.

for. The chief formal requirement of modern enterprise is thus to demonstrate the practical and rational pursuit of self-interest.

c. Practical Limitations of the Market Mechanism

Modern economic life is also resistant to substantive considerations because the market mechanism simply cannot reward such things as virtue properly. This was one of Alasdair MacIntyre's contentions in his influential study *After Virtue* (1981).[33] MacIntyre distinguished two kinds of "goods" that it is possible to seek in economic activity. "Internal goods," he argued, are those which have to do with doing something well or with achieving excellence in a classical philosophical or teleological sense. "External goods," on the other hand, do not relate to excellence or goodness as such, but instead have to do with *effectiveness* in garnering external rewards like money, power, prestige, status, etc. External goods, MacIntyre continued, are typically objects of the kind of competition in which there must, by definition, be losers as well as winners. Internal goods, on the other hand, may result from the competition to excel, but when someone achieves an internal good it does not necessarily imply someone else's loss. On the contrary, internal goods benefit the entire community. They both require and sustain virtue. The problem with the market economy, MacIntyre suggested, is that it is only able to recognize and reward external goods. Virtues and internal goods, it seems, do not lend themselves to the objective reduction of quality to quantity necessary for practical rational calculation.

Admittedly, the market system has never claimed to be able to reward virtue. Indeed, market apologists from Adam Smith to the present have made a point of stressing that the genius of the market mechanism lies precisely in the fact that it is able to facilitate peaceful exchange even in the absence of consensus on the knotty issues of "virtue" and ultimate purposes. The social value of this facility should not be underestimated; for free and peaceful exchange is difficult to sustain, especially in pluralistic social environments. Still, it must be recognized that the market system is necessarily oriented more toward external rewards than toward the pursuit of goodness or excellence as

33. Alasdair MacIntyre, *After Virtue: A Study in Moral Theory*, 2nd edition (Notre Dame: University of Notre Dame Press, 1984), 190-91.

such. Indeed, the pursuit of excellence is actually redefined in capitalist society in terms of effectiveness. Thus MacIntyre concludes that:

> In any society which recognized only external goods competitiveness would be the dominant and even exclusive feature. . . . We should therefore expect that, if in a particular society the pursuit of external goods were to become dominant, the concept of the virtues might suffer first attrition and then perhaps something near total effacement, although simulacra might abound.[34]

d. The Cash Nexus

The elimination of substantive concerns from modern economic life is also a by-product of the pervasive use of *money*. While the use of money makes rational calculation and accounting possible by rendering formerly noncomparable objects commensurable, it also reduces all qualities to mere quantities. Marx was among the first to recognize the conceptual significance of this within the modern social system:

> Since money does not disclose what has been transformed into it, everything, whether a commodity or not, is convertible into gold. Everything becomes salable and purchasable. Circulation is the great social retort into which everything is thrown and out of which everything is recovered as crystallized money. Not even the bones of the saints are able to withstand this alchemy; and still less able to withstand it are more delicate things, sacrosanct things which are outside the commercial traffic of men. Just as all qualitative differences between commodities are effaced in money, so money, a radical leveler, effaces all distinctions. But money itself is a commodity, an external object, capable of becoming the private property of an individual. Thus social power becomes private power in the hands of a private person.[35]

Although we are occasionally encouraged to reflect about the ethical implications of the ways that we spend money, the implications

---

34. Ibid., 196.
35. Marx, cited in Lewis Mumford, *Technics and Civilization* (London: Routledge & Sons, 1934), 23-24.

of assigning monetary values to things are not typically something we worry very much about. For the most part, we simply take this for granted. Yet it is important to stress that *everything* — including even religious understanding — is indeed transformed in the alchemy of monetary commodification. The secular and impersonal character of modern worldliness owes much to this transformation. In this connection, in an extraordinarily insightful essay entitled "The Metropolis and Mental Life," German social philosopher Georg Simmel linked the self-consciousness, intellectuality, and rationality of modern urban life with the pervasive use of money. Simmel observed that the modern urban dweller is faced with a vast number of novel situations, persons, and choices. This "intensification of nervous stimulation," as Simmel terms it, would be intolerable were it not for the fact that money is able to render the flood of objects and relations easier to cope with by making them comparable in terms of price.[36] It is money's mathematical character that enables it to do this, for numerical abstraction is precise, reliable, repeatable, and relatively easy to learn. The key to money's alchemy, in other words, is simple arithmetic. It quickly and conveniently reduces concrete and qualitative relationships to comparability, thereby rendering rational choice possible. Money thus offers us a kind of absolutely general instrumentality.[37]

Not surprisingly, the pervasive use of money has had a significant psychological impact in the modern situation. The modern mind, Simmel observed:

> has become more and more calculating. The calculative exactness of practical life which the money economy has brought about corresponds to the ideal of natural science: to transform the world into an arithmetic problem, to fix every part of the world by mathematical formulas. Only money economy has filled the days of so many people with weighing, calculating, with numerical determinations, with a reduction of qualitative values to quantitative ones.[38]

36. Georg Simmel, "The Metropolis and Mental Life," in *The Sociology of Georg Simmel*, trans. and ed. Kurt H. Wolff (Glencoe, IL: The Free Press, 1950), 410.

37. See Donald N. Levine's discussion of Simmel in "Rationality and Freedom: Weber and Beyond," *Sociological Inquiry* 51, no. 1 (1981): 5-25.

38. Simmel, "The Metropolis and Mental Life," 412.

Simmel went on to suggest that the preoccupation with calculation has given rise to that distinctly modern attitude captured in the term "blasé." It is an attitude in which all qualities have been flattened out into the calculations of quantity. The blasé attitude, Simmel felt, is simply the subjective reflection of the money economy. As money levels our experience by making everything conveniently comparable in terms of simple arithmetical calculations, so we actually begin to experience the world as a place devoid of qualities in which "all things lie on the same level and differ from one another only in the size of the area which they cover."[39] Kierkegaard captured this a century and a half ago with characteristic irony:

> In the end, therefore, money will be the one thing people will desire, which is moreover only representative, an abstraction. Nowadays a young man hardly envies anyone his gifts, his art, the love of a beautiful girl, or his fame; he only envies him his money. Give me money, he will say, and I am saved. . . . He would die with nothing to reproach himself with, and under the impression that if only he had had the money he might really have lived and might even have achieved something great.[40]

Glenn Tinder distilled the insidious impact of money more recently in *The Political Meaning of Christianity* (1989):

> The subversion of physical reality reaches its logical climax when wealth is money. The amount that a person owns (his worth!) can be precisely calculated, thus giving to the independence and security wealth supposedly provides an appearance of unassailable objectivity. Holdings in money can be indefinitely increased; one's barns become infinitely capacious. And since money is readily convertible into a variety of physical possessions and personal services, it adds to the charm of ownership the allure of power. It is not surprising that "the love of money" is characterized in the New Testament as "the root of all evils."[41]

39. Ibid., 414; see also Georg Simmel, *The Philosophy of Money* (London: Routledge & Kegan Paul, 1978), 443ff.

40. Søren Kierkegaard, *The Present Age & Of the Difference between a Genius and an Apostle*, trans. Alexander Dru (New York: Harper & Row, 1962), 40-41.

41. Glenn Tinder, *The Political Meaning of Christianity: The Prophetic Stance, An Interpretation* (San Francisco: HarperSanFrancisco, 1989), 184.

The formal necessity of monetary abstraction within rational accounting and the subjective impact of the pervasive use of money thus go some distance toward explaining the peculiar habits of practical rationality that have become the trademarks of modern industrial societies. The "net effect" of these habits is captured in the phrase, reputedly coined to describe Singaporean merchants: "they know the price of everything, but the value of nothing."

As we noted at the outset, the habit of practical rationalization has shown an insidious tendency to spill out of the economic sphere and into other areas of our lives. This "spillover" effect accounts for the practical rationalization of modern philosophies, of our understanding of nature, of our concepts of beauty and justice, and of our spiritual ambitions: in short, it accounts for the practical rationalization of our whole outlook on life.[42] Not surprisingly, modern capitalism has produced, most notably in formerly Protestant countries, distinctively practical people. This, after all, is the meaning of the term "bourgeois." The typically bourgeois individual is one who tends both to value and to

---

42. Joseph A. Schumpeter, *Capitalism, Socialism, and Democracy* (1942; New York: Harper & Row, 1975), 123-24. Schumpeter suggested (pp. 157-58), for example, that it was the application of a kind of "inarticulate system of cost-accounting" to family life that accounted for the phenomenon of bourgeois couples having fewer and fewer children. The prevalence of this "habit of rationality" in contemporary capitalist culture is also indicated by the notoriety (including the 1992 Nobel Prize for Economics) Gary S. Becker has received for his "economic approach to human behavior." See, for example, his book of that title (Chicago: University of Chicago, 1976). Becker suggests that his approach — which he applies to behaviors ranging from criminal to courtship — simply assumes maximizing behavior, market equilibrium, and stable preferences, and is applicable in principle to all human behavior. "The heart of my argument," Becker writes (p. 14), "is that human behavior is not compartmentalized, sometimes based on maximizing, sometimes not, sometimes motivated by stable preferences, sometimes by volatile ones, sometimes resulting in an optimal accumulation of information, sometimes not. Rather, all human behavior can be viewed as involving participants who maximize their utility from a stable set of preferences and accumulate an optimal amount of information and other inputs in a variety of markets." Admittedly, Becker's approach is somewhat at odds with the gist of the present argument (i.e., that a pervasively "calculating" mentality is the relatively unique product of a capitalist culture). Still, one cannot help but wonder if the success of Becker's approach *is not itself a reflection of the capitalist cultural milieu*, a milieu in which we are constantly encouraged to calculate, to "maximize," and, in Schumpeter's terms, to apply a kind of "inarticulate system of cost accounting" to all of life.

exhibit a high degree of individual autonomy, and to place a premium on worldly, practical rationality. This individual is characterized, as Peter Berger noted in *The Capitalist Revolution* (1986):

> by functional rationality, by a sober, no-nonsense, problem-solving attitude to life in general and, of course, to economic life in particular. . . . Put differently, what we have here is a "calculating" individual — not, or not necessarily, in the sense that all human relations are perceived in terms of some sort of economic costs/benefits analysis (that is the anticapitalist stereotype) — but rather in the sense that specific sectors of life, and notably the sector of economic activity, are approached in a rationally calculating and planning manner. This individual is also animated by a strong sense of ambition and the goals of this ambition are to be reached by way of competitive achievement. Finally, here is an individual who is open to innovation, as against one bound by the past. Indeed, there is a tendency within this individual to regard anything as better just because it is new.[43]

The practical, activistic, and this-worldly bourgeois outlook is not particularly conducive to the religious view of life, especially to the extent that religion occasionally enjoins contemplation and the cessation of activity.

e. The Practical Effects of Specialization

The practical rationalization of modern economic life has also been encouraged by the increasingly complex division of labor that rational economic exchange naturally and inevitably gives rise to. This was Adam Smith's opening observation in *The Wealth of Nations* (1776), the observation his famous example of pin-making was meant to illustrate. "The greatest improvement in the productive powers of labour," Smith observed:

> and the greater part of the skill, dexterity, and judgment with which it is anywhere directed, seem to have been the effects of the division

43. Peter L. Berger, *The Capitalist Revolution: Fifty Propositions about Prosperity, Equality, and Liberty* (New York: Basic Books, 1986), 107-8.

of labour. . . . It is the great multiplication of the production of all the different arts, in consequence of the division of labour, which occasions, in a well-governed society, that universal opulence which extends itself to the lowest ranks of the people.[44]

Specifically, Smith contended that specialization improved the productive powers of labor because it enhanced the skills of individual specialists and saved time by not requiring them to move back and forth between too many different tasks. Specialization also spurs the development of specialized tools and machinery which further increases the productivity of the individual specialists. In Smith's studied opinion, the prospect of profit provided the universal impulse toward specialization and toward the division of labor, that is, the prospect of practically and rationally maximizing one's own self-interest by means of peaceful and ordered exchange. In the absence of external interference, Smith felt, human behavior naturally tended in the direction of practical rationalization.

It is important to stress, however, that the specialization of enterprise, which has by now become such a central feature of modern life, severely hampers the ability of any kind of substantive rationality — including religious understanding — to discipline the process of practical rationalization. This is because ongoing specialization engenders relentless social change which is difficult to interpret and evaluate. It is not terribly surprising, for example, that modern ethicists have found it so difficult to keep pace with the issues and problems generated by the modern technological economy; for the pace with which the practical rationalization of economic life has specialized and differentiated products, roles, and social relationships has increased at an almost exponential rate in the last hundred and fifty years.

The Secularity and Impersonality of Modern Work

The sorts of considerations just discussed above go some distance toward interpreting the secular and impersonal quality of a great deal of modern

44. Adam Smith, *An Inquiry into the Nature and Causes of the Wealth of Nations*, Great Books of the Western World, no. 39 (1776; Chicago: Encyclopedia Britannica, 1952), 3, 6.

work. In the first instance, the practical-rational logic of enterprise requires monetary abstraction, and so requires us to reduce all qualities to mere quantities. The practical-rational logic of enterprise also fosters specialization and a seemingly relentless differentiation of skills, roles, and relations in the workplace. The institutional logic of modern business corporations, furthermore, necessitates abstracting away from the uncertainties and contingencies that attach to individual personality. Taken together, these requirements mean that the narrative structure of the modern workplace is fundamentally at odds with the lives of the individuals involved in it. Unlike human persons, the modern firm does not really grow old or die, and does not need to question the meaning of its existence in the light of these contingencies. Instead, the logic of the firm is simply geared toward perpetual, quantitatively measured growth, something actually unachievable by real persons.[45] The incommensurability between the modern economic system and the people who staff it explains why modern workers have so often been depicted as "cogs" in the larger "machinery" of industrial civilization; for while the practical rationalization of enterprise does require workers to be consistent, predictable, precise, uniform, and even to a certain extent creative, it does not really require them to be persons, that is, to live examined lives, to grow, to develop character, to search for truth, to know themselves, etc.

Of course, the alienating character of modern work has been grossly exaggerated by those who hoped that the "immiseration" of the worker predicted by Marx and others would give way to revolutionary social change; and, contrary to revolutionary expectations, the modern workplace has by-and-large grown increasingly humane over the course of this last century. And yet, however comfortable the modern workplace may have become, the practical rationalization of work still prevents most of us from being persons "on the job," as it were. Truly personal existence is impeded by work that is simply too practical and too specialized to do justice to the formation of character. Indeed, most of the jobs we do really cannot be discussed in anything beyond merely functional and/or quantitative terms.

Yet when the scope of a job is narrowed to the extent that it simply

45. See, for example, Agnes Heller, "The Dissatisfied Society," *Praxis International* 2, no. 4 (January 1983): 359-70.

becomes a kind of "fate," it must be judged from a Christian perspective to be wasteful, no matter how necessary the job might appear to be and no matter how willingly this fate is accepted. Indeed, it is wasteful of the only thing in this world that really matters, namely, of the opportunity to exercise and to develop personal responsibility in the world before God. This fateful wastefulness, as Tinder observes, is ultimately linked with the prideful human desire for autonomous control over the world:

> The fatefulness of modern work can be seen in the ways it reflects the blindness of pride. In its most commonly noted characteristic, the mechanization of the worker, for example, it reflects blindness to the mystery and plenitude of being. It partakes of the deadly objectification inherent in the will to mastery. It does this not only in factories but in almost all organizations, and thus it affects all classes. Treated as things of the same order as machines and raw materials, human beings are reduced not merely to nature but to nature that has itself been reduced to causal relationships. Fate appears as an efficient but humanly destructive system of over-simplification.[46]

Perhaps the chief reason the modern rationalized economic order has so often been experienced as an "iron cage" is that its tendency, as Weber put it (following Nietzsche), is to produce "specialists without spirit" and "sensualists without heart,"[47] mere functionaries who become so thoroughly integrated into the machinery of modern rationalized existence that they cease to be persons. This tendency is directly linked to the ascendancy of the peculiarly practical modern outlook, an outlook which is literally *built into* the logic of modern economic enterprise and which has become almost the sole standard by which the "rationality" or "irrationality" of economic actions is assessed. While this practical outlook is only formally required to make economic decisions by means of rational accounting procedures, it has shown a tendency to spill over into other areas of life, such that the practical-rational

---

46. Tinder, *Against Fate*, 75.

47. Weber, *The Protestant Ethic*, 182; see also Arnold Gehlen, *Man in the Age of Technology*, trans. Patricia Lipscomb (New York: Columbia University Press, 1980), 50.

virtues of "efficiency," "maximization," "least cost," "productivity," etc. have become paramount within bourgeois culture and have replaced the traditional concerns for the formation of character and for the discipline of contentment. The hegemony of practicality has most commonly been legitimated, furthermore, under the ideological banner of liberalism, which, as we have seen, promises rational mastery over the social world by means of science, technology, and the freeing of individuals to pursue their own self-interests.[48]

The plausibility of secularity and practical atheism in the contemporary situation thus owes a great deal to the practical rationalization of modern economic life. The spirit of enterprise is simply too practical and too impatient to devote much time — which, after all, is money — to considering religious matters. This spirit has, by now, overrun much of the rest of our lives. That Christianity, and in particular Calvinism, appears to have contributed quite significantly to the ascendancy of this worldly and practical spirit is another one of the peculiar ironies of modern history.

The Theological Origins of Modern Economic Rationality

We have stressed that recent centuries have witnessed the ascendancy of a peculiar kind of worldly pragmatism, particularly in the area of economic life. And yet how can we account for this given the fact that practical rationality, depending as it does upon individual self-interest, normally possesses only a very limited capacity to catalyze historical social change, and is most commonly disciplined, either by tradition and the force of habit, or by some sort of substantive rationality? Weber felt that the answer to this important question lay in the fact that at a particular juncture in Western history practical rationality became substantively significant within a larger theoretical conception of the world. Indeed, Weber's central thesis in *The Protestant Ethic and the Spirit of Capitalism* is that it was the *ethical* rationalization of the world wrought within Calvinist Protestantism that gave rise to an essentially new kind of practical rationality, one that was both profoundly acquisitive and yet also disci-

48. See Harold J. Laski, *The Rise of European Liberalism: An Essay in Interpretation* (1936; London: Unwin Books, 1962).

plined and suspicious, as he put it, of "the spontaneous enjoyment of possessions."[49] Weber captured the gist of this new practical rationality in the term "worldly asceticism." It was, he stressed, the combination of limited consumption with the release of acquisitive activity that first gave rise to practical rational capital accumulation. And Calvinism's — and particularly Puritanism's — uniquely practical, disciplined, and this-worldly "spirit" would not simply animate early capitalistic economic development, but would eventually result in the practical rationalization of all of modern life. "As far as the influence of the Puritan outlook extended [and] under all circumstances . . . ," Weber insisted, "it favoured the development of a rational bourgeois economic life. . . . It stood at the cradle of the modern economic man."[50]

Calvinism's powerful synthesis of practical and substantive rationality appears to have been both intentional and unintentional. It was intended to the extent that it followed from the Protestant repudiation of the medieval distinction between "sacred" and "secular" work in the world. This meant that Protestants were more comfortable in affirming everyday work in the world than their Roman Catholic counterparts, who tended, theologically speaking, to view work only as a kind of necessary evil. Indeed, the Reformers insisted that all practical activity in the world — or at least all practical activity not otherwise at odds with the moral law — was not only religiously legitimate, but was to be considered an essential aspect of Christian obedience to the divine *calling*. For Lutherans, the radical social implications of this new understanding were mitigated to some extent by the fact that Luther only envisioned the callings against the traditional backdrop of the late medieval social order. The practical and worldly aspects of the work entailed in one's calling were also consistently relativized over and against "the life to come" in Lutheran understanding. As we have already seen in connection with the rise of early modern science, however, Calvinists appear to have unleashed the radical social potential of the Protestant redefinition of calling by insisting that the Christian is called to the deliberate and energetic *reform* of the social order itself such that it may be brought into accord with the divine commands. Practical, instrumental rationality was held to be crucial to this reform

49. Weber, *The Protestant Ethic*, 171.
50. Ibid., 174.

process. This, according to Weber, is what explains the curious admixture of otherworldliness and utilitarianism in Calvinist ethics:

> It seems at first a mystery how the undoubted superiority of Calvinism in social organization can be connected with this tendency to tear the individual away from the closed [traditional social] ties with which he is bound to this world. . . . But God requires social achievement of the Christian because He wills that social life shall be organized according to His commandments, in accordance with that purpose. . . . For the wonderfully purposeful organization and arrangement of this cosmos is, according to both the revelation of the Bible and to natural intuition, evidently designed by God to serve the utility of the human race. This makes labour in the service of impersonal social usefulness appear to promote the glory of God and hence to be willed by him.[51]

Calvinists, in other words, tended to be somewhat more pragmatic than their Roman Catholic and/or Lutheran counterparts in assessing the actual results of economic actions. If something worked and was useful, it was deemed Christianly acceptable. The Christian was not to be bound by moribund tradition in economic matters, but was instead expected to be open to practical-rational innovation in the service of his or her neighbor and in the interests of the common good.[52] Richard

---

51. Ibid., 108-9.

52. In his well-known study *Religion and the Rise of Capitalism: A Historical Study* (New York: Harcourt, Brace & Company, 1952), R. H. Tawney contended that this freedom from tradition is clearly evident in Calvin's treatment of "capital." "What [Calvin] did," Tawney writes (pp. 107-8), "was to change the plane on which the discussion was conducted, by treating the ethics of money-lending, not as a matter to be decided by an appeal to a special body of doctrine on the subject of usury, but as a particular case of the general problem of the social relations of a Christian community, which must be solved in the light of existing circumstances. The significant feature in his discussion of the subject is that he assumes credit to be a normal and inevitable incident in the life of society. He therefore dismisses the oft-quoted passages from the Old Testament and the Fathers as irrelevant, because [they were] designed for conditions which no longer exist, argues that the payment of interest for capital is as reasonable as the payment of rent for land, and throws on the conscience of the individual the obligation of seeing that it does not exceed the amount dictated by natural justice and the golden rule."

Baxter's advice is commonly cited in this connection. "If God show you a way in which you may lawfully get more than in another way (without wrong to your soul or to any other)," Baxter insisted, "if you refuse this, and choose the less gainful way, you cross one of the ends of your Calling, and you refuse to be God's steward, and to accept His gifts and use them for Him when He requireth it: you may labour to be rich for God, though not for the flesh and sin."[53]

Weber also believed that Calvinism's synthesis of practical and substantive rationality was partly accidental. Indeed, one of his most contentious suggestions in *The Protestant Ethic and the Spirit of Capitalism* was that the utilitarian character of Calvinist ethics was a kind of unintended by-product of pastoral advice aimed at lessening the anxiety aroused by the doctrine of double predestination. This pastoral advice affirmed that diligent work in the world is the best remedy for anxiety about one's election, especially if this work reveals itself to be consonant with God's purposes by effectively advancing the common good. "The religious believer can make himself sure of his state of grace," Weber noted:

> either in that he feels himself to be the vessel of the Holy Spirit or the tool of the divine will. In the former case his religious life tends to mysticism and emotionalism, in the latter to ascetic action; Luther stood close to the former type, Calvinism belonged definitely to the latter. The Calvinist also wanted to be saved *sola fide*. But since Calvin viewed all pure feelings and emotions, no matter how exalted they might seem to be, with suspicion, faith had to be proved by its objective results in order to provide a firm foundation for the *certitudo salutis*. It must be *fides efficax*, the call to salvation to be an effectual calling. . . .[54]

Weber went on to suggest that this emphasis upon effectual calling devolved in practice into little more than the belief that God helps those who help themselves.[55] Yet it was this belief, he felt, that inter-

---

53. Richard Baxter, cited in Weber, *The Protestant Ethic*, 162; also Tawney, *Religion and the Rise of Capitalism*, 243.

54. Weber, *The Protestant Ethic*, 113-14.

55. Ibid., 115.

preted the tremendous diligence with which subsequent generations of Calvinists sought to reform this worldly existence by means of practical rationality. The Protestant ethic proved to be a very powerful catalyst of social change and innovation, particularly in the area of economic life.

Weber has been criticized for misunderstanding and misinterpreting the counsel of the Puritan divines on matters having to do with the pursuit of wealth. Leo Strauss, for example, observed that, while Weber's argument depended upon establishing a credible link between Puritanism and the view that held the limitless accumulation of capital to be an end in itself, he never actually established such a link.[56] In this connection, it is one thing to value practicality, as Baxter and the Puritans most certainly did, but it is quite another to suggest that therefore the Puritans somehow sanctioned acquisitiveness, for they most certainly did not. Put somewhat differently, there is obviously a considerable difference between the Puritan stress upon working hard for the sake of the common good and the subsequent liberal assumption that in serving oneself one is thereby also automatically serving the common good. Indeed, with reference to the social-ethical teaching of the English Puritans between 1570 and 1640, Charles and Katherine George contended that this teaching was "unreservedly anticapitalistic."[57] It explicitly condemned the continuous rational pursuit of wealth for its own sake which, according

56. Leo Strauss, "Comment on the Weber Thesis Reexamined," *Church History* 30 (1961): 100-102. Strauss contends that the "spirit" of modern capitalism actually originated in the political "realism" of Machiavelli, which encouraged intellectuals to conceive of social order as being based upon socially useful passions or vices and not upon piety and virtue. "Generally speaking," he notes (p. 102), "the Puritans were more open to the new philosophy or science both natural and moral than, e.g., Lutherans because Calvinism had broken with 'pagan' philosophy (Aristotle) most radically; Puritanism was or became the natural *carrier* of a way of thinking which it had not originated in any way. By looking for the origin of the capitalist spirit in the way of thinking originated by Machiavelli one will also avoid an obvious pitfall of Weber's inquiry: Weber's study of the origin of the capitalist spirit is wholly unconcerned with the origins of the science of economics; for the science of economics is the authentic interpretation of the 'capitalist spirit.'"

57. Charles and Katherine George, "Protestantism and Capitalism in Pre-Revolutionary England," in *The Protestant Ethic and Modernization: A Comparative View*, ed. S. N. Eisenstadt (New York: Basic Books, 1968), 165.

to Weber, was the distinguishing characteristic of the spirit of modern capitalism.[58] Others have wanted to place a stronger emphasis than Weber did upon the significance of Calvinism's destruction of the traditional feudal order, arguing that this is really where Calvinism's signal contribution to modernity lay.[59] Still others have suggested that the critical impetus to modern rationalization came not from the Puritan theology of calling and election so much as from Protestantism's voluntarist and nominalist epistemology, which exploded the medieval understanding of "natural theology."[60] In this connection, John Milbank has recently suggested that purely secular social space only opened up as the Protestant reinterpretation of calling was united with the Reformers' anti-teleological epistemology. It was this combination that led to the modern belief that certain areas of social life are subject *only* to practical-rational assessment and manipulation.[61] Milbank has also stressed the importance of the Protestant recovery of Roman Law with its emphasis upon individual autonomy and sovereignty.[62] The practical rationalization of modern life may also have stemmed from the Puritan emphasis upon literacy and upon the rational formulation of doctrine.[63] Or it may have issued from the insistence of post-Reformation sects upon the rights of individual conscience over and against state-sponsored churches, for this appears

58. See Weber, *The Protestant Ethic*, 17.

59. See Michael Walzer, "Puritanism as a Revolutionary Ideology," in *The Protestant Ethic and Modernization: A Comparative View*, ed. S. N. Eisenstadt (New York: Basic Books, 1968), 109-34.

60. See, for example, Leo Strauss, *Natural Right and History* (Chicago: University of Chicago Press, 1950). "What [Weber] failed to consider," Strauss suggested (note p. 61), "was that in the course of the sixteenth century there was a conscious break with the whole philosophic tradition, a break that took place on the plane of purely philosophic or rational or secular thought. This break was originated by Machiavelli, and it led to the moral teachings of Bacon and Hobbes: thinkers whose writings preceded by decades those writings of their Puritan countrymen on which Weber's thesis is based. See also George Grant, "In Defense of North America," in *Technology and Empire: Perspectives on North America* (Toronto: Anansi, 1969), 21.

61. John Milbank, *Theology and Social Theory: Beyond Secular Reason* (Oxford: Basil Blackwell, 1990), 90.

62. See Milbank, *Theology and Social Theory*, chapter 1: "Political Theology and the New Science of Politics."

63. See Harry S. Stout, "Puritanism Considered as a Profane Movement," *Christian Scholar's Review* 10 (1980): 3-19.

to have led to the formulation of the notion of individual "rights."[64] In short, Protestantism appears to have contributed to the practical and utilitarian temper of modern social life in a number of ways not specifically emphasized by Weber. In spite of all of the criticism and qualification of Weber's thesis, however, it has undoubtedly served to draw attention to the intriguing similarities between seventeenth-century Calvinism and the secular utilitarianism that would emerge a century later. The difference between Puritanism's practical-rational commitment to mastering the world for the sake of God's kingdom and the secular commitment to scientific mastery for the sake of rational "progress" devolved, in practice, into little more than a slight difference in orientation.[65]

The devolution of Puritanism into utilitarianism is the subject of R. H. Tawney's celebrated study *Religion and the Rise of Capitalism* (1926). Tawney's thesis is that Puritanism paved the way for the practical rationalization of modern economic and social life by repudiating medieval Christian (Aristotelian) social ethics:

> The shrewd, calculating commercialism which tries all human relations by pecuniary standards, the acquisitiveness which cannot rest while there are competitors to be conquered or profits to be won, the love of social power and hunger for economic gain — these irrepressible appetites had evoked from time immemorial the warnings and denunciations of saints and sages. Plunged in the cleansing waters of later Puritanism, the qualities which less enlightened ages had denounced as social vices emerged as economic virtues. They emerged as moral virtues as well. For the world exists not to be enjoyed, but to be conquered. Only its conqueror deserves the name of Christian.[66]

While Tawney's acerbic comments are not entirely fair, historian Robert Michaelson shed interesting light on the evolution of later Puri-

---

64. See Guenther Roth, "Religion and Revolutionary Beliefs: Sociological and Historical Dimensions in Max Weber's Work — In Memory of Ivan Vallier (1927-1974)," *Social Forces* 2 (December 1976): 257-72.

65. Alan D. Gilbert, *The Making of Post-Christian Britain*, 33.

66. R. H. Tawney, *Religion and the Rise of Capitalism*, 248.

tanism in an essay entitled "Changes in the Puritan Concept of Calling or Vocation" (1953).[67] Michaelson observed that in early Puritan understanding (c. 1600), one's "particular vocation," or work in the world, was wholly circumscribed by one's "general calling" to Christian faith and obedience. By the end of the seventeenth century, however, the Puritan understanding of the "particular vocation" had been modified to suggest simply that it ought not to interfere with religious duties such as Sabbath observance. It was this subtle shift, Michaelson suggested, that eventually led to the secularization of the notion of vocation. Michaelson also noted that this same period witnessed a gradual transformation in the sorts of sins Puritan preachers were most concerned to censure. Whereas early Puritan divines had repeatedly denounced the sin of covetousness, later preachers focused most of their attention on the sins of sensuality, including those of laziness and idleness. In shifting attention to the sins of the flesh, however, the sins of the spirit, such as covetousness and ambition, were allowed a certain degree of latitude.[68] In addition, by encouraging labor and industry as a way of avoiding fleshly indulgence, later Puritans came very close to blessing secular industry in and of itself and, by extension, the material wealth gained by this industry. Along this line, recall that only fifty years separate the England of Richard Baxter from the England of Wesley's famous lament cited above. The Puritan sanctification of worldly vocations, Michaelson concluded, was a significant boon to the developing commercialism of the late seventeenth century:

> The changes within the Puritan concept of vocation prepared the way for significant and influential later developments. In England they helped produce Daniel Defoe's "complete English tradesman," whose religious life — it could be called that — was all but completely separated from his business. In America they contributed to the "wisdom" of Poor Richard as it came to be expressed in his almanacs and in *The Way to Wealth*. The separation between religion and business was completed with Poor Richard.[69]

67. Robert S. Michaelson, "Changes in the Puritan Concept of Calling or Vocation," *New England Quarterly* 26 (1953): 315-36.

68. Ibid., 329.

69. Ibid., 336.

The most crucial figure in the devolution of Puritanism into secular utilitarianism in the English-speaking world was probably John Locke. More than anyone else, Locke was responsible for the amalgamation of Protestantism's affirmation of worldly work and the Cartesian ideal of disengaged and autonomous rationality.[70] As Charles Taylor has noted in his thoughtful study, *Sources of the Self: The Making of the Modern Identity* (1989), while the Reformers had stressed living worshipfully before a Scripturally revealed God, Locke shifted the emphasis toward worshipping a naturally revealed God by living practically and rationally before him. This was accomplished by means of a new, purportedly "scientific," anthropology which stressed that the most important thing that needed to be said about human beings is that they are, like other creatures, oriented toward their own self-preservation. Locke Christianized this essentially secular view by insisting that this natural impulse toward self-preservation is actually providentially ordained, and that Christians therefore served and pleased God by acting rationally and in the best interests of their own self-preservation.[71] Already by the beginning of the eighteenth century, then, God was indeed believed to help those who helped themselves, and Lockean Christians helped themselves by acting practically and rationally to improve their own material circumstances.

Yet however the devolution of English Puritanism is recounted, the Protestant affirmation of worldly work by means of a redefinition of Christian "calling" does appear to have suffered a kind of ironic reversal toward the end of the seventeenth century. While the Protestant understanding of calling had only been intended to refute the mistaken medieval distinction between "sacred" and "secular" work, and although the Reformers obviously had no intention of shifting the

70. See Charles Taylor, *Sources of the Self: The Making of the Modern Identity* (Cambridge, MA: Harvard University Press, 1989), 239. Alasdair MacIntyre has also described the history of this devolution of the Christian moral tradition into modern liberal individualism in great detail. See especially *Whose Justice? Which Rationality?* (Notre Dame, IN: University of Notre Dame, 1988). MacIntyre identifies David Hume as a key figure in this development, for he believes that it was due to the radical suspicion that Hume cast upon all substantive reasoning that it became increasingly difficult to question (or to discipline) an individual's desires or wants on the basis of any kind of substantive position.

71. Taylor, *Sources of the Self*, 238-39.

religious stress away from eternal life, this is what eventually happened. By the time of Locke (d. 1704), the Protestant affirmation of everyday life had come to mean the affirmation of the fundamental importance of the practical improvement of life in this world, whatever "the world to come" might eventually hold in store. Indeed, the Christian religion itself came to be understood as chiefly a matter of the practical improvement of this-worldly social conditions.[72]

The radical implications of this relativization of eternal life over and against the practical exigencies of this life seem not to have been noticed at first. Locke, John Tolland, and others simply assumed that Christian doctrine — at least to the extent that it was freed of the mysterious and superstitious elements with which it had become encrusted — *must* function in practice to improve human life, and that obedience to the Law of God must give rise to happiness here and now as well as, presumably, in the "age to come." But Lockean Christianity continued to devolve into Deism, and the requirements of human happiness altogether ceased to be determined theologically and came instead to be determined naturalistically and scientifically. Hence, as Taylor has noted, "Locke helped to define and give currency to the growing Deist picture, which will emerge fully in the eighteenth century, of the universe as a vast interlocking order of beings, mutually subserving

---

72. As we noted in Chapter 1, Karl Barth coined the interesting term "humanization" to describe this absorption of Christian theology into the practical exigencies of bourgeois life during the eighteenth century. See *Protestant Theology in the Nineteenth Century: Its Background and History* (London: S.C.M., 1972), 84ff. Interestingly, both the more "conservative" Pietists and the more "liberal" rationalists took part in this process. "Both Pietists and rationalists," Barth noted (pp. 98-99), "were modern men and, more particularly, modern citizens, who applied to traditional Christianity a particular presupposition, namely the presupposition, the idea, the systematic principle that in all circumstances Christianity must serve to improve life." Here we might also recall Klaus Bockmuehl's contention that the Reformers overemphasized the importance of the so-called "civil" vocation for Christian faith and life. This overreaction appears to have stemmed from their fear of Anabaptist "spirituality" and their stress upon the possibility of immediate divine guidance. "No," the Reformers said in effect, "one's service to God in the world is to be understood entirely in terms of one's civil vocation and obedience to the ten commandments." Yet this had the effect, Bockmuehl asserts, of secularizing the notion of vocation within European Protestantism. See Klaus Bockmuehl, "Recovering Vocation Today," *Crux* 24, no. 3 (1988): 25-35.

each other's flourishing, for whose design the architect of nature deserves our praise and thanks and admiration. . . ."[73] The Deist picture, with its stress upon reshaping the social world by means of practical-rational effort, subsequently became a kind of philosophical backdrop for bourgeois civilization. Indeed, apologies for market capitalism and for liberal democratic polity still most often presuppose just such a picture of the world.

The practical rationalization of modern economic life thus appears to be linked, at least initially, to a number of Protestant theological innovations. Chief among these innovations were the redefinition of the notion of Christian "calling" with its resulting affirmation of work, the nominalist (anti-teleological) conception of nature, and, following on from both of these, a revised theological anthropology which stressed that the human task in the world is not simply to admire it,[74] but to actively reshape it for the glory of God. None of these innovations was conceived with practical economic activity in mind, but together they appear — accidentally and ironically — to have had a profound effect upon the emergence of the modern economic order. As the religious energy of the Reformation waned toward the end of the seventeenth century, the legacy of these theological innovations was such as to have enhanced the secular quality of modern life. As R. H. Tawney observed:

> When the age of the Reformation begins, economics is still a branch of ethics, and ethics of theology; all human activities are treated as falling within a single scheme, whose character is determined by the spiritual destiny of mankind . . . [but] by the Restoration the whole perspective, at least in England, had been revolutionized. Religion has been converted from the keystone which holds together the social edifice into one department within it, and the idea of a rule of right

73. Taylor, *Sources of the Self,* 244.

74. See Grant, "In Defense of North America." Grant observes: "Perhaps [as a result of the devolution of Calvinist nominalism] we are lacking the recognition that our response to the whole should not most deeply be that of doing, nor even that of terror and anguish, but that of wondering or marveling at what is, being amazed or astonished by it, or perhaps best, in a discarded English usage, admiring it; and that such a stance, as beyond all bargains and conveniences, is the only source from which purposes may be manifest to us from our necessary calculating" (p. 35).

is replaced by economic expediency as the arbiter of policy and the criterion of conduct. From a spiritual being who, in order to survive, must devote a reasonable attention to economic interest, man seems sometimes to have become an economic animal, who will be prudent, nevertheless, if he takes due precautions to assure his spiritual well-being.[75]

The move from the medieval to the modern economic order may thus be said to have been a move from a world in which the chief concern was to protect the possibility of eternal blessedness from mundane economic activity, to a world in which free, practical, rational, and individual economic activity is considered crucial to the pursuit of temporal and, by extension, of eternal happiness.

Yet it is important to stress that whatever the impact of Protestantism may have been, the practical rationalization of modern economic life also bears the marks of the characteristically modern conceit that it is up to us to create — either individually or collectively — our own meanings and purposes. For us to have extended the logic of practical rationality as far as we have in contemporary society and culture, in other words, betrays a deliberately chosen and fundamentally subjective orientation toward the world.[76] Practical rationalization, after all, is about control. Social life is only surrendered to practical-rational methods for the sake of achieving rational mastery over it. Modern economic life thus reveals a deep self-centeredness. After all, what does our obsession with money and with monetary values disclose beyond the fact that we are obsessed with controlling our own circumstances and committed to the notion that it is up to us to determine and to attribute our own "values" to the stuff of the world?

---

75. Tawney, *Religion and the Rise of Capitalism*, 278-79.

76. Interesting discussions of this are given by Louis Dupré, "The Closed World of the Modern Mind," *Religion and Intellectual Life* 1 (Summer, 1984), and Steven Seidman, *Liberalism and the Origins of European Social Theory* (Berkeley, CA: University of California Press, 1983); see also Milbank, *Theology and Social Theory*, 241ff.

Economic Practicality and Modern Worldliness

Needless to say, the practical rationalization of modern economic life has greatly enhanced the *plausibility* of worldliness in contemporary society and culture. Not only has the market system's remarkable productivity tempted us to locate more and more of our aspirations in this world; but the alchemy and "absolutely general instrumentality" of monetary abstraction have largely evacuated the world of all meanings and values save those which *we* choose to attribute to it. It is no wonder that the New Testament considers the love of money to be the root of many evils, for it insidiously encourages us to substitute our own humanly created "values" for those of God's good creation. By exalting the practical-rational pursuit of self-interest, furthermore, the logic of the market is intrinsically resistant to substantive religious critique. Indeed, to suggest that economic affairs ought to be disciplined by religious understanding is, from the modern point of view, to pose a somewhat irrational threat to productivity and consumption and thus to the experience of well being.

And so we face quite a dilemma with respect to the practical rationalization of economic activity in modern society. On the one hand, the process has proven tremendously productive and we have come to depend upon its continuing productivity. On the other hand, this productivity appears to be intrinsically and perhaps inextricably linked to the secularity and impersonality of contemporary culture. The practical, subjectivistic, egoistic, and individualistic orientation toward the world which Weber contended is sadly incapable of making sense of the world in any humanly meaningful way now presents itself — with the formal force of law, and with the theoretical support of any number of compelling modern ideologies — as the only rational way forward, as our fate. While Weber may well have overstated the matter by contending that the modern situation has become a kind of "iron cage," it is at the very least an ironic one.

Christian Calling Revisited

Immediately following his suggestion that industrial capitalism had become an "iron cage," Weber went on to remark:

No one knows who will live in this cage in the future or whether at the end of this tremendous development entirely new prophets will arise, or whether there will be a great rebirth of old ideas and ideals, or, if neither, mechanized petrification, embellished with a sort of convulsive self-importance. For of the last stage of this cultural development, it might well be truly said: "Specialists without spirit, sensualists without heart; this nullity imagines that it has attained a level of civilization never before achieved." . . . But this brings us to the world of judgments of value and of faith, with which this purely historical discussion need not be burdened. . . .[77]

Although Weber refrained from burdening his historical discussion with judgments of value and faith, we must obviously do so if we are to render the practical rationalization of modern economic life less secularizing and dehumanizing. We must, as Weber's own analysis suggests, rediscover and reassert some kind of substantively rational understanding of economic action. As we have already noted, however, the peculiar genius of the market mechanism lies precisely in its ability to coordinate peaceful and ordered economic exchange *in the absence* of consensus on religious matters of substance. Oddly enough, it is the worldly and anti-heroic quality of the market that appears to account for its remarkable productivity.

Here we face a peculiarly modern dilemma: we cannot afford *not* to utilize the genius of the market mechanism, and yet we cannot afford to simply surrender ourselves and our culture to its radical secularity and impersonality either. We apparently cannot survive without modern capitalism, and neither can we really *live* with it. The depth of this dilemma is indicated by the number of observers who have argued that we face something of a fork in the road with respect to the market system: either we surrender all hope of preserving (or recovering) substantive culture, or we must reject the market system altogether in favor of an alternative that is more open to substantive discipline. As twentieth-century developments have made quite clear, however, fascism, Marxism, various kinds of socialism, and other alternatives to the market have, under modern conditions, not only proven to be economically inefficient, but they have also proven to be profoundly secularizing and

77. Weber, The Protestant Ethic, 182.

dehumanizing, for they inevitably exacerbate the temptation to manipulative anthropocentrism by rationalizing and consolidating economic and political power.

I would argue that what the present situation calls for, then, is not the collective implementation of some kind of alternative to the market system, so much as for us to decide individually not to surrender ourselves to the logic of practical rationality and to try, where possible, to resist it. Each of us needs to decide, in other words, to act ethically and substantively within the system no matter how *im*practical we may occasionally have to appear in doing so. Of course, this will not come easily, and the following reflection only scratches the surface of issues that will call for more extensive and careful treatment. Still, long journeys, as they say, begin with small steps.

So how do we go about resisting the secular and impersonal logic of practical rationality? At the very least, it will require us to *think* about economic activity in a way that extends beyond efficiency, effectiveness, feasibility, and other purely practical considerations. In this connection, it occurs to me that the time may ironically be ripe for the rediscovery of one of the doctrines that, as we have seen, may have been responsible for catalyzing the practical rationalization of economic life to begin with, namely, the Protestant doctrine of *calling*. There are two reasons for this. The first is that this doctrine is deeply individuating and personalizing. The second is that the notion of calling does not allow us to separate our work in this world from our faith *in* and our responsibility *before* God.[78] The notion of calling simply cannot be understood in a secular fashion, at least not if it is taken at all seriously.

As we have seen, many of the thorniest problems associated with the practical rationalization of modern economic life have to do with objectification and abstraction, and particularly with abstracting away from *persons*. Whatever else we may want to say about economic justice and about the substantive ordering of economic life, then, we must begin by trying to exempt persons — including ourselves — from rationalized abstraction. It is precisely the failure to do this that has hamstrung the proposed alternatives to modern capitalism. None has been

78. Many of the following insights are taken from Karl Holl's historical discussion in "The History of the Word Vocation (Beruf)," *Review and Expositor* 55 (April 1958): 126-54.

able to provide a solid foundation for individual and personal existence, and so they have not been able, their ideological rhetoric notwithstanding, to preserve freedom and justice for real persons. The Christian understanding of calling, however, while affirming rationality as such, arrests the abstraction of practical rationalization by insisting that the crux of human existence lies in an intentional and personal response to God's intentional and personal address. As Emil Brunner observed a number of years ago:

> [The] dignity of human personality is not grounded in an abstract, general element in all men, namely reason [as in Greek thought], but individual personality as such is the object of this appreciation because it is deemed *worthy of being called by God* [emphasis added]. Only the personal God can fundamentally establish truly personal existence and responsibility, responsibility being the inescapable necessity to answer God's creative call, and to answer it so that this answer is also a decision. . . . The love of the personal God does not create an abstract, impersonal humanity; it calls the individual to the most personal responsibility.[79]

We are enabled to truly become responsible persons, furthermore, only to the extent that we *respond* to God's gracious call in love and in the obedience of faith. This is the "general" call to Christian faith. From a Christian perspective, then, the fundamental call is thus to *personal* existence and to personal "response-ability." Persons thus called are obviously not to be treated simply as objects in economic calculation.

That the Protestant understanding of calling appears to have contributed to the practical rationalization of modern life is not simply ironic, then, but it discloses a serious theological misunderstanding. If Weber's analysis is at all correct, furthermore, this misunderstanding may have had something to do with the logic of double predestination. After all, if this logic is pursued too relentlessly (as Calvinists have occasionally shown a tendency to do), it has the effect of obliterating human personality by collapsing human "response-ability" into the doctrine of election. To the extent that this happened toward the end of

---

79. Emil Brunner, *Christianity and Civilisation*, Vol. 1, "Foundations" (New York: Charles Scribner's Sons, 1948), 94.

the seventeenth century within English Puritanism, it is not difficult to imagine why anxious souls might have tried to lose themselves in diligent labor, and why they might have surrendered so willingly to the practical rationalization of social and economic life. Practical-rational effectiveness would have seemed to them a way of proving, not really a divine call, but a *fate*. The problem may not have had so much to do with the doctrine of election, however, as with the rationalistic — one is tempted to say "Newtonian" — assumption that the logic of election is humanly comprehensible, and hence that all sorts of mechanical implications can be logically drawn from it. This tendency toward excessive rationalism has characterized what has been labeled "hyper-Calvinism." Yet regardless of what did or didn't happen toward the end of the seventeenth century in England or Holland, the point to stress here is simply that a truly biblical understanding of calling preserves the centrality of the *person* in Christian ethical reflection. It therefore immediately challenges the objectification, abstraction, and impersonal logic of much of modern economic life.

The Christian calling neither encourages nor permits us simply to withdraw from the realm of economic activity, however. On the contrary, we are each called to real work in the world. This was Luther's critical discovery and it has subsequently been discussed under the heading of "particular calling" in Protestant theology. That we are called to particular work in the world implies that it is precisely in the context of worldly work that our salvation is to be worked out "in fear and trembling" (Phil. 2:12); and it is in the real world of work that God promises to be present to us. Worldly work is not to be envisioned simply as a proving ground for eternal life either. Rather, as we stressed at the end of the last chapter, it is by means of creative human work that the created order is, mysteriously by the Son and through the Spirit, to be returned to the Father in love and worship. Indeed, we are told that the glory and honor of all the nations is to be brought into the New Jerusalem (Rev. 21:26). Christianly understood, then, economic activity is of tremendous religious significance. The obedience of faith recognizes an essential consonance between God's inward call to the heart and his address to us outwardly in the circumstances of our worldly work.

Naturally, God's intentional, personal, and particular address to us calls for a personal and intentional response. Our work, in other words, must be undertaken in *faith*. This is sobering, but also profoundly liberating, for it means that we are not so much responsible for achieving "results" in the world, as for simply walking before the LORD in humility and for showing justice and mercy to our neighbor (Mic. 6:8). Indeed, even the most outwardly insignificant work performed in the consciousness that it is undertaken in response to the divine commission — performed, that is, in faith — stands ethically on a higher level than even the most exalted work measured outwardly and objectively. The success or failure of our own work in the world is thus not finally our responsibility. Even trying to distinguish the one from the other is problematic, for we know that God "causes his sun to rise on the evil and the good, and sends rain on the righteous and the unrighteous" (Matt. 5:45).

Of course, we know that while we are in the world our "worth" will inevitably be judged on the basis of objective measures, and this will be a source of pain. Such, after all, is the way of the world. But we are not called to judge ourselves in this harsh fashion. Rather, we are called to mitigate the impact of the world's harsh objective assessment by continually reminding each other that what the world calls success God calls foolishness, and that what is of little value in the world is of great value to God (cf. 1 Cor. 1:20).

The emphasis upon faithful and responsible work also opens up the consideration of what we discussed above under the heading of "internal goods." It encourages us to reflect upon the matters of integrity and excellence and other goods that may well be undervalued by the market. While this reflection must be realistic, bound to the conditions of real life and work, it stems from the recognition that we are responsible for submitting our work to a discipline that is far more searching than simply that of efficiency, effectiveness, and the other considerations often associated with the practical realization of self-interest. Reflecting about the internal integrity of our work in the world will undoubtedly make it more difficult, but it may also make it more satisfying. Such reflection is, in any event, our responsibility before God.

If Christian faith assures us that our salvation does not ultimately depend upon "objective" assessment and our having achieved practical "results" in the world, then neither can we simply rest content with an economic system that treats people as if it does. Christian faith does not permit us to treat our neighbor as an object to be manipulated for the sake of practical purposes, or to reduce his or her "worth" to a digit within the economic calculus. Indeed, Christian faith does not even allow us to objectify the natural world, for we are responsible before God for caring for it. It is not to be treated simply as "stuff" that we are free to conceive as "resources" and to which we are free to assign monetary values. In short, Christian faith insists that economic activity be envisioned responsibly before God. How we perform our work in the world is evidence of the quality of our relation to the world, to our neighbor, and ultimately to God. This is why the apostle Paul reminds us (Rom. 14:23) that everything that does not come from faith — including our everyday work in the world — is *sin*. While this obviously does not mean that we can ignore practical realities, or shun the considerations of effectiveness and efficiency altogether, it does mean that we cannot simply surrender the world — including ourselves — to the secular and impersonal logic of practical rationalization. To do so would be to act in bad faith.

To conclude, the "iron cage" of modern rationalized economic existence has become a cage only to the extent that we have collectively chosen to make it so, that is, to the extent that we have submitted — more or less willingly — to its inherent abstractions and dehumanization in the vain hope of achieving a kind of collective mastery over the world. We might have chosen differently; and, indeed, we still can. But, of course, choosing differently requires the reopening of a number of difficult questions that even Christians have gotten out of the habit of asking in the modern period, questions like: Who are we? What are we here for? and How should we live and work in light of who we are and what we are here for? Along this line, the centrality of persons and of personal responsibility implied in the Christian understanding of calling — grounded as it is in the personal existence of the triune God — is capable of restraining and ordering practical rationality. Indeed, our only hope of restraining the impersonal logic of the modern rationalized economic order may lie in just this kind of substantive reorientation in which we are able to criticize and reform economic systems on the basis of how persons are treated within them, protesting and hopefully preventing the abolition of persons within modernity's "iron cage."

CHAPTER FOUR

The Worldly Self at the Heart of Modern Culture

The modern man is in general, even with the best will, unable to give religious ideas a significance for culture and national character which they deserve.

Max Weber[1]

We have entered on a new phase of culture — we may call it the Age of the Cinema — in which the most amazing perfection of scientific technique is being devoted to purely ephemeral objects, without any consideration of their ultimate justification. It seems as though a new society was arising which will acknowledge no hierarchy of values, no intellectual authority, and no social or religious tradition, but which will live for the moment in a chaos of pure sensation.

Christopher Dawson[2]

1. Max Weber, *The Protestant Ethic and the Spirit of Capitalism*, trans. Talcott Parsons (New York: Charles Scribner's Sons, 1958), 183.
2. Christopher Dawson, *Progress and Religion: An Historical Inquiry* (1931; Peru, IL: Sherwood Sugden & Co., 1991), 228.

The contemporary climate is therapeutic, not religious. People today hunger not for personal salvation, let alone for the restoration of an earlier golden age, but for the feeling, the momentary illusion, of personal well-being, health, and psychic security.

Christopher Lasch[3]

The practical-rational spirit of modern enterprise, aided by technological expertise and protected under the aegis of the liberal welfare-state, has by now so overwhelmed all other lines of historical development that it has led many of the most astute observers of modernity to announce that we have arrived at the end of history. Of course, time will continue to pass, and generations of people will continue to live and die, but to the extent that meaningful history consists in the evolution of fundamentally new ideas and new cultural ideals, so Hegel and others have reasoned, modernity admits of no further development. It is permanent and irresolvable. Indeed, all that remains is for certain pockets of resistance — including what is left of traditional religious culture — to be absorbed into the modern system. Along this line, the hegemony of distinctively modern ideas and methods moved Heidegger to predict the onset of what he called "the night of the world," in which all cultural development will be collapsed into technical uniformity and mindless consumption.[4] Weber described this outcome in terms of "mechanized petrification embellished with a sort of convulsive self-importance," an endless era ruled only by "specialists without spirit" and "sensualists without heart."[5] "The end of history will be a very sad time," Francis Fukuyama lamented most recently in his provocative essay entitled "The End of History?" (1989):

The struggle for recognition, the willingness to risk one's own life for a purely abstract goal, the worldwide ideological struggle that calls

3. Christopher Lasch, *The Culture of Narcissism: American Life in an Age of Diminishing Expectations* (New York: Warner Books, 1979), 33.

4. See Leo Strauss, "An Introduction to Heideggarian Existentialism," in *The Rebirth of Classical Political Rationalism: An Introduction to the Thought of Leo Strauss,* ed. Thomas L. Pangle (Chicago: University of Chicago Press, 1989), 42.

5. Weber, *The Protestant Ethic,* 182.

forth daring, courage, imagination, and idealism, will be replaced by economic calculation, the endless solving of technical problems, environmental concerns, and the satisfaction of sophisticated consumer demands. In the post-historical period there will be neither art nor philosophy, just the perpetual caretaking of the museum of human history.[6]

Fukuyama concluded by suggesting that our only hope is that the dreary prospect of centuries of spiritual emptiness and boredom will set the historical process in motion again, but he did not say how.

Of course, from a Christian point of view, this Hegelian reading of modern history is fundamentally mistaken in its faithless equation of worldly success and ultimate significance. It assumes that the only history worth talking about is that which is more or less obviously given in purportedly "world historical" social and political developments like the apparently global triumph of capitalism over socialism in recent years. Such a reading simply does not see anything that does not exert a significant amount of social, and particularly political, force. It is therefore completely incapable of appreciating the *spiritual* advance of God's Kingdom in the Church.

Yet the suggestion that we have reached a kind of "end of history" is notable for several reasons. In the first instance, it indicates the gravity of the modern predicament. As our previous discussions have hopefully shown, the institutional infrastructure of modernity is monolithic, entrenched, and almost entirely immune to substantive criticism. It is difficult to imagine how it could ever really be substantively reformed. In addition, the prediction that the hegemonic quality of technical and practical rationality will impede further cultural and historical development underlines the tragedy and inhumanity of the modern situation, as well as the fact that modernity's inhumanity is inextricably linked to its secularity. Even explicitly atheistic observers have lamented this fact, for although the development of the secular modern system may well be celebrated as a remarkable historical achievement, it spells the end of religious striving and of heroic culture and signals the death of meaningful human existence. This is why Nietzsche was so concerned

6. Francis Fukuyama, "The End of History?" *The National Interest* (Summer 1989): 18.

to stress that the death of man in modern times is the inevitable result of the death of God, even if he could not personally bring himself to believe in God.

Lastly, we note that the proposition that we have arrived at the end of history is derived from an analysis that suggests the paramount importance of *ideas* in historical development. The Hegelian reading of history does not allow us to simply reduce history to material — say, to technological or economic — developments, but insists that history is always animated by *spirited* human agents who have something in mind, something after which they are striving and for which they are willing to risk. Indeed, we note that it is precisely the ability to strive and to risk that is imperiled by modern technological affluence, for this affluence tends to make us self-satisfied and complacent. From the Hegelian point of view, then, the extent to which we have arrived at the end of history discloses a distinctive desire and motivation, indeed a distinctive *consciousness*. We want to explore the various dimensions of this distinctive consciousness in this fourth chapter, for it cuts to the heart of the problem of worldliness in modern society and culture. Along this line, I will argue that the peculiar consciousness disclosed by modern developments is marked by the desire for *autonomy* and by what might be called the *will-to-self-definition*. After all, it has been largely for the sake of autonomous self-definition that we have surrendered sector after sector of modern society and culture to secularity and to rationalized methods and techniques, in spite of the fact that this surrender has, in almost every instance, failed to live up to its initial promise of liberation and fulfillment. It appears that, collectively speaking at least, we would rather suffer extreme deprivation and impoverishment — even the death of the soul — than confess that we are not, finally, able to define and create ourselves all by ourselves.

Admittedly, this assertion that a kind of secular consciousness is finally what accounts for the godlessness of modern society and culture may seem at odds with our thesis that practical atheism rests upon the foundation of *plausibility*, and hence that it is somewhat *unconscious* and simply taken-for-granted. Yet to focus upon the distinctive self-consciousness that appears to animate so much of modern history only affirms the ultimately spiritual quality of human existence and the dialectical nature of the relation between spirituality and society. Consciously willed secularity and the more or less unconscious habit of practical atheism are, after all, dialectically related. As our previous discussions have shown, the same institutions which underwrite the plausibility of practical atheism in contemporary culture were, by and large, conceived and designed to function in a secular fashion. Indeed, philosophical and/or theological commitments underlie all of the institutional realities of modern society and culture, and although modern realities have frequently reshaped these initial philosophical and/or theological commitments in ironic and sometimes in completely unintended ways, it is still possible to trace a peculiar self-understanding through modernity's entire development. This distinctively secular self-consciousness goes some distance toward shaping the character of modern, and now postmodern, worldliness. It also explains why we may well have arrived at the end of history, or at least at the end of a particular line of historical development, for it is difficult to imagine how the modern will-to-self-definition could be extended much further than it has been already in contemporary culture.

The Triumph of the Therapeutic

Modern secular self-consciousness is most immediately evident in the contemporary preoccupation with psychological techniques and therapies of *self-help*. As Philip Rieff contended a number of years ago in an important polemic entitled *The Triumph of the Therapeutic* (1966),[7] our culture's preoccupation with psychological therapies suggests a fundamental narrowing of human aspirations. While "therapy" once simply denoted the remedial treatment of physical disorders, and while a variety of psychological as well as strictly physical therapies have been of inestimable benefit to many of us, therapy has also become the focus of essentially religious devotion in contemporary culture. This is disturbing. Indeed, beyond simply seeking therapeutic treatment for specific ailments, more and more people today are taking a therapeutic approach to the problems associated with relationships and self-esteem, to the problems of ultimate meaning and purpose, in short, to life itself and to life's most basic existential questions. Yet because the therapeutic stress is necessarily upon immediate relief and rehabilitation, and because its

7. Philip Rieff, *The Triumph of the Therapeutic: Uses of Faith after Freud* (London: Chatto & Windus, 1966).

only final criterion is the *subjective experience of well-being,* the therapeutic orientation provides no serious discipline for the soul. Taking a therapeutic approach to life, in other words, does not lead — or, at best, only accidentally leads — to the formation of character and to the acceptance of responsibility before God and neighbor.

At first glance the therapeutic culture appears to be quite open to the possibility of religious faith. After all, tolerance has become an accepted social virtue in contemporary culture, and religion is no longer necessarily considered offensive to intellectual integrity or an impediment to authentic self-development. Recent decades have witnessed a virtual explosion of interest in traditional beliefs as well as in "new age" alternative religions. As Rieff observed, however, truly religious faith and the therapeutic *use* of religion represent two very different, indeed mutually exclusive, dispositions. The Christian religion, for example, draws the believer *out* of him or herself and into the obedience of faith, thus opening up the possibility of *self-transcendence.* The therapeutic disposition, on the other hand, tends to leave the individual more or less in control of his or her own self-development. This is not to say that it is not possible to lose oneself in therapy, for it is indeed, and people willingly surrender themselves to therapeutic regimens all the time. But these same individuals do not generally surrender to therapeutic techniques because they are convinced that they are true or good or beautiful, so much as because they have become convinced that these techniques stand a good chance of yielding the experience of well-being. Put differently, there is little genuine self-transcendence in the surrender to therapy. "Religious man was born to be saved," Rieff lamented, "psychological man is born to be pleased."[8]

Of course, therapeutic ambivalence with respect to religious belief may simply stem, at least in part, from the uncertainty associated with the fact of cultural plurality. The pluralistic environment is one in which questions about the nature of the good, the meaning of truth, the existence of God, etc., may understandably be taken to be unanswerable and hence in a certain sense insignificant.[9] In the final analysis, however,

8. Ibid., 24-25.

9. Roger Lundin, *The Culture of Interpretation: Christian Faith and the Postmodern World* (Grand Rapids, MI: Eerdmans, 1993), 5-6; see also John Murray Cuddihy, *No Offense: Civil Religion and Protestant Taste* (New York: Seabury, 1978).

therapeutic agnosticism reflects more than simple ambivalence. Rather, it reflects the inherent tension that exists between the goals of therapy and those of traditional religious commitment. As we have seen, the dignity of the human person, understood Christianly, lies in "response-ability," in the possibility of freely and consciously giving oneself in love to God and to one's neighbor. Therapy, on the other hand, tends to dissolve responsibility into prior causes. Scientific psychological paradigms, for example, ultimately dismiss conscious moral agency as the source of behavior in favor of such things as childhood trauma, unconscious conflict, or biochemistry.[10] In addition, therapy's commitment to the present experience of well-being means that it must either reject the belief that some higher purpose — say, eternal life — relativizes our present experience, or that it must somehow absorb this belief and put it to good therapeutic use.

Along this line, Rieff observed that, in his independence from all gods, modern "psychological man" feels free to use god language and, indeed, to use any faith that lends itself to therapeutic use, but he cannot really *believe* anything.[11] This is what explains the complete absence of asceticism from contemporary culture. For to the extent that we are preoccupied with the present experience of well-being, we are not likely to see the point of ascetic self-denial. In effect, the modern therapeutic disposition mortgages eternal destiny for the sake of comfort.[12] It reverses Jesus' question about the prudence of gaining the world at the cost of one's soul (Matt. 16:26) and asks instead: What good will it be for someone to gain his "soul," yet lose this

10. See Jeffrey Burke Satinover, "Psychology and the Abolition of Meaning," *First Things* (February 1994): 14-18.

11. Rieff, *The Triumph of the Therapeutic*, 25.

12. For an interesting discussion of this trade-off, see Leszek Kolakowski, *Modernity on Endless Trial* (Chicago: University of Chicago Press, 1990), 97ff. The real issue with respect to the matter of secularization, Kolakowski suggests, is not the conflict between religious faith and science, but the conflict between our desire for meaning and our desire for comfort. "The conflict is cultural," Kolakowski writes (p. 99), "and it is about our hierarchy of preferences: our *libido dominandi* against our need to find meaning in the universe and in our lives. Both desires, *libido dominandi* and the search for meaning, are rooted inalienably in the very act of being human, but they limit each other instead of coexisting peacefully." In contemporary culture, the former decisively limits the latter. We would much rather be comfortable than heroic or saved.

world?[13] "The therapy of all therapies," Philip Rieff commented at the conclusion of The Triumph of the Therapeutic:

> is not to attach oneself exclusively to any particular therapy, so that no illusion may survive of some end beyond an intensely private sense of well-being to be generated in the living of life itself. That a sense of well-being has become the end, rather than a by-product of striving after some superior communal end, announces a fundamental change of focus in the entire cast of our culture — toward a human condition about which there will be nothing further to say in terms of the old style of despair and hope.[14]

If there is nothing further to say in terms of hope in our culture, then of course there is nothing truly Christian to be said either. While Christian terms and concepts will undoubtedly be made to serve therapeutic purposes in contemporary culture, then, we must not allow ourselves to be deceived by this. The Christian faith is indeed a matter of healing and rehabilitation — indeed of resurrection — but it cannot be construed therapeutically, which is to say instrumentally. Faith in God through Jesus Christ and by the power of the Spirit is not a means, but is, along with hope and love, the end or purpose of human existence.

Of course, the triumph of the therapeutic has attracted a great deal of criticism in recent years. In his influential study The Culture of Narcissism (1979), Christopher Lasch castigated the modern obsession with self-realization and self-development.[15] Wendy Kaminer has criticized the radical subjectivity of the self-help movement most recently in a book

13. As Freud clearly recognized, and as Feuerbach had already seen several generations earlier, ascetic other-worldliness must be deemed intolerable from the modern point of view because it diminishes the importance of temporal happiness and well-being. "[S]urely [religious] infantilism is destined to be surmounted," Freud wrote in The Future of an Illusion (1927; New York: W. W. Norton & Co., 1961), 49, 50: "Men cannot remain children forever. . . . Need I confess to you that the sole purpose of my book is to point out the necessity for this forward step? . . . By withdrawing their expectations from the other world and concentrating all their liberated energies into their life on earth, they will probably succeed in achieving a state of things in which life will become tolerable for everyone and civilization no longer oppressive to anyone."

14. Rieff, The Triumph of the Therapeutic, 261.

15. Christopher Lasch, The Culture of Narcissism: American Life in an Age of Diminishing Expectations (New York: Warner Books, 1979).

mockingly titled *I'm Dysfunctional, You're Dysfunctional* (1993)[16] after the best-selling manifesto of "transactional analysis," *I'm O.K., You're O.K.*[17] Yet it is perhaps important to stress that the problem is not with the notion of therapy *as such,* nor even with specific therapies which often are of real benefit. Instead, the problem lies in the contemporary tendency to focus religious aspirations on the possibilities of therapy, as though therapy could resolve the problems of the human condition. It is also important to recall that contemporary society and culture disclose an excess of concern with the self in any number of other ways besides the overt preoccupation with therapy. Our rapt fascination with science and technology suggests that we are eager to be impressed by anything that promises to expand the boundaries of our experience. More ominously, we appear to be committed to the project of using technology to redefine human experience *as such.* The technologies of birth control and abortion are, for example, most often advocated by those who would, in the name of equality, social justice, or other typically modern liberal values, re-design human sexuality and the relations between men, women, and children. Indeed, sexuality and procreation, once understood in terms of created nature, are today increasingly construed in terms of "gender," "sexual preference," "lifestyle," in short, they are envisioned only as social constructs and conventions which may be redesigned at any time to suit our changing tastes and preferences.[18] Modern politics, furthermore, is fast becoming simply the

16. Wendy Kaminer, *I'm Dysfunctional, You're Dysfunctional: The Recovery Movement and Other Self-Help Fashions* (New York: Vintage, 1993).

17. Thomas A. Harris, *I'm O.K, You're O.K.* (New York: Avon, 1973).

18. It is not particularly surprising that the issue of homosexuality has emerged as such a visible and pivotal public issue in recent years, for homosexuality is emblematic of the distinctively modern self-understanding and further discloses — and in a particularly striking fashion — the distinctively modern will-to-self-definition and rejection of created nature. As we have seen, modern self-understanding has from the very beginning placed "nature" in quotation marks to indicate that whatever passes for "nature" simply masks prior human decision. Nietzsche, for example, already captured the spirit of this radically anthropocentric modern self-understanding over a century ago when he insisted that "truths are illusions which we have forgotten are illusions, worn-out metaphors now impotent to stir the senses, coins which have lost their faces and are considered now as metal rather than currency." Acting out of concern for "the truth of things," Nietzsche insisted, simply conceals the fact that it is finally only the will to power which really motivates any of us. Nietzsche, cited in Alasdair MacIntyre, *Three Rival Versions of Moral Inquiry: Encyclopedia, Genealogy, and Tradition* (Notre Dame, IN: University of Notre Dame, 1990), 35.

"politics of felt need" in which various groups of individuals compete with one another for recognition and subsidy from an increasingly therapeutic state. And the so-called "consumer revolution" presupposes a mass audience who view consumption as a means toward the end of self-realization. Indeed, a veritable identity industry has emerged in recent years in response to consumer demand for products and services designed to help us discover and improve ourselves. If there has been a triumph of the therapeutic in contemporary culture, then this cannot simply be blamed upon secular psychological theorists or upon the emergence of the so-called helping professions, but it reflects an entire cultural ethos characterized by profound *self*-centeredness.

Western Individuality and Loneliness

Concerns about our culture's preoccupation with therapies of self-help converge with similar concerns that have been voiced about the exaggerated importance modern Western society and culture has assigned to *individuality*. Indeed, in an interesting essay entitled "Western Individuality: Liberation and Loneliness" (1985), Peter Berger went so far as to suggest that the concept of the "autonomous individual" is the strategically central component of the modern Western world.[19] It animates modern jurisprudence, modern liberal democracy, the market economy, modern higher education, and other primary institutional features of modern societies. Berger went on to describe the peculiarly Western understanding of individuality in terms of six propositions: a) that the uniqueness of the individual represents his or her essential reality; b) that individuals are and ought to be free; c) that individuals are to be held responsible for their own actions, but only for their own actions; d) that an individual's subjective experience of the world is "real" by definition; e) that individuals possess certain rights over and against all collectivities; and f) that individuals are ultimately responsible for creating themselves.[20]

The ideational origins of Berger's six propositions are commonly

---

19. Peter L. Berger, "Western Individuality: Liberation and Loneliness," *Partisan Review* 52 (1985): 324.

20. Ibid., 326-27.

traced to the classical philosophical commitment to the disciplined use of *reason* and to the biblical affirmation of conscience and of the possibility of responsible individual existence before God. Both beliefs were subsequently amalgamated within the Christian tradition and inform much of Western history. For a number of reasons that we will discuss at greater length below, however, the ideal of autonomous individuality surfaced with unusual social power in the intellectual events that marked the beginning of the modern era, the Renaissance, the Reformation, and the Enlightenment. "Relentless reason" and "relentless conscience," as Berger put it, have together had a great deal to do with the development of modern society and culture, particularly since the sixteenth century.

Western individuality has been and continues to be experienced as a great *liberation*. The modern individual has been freed from the repressive constraints of tradition, of caste and clan, and indeed even from the limitations of nature itself. We are free now to make something of ourselves if we can, to better our position in the social order, and/or simply to be left alone, and we are protected by laws and institutions which guarantee our rights over and against the larger society. Not surprisingly, then, modern Western history has exhibited a steady procession of characters who embody the ideal of autonomous individuality: the conquistador, the entrepreneur, the citizen, the bourgeois gentleman, the romantic artist-hero, the existential hero, and, most recently, the sexual revolutionary.[21]

Yet the modern commitment to individuality extends far beyond the simple belief that one ought to be left free to think for oneself and to obey the dictates of one's own conscience. Also entailed within the modern view is the conviction that it is morally legitimate for individuals to pursue their own happiness and, indeed, that the pursuit of this-worldly happiness and satisfaction is, finally, the only truly human *telos*. In addition to the original commitments to reason and conscience, then, the distinctively modern ideal of individuality includes the commitment to autonomous self-creation. German social philosopher Arnold Gehlen described this development as a virtual "second Enlightenment" that appears to have taken place during the eighteenth century and that heralded an entirely new style of subjec-

21. Ibid., 331-32.

tivity.[22] As a result of this "second Enlightenment," *self*-realization and even *self*-gratification have become the master principles of modern culture.[23] From this perspective, the relatively recent arrival of "psychological man" announced by Rieff, Lasch, and others is really only the latest expression of a kind of self-centered subjectivity that has been developing within Western culture for several centuries.[24]

Here again, the fact that a number of influential eighteenth-century thinkers became "enlightened" to the possibilities of self-realization and self-gratification helps to explain the remarkable absence of ascetic ideals from modern industrial culture. Yet it is also important to stress that asceticism is also ruled out of modern life *practically* on the basis of economic realities. After all, the ascetic renunciation of well-being, which under modern conditions means the failure to pursue one's own self-interest by means of consumption, is held to threaten the viability of our entire economic system and invites the reproach of being "irrational." Along this line, Gehlen argued that it was this economic pressure toward hedonism that lay at the root, as he put it, of "all currently dominant forms of unfreedom."[25]

Gehlen's juxtaposition of the liberal emphasis upon individual

22. Gehlen, *Man in the Age of Technology*, trans. Patricia Lipscomb (New York: Columbia University Press, 1980), 73ff.

23. Daniel Bell, "The Return of the Sacred?: The Argument on the Future of Religion," in *British Journal of Sociology* 28, no. 4 (1977): 424.

24. See, for example, Lionel Trilling's discussion of the emergence of modern autobiography in *Sincerity and Authenticity* (Cambridge, MA: Harvard University Press, 1971). The popularity of "postmodern" theories of language is also instructive in this connection. It is frequently observed that we no longer share the eighteenth century's optimism with respect to the achievement of moral perfection or to the acquisition of certain knowledge. Yet we have obviously not surrendered the Enlightenment belief that the self can create itself. "In the secular eschatology of desire," Roger Lundin noted in *The Culture of Interpretation*, 37, "the kingdom to come at the end of history is a realm in which expressive individuals enjoy expansive and flexible freedom. That freedom is put into the service of the self's quest for expression, acquisition, and satisfaction." Lundin traces this commitment to self-expression back to the early Romantic quest for authentic experience. As we have already noted, the emphasis upon the creative use of language has by now been extended to the point that it has all but severed the connection between language and reality. We can change the very nature of reality for ourselves, so contemporary literary theorists suggest, simply by speaking it differently.

25. Gehlen, *Man in the Age of Technology*, 108.

well-being and the loss of freedom is significant, for it suggests that the otherwise optimistic stress upon liberated individuality may have ironic and unintended consequences. In this connection, Berger has contended that a certain measure of alienation is simply the price we must pay for individual autonomy, for to the extent that we are free from others, we are also alienated from them.[26] Yet the dimensions of contemporary alienation seem to extend well beyond occasionally having to stand alone over and against the group. Indeed, more and more people today appear to stand alone over and against *all* communities *all* of the time. Robert Nisbet coined the term "loose individuals" to describe this peculiar problem. "Without a doubt," Nisbet observed:

> there are a great many loose individuals in American society at the present time: loose from marriage and family, from the school, the church, the nation, job, and moral responsibility. What sociologists are prone to call social disintegration is really nothing more than the spectacle of a rising number of individuals playing fast and loose with other individuals in relationships of trust and responsibility.[27]

What makes this phenomenon of the "loose individual" most disturbing, however, is not simply the lack of relationships based on trust and responsibility, for there is obviously nothing particularly new about dishonesty, betrayal, and infidelity. What is new is the fact that an increasing number of individuals actually *defend* infidelity and betrayal as the prerogatives of authentic selfhood. Indeed, the modern, and now "postmodern," ideal of absolute individual autonomy demands the freedom from even the possibility of moral judgment pronounced on the self.[28]

That there are a great many people today who appear to be largely incapable of making commitments to each other is the facet of contemporary social life so lamented by Robert Bellah et al. in their celebrated study *Habits of the Heart: Individualism and Commitment in American Life*

---

26. Berger, "Western Individuality: Liberation and Loneliness," 324.

27. Robert Nisbet, *The Present Age: Progress and Anarchy in Modern America* (New York: Harper & Row, 1988): 84.

28. James Hitchcock, "Self, Jesus, and God: The Roots of Religious Secularization," in *Summons to Faith and Renewal: Christian Renewal in a Post-Christian World*, ed. Peter S. Williamson and Kevin Perotta (Ann Arbor, MI: Servant, 1983), 29.

(1985).[29] The problem of destructive individualism has subsequently led many contemporary observers to emphasize the importance of community, and to contend for a return to communitarian values.[30] Yet it is important to stress that the contemporary impotence with respect to commitment cannot itself be remedied by the simple decision to reestablish "community," for community already presupposes the capacity of individuals to make lasting commitments and this capacity is precisely what contemporary "loose individuals" lack. As Kierkegaard observed: "It is quite impossible for the community or the idea of association to save our age. . . . Nowadays the principle of association . . . is not positive but negative; it is an escape, a distraction and an illusion . . . the association of individuals who are themselves weak, is just as disgusting and as harmful as the marriage of children."[31]

Just as modern individuals have tended to tear themselves loose from each other, so they have also torn themselves "loose" from God, or at least from any conception of God implying limits to autonomous self-definition. Of course, this is obviously evident in the various ex-

---

29. Robert N. Bellah, Richard Madsen, William M. Sullivan, Ann Swidler, and Steven M. Tipton, *Habits of the Heart: Individualism and Commitment in American Life* (Berkeley, CA: University of California Press, 1985). See also David Riesman, *The Lonely Crowd: A Study in Changing American Character* (Garden City, NY: Anchor, 1956). In this connection, it has been observed that the modern commitment to autonomous individuality has precipitated a crisis of moral and cultural authority. In a study entitled *The American Hour: A Time of Reckoning and the Once and Future Role of Faith* (New York: The Free Press, 1993), Os Guinness recently argued that the contemporary crisis of cultural authority is America's most pressing problem. James Davison Hunter has gone so far as to describe the conflict over moral authority in terms of cultural warfare in *Culture Wars: The Struggle to Define America* (New York: Basic Books, 1991). Unfortunately, the conflict over moral authority has only contributed to the further politicization of modern culture discussed in our first chapter, for the combatants on either side of various fronts in the contemporary "culture war" are quick to call for a political resolution to moral and cultural ambiguity. Because "loose individuals" are increasingly unable to get along with each other, it seems, the political apparatus itself becomes the only means by which civil society is possible. This virtually ensures the emergence of totalitarian, or at least of authoritarian, regimes in the future.

30. See, for example, Amitai Etzioni, *The Spirit of Community: Rights, Responsibilities, and the Communitarian Agenda* (New York: Crown, 1993).

31. Søren Kierkegaard, *The Present Age & Of the Difference between a Genius and an Apostle*, trans. Alexander Dru (New York: Harper & Row, 1962), 79.

pressions of explicit atheism that have become so commonplace in modern culture. But it is important to stress that this "liberation" from God is also given in the subjective quality of modernity's remaining religious sensibilities. Eric Voegelin suggested, for example, that modern religiosity entails the absorption of divine predicates into the realm of human culture, a process he termed "immanentization."[32] Where it is successful, the process of immanentization transforms the universe of traditional religion, once the dominion of the transcendent God, into an exclusively human universe, a universe in which God is held to stand "behind" or "within" humanity's conscious manipulation of history, meaning, and value. The fact that individual experience has by now assumed the place of divine revelation for many of our contemporaries is the reason that Daniel Bell described modern culture in terms of a "great profanation."[33] "To use a term which has become popular in some theological circles," evangelical theologian Oliver O'Donovan has also commented describing this process, "the end of history is the 'hominization' of the world: all events are to fall under the conscious direction of human culture, so that the world itself becomes, so to speak, a human artifact."[34] Contemporary culture — even contemporary religious culture — has thus shown an insidious tendency to collapse the sacred into the profane. Indeed, even to distinguish between these two is sometimes protested because it denies absolute autonomy of the secular realm, and inhibits the modern self's freedom of movement.[35]

"New age" religion is once again instructive in this connection. For although "new age" religion is concerned with human limits — chiefly with the limits of science and technology, and with the limits of the human development of natural resources — it is at the same time committed to the notion of *unlimited* human potential. Thus while we might expect advocates of the "new age" to be attracted to religions of obedience — obedience to God, to truth, to natural law, indeed to anything that might limit and order human experience — we find them

32. Eric Voegelin, *The New Science of Politics: An Introduction* (Chicago: University of Chicago Press, 1952), 163.

33. Daniel Bell, "The Return of the Sacred?: The Argument on the Future of Religion," in *British Journal of Sociology* 28, no. 4 (1977): 419-49.

34. Oliver O'Donovan, *Resurrection and Moral Order: An Outline for Evangelical Ethics* (Grand Rapids, MI: Eerdmans, 1986), 68.

35. See Kolakowski, *Modernity on Endless Trial*, 63ff.

attracted instead to religious *gnosis* and to spiritual techniques that promise *mastery*. Mastery is sought over physical limitations, over death, and finally over the self itself. The term "transcendence" in "new age" parlance, then, does not really point *beyond* the self so much as it points to the absolute transcendence *of* the self in the world. The protest against the *hubris* of modern technologism and against its material transformation of the world does not give way to humility so much as it leads to an even more ambitious attempt to engineer the world *spiritually* as well as technologically. As Reinhold Niebuhr observed a number of years ago, contemporary interest in religion usually masks either a pantheism in which existence in its totality is considered holy, a rationalistic humanism in which human reason is considered holy, or a vitalistic humanism in which some vital human drive is held to be holy.[36] All three, Niebuhr concluded, really only amount to a kind of religion of *self*-glorification.[37]

The individual has thus become something of a god in contemporary culture. Not only has the self become the object of essentially religious devotion, but the attributes once reserved for divinity, particularly aseity (self-existence) and absolute creativity, are now assigned to self-constructing individuals. It is perhaps not surprising, therefore, to find that solipsism is one of the more representative infirmities of the modern soul.[38] As Martin Buber commented: "Something has stepped between our existence and God to shut off the light of heaven . . . , [and] that something is in fact *ourselves*, our own bloated selfhood."[39]

Self and Society

The distinctively modern self-understanding is often said to be a reflection of the complexity of modern society and culture. Compared to traditional or premodern societies, modern societies are not simply more

36. Reinhold Niebuhr, "The Christian Church in a Secular Age," in *The Essential Reinhold Niebuhr: Selected Essays and Addresses*, ed. Robert McAfee Brown (New Haven: Yale University Press, 1986), 79-92.

37. Ibid., 80.

38. Hitchcock, "Self, Jesus, and God," 35.

39. Martin Buber, quoted in Thomas F. Torrance, *God and Rationality* (Oxford: Oxford University Press, 1971), 29.

complicated, but their complexity is also far less coherent and integrated. The various sectors of modern society and culture are difficult, if not impossible, to fit into a unified interpretation or system of explanation. The subjective consequences of the complexity and of the dis-integrated quality of modern societies have been the focus of a number of theories of modernization. Toennies' thesis that the process of modernization entails a shift from "community" (*Gemeinschaft*) to "society" (*Gesellschaft*) implies a rapid multiplication of social roles and relationships.[40] The subjective impact of the complexity of modern society and culture figured prominently in the work of Durkheim, and was taken up by Parsons in his work detailing the vastly increased "differentiation" of institutions and roles in modern societies. In a fascinating study entitled *The Homeless Mind: Modernization and Consciousness* (1973), Peter Berger et al. actually define modernity in terms of a "plurality of life worlds."[41] Most recently, in a study entitled *The Saturated Self: Dilemmas of Identity in Contemporary Life* (1991), Kenneth Gergen contends that the rapid expansion of relational possibilities created by modern communications technology has overwhelmed our ability to maintain the coherence of our own individual identities.[42] Indeed, many people today appear to have reached a kind of saturation point and their identities appear to have all but disappeared beneath the waves of possibility. Thus Gergen observes that "the fully saturated self becomes no self at all."[43]

While Gergen's recent thesis is perhaps a bit exaggerated, Berger et al. suggest that modern individuals do exhibit a kind of "urbanized" consciousness which does indeed appear to be a reflection of the complexity of modern social life.[44] As the larger society has become dis-integrated, modern subjectivity has grown increasingly complex and segmented. From this perspective, the individualistic attitude discussed above may simply be the subjective reflection of the fact that we are

40. See Ferdinand Toennies, *Community and Society*, trans. Charles P. Loomis (East Lansing, MI: Michigan State University Press, 1957).

41. Peter L. Berger, Brigitte Berger, and Hansfried Kellner, *The Homeless Mind: Modernization and Consciousness* (New York: Vintage Books, 1973), 64.

42. Kenneth J. Gergen, *The Saturated Self: Dilemmas of Identity in Contemporary Life* (New York: Basic Books, 1991).

43. Ibid., 7.

44. Berger et al., *The Homeless Mind*, 67.

required to function as semi-autonomous individuals in any number of social contexts. In addition, the excessive introspection and reflection so characteristic of the therapeutic revolution may only reflect the fact that we are required to participate in a complicated society in a wide variety of more or less discrepant roles and relationships. We are thus constantly changing roles, moving back and forth between various "life-worlds," and trying to remember who we are in the process. This takes time and effort, and occasionally requires professional assistance. Finally, as the larger society has ceased to make sense in any kind of holistic and integrated way, so we have been forced to look to ourselves in the search for meaning and truth. There is strong socio-structural basis, in other words, for the modern preoccupation with self.

It is important to stress that these same social conditions con-tribute to the *implausibility* of traditional religious belief. Although the various component parts of modern society and culture are formally and technically related to each other, the generally dis-integrated quality of modern social life has made it increasingly difficult, if not impossible, for religion to provide an interpretive canopy over the whole. Instead, each component piece of the larger society tends to have its own internal rationale and even its own language. Not only does this help to explain the stubborn plausibility of modern skepticism and agnosticism, but it also interprets the subjective quality of modern religious adherence, for while religious faith remains a possibility in the modern situation, it can never be simply taken for granted. It must always be rather self-consciously *willed* over and against any number of conflicting and competing alternatives. Of course, from a Christian point of view this is not necessarily a problem, for Christian faith always presupposes the freedom of the will and conscious decision. Still, under modern conditions the decision *to* believe has a way of eclipsing the object *of* belief, and often seems to give way to subjectivism. Along this line, Berger has suggested that the slide into subjectivism is all but unavoidable in modern society and that *heresy* — with its stress upon the subjective will-to-believe — has become a kind of imperative for all contemporary religious affirmation.[45] Modern highly differ-

45. Peter L. Berger, *The Heretical Imperative: Contemporary Possibilities of Religious Affirmation* (Garden City, NY: Anchor, 1979). Interestingly, this slide into subjectivism appears to have been initially precipitated by the Reformation's pluralization of eccle-

entiated society is not, in short, a particularly hospitable environment for a traditionally religious view of the world.[46]

In speaking of the "saturated self" and the "urbanization of consciousness" it is perhaps important to point out that we do not actually experience much of the complexity of modern social life directly. Rather, it is mediated to us by means of mass communications media. Indeed, the mass media expand our awareness of the many possibilities of action and affirmation while simultaneously rendering these possibilities easier to cope with by allowing us to hold them at arm's length. Daniel Lerner coined the term "psychic mobility" a number of years ago to describe the heightened capacity to deal with choice and change made possible by modern mass media.[47] Lerner observed that, on the one hand, radio, television, and film extend the revolution begun by Gutenberg and open up a bewildering universe of possibilities to us. Yet the mediated quality of this universe prevents it from overwhelming us. In fact, it is exposure to what Lerner termed "the infinite vicarious universe" of mass-mediated possibilities that actually prepares us mentally and emotionally to adapt to the complexity of modern social conditions.[48] Mass media, then, play a crucial psychological role in modern society by insulating us from the harsh realities of complexity and differentiation.

Yet the quality of mass-mediated experience may insulate us from more than simply the harsh reality of social complexity. Indeed, it has been suggested that modern mass media actually have the effect of

---

siastical, political, and moral authority. As social theorist Karl Mannheim has noted in *Ideology and Utopia: An Introduction to the Sociology of Knowledge,* trans. Louis Wirth and Edward Shils (New York: Harcourt, Brace, & World, 1936), 12-13: "The disruption of the intellectual monopoly of the church [by the Reformation] brought about a sudden flowering of an unexampled intellectual richness. But at the same time we must attribute to the organizational disintegration of the unitary church the fact that the belief in the unity and eternal nature of thought, which had persisted since classical antiquity, was again shaken. The origins of the profound disquietude of the present day reach back to this period, even though in most recent times additional causes of a quite different nature have entered into the process."

46. Berger et al., *Homeless Mind,* 79-80; see also Bryan Wilson, *Religion in Sociological Perspective* (New York: Oxford University Press, 1982), 176.

47. Daniel Lerner, *The Passing of Traditional Society: Modernizing the Middle East* (New York: The Free Press, 1958), 51.

48. Ibid.

insulating us from reality altogether, and specifically from the reality of our own limitations and the limitations inherent in the human condition. This was the thesis of Daniel Boorstin's celebrated study *The Image: A Guide to Pseudo-Events in America* (1961). We have used our literacy and our wealth of technology, Boorstin suggested:

> to create the thicket of unreality which stands between us and the facts of life. . . . We want to believe these illusions because we suffer from extravagant expectations. . . . When we pick up the newspaper at breakfast, we expect — we even demand — that it bring us momentous events since the night before. . . . We expect our two-week vacations to be romantic, exotic, cheap, and effortless. . . . We expect anything and everything. We expect the contradictory and the impossible. We expect compact cars which are spacious; luxurious cars which are economical. We expect to be rich and charitable, powerful and merciful, active and reflective, kind and competitive. We expect to be inspired by mediocre appeals for excellence, to be made literate by illiterate appeals for literacy . . . to go to a "church of our choice" and yet feel its guiding power over us, to revere God and to be God. Never have people been more the masters of their environment. Yet never has a people felt more deceived and disappointed. For never has a people expected so much more than the world could offer.[49]

On an even more ominous note, Malcolm Muggeridge contended that modern mass media — and particularly television — insulate us from the reality of moral order.[50] By making moral evil appear attractive, and by rendering goodness in such a way as to make it appear dull and boring, mass media — and particularly visual media — have literally *de*moralized modern society and culture. Indeed, Muggeridge felt that media have by now so denigrated traditional standards and commitments that all that is left of contemporary culture is a kind of void in which even the notions of good and evil have ceased to have any real meaning. "I have tried to show," Muggeridge concluded in his classic

---

49. Daniel Boorstin, *The Image: A Guide to Pseudo-Events in America* (New York: Harper & Row, 1961), 3-4.

50. Malcolm Muggeridge, *Christ and the Media* (Grand Rapids, MI: Eerdmans, 1977).

study *Christ and the Media* (1977), "that, as I see it, the media have created, and belong to, a world of fantasy, the more dangerous because it purports to be, and it is largely taken as being, the real world."[51]

We would be mistaken to blame the secularity and immorality of modern mass media solely on the ideological commitments of those responsible for producing and distributing its contents, however, for its unreality also stems from the fact that secularity and immorality are essentially structured into the media themselves. Modern journalism is instructive in this connection, for by focusing exclusively on the events of the day, journalism all but severs the connection between time and eternity. It makes the world appear to be nothing but an endless jumble of events through which it is difficult, if not impossible, to discern anything beyond the relatively base motivations of lust, calculated self-interest, and the will to power. In short, journalism is not able to communicate wisdom. Rather, it is only able to report on the surface of things and events. As historian John Sommerville has recently noted, the invention of the journal, or regular periodical, was thus a significant milestone in the development of modern secular consciousness. "Periodical publication suggests a new tempo and urgency in the world's affairs," Sommerville notes: "Being informed replaces the ideal of being wise, and the day or the week becomes the focus of attention, rather than eternity."[52] Perhaps needless to say, then, journalism's constriction of the temporal horizon to discrete twenty-four-hour, weekly, or monthly periods has contributed quite substantially to the secular quality of modern society and culture. By completely relativizing eternity over and against the events of the day, or week, journalism renders such things as character, perseverance, fidelity, and hope largely meaningless.[53] As George Steiner observes:

51. Ibid., 60.

52. C. John Sommerville, *The Secularization of Early Modern England: From Religious Culture to Religious Faith* (New York: Oxford University Press, 1992), 182.

53. Ironically, Protestant churchmen appear to have had a lot to do with the spread of mass media, particularly in the nineteenth century. See R. Laurence Moore, "Religion, Secularization, and the Shaping of the Culture Industry in Antebellum America," *American Quarterly* 41 (June 1989): 216-42. Moore notes how Bible and tract societies contributed to the rise of mass media in America during the early nineteenth century by creating a commercially exploitable reading public.

The root-phenomenology of the journalistic is, in a sense, metaphysical. It articulates an epistemology and ethics of spurious temporality. Journalistic presentation generates a temporality of equivalent instantaneity. All things are more or less of equal import; all are only daily. Correspondingly, the content, the possible significance of the material which journalism communicates, is 'remaindered' the day after. The journalistic vision sharpens to the point of maximum impact every event, every individual and social configuration; but the honing is uniform. Political enormity and the circus, the leaps of science and those of the athlete, apocalypse and indigestion, are given the same edge. Paradoxically, this monotone of graphic urgency anaesthetizes. The utmost beauty or terror is shredded at close of day. We are made whole again, and expectant, in time for the morning edition.[54]

The Education of Self

Of course, in addition to being communicated by mass media, the distinctively secular and autonomous modern self-understanding is also conveyed by institutions of higher education today. In fact, universities and colleges have become quite crucial "carriers" of secularity in modern societies. Not only is the modern university the crucial locale of scientific and technological research, and of research into economic and political policy and management, but institutions of higher education increasingly proffer professional training in therapies of various kinds as well. Even more significantly, modern universities and colleges are the chief wardens of any number of distinctively modern ideologies, many of which may be said to fall under the general heading of "secular humanism."

While the moniker "secular humanism" has acquired somewhat unhelpful political connotations in recent decades, it remains a useful term to describe the predominant ideology of the modern academic life. "Secular" refers to its purely practical and temporal horizon, as well as to its pronounced skepticism with respect to all sources of traditional religious authority. Religious doubt, especially doubt about traditional

54. George Steiner, *Real Presences* (Chicago: University of Chicago, 1989), 26-27.

religion, is automatically more credible in modern intellectual circles than belief. Indeed, even in the field of "religious studies," traditional religious commitment — and in particular Christian commitment — is something of a rarity. After all, to believe anything too unreservedly bespeaks a potentially embarrassing lack of secular and worldly sophistication. "Humanism," on the other hand, refers to the intellectual commitment to human potential and to the possibilities of human development by means of rational human effort. As James Davison Hunter has noted:

> Humanism is . . . a meaning system or a cosmology. It is built upon certain unstated assumptions, as well as formal propositions about the nature of the universe (a closed, naturalistic system), the origin of the human race (evolutionary), the nature and origin of knowledge (scientistic if not positivistic), the nature of human values (relativistic, subjectivistic and, in part, scientifically derived), and the goal of human life (the full "realization" and "actualization" of human potentiality at both the individual and societal level). . . . Humanity as a symbol and as a reality is, for all practical purposes, sacralized, as is the chief mechanism for humanity's progress and development — science/technology.[55]

Secular humanism thus functions somewhat paradoxically as a kind of irreligious substitute religion in the modern context, and particularly in the context of the modern academy. As it emerged historically out of a Christian civilization, however, and because it was envisioned in reaction to Christian theology, secular humanism's values and sensibilities have a distinctively "Christian" flavor. Indeed, secular humanism really only differs with traditional Christianity on the question of the means of human fulfillment, preferring to sacralize human agency instead of God's.[56]

Interestingly, the sacralization of human agency has become more explicitly "religious" of late, but in a largely pantheistic fashion. Along

55. James Davison Hunter, "'America's Fourth Faith': A Sociological Perspective on Secular Humanism," *This World* 19 (Fall 1987): 103-4.
56. See Carl L. Becker, *The Heavenly City of the Eighteenth Century Philosophers* (New Haven, CT: Yale University Press, 1932).

this line, Colin Campbell has recently suggested (following Troeltsch) that the educated classes in modern societies are not at all irreligious; rather, they are just religious in a different, secret, and quasi-mystical way. Indeed, they are quite open to religious belief as long as it does not impinge upon their commitment to autonomous individuality:

> The characteristics which give mystical religion its adaptive advantage are its monism, relativism, tolerance, syncretism, and above all, its individualism. . . . The individual is the vehicle for religious experience and hence each person becomes his own high priest and theologian but without any grounds for an intolerant rejection of his neighbor's interpretation. The negative consequence of this emphasis is the absence of a religious community in any formal sense, while the positive one is that it enables the religious commitment to exist without there being any threat to the personal autonomy of thought or action of one's neighbor.[57]

Of course, Campbell's comments simply corroborate the observations we have already made about the "triumph of the therapeutic" and the "ordeal of civility." Secular-humanist ideology is only rarely explicitly atheistic. More commonly secular humanism simply requests that religious commitment be construed in such a way as not to endanger the therapeutic pursuit of well-being in the modern pluralistic environment.

The evolution of secular humanism in modern higher education in North America has an interesting history. For the most part, it appears to have occurred gradually and not altogether intentionally. Higher education in North America began as an explicitly Christian endeavor, with colleges and universities founded under churchly auspices, primarily for the training of pastors. Between the seventeenth and the nineteenth centuries, however, the ties that bound higher education to the churches gradually weakened, though for the most part without significant cultural controversy.[58] Even as these ties weakened, colleges

57. Colin Campbell, "The Secret Religion of the Educated Classes," in *Sociological Analysis* 39 (1978): 153.

58. See D. G. Hart, "The Troubled Soul of the Academy: American Learning and the Problem of Religious Studies," *Religion and American Life: A Journal of Inter-*

and universities were still understood to stand in the service of explicitly Christian, and typically conservative Protestant ends, right until the final decades of the nineteenth century. Toward the close of the nineteenth century, however, the breach separating the universities and the churches widened suddenly, and culminated in the extraordinarily rapid and dramatic "disestablishment" of conservative Protestantism from North American academic life between roughly 1890 and 1930.[59] It would not be an exaggeration to say that North American conservative Protestants have been reeling from the effects of this dramatic cultural defeat ever since.[60]

In part, the ejection of conservative Protestantism from North American colleges and universities after 1890 had to do with the insurgency of secular-humanist ideology. Influential proponents of secular rationality like John Dewey openly advocated the substitution of an "intellectual gospel" of naturalism and pragmatic liberalism for traditional religious understanding.[61] Yet it also appears that conservative Protestant educators willingly surrendered higher education to secularity rather than be seen to be illiberal and/or sectarian in the context of an increasingly secular culture, and especially in the eyes of their increasingly secularized political and industrial benefactors. Of course, at the time this surrender was not really viewed as such because conser-

---

pretation 2 (Winter 1992): 49-77. It has been suggested that the separation of higher education from the Church may actually have begun as early as the fifteenth century in Europe with the separation of the "bachelor of arts" from theological study as such. See Sommerville, *The Secularization of Early Modern England,* 160.

59. George M. Marsden, *Reforming Fundamentalism: Fuller Seminary and the New Evangelicalism* (Grand Rapids, MI: Eerdmans, 1987), 4.

60. See Mark A. Noll, *The Scandal of the Evangelical Mind* (Grand Rapids, MI: Eerdmans, 1994).

61. See Bruce Kuklick, "John Dewey, American Theology, and Scientific Politics," in *Religion and Twentieth-Century American Intellectual Life,* ed. Michael J. Lacey (New York: Cambridge University Press, 1989), 78-93; also David A. Hollinger, "Justification by Verification: The Scientific Challenge to the Moral Authority of Christianity in Modern America," in *Religion and Twentieth-Century American Intellectual Life,* ed. Michael J. Lacey (New York: Cambridge University Press, 1989), 116-35; and D. G. Hart, "Faith and Learning in the Age of the University: The Academic Ministry of Daniel Coit Gilman," in *The Secularization of the Academy,* ed. George M. Marsden and Bradley J. Longfield (Oxford: Oxford University Press, 1992), 107-45.

vative Protestants simply assumed the unshakably Christian character and identity of their institutions and of the nation. As we have already seen in connection with the rise of modern science, conservatives were also convinced that the findings of secular science must necessarily corroborate biblical truth. Needless to say, they were wrong on both counts. The Christian character of various universities proved remarkably easy to efface, and the findings of secular science only legitimated the effacement. In retrospect, it appears that Protestant educators were simply cognitively unprepared to deal with the growing secularization and pluralization of American culture. By the time they became aware of the problem of secularization, furthermore, it was too late for them to do anything about it, as least insofar as the established academy was concerned. "Why is it that Protestants have [by now] voluntarily abandoned their vast educational enterprise and are even embarrassed to acknowledge that they ever ran such a thing?" evangelical historian George Marsden recently queried:

> The answer is that, on the one hand, they were confronted with vast cultural trends, such as technological advance, professionalization, and secularism, which they could not control; but, on the other hand, the combination of pressures of cultural pluralism and Christian ethical principles [i.e., the commitments to tolerance and to "nonsectarianism" as well as an epistemological commitment to the unity of all truth] made it awkward if not impossible to take any decisive stand against the secularizing trends.[62]

Marsden went on to suggest that by the end of the nineteenth century Protestant educators had maneuvered themselves into a very difficult

---

62. George M. Marsden, "The Soul of the American University: A Historical Overview," in *The Secularization of the Academy*, ed. Marsden and Longfield, 28; see also George M. Marsden, *The Soul of the American University: From Protestant Establishment to Established Nonbelief* (New York: Oxford University Press, 1994); Michael J. Lacey, "Introduction: The Academic Revolution and American Religious Thought," in *Religion and Twentieth-Century American Intellectual Life*, ed. Michael J. Lacey (New York: Cambridge University Press, 1989), 1-11. Interestingly, the same thing appears to have occurred in British universities at about the same time. See David Bebbington, "The Secularization of British Universities since the Mid-Nineteenth Century," in *The Secularization of the Academy*, ed. Marsden and Longfield, 259-77.

situation. Committed as they were to the practical improvement of life by means of scientific and technological advancement, they could hardly object to educational strategies that promised to aid this advancement, even if these strategies also undermined traditional theological commitments.[63] After all, to defend traditional theological commitments over and against the advancing sciences would have meant impeding the very social progress that the Christian religion was at that time understood to be principally concerned with.

The rapid secularization of North American academic life at the turn of the century also appears to have been due to the emergence of the modern research university, with its strict delimitation of scientific disciplines and specialties, each committed to its own inner logic and method. Indeed, quite apart from any explicit intellectual hostility to religion, the modern intellectual habits of criticism, analysis, redefinition, and rearticulation, and even of simplification may be said to pose a threat to religious belief almost by definition, or at least to the belief in eternal and unchanging truth. And even if these habits do not actually necessitate the rejection of religious belief, they do point in the direction of agnosticism. A number of other structural features of modern academic life point in an agnostic direction as well: the academic commitment to plurality and to the due consideration of all points of view, a consideration that requires the protracted suspension of judgment until "all the facts are in," as it were; the tendency toward the ever increasing specialization of knowledge, a tendency which, as we have seen, has rendered the task of integrating disciplines more and more difficult; the professionalization of academic standing, a process in which performance is no longer measured against any kind of authoritative standard of character or belief, but is instead evaluated solely on the basis of professional competence as measured chiefly by a record of increasingly specialized publications; the relentless pressures to publish and the tacit valuation of innovation and experimentation this kind

---

63. This dilemma appears to have been most acute for Protestant proponents of the emerging social sciences. Along this line, those Protestant clergymen most enthusiastic about the potential of the social sciences appear to have had no idea that the impact of these new disciplines would be profoundly secularizing. See R. Laurence Moore, "Secularization: Religion and the Social Sciences," in *Between the Times: The Travail of the Protestant Establishment in America 1900-1960*, ed. William R. Hutchison (Cambridge: Cambridge University Press, 1989), 233-52.

of pressure presupposes. All of these factors are inherently secularizing and, in conjunction with the intrinsically secular logic of modern science and the ideology of secular humanism, go some distance toward explaining the secular quality of modern academic culture. Indeed, university culture is one in which largely secular rules of discourse have by now almost completely replaced religious commitment as the standard and measure of rationality.[64]

Of course, the secularization of modern higher education would not be such a significant problem were it not for the fact that so many of us are required to pass through the university system. Indeed, the threat posed to the Church by relentlessly skeptical intellectuals was limited even in the relatively recent past by the fact that there simply weren't that many of them around. The threat was probably also reduced because the few intellectuals who were around tended to understand themselves as a marginalized elite with a consciousness thankfully removed from that of the person-on-the-street. Since the turn of this century, however, and especially with the rapid expansion of the "knowledge industry" since mid-century, the number of intellectuals, or at least the number of those who identify with the characteristically intellectual outlook, has exploded. In fact their numbers have increased to the extent that, as we have seen, not a few social theorists have been tempted to group intellectuals and other knowledge workers into an entirely new "knowledge class" within modern society,[65] a class which is markedly more secularized than other groups. One of the consequences of this rapid increase in the number of intellectuals in recent years, undoubtedly also stemming from an enduring populist impulse within North American culture, is that the intellectual sense of marginality vis-à-vis the larger community has ceased to be distinctively intellectual. Whereas the adversarial and radically suspicious outlook may once have been jealously reserved, by the intellectuals' own admission, to the salon and café, agnosticism and the disposition toward

64. See, for example, Alvin Gouldner's discussion of the "culture of critical discourse" in *The Future of Intellectuals and the Rise of the New Class* (New York: Seabury, 1979), 1, 28ff.; see also Richard K. Fenn, "Secular Constraints on Religious Language," *The Annual Review of the Social Sciences of Religion* 4 (1980): 61-83.

65. Gouldner, *The Future of Intellectuals*; see also B. Bruce-Briggs (ed.), *The New Class?* (New Brunswick, NJ: Transaction Books, 1979); and Peter L. Berger, "Ethics and the Present Class Struggle," *Worldview* (April 1978): 6-11.

permanent reflection have now become, for a very large number of people in modern society, the *normal* attitudes to be expected of all educated and reasonable persons.

The enormous increase in the number of self-conscious intellectuals, then, people for whom belief has always been a problem, obviously has a good deal to do with the plausibility of secularity in modern society and culture.[66] Secular humanism has become, as the title of Hunter's article cited above suggests, North America's "fourth faith." Yet perhaps this actually understates the problem. Given its close affinities with liberal ideology, and given its commitment to the characteristically modern ideal of self-constructing individuality, quasi-religious secular humanism should probably be ranked *first* in terms of its impact upon modern social and cultural life.

The Private Pursuit of Happiness

Returning to our consideration of the subjective impact of the complexity of modern society, perhaps the most basic reflection of the dis-integrated quality of modern social life is evident in the bifurcation of self into "public" and "private" identities. This odd division appears to reflect the disparity that exists between the rationalized and impersonal logic of modern institutional life and the ongoing human need for personal meaning and fulfillment. Indeed, it is precisely because the impersonality of much of modern *public* life is so substantially at odds with meaningful existence that we are compelled to seek for personal meanings elsewhere and largely in *private*. A private sphere of life has thus been invented in modern society to compensate for the sterility and impersonality of the public workplace. As Thomas Luckmann has noted:

> In comparison to traditional social orders . . . primary public institutions no longer significantly contribute to the formation of individual consciousness and personality, despite the massive performance con-

66. Robert N. Bellah, "The Historical Background of Unbelief," in *The Culture of Unbelief,* ed. Rocco Caporale and Antonio Grumelli (Berkeley: University of California, 1971), 41.

trol exerted by their functionally rational "mechanisms." Personal identity becomes, essentially, a private phenomenon. This is, perhaps, the most revolutionary trait of modern society. Institutional segmentation left wide areas in the life of the individual unstructured and the overarching biographical context of significance undetermined. From the interstices of the social structure that resulted from institutional segmentation emerged what may be called a "private sphere." The "liberation" of individual consciousness from the social structure and the "freedom" in the "private sphere" provide the basis for the somewhat illusory sense of autonomy which characterizes the typical person in modern society.[67]

This division of individual biography into public and private aspects helps to interpret the problem of therapeutic self-absorption and the phenomenon of modern individualism. It also helps to explain the odd coincidence of individualistic self-absorption and mass conformity within contemporary culture. As the discovery and formation of individual identity has become a predominantly private activity, it seems, we have been cut loose from the discipline of community.[68] Indeed, we have been left largely to our own devices in trying to construct our own identities. This has left us highly vulnerable to fashion, however, and to the seductive claims of various mass-marketed products and techniques that have been developed in recent years to facilitate private self-construction. Authentic individuality, which has such a distinguished intellectual history in the West, has thus devolved into mere individualism and conformism. Put somewhat differently, individuality has been an unintended casualty in the rationalization of social order.

---

67. Thomas Luckmann, "The Invisible Religion," in *Secularization and the Protestant Prospect*, ed. James F. Childress and David B. Harned (Philadelphia: Westminster, 1970), 74; Luckmann's insights were developed by Anton Zijderfeld in *The Abstract Society: A Cultural Analysis of Our Time* (Garden City, NY: Anchor, 1971). Of course, Luckmann's analysis was already anticipated in Georg Simmel's essay, cited in the last chapter, "The Metropolis and Mental Life." Simmel commented on the modern divorce of the "objective spirit" of modern rationalized institutions from the "subjective spirit" of individual consciousness. The divorce between these two helps to explain the "blasé" indifference of the modern urban dweller toward society in general; for subjectivity must be protected from the harsh and impersonal realities of the larger society.

68. Peter L. Berger, *Facing Up to Modernity* (New York: Basic Books, 1977), 133.

Religion has, for the most part, been relegated to the private sphere of subjective autonomy.[69] But, of course, to the extent that religion is disconnected from public life, and so ceases to provide an interpretive canopy over *all* of life, it becomes vulnerable to individual whim. Indeed, religious commitment begins to be seen as something to be chosen or discarded, not on the basis of truth, but only on the basis of its perceived value in the process of self-construction. There is a great deal of irony in this. For the reason religious ideas figure so prominently in contemporary therapy is undoubtedly that we crave the certainty and rootedness religion seems once to have provided our ancestors. Yet certainty and rootedness are precisely what the subjective autonomy and privateness of self-construction prevent us from finding even in traditional religion. Again, to the extent that we understand religion therapeutically we will be prevented from finding genuine self-transcendence in religious belief. The fact that even Christian churches have become largely preoccupied with the provision and administration of therapies today is quite rueful. Far from demonstrating the prophetic relevance of the gospel in contemporary culture, the triumph of therapeutic sensibilities in our churches signals an advanced stage of privatization and secularization. "The findings are in and the message is clear," Canadian sociologist Reginald Bibby has commented, "Religion . . . is mirroring culture. A specialized society is met with specialized religion. Consumer-minded individuals are provided with a smorgasbord of fragment choices. Culture leads; religion follows."[70]

69. See, for example, Peter L. Berger and Thomas Luckmann, "Secularization and Pluralism," *International Yearbook for the Sociology of Religion* 1 (1966): 73-84. The phenomenon of denominationalism should probably be noted in this connection as well; for this appears to be yet another reflection of the voluntary status of competing religious options on the private market. See, for example, Berger's discussion of this in *The Sacred Canopy: Elements of a Sociological Theory of Religion* (Garden City, NY: Anchor, 1969), #137ff. Of course, until relatively recently, denominational diversity in North America fell within the broad confines of Judeo-Christianity, thus mitigating the psychic stress of competition between camps. Most recently, however, non-Christian religions and traditions have sought refuge under the denominational heading as well, making the ordeal of denominational civility quite a bit more difficult. See John Murray Cuddihy, *No Offense: Civil Religion and Protestant Taste.*

70. Reginald W. Bibby, *Fragmented Gods: The Poverty and Potential of Religion in Canada* (Toronto: Irwin, 1987), 233.

The Weightlessness of Modern Culture

Any number of observers have commented upon the ephemeral quality or, as Nietzsche put it, the "weightlessness" of modern culture.[71] In part, this superficiality may be interpreted by the obvious affinities that exist between therapeutic and individualistic sensibilities and consumer capitalism. As the consumption of things and experiences has proven instrumentally useful to the subjective construction and maintenance of the self, it seems, so the creation of culture has been increasingly surrendered to the logic of mass production and distribution. In the first instance, the quality and pervasiveness of modern advertising provide a good indication that there are quite a few individuals who are more or less "sold" on the project of self-construction-by-consumption. It also indicates that modern business firms are very well aware of the social psychology of therapy, and that they have become remarkably accurate judges of cultural sensibilities. After all, most if not all of this advertising is quite carefully crafted to stimulate consumer demand by associating particular products with images of personal fulfillment and successful self-construction.

Of course, it may be argued that the confluence of therapeutic sensibilities and consumer capitalism has given rise to an unprecedented diffusion of cultural products and services geared toward self-enrichment and self-enhancement, and that this has enabled many groups that have not traditionally participated in cultural consumption to participate in modern culture.[72] This may well be the case, but at the same time it must be admitted quite frankly that the costs of this wide diffusion of cultural products and services have been mediocrity and, more importantly with respect to our concerns, *secularity*. Economies of scale simply dictate that cultural products be inoffensive and relatively easy to consume, and that they appeal to the broadest possible market. Indeed, economic realities virtually ensure that most popular cultural products will be designed to appeal to universal in-

71. See, for example, T. J. Jackson Lears's discussion of both Nietzsche's and Marx's critical diagnosis of bourgeois culture in *No Place of Grace: Antimodernism and the Transformation of American Culture, 1880-1920* (New York: Pantheon, 1981), 41ff.

72. See Edward Shils, *The Intellectuals and the Powers* (Chicago: University of Chicago Press, 1972); in particular chapter 11, "Mass Society and its Culture," 229ff.

stincts such as sex, envy, anger, and the will to power.[73] As the advertising adage suggests: "Sex sells"; and so apparently do violence and resentment. On the other hand, the exigencies of mass production and distribution insure that the aesthetic quality of so-called "high" cultural products will be rather bland, for to be economically viable these products must be made to appeal to the broadest possible audience. Both strategies result in the secularization of cultural production; for it is safer to dissociate cultural products from religious affirmation altogether than it is to risk alienating potentially significant market segments in a multi-cultural environment. It is the convergence of therapeutic sensibilities and market realities, then, that really shapes the secularity of contemporary culture, and not simply the explicit secular humanism of the "cultural elite," though this is undoubtedly a factor as well. As Jonathan Alter a few years ago commented in *Newsweek* in an article on "The Cultural Elite" in America, "People in Hollywood don't have a shred of honest ideology among them. . . . 'Murphy Brown' and a few plugs for AIDS prevention notwithstanding, the mass media are so politically incorrect, its affronts to taste so numerous, that legions of p.c. professors make careers of deconstructing the racism and sexism they see in it."[74] Far from conspiring to advance any particular point of view, Alter suggests, contemporary media personnel simply believe that, on the contrary, they must function amorally so as not to seem to favor any particular point of view.

The odd weightlessness of contemporary culture may also be ascribed to the fact that both consumer capitalism and therapy share an inherently anti-teleological ethos. Neither, it seems, is particularly concerned with the identification of transcendent purposes, so much as it is with simply "getting by" in this world. Along this line, Bellah et al. suggested that the two principal character-types in contemporary society are the therapist and the manager.[75] Just as the therapist is committed to the ongoing maintenance of the experience of well-being, so the manager is dedicated to the survival of the firm in the

---

73. Kenneth A. Myers, *All God's Children and Blue Suede Shoes: Christians and Popular Culture*, Turning Point Christian World View Series, ed. Marvin Olasky (Wheaton, IL: Crossway, 1989), 99.

74. Jonathan Alter, "The Cultural Elite," *Newsweek* (October 5, 1992).

75. Bellah et al., *Habits of the Heart*, 44ff.

marketplace. Both, in effect, renounce ultimate concerns for the sake of comfort, convenience, and survival. Rieff made a similar observation. "Psychological man may be going nowhere," he noted, "but he aims to achieve a certain speed and certainty in going. Like his predecessor, the man of the market economy, he understands morality as that which is conducive to increased activity. The important thing is to keep going."[76]

David Riesman tried to capture the difference between the contemporary therapeutic ethos and its predecessor in his influential study *The Lonely Crowd* (1956) by developing a distinction between what he termed "inner-directed" and "other-directed" personality. The "inner-directed" self, Riesman suggested, is motivated by ultimate, typically religious, purposes and by the dictates of conscience shaped by religious belief. Such characters fill the annals of North American history from the seventeenth through the early twentieth centuries. But Riesman observed that the North American character has since become primarily "other-directed," in the sense that we now rely mostly upon the crowd and upon the mass media to tell us who we are and what is worth pursuing at any given moment. The only real *telos* of the "other-directed" personality, then, is to try to move in whatever direction promises to produce the least resistance and least drag. "It is only the process of striving itself," Riesman wrote, "and the process of paying close attention to the signals from others that remain unaltered throughout life."[77] The anti-teleological bias of "other-directed" personality helps to interpret the uniquely absorptive quality of contemporary consumer culture; for it is one in which virtually any idea is

76. Rieff, *The Triumph of the Therapeutic*, 41.

77. Riesman, *The Lonely Crowd*, 37. The apathy of the "other-directed" personality concerning traditional religious answers to ultimate questions is perhaps what accounts for the prevalence of what are termed "religious nones" in sociological circles. These are people who profess no adherence to religion, not because they are atheists, but simply because they are completely uninterested in the sorts of questions that religion claims to provide the answers to. While "religious nones" remain a minority even in modern secular culture, there appear to be far more of them today than in traditional cultures, and this increase may well have to do with the anti-teleological bias of modern institutions and ideologies. See, for example, Reginald W. Bibby, "Religion and Modernity: The Canadian Case," *Journal for the Scientific Study of Religion* 18, no. 1 (1979): 1-17.

welcome so long as it can be utilized in the ongoing construction and management of self. Indeed, the plasticity and absorptive capacity of contemporary Western culture have no precedent. "Nothing much can oppose it really, and it welcomes all criticism," Rieff commented, "for, in a sense, it stands for nothing."[78]

In a recent study entitled *The Romantic Ethic and the Spirit of Consumerism* (1987), British sociologist Colin Campbell provided an interesting glimpse into the possible origins of the narcissistic consumer ethic.[79] Campbell's provocative thesis is a variation on Weber's Protestant ethic theme. Just as the Protestant ethic appears to have led to a revolution in production, so eighteenth-century Romanticism appears to have precipitated something of a revolution in consumption. Indeed, this latter revolution in consumption may actually have had more to do with the development of industrial capitalism than with the inner-worldly asceticism of later Puritanism.[80] The key to this revolution in consumption, Campbell suggested, was Romanticism's distinctive understanding of the self. This Romantic self-understanding led to the spirit of modern consumption, which is, as he put it, "to want to want under all circumstances and at all times irrespective of what goods or services are actually acquired or consumed." Specifically, Campbell contended that this unique spirit of insatiable wanting,

---

78. Rieff, *The Triumph of the Therapeutic*, 65.

79. Colin Campbell, *The Romantic Ethic and the Spirit of Consumerism* (Oxford: Basil Blackwell, 1987); see also "Romanticism and the Consumer Ethic: Intimations of a Weber-style Thesis," in *Sociological Analysis* 44 (Winter 1983): 279-96.

80. Supporting Campbell's thesis, in his discussion of Weber's Protestant ethic thesis in *Theology and Social Theory: Beyond Secular Reason* (Oxford: Basil Blackwell, 1990), John Milbank writes (p. 33): "The capitalist take-off presupposed a shift in the very economy of desire. Previously, modes of public style and behaviour were regarded as desirable or otherwise because they were ultimately related to accepted standards of the common good. Now, by contrast, public style and behaviour becomes the subject of fashion and of an endless 'diversion.' What now matters, as thinkers like Montesquieu and Helvetius noted, is not the 'proper' object of desire but rather the promotion of desire itself, and the manipulation and control of the process. Only this reversal of the order of priority between desire and goal permitted a new code of social practice where people could start to see themselves as primarily 'producers' and 'consumers.' For to 'abstract desire' corresponded a new 'abstract wealth,' meaning the maximum diversification and increase of production, and the maximum circulation of products and their representative species through exchange."

which is very much at odds with the ascetic spirit of early capitalist production, descended from Romanticism's commitment to creative individuality and to the liberation of the self by means of immediate experience. Describing the novelty of the eighteenth-century Romantic ethic, Campbell notes:

> The "self" becomes, in effect, a very personal god or spirit to whom one owes obedience. Hence "experiencing," with all its connotations of gratificatory and stimulative feelings, becomes an ethical activity, an aspect of duty. This is a radically different doctrine of the person, who is no longer conceived of as a "character" constructed painfully out of the unpromising raw material of original sin, but as a "self" liberated through experiences and strong feelings from the inhibiting constraints of social convention.[81]

Thus, while consumerism is often thought to be simply a kind of by-product of capitalist production that is foisted upon hapless consumers by means of manipulative advertising, Campbell's historical study suggests that, although contemporary patterns of consumption are quite closely linked to the means of production, the peculiar *spirit* of consumerism — the insatiable "want to want" — appears to have emerged initially out of a Romantic understanding of the individual self. Of course, the heroic quest for experience has by now devolved into a kind of vicious cycle of restlessness and continuous consumption. Indeed, in the absence of any kind of religious (ascetic) restraint, the contemporary "structure of needs" is such that it must necessarily produce endless frustration and dissatisfaction.[82] What is good for the modern economy, it seems, is not necessarily very good for the soul.

The historical coincidence of therapeutic sensibilities and con-

---

81. Campbell, "Romanticism and the Consumer Ethic," 285-86. Indeed, as Lionel Trilling noted in his study of modern character, *Sincerity and Authenticity* (Cambridge, MA: Harvard University Press, 1971), intellectual historians are in substantial agreement that a new conception of personality began to emerge in Europe even as early as the late sixteenth and early seventeenth centuries. This appears to have been the period in which being "true to oneself" first began to be seen as a virtue in and of itself.

82. See Agnes Heller, "The Dissatisfied Society," *Praxis International* 2 (January 1983): 359-70.

sumer capitalism has thus contributed quite substantially to the secularization of modern society and culture. The therapeutic individual is not really interested in religious truth except insofar as it can be made to serve the secular interests of well-being. The secular logic of the market, furthermore, fosters egoism and requires only that subjective preferences be expressed in an orderly and disciplined fashion in the marketplace and that they be backed by money. Religion has, for the most part, been a victim of this process of therapeutic commodification. It has been reduced to the status of a therapeutic product in the contemporary marketplace of ideas, available for private consumption but not of much interest or importance otherwise.[83] Indeed, all serious attempts to make sense of human life have suffered this fate. It has become simply inconvenient to believe anything too unreservedly, or to be committed to anything too unconditionally. Such is the weightlessness of contemporary consumer culture.

Søren Kierkegaard was an early critic of modern consumer behavior, and his insights remain among the most incisive. The inventive term Kierkegaard coined to describe modern consumer culture was the "philistine-bourgeois mentality," a mentality so mired in this-worldly probability that it cannot even bring itself to imagine the possibility of a human destiny that transcends this world. The "philistine-bourgeois mentality," Kierkegaard observed:

> lacks every qualification of spirit and is completely wrapped up in probability, within which possibility finds its small corner; therefore it lacks the possibility of becoming aware of God. Bereft of imagination, as the philistine-bourgeois always is, whether alehouse keeper or prime minister, he lives within a certain trivial compendium of experiences as to how things go, what is possible, what usually happens. In this way, the philistine-bourgeois has lost his self and God. In order for a person to become aware of his self and of God, imagination must raise him higher than the miasma of probability, it must tear him out of this and teach him to hope and to fear — or to fear and to hope — by rendering possible that which surpasses the *quan-*

83. See Thomas Luckmann, "On Religion in Modern Society: Individual Consciousness, World View, Institution," *Journal for the Scientific Study of Religion* 2 (Spring 1963): 147-62.

tum satis [sufficient standard] of any experience. But the philistine-bourgeois mentality does not have imagination, does not want to have it, abhors it. So there is no help to be had here. And if at times existence provides frightful experiences that go beyond the parrot-wisdom of routine experience, then the philistine-bourgeois mentality despairs, then it becomes apparent that it was despair; it lacks faith's possibility of being able under God to save a self from certain downfall.[84]

Of course, to be "completely wrapped up in probability," as Kierkegaard put it, is simply to be committed to the typically modern assumption, following the likes of David Hume, that "reasonable" discourse must be enclosed within the boundaries of probability, and that imagination must never be allowed to extend beyond this-worldly experience.

If contemporary culture has become superficial, however, it has also become profoundly unsatisfying, for human beings desperately *need* to believe in something that can carry them out beyond the limited orbit of individual self-interest, and they desperately *need* to be able to make substantive commitments that contain at least the possibility of self-transcendence. Yet amazingly, contemporary consumer culture is even able to absorb, and indeed to thrive upon, the very dissatisfaction its ephemerality and superficiality generate. After all, it is the weight-lessness of consumer culture that fuels the contemporary demand for *real* experience and creates a large market for therapies designed to alleviate the nagging problem of meaninglessness. The so-called "sexual revolution" of the last several decades might be mentioned in this connection. Indeed, one gets the impression that sexuality has become a kind of last sacrament in a secular and materialistic culture, a last link to the possibility of self-transcendence.

When reality is reduced to "experiences" to be consumed, however, it is rendered all the more unreal and unsatisfying. It is also damaged; and therapies of self-help can only with considerable cognitive and emotional effort be made to function as a substitute for real meaning. Contemporary consumer demand for substance thus only stimulates

84. Søren Kierkegaard, *The Sickness Unto Death: A Christian Psychological Exposition for Upbuilding and Awakening*, trans. Howard and Edna Hong (Princeton: Princeton University Press, 1980), 41.

the development of therapeutic products and strategies which further undermine the substance of culture, further intensifying consumer demand for substance, and so forth. This is yet another one of the viciously cyclical patterns that seem to energize modern society and culture. An awareness of this viciousness figures significantly in post-modern nihilism, and it is the reason that so many have reasoned that we have reached the end of history. Contemporary despair over the possibility of ever really grounding the self also creates a large market for diversion and distraction. As Ernest Becker noted in his provocative study *The Denial of Death* (1973):

> Modern man is drinking and drugging himself out of awareness, or he spends his time shopping, which is the same thing. As awareness calls for types of heroic dedication that his culture no longer provides for him, society contrives to help him forget. Or, alternatively, he buries himself in psychology in the belief that awareness all by itself will be some kind of magical cure for his problems. But psychology was born with the breakdown of shared social heroisms; it can only be gone beyond with the creation of new heroisms that are basically matters of belief and will, dedication to a vision.[85]

But, of course, to recommend the human creation of "new heroisms" is simply to exacerbate the problem of modern narcissism and anthro-pocentrism. As Walker Percy observed so penetratingly in his strange little book *Lost in the Cosmos: The Last Self-Help Book* (1983), there is, finally, no self-help. If help is going to come, it is going to need to come *to* us from *outside* of ourselves.[86]

The Rise of the Secular Self

We have said that the roots of the consumer ethic extend back into Romanticism. Yet the roots of the distinctively secular and autonomous modern subjectivity extend back even farther than the eighteenth cen-

85. Ernest Becker, *The Denial of Death* (New York: The Free Press, 1973), 284.
86. Walker Percy, *Lost in the Cosmos: The Last Self-Help Book* (New York: Washington Square Press, 1983).

tury. That modern culture is populated by a significant number of "despisers of religion," for example, was recognized long before Friedrich Schleiermacher penned his famous *Speeches on Religion* in 1799.[87] Indeed, the emergence of the modern view of the self dates back at least as far as the sixteenth and seventeenth centuries with the emergence of early modern natural science.[88] Specifically, it may be linked to the critical rational epistemology of René Descartes. Discouraged by the uncertainties and ambiguities inhering in traditional sources of authority, Descartes resolved to discard all of them and to start over again "from scratch," as it were, by retreating into his own subjectivity. "Like one walking alone and in the dark," Descartes confessed, "I resolved to proceed so slowly and with such circumspection, that if I did not advance far, I would at least guard against falling."[89] By beginning with the purportedly indubitable principle "I think therefore I am," Descartes was able to guarantee the certainty of his method, and to rationally re-establish such things as the existence of the soul and of God. "Whether awake or asleep," Descartes insisted, "we ought never to allow ourselves to be persuaded of the truth of anything unless on the evidence of *our* Reason [emphasis added]."[90] Nothing, in other words, was to be taken on faith.

Descartes thus inaugurated an entirely new understanding of what it means to "know thy*self*," and a new account of what is entailed in *self*-control. While the problem of self-control had been an object of philosophical contemplation in the West since Plato, the whole point of this effort had been to bring the self into line with Nature, or with the Eternal Forms, or with God, with something, in other words, that transcended the self and was thus capable of grounding it. By contrast, Descartes construed self-control in terms of self-exploration, and ultimately in terms of self-construction. The order of Nature was thus no longer held to present an intrinsically meaningful order to which even

87. Friedrich Schleiermacher, *On Religion: Speeches to its Cultured Despisers*, trans. John Oman (1799; New York: Harper & Row, 1958).

88. See Franklin L. Baumer's discussion of the "skeptical tradition" in *Religion and the Rise of Skepticism* (New York: Harcourt, Brace & World, 1960).

89. René Descartes, *Discourse on Method*, in *Classics of Western Thought, Volume III: The Modern World*, ed. Charles Hirschfeld (New York: Harcourt, Brace & World, 1964), 15.

90. Ibid., 24.

reason must submit itself in faith if it is to be fulfilled. Rather, the individual rational self was held to possess the ability to ascribe its own internal order *to* reality, thereby *rendering* it meaningful. As Charles Taylor has noted, a fundamentally new conception of the self lay at the heart of Descartes's "new philosophy," a conception that subsequently animated the Cartesian revolution:

> What one finds running through all the aspects of this [Cartesian] constellation: the new philosophy, the methods of administration and military organization, the new spirit of government, and methods of discipline, is the growing ideal of a human agent who is able to remake himself by methodical and disciplined action. What this calls for is the ability to take an instrumental stance to one's given properties, desires, inclinations, tendencies, habits of thought and feeling, so that they can be worked on, doing away with some and strengthening others, until one meets the desired specifications.[91]

Of course, the initial plausibility of the Cartesian ideal of the human agent who is able to remake him or herself by means of methodical and disciplined action was buttressed by the successes of early modern science. This new view of self was subsequently affirmed during the eighteenth century by increasing doubts about the possibility of the miraculous, and hence about the possibility of revelation, by the presumed social advantages of rejecting original sin in favor of a more purely rational philosophical anthropology,[92] by the emergence of profane historiography, and by a number of secular theories about the natural origins of religion. With respect to the latter, it was suggested that religious sentiment only originates in fear and/or ignorance or that religion is really only the manipulative creation of priests and kings.

---

91. Charles Taylor, "Inwardness and the Culture of Modernity," in *Zwischenbetrachtungen: Im Process der Aufklärung*, ed. Axel Honneth, Thomas McCarthy, Claus Offe, and Albrecht Wellmer (Frankfurt am Main: Suhrkamp Verlag, 1989), 612-13. See also Taylor, *Sources of the Self: The Making of the Modern Identity* (Cambridge, MA: Harvard University Press, 1989).

92. See David Spadafora, "Secularization in British Thought, 1730-1789: Some Landmarks," in *The Secular Mind: Transformations of Faith in Modern Europe*, ed. W. Warren Wager (New York: Holmes & Meier, 1982), 35-56. See also Trilling, *Sincerity and Authenticity*.

Both theories had been around for centuries, but they experienced something of a renaissance in Western intellectual culture toward the end of the seventeenth century,[93] and became stock-in-trade objections to Christianity during the Enlightenment.[94] All of these developments tended to warrant the new conception of the self. The central article of this emergent faith in the self was not so much the belief in reason *as such,* as it was in the capacity of reasonable individuals to reconstruct a more perfect social order based upon their mutual commitment to employ rational methods. Belief in this possibility is implicit in Kant's celebrated definition of enlightenment as "having the courage to use one's *own* understanding" and renouncing the childish need for guidance from any source of authority other than that contained *within* oneself. Indeed, Kant's "transcendental ego," who "dares to know" and who lays a claim upon eternity by virtue of the practical moral decision to do one's duty even in the absence of all external support, was perhaps the supreme expression of Western philosophical individualism. Few have since dared to place quite this much emphasis upon the individual reasoning self.

It is important to stress that, on the way from Descartes to Kant and into the nineteenth century, it became rationally defensible, and indeed morally legitimate, to understand the project of self-creation in terms of the pursuit of happiness. Hobbes and Locke, for example, redefined "rationality" in terms of successful self-preservation. As Christian asceticism continued to wither under the assaults of enlightened criticism, self-preservation was increasingly interpreted hedonistically in terms of the satisfaction of natural appetites.[95] While Romantic hedonism and the Romantic emphasis upon the creative self are often represented as reactions to the Enlightenment's rational negation of individuality, then, the intellectual transition from rational individual-

---

93. See Sommerville, *The Secularization of Early Modern England,* 162.

94. Any number of authors have commented upon the decline of traditional religious belief toward the end of the seventeenth century. In addition to Baumer and Spadafora, see, for example, Michael J. Buckley, *At the Origins of Modern Atheism* (New Haven: Yale University Press, 1987); and C. John Sommerville, "The Destruction of Religious Culture in Pre-Industrial England," *The Journal of Religious History* 15 (June 1988): 76-93.

95. Harold J. Laski, *The Rise of European Liberalism: An Essay in Interpretation* (1936; London: Unwin Books, 1962), 84.

ism to the romantic quest for individual experience actually appears to have been a rather natural one. Both represented what Taylor has called "the massive subjective turn" of modern self-understanding.[96] As Lundin has recently noted:

> Although the Enlightenment differed markedly in a number of respects from the romantic era that followed in its wake, these two movements shared a distinct perspective upon the place of the self in nature and society. Both emphasized the self as an entity in isolation, equipped in its solitude with a panoply of powers. In the Enlightenment, to be sure, faith was centered upon rationality as the instrument of power, while in romanticism it was the intuition or imagination that promised to deliver human beings from their bondage to ignorance and injustice. But the adherents of the Enlightenment and romanticism were more united by their unshakable faith in the self than they were divided by their disagreements about the mechanisms through which that self did its work.[97]

The distinctively modern view of self has been given optimistic as well as pessimistic expression in more recent philosophy. On the one hand, Hegel's philosophy of dialectical idealism is one of seemingly unalloyed self-confidence, in which the predicates of divinity are quite openly and hopefully ascribed to human self-consciousness.[98] Yet a kind of "massive subjectivity" obviously also characterizes Nietzschean nihilism, in which it is held that humanity, having done away with God, is now diabolically free either to save or to destroy itself against the backdrop of an absolutely indifferent universe. The fact that genuine individuality is obliterated in both of these expressions is one of the peculiar ironies of modern intellectual history, of which we will have more to say in our final chapter. The point to note here is simply that, while the twentieth century has witnessed intellectuals oscillating nervously back and forth between extravagant optimism and absolute

96. Charles Taylor, *The Malaise of Modernity* (Concord, Ontario: Anansi, 1991), 26.

97. Lundin, *The Culture of Interpretation*, 5.

98. See Karl Barth, *Protestant Theology in the Nineteenth Century: Its Background and History* (London: S.C.M. Press, 1972), 385ff.

despair with respect to the self, no one today is prepared to surrender the will-to-self-definition. The "modernism" fashionable at the beginning of the century, for example, was quite optimistic about the possibility of our being able to construct a unified culture on the basis of a kind of rational consensus on the meaning and purpose of human life. "Postmodernism" has by now surrendered this hope, but it has not surrendered the will-to-self-definition. Indeed, the "postmodern" commitment to autonomous self-creation is, if anything, even more radical than that of the "modernists." As Lundin has noted:

> At a time when confidence in epistemology has eroded significantly, perspectivism appears to afford an opportunity for the isolated self — which has been at the center of Western science, philosophy, and art for more than three centuries — to sustain its faith in its own powers. Even though we may no longer believe in the ability of the self to achieve moral perfection or to acquire indubitable knowledge, we are still able, through our contemporary theories of interpretation, to sustain faith in that self's ability to find satisfaction through the exercise of its creative powers. In postmodern America, we can observe this faith in "perspective" at work in everything from the self-help regimens promising easy wealth and psychic health to the fantastic visions of academic critics who see creative interpretation as a kind of explosive charge for blasting through the imprisoning walls of the metaphysical past.[99]

The distinctively modern commitment to the self-creating self has thus remained quite constant throughout the modern, and now purportedly "postmodern," periods, even if this commitment has been expressed rather anxiously of late.

Christianity and the Modern Self

While the distinctively modern will-to-self-definition only emerged as a potent social force toward the end of the seventeenth century, it would be mistaken to lay the blame for the contemporary preoc-

99. Lundin, *The Culture of Interpretation*, 33.

cupation with the self solely upon secular humanism. In the first instance, this is simply because self-absorption is perhaps the most basic mark of the fallen human condition in sin. As Luther observed, following Augustine and the apostle Paul: "[Fallen human nature] is completely self-centered. . . . It puts itself in the place of everything else, even in the place of God himself and seeks only its own purposes and not God's. For this reason it is its own chief and most important idol."[100] It is also important to stress that the distinctively modern self-understanding exhibits the stamp of Christian, and particularly Protestant, theology in a number of significant respects. The skepticism with which modern intellectuals regard religion has a clear precedent in the Protestant criticism of medieval religiosity. Indeed, the "enlightened" characterization of the Middle Ages as a period of darkness, ignorance, and superstition was initially espoused by the Reformers. Along a similar line, it has been suggested that Calvinist iconoclasm may well have led to the development of secular biblical criticism. Given their repudiation of liturgy and ceremony, and given their near exclusive focus upon the text of Scripture, Puritan scholars appear to have paved the way for taking a rationalized attitude toward *all* texts and *all* traditions.[101] Puritanism's "typological" interpretation of Scripture, in which believers were encouraged to understand their own individual biographies as reduplicating events in the biblical narrative, may also have contributed to the rise of the profoundly individualistic Romantic hermeneutic, in which the self creatively makes use of the biblical text in the process of its own self-actualization, but does not submit to it.[102]

Yet beyond their disciplined repudiation of magical and superstitious religiosity, perhaps the most important Protestant contribution to the distinctively modern self-understanding lay in the Reformers use of "nominalism" in criticizing Scholastic (Aristotelian) ontology. As we have seen, this had the effect of shifting the philosophical focus away from ontology and toward epistemology, and thus toward the workings

100. Martin Luther, quoted in Paul Althaus, *The Theology of Martin Luther* (Philadelphia: Fortress Press, 1966), 147.

101. Jeffrey Stout, "Liberal Society and Language of Morals," *Soundings* 69 (Spring-Summer 1986): 32-59.

102. Lundin, *The Culture of Interpretation*, 63ff.

of the human mind. Of course, the Reformers' intention in reemphasizing the Augustinian account of personality and responsibility over and against the Scholastic conception of the "great chain of being" — within which freedom was, as already implied by the word "chain," somewhat limited — was to refocus the matter of faith upon the *grace* of God and upon the quality of the individual's *response* to this grace. Protestant theology thus laid the stress upon faith and responsibility, and hence upon the freedom of conscience before God. It exalted the individual. Yet Protestant theology thereby exacerbated the temptation, as Luther himself had warned, for individuals to make idols of themselves. Indeed, modern culture's seemingly unending preoccupation with psychology may be traced to the Reformers' emphasis upon conscience and conviction. It appears that the emphasis upon conviction quickly led to introspection and to concern about the subjective certainty of salvation. The subjective concern for assurance, in turn, appears to have occasioned a more general, and eventually entirely secularized, interest in the workings of the human psyche. "It was not a long step," Mannheim noted, following Troeltsch, "from the doctrine of the subjective certainty of salvation to a psychological standpoint in which gradually the observation of the psychic process, which developed into a veritable curiosity, became more important than the harkening to the criteria of salvation which men had formerly tried to detect in their own souls."[103] The Protestant theology of conscience thus lies behind the distinctively modern understanding of individuality. Indeed, modernity's characteristic emphases upon individuality and rational autonomy were, by and large, championed by Protestants who often explicitly defended the modern self-understanding on the basis of the rights of conscience and conviction. This stance was viewed as a logical extension of the principles of the Reformation.

Interestingly, the Protestant theology of conscience also appears to lie behind the distinctively modern conception of *privacy*. As the Protestant ethic fostered rational and disciplined activity in the public realms of science and the economy, so it also appears to have encouraged disciplined rationality in the private world of the bourgeois home. Along this line, it has been suggested that Protestant family life contributed substantially, perhaps even crucially, to the socialization of autonomous

103. Karl Mannheim, *Ideology and Utopia*, 34.

individuality since the seventeenth century.[104] The Protestant ethic thus appears to lie behind the modern notion of the right to privacy, and behind the emergence of the basic liberal commitment to rationalizing such public concerns as health care and public education, as well as behind the rationalization of modern science and the industrial economy.[105] The odd bifurcation of the modern self into public and private identities also appears to issue from an originally Protestant source, for while the stress upon rational self-discipline was in principle the same in the home as it was in the workplace, Protestants allowed for a separation of these activities, a separation that would eventually become a divorce.

Admittedly, early modern scientific epistemology and the Protestant theology of conscience did not, in and of themselves, produce modern individualism. Indeed, the phenomenon of the "loose individual" only began to surface toward the end of the seventeenth century as the religious energy of the Reformation began to wane. More specifically, the modern optimistic and individualistic "scientific" anthropology only emerged after the Protestant commitment to radical self-suspicion implied in the doctrine of original sin had become intellectually incredible.[106] This, for example, is Campbell's conclusion in

104. See Peter L. Berger and Brigitte Berger, *The War over the Family: Capturing the Middle Ground* (Garden City, NY: Anchor, 1983), 109.

105. Ibid., 115.

106. In his article entitled "Changes in the Puritan Concept of Calling or Vocation," *New England Quarterly* 26 (1953): 315-36, Robert S. Michaelson suggested that the movement away from radical self-suspicion was evident in English Puritanism even before the Restoration. Still, there does appear to have been a rather substantial gap between the Protestant and the "humanist" understanding of the self. In an interesting study entitled *The Puritan Origins of the Self* (New Haven: Yale University Press, 1975), Sacvan Bercovitch argues, for example, that while Protestantism and humanism shared an emphasis upon the individual over and against institutions as such, Protestants insisted upon the need for the radical reconstitution of the individual such that he or she reflected the life of Christ as embodied in the Church. Needless to say, secular humanists did not see the need for this, and their emphasis was upon the "self-fulfillment" of the individual who already possesses within himself the means for this task. "The humanists differed from the Reformers," Bercovitch writes (pp. 11-12), "neither in their worldliness nor in their optimism, but in their individualism. Whether they saw man as the quintessence of dust or as the paragon of creation, a very god in action and apprehension, it was the microcosm that held their attention . . . each of these writers [Petrarch, Montaigne, etc.] declares the primacy of the single

The Romantic Ethic and the Spirit of Consumerism. English Sentimentalism and eventually Romanticism, he suggests, emerge out of the Arminian repudiation of strict Calvinism on the part of the Cambridge Platonists and Latitudinarian Anglican divines. The rejection of the doctrines of original sin and predestination, Campbell observes, as well as the distaste of "dogma" generally, had the effect of shifting the religious focus away from salvation *per se,* to the present *experience* of "spirituality" within eighteenth-century bourgeois culture.[107]

Still, the basic Protestant emphases upon individual conscience and upon such things as the practical improvement of the material conditions of life do appear to have laid a foundation for the emergence of a distinctively modern self-understanding, and they are still dimly discernible beneath the surface of the contemporary therapeutic preoccupation with self-development and self-construction. This is yet another reason why the distinctively modern form of worldliness has proven so difficult for Protestants to recognize and to resist. Indeed, contemporary Protestant churches have themselves become primary carriers of therapeutic sensibilities. As Marsha Witten observed recently after surveying the content of contemporary Protestant sermons in *All Is Forgiven: The Secular Message in American Protestantism* (1993):

> The language of many of the sermons [today] . . . does not merely restrict God to the realm of subjective apprehension; it also provides an important mechanism for the reinforcement and continuation of this practice. As this God speaks to our own subjectivities in reflecting them, he justifies our concern with them. The God created in this speech validates human beings' incessant interest in their private inner workings. God legitimates people's fascination with the depths of their emotional experiences. This is a God whose transcendent qualities have, for the most part, disappeared; a God who, in his

---

separate person, and justifies his self-study on its intrinsic merits, without pretense at religious or even moral instruction. He assumes that what he has thought and done will interest others because it is authentically his, the product of his own personality in all its rich uniqueness. . . ."

107. See Campbell, *The Romantic Ethic and the Spirit of Consumerism,* chapter 6: *The Other Protestant Ethic,* 99ff.; Campbell's source for much of this material is John W. Draper, *The Funeral Elegy and the Rise of English Romanticism* (London: Frank Cass, 1929).

immanence and understanding, smiles benevolently on the age of psychology.[108]

To the extent that Witten's reading of the situation is accurate, it does indeed suggest the *triumph* of therapeutic sensibilities in contemporary culture, for they appear now to have supplanted even the Protestant insights that initially gave rise to them. We do indeed appear to have arrived at the end of a particular line of historical development.

Modern Self-Absorption and the Destruction of Personality

In spite of the contemporary preoccupation with individuality and with the autonomous construction and reconstruction of the self by means of psychological insights and therapeutic regimens of self-help, genuine self-knowledge continues to elude our grasp. Indeed, real self-understanding appears further removed today than it was when the distinctively modern project of self-construction by means of rational technique began three hundred years ago. The plight of the modern therapeutic individual is thus, as Ernest Becker put it in *The Denial of Death* (1973), that he or she is "a sinner with no word for it or worse, who looks for the word for it in a dictionary of psychology and thus only aggravates the problem of his separateness and hyper-consciousness."[109] The contemporary quest for self-realization by means of psychological therapies of self-knowledge is, in other words, a cul-de-sac. By its very nature, the therapeutic quest for self-discovery must end in self-deception and, finally, in self-annihilation. In the first instance, turning to psychological therapies tends only to exacerbate the problem of individualism, thereby aggravating the alienation that made us turn to therapy in the first place.[110] Add to

108. Marsha G. Witten, *All Is Forgiven: The Secular Message in American Protestantism* (Princeton: Princeton University Press, 1993), 132.

109. Becker, *The Denial of Death*, 198.

110. Peter and Brigitte Berger make this point in *The War over the Family*. Modern psychology and psychotherapy, they write (p. 121), serve to legitimate "the normative assumptions of hyper-individualism. The latter is based on two psychological presuppositions: that the individual self is the *only reality* in the human sphere, and that this

this the fact that scientific psychology typically dissolves human moral agency into prior causes, and it is no wonder that modern psychological man is confused and frustrated. Indeed, it has been suggested that psychoanalysis is itself the disease for which it claims to be the cure.[111] As Becker noted:

> All the analysis in the world doesn't allow the person to find out *who he is* and why he is here on earth, why he has to die, and how he can make his life a triumph. It is when psychology pretends to do this, when it offers itself as a full explanation of human unhappiness, that it becomes a fraud that makes the situation of modern man an impasse from which he cannot escape.[112]

The supreme irony of the contemporary "culture of narcissism," a culture obsessed with self-development and self-actualization, is thus that it fails, finally, to produce real human persons. Neither self-realization by means of therapeutic technique, nor by means of the sheer will-to-self-definition, is capable of bearing the full weight of human personality. Christianity is able to bear this weight, and did in fact bear it for much of our culture's long history, but the quasi-religious therapeutic regimens which have arisen to replace Christianity in the name of individual liberty and/or rational science are simply not up to the task. As a result, contemporary culture is characterized either by ever-more-fascinating distractions that temporarily shield us from the pain of not knowing who we are, or by ever-more-inventive therapeutic options which hold out the hope that perhaps we can construct ourselves by ourselves after all. Both obstruct the development of real personality.

---

reality is the result of a *process* that in principle can be interfered with in a deliberate way. In other words, only the individual is real, as against the pseudo realities of all and any collective entities; and the individual, by himself or with the help of experts, can go about modifying and styling his own self — identity ceases to be a given and becomes a project. . . ."

111. Karl Krauss, cited in Neil Postman, *Technopoly: The Surrender of Culture to Technology* (New York: Vintage, 1993), 86.

112. Becker, *The Denial of Death*, 193.

The Self before God

Ernest Becker's dramatic assertion that all the analysis in the world does not finally allow a person to know who he or she is, was inspired by a little book written almost a hundred and fifty years ago entitled *The Sickness unto Death: A Christian Psychological Exposition for Upbuilding and Awakening* (1849) by Søren Kierkegaard. The human person, or *self*, Kierkegaard observed, is essentially relational and is, within certain limits, essentially free. For this reason, human beings achieve genuine selfhood only in freely relating to others, and in allowing others freedom in this relation. Thus, for example, the master of a slave could not be said to possess a genuine self, for in denying freedom to the one to whom he is related — his slave — the master undermines the possibility of realizing his own selfhood, as well as that of his slave. The quality of our own self-consciousness, in other words, will depend upon the quality of our relations with others. For us to experience freedom, we must preserve the freedom of those to whom we relate; and we must enhance the quality of their self-consciousness if we are to enhance the quality of our own. The others to whom we relate, Kierkegaard observed furthermore, determine the degree of self-consciousness it will be possible for us to achieve. Thus the self-development of a farmer who related only to his animals must necessarily be rather stunted and limited by the possibilities of animal communication. Along this line, Kierkegaard insisted that we are ultimately enabled to achieve full and authentic selfhood only as we are called into relation with the Person of God, the ultimate Self and the creator of human selfhood, and only if we respond to his call in love and trust. Only in such a relation is genuine self-transcendence and true self-consciousness possible.

"Generally speaking," Kierkegaard observed, "consciousness — that is, self-consciousness — is decisive with regard to the self. The more consciousness, the more self; the more consciousness, the more will; the more will, the more self. A person who has no will at all is not a self; but the more will he has, the more self-consciousness he has also."[113] Kierkegaard went on to observe that self-consciousness is requisite for salvation, Christianly understood, for salvation consists in willing to be freely and intimately related to God in love and trust. Self-consciousness

113. Kierkegaard, *The Sickness unto Death*, 29.

is also enhanced by faith, however, for, again, the quality of the relation to God is such that we are enabled to become what we could not become apart from it. "I no longer call you servants," Jesus says to us (John 15:15), "because a servant does not know his master's business. Instead, I have called you friends, for everything that I learned from my Father I have made known to you." Needless to say, friendship with Jesus and knowledge of the Father's business fantastically amplify the possibilities of our existence. Indeed, self-consciousness, individuality, and selfhood are God's greatest gifts to us, and an inevitable consequence of becoming a Christian is — or ought to be — a kind of "intensification" of one's own self-consciousness in which one's love for God and neighbor is progressively realized and deepened.

The problem, of course, is that we stubbornly and persistently refuse to be related to God in love and trust. In fact, this stubborn and persistent refusal is what, Christianly speaking, defines the fallen human condition in sin, for sin is ultimately a relational disorder. This, after all, is why David confessed (Ps. 51:4): "Against you, you only, have I sinned and done what is evil in your sight." While the reasons for our refusal to be related to God are hidden in the mystery of freedom, the Scriptures suggest that this refusal has something to do with the fact that we would rather try to realize our selfhood *by ourselves* than to realize ourselves in relation to God. Again, as the Psalmist says (Ps. 2:3): "The kings of the earth take their stand and the rulers gather together against the LORD and against his Anointed One. 'Let us break their chains,' they say, 'and throw off their fetters.'" The consequences of this rebellion and of our stubborn refusal to submit to God in love and trust surround us on all sides in the form of twisted and damaged relationships and in the way of distorted selfhood. Kierkegaard labeled our sorry condition "despair."

Kierkegaard also made the sobering observation that just as the intensification of self-consciousness is the requisite of genuine faith, so it also discloses the possibility of true spiritual evil, that is, the possibility of *conscious* repudiation of the things of God. When this repudiation achieves full consciousness, furthermore, it may be said to be demonic. After all, the New Testament tells us that the demons *knew* who Jesus was, and hated him anyway. The unforgivable sin against the Holy Spirit (Matt. 12:32; Mark 3:29; Luke 12:10) may be cited in this connection as well. Although self-consciousness — freedom — is God's greatest gift to us, then, it is also our greatest burden, for it exposes us to the awesome necessity of having to choose how we will respond to God's call to us. "No man," Kierkegaard observed:

> shall presume to leave Christ's life in abeyance as a curiosity. When God lets himself be born and become man, this is not an idle caprice, some fancy he hits upon just to be doing something, perhaps to put an end to the boredom that has brashly been said must be involved in being God — it is not in order to have an adventure. No, when God does this, then this fact is the earnestness of existence. And, in turn, the earnestness in this earnestness is: that everyone *shall* have an opinion about it.[114]

When we are confronted by the gospel of grace, then, we must choose to give ourselves to God in faith or to resort either to the project of autonomous self-realization or to a kind of pathological attempt to escape from freedom and selfhood altogether. The latter two are the avenues of despair, the sickness unto death.

Of course, the secular quality of modern social life betrays a kind of collective *refusal* to relate a great many of the things we do in the world to God. And so, although the term "despair" is usually only used to refer to an individual state of mind, it is a useful concept in describing the quality of our culture as a whole. Contemporary culture is one in which genuine individuality and true self-consciousness have, precisely as a result of its secularity and will-to-self-definition, become increasingly problematic. Contemporary culture is indeed sick unto death. It inhibits the possibility of genuine relatedness, both to God and to others. In this connection, Kierkegaard observed that the secular mentality always attributes infinite worth to objects unworthy of it, and attributes finite worth to truly infinite objects. Secular society thus tempts us to focus a great deal of our time and energy on matters which are merely accidental to our true selves, and consequently to neglect those things which are essential to ourselves and our persons:

> Surrounded by hordes of men, absorbed in all sorts of secular matters, more and more shrewd about the ways of the world — such a person

114. Ibid., 130.

forgets himself, forgets his name divinely understood, does not dare
to believe in himself, finds it too hazardous to believe in himself and
far easier and safer to be like the others, to become a copy, a number,
a mass man. . . . In fact, what is called the secular mentality consists
simply of such men who, so to speak, mortgage themselves to the
world. They use their capacities, amass money, carry on secular enterprises, calculate shrewdly, etc., perhaps make a name in history,
but themselves they are not; spiritually speaking, they have no self,
no self for whose sake they could venture everything, no self before
God — however self-seeking they are otherwise.[115]

The little phrase "no self before God — however self-seeking they are
otherwise" is pointed quite deliberately at modern culture. With these
few words, Kierkegaard both anticipated and condemned the modern
will-to-self-definition and the contemporary culture of therapeutic narcissism. The typically modern project of self-development and self-
construction cannot succeed, Kierkegaard saw, precisely because of its
self-centeredness and secularity. The project is premised upon a refusal
to enter into the only relation that can possibly make genuine self-
consciousness possible. In effect, precisely to the extent that we have
allowed our bloated subjectivity to eclipse the reality of God from view,
we have eliminated the possibility of becoming truly ourselves. In short,
as Becker observed, we are simply not capable of constructing ourselves.
Rather, we are only *enabled* to become ourselves in and through the
power of the Creator of selfhood. "For whoever wants to save his life
will lose it," Jesus says to us (Matt. 16:25), "but whoever loses his life
for me will find it." Living in this knowledge, Kierkegaard insisted, is to
live *before God*.

Of course, it has been suggested that modern society and culture

115. Ibid., 33-34, 35. In his *Concluding Unscientific Postscript*, trans. David F.
Swenson and Walter Lowrie (1846; Princeton: Princeton University Press, 1941),
Kierkegaard commented (p. 219): "Essentially it is the God-relationship that makes a
man a man, and yet [the secular mass man] lacked this. No one would hesitate, however,
to regard him as a real man (for the absence of inwardness is not directly apparent); in
reality he would constitute a sort of marionette, very deceptively imitating everything
human — even to the extent of having children by his wife. At the end of his life, one
would have to say that one thing had escaped him: his consciousness had taken no note
of God."

are not simply characterized by secularity but by a kind of *anti*-theology and by the more or less *conscious* rejection of the things of God, and specifically by a conscious rejection of Christianity. Indeed, as any number of observers have lamented, our modern will-to-self-definition by means of scientific, technological, and/or economic progress and by means of ideological programs of social change, and our modern willingness to ecstatically surrender ourselves to such programs, are both linked to the repudiation of the Christian tradition.[116] The ambiguous quality of modernity's "liberation" is thus dialectically related to the Christian religion. As George Steiner observed in a series of lectures entitled *Nostalgia for the Absolute* (1974):

> The major mythologies constructed in the West since the early nineteenth century are not only attempts to fill the emptiness left by the decay of Christian theology and Christian dogma. They are themselves a kind of *substitute theology*. They are systems of belief and argument which may be savagely antireligious, which may postulate a world without God and may deny an afterlife, but whose structure, whose aspirations, whose claims on the believer, are profoundly religious in strategy and effect.[117]

The typically modern virtues of individual autonomy, freedom, progress, etc., in other words, while all Christian in origin, have by now been more or less consciously employed to undermine the authority, first of the Christian Church, and now even of God himself. This intentional secularization has, ironically, made genuine individuality, true freedom, and real progress impossible for us. And so the modern world has become fateful and incapable of sustaining human personality. Such is the earnestness of existence.

Yet before we become too discouraged by this result, it may help to recall that Kierkegaard suggested that the secular mentality represented only a fairly low level of self-consciousness, and indeed that the

116. See, for example, Karl Löwith, *Meaning in History: The Theological Implications of the Philosophy of History* (Chicago: University of Chicago Press, 1949); and, more recently, David Walsh, *After Ideology: Recovering the Spiritual Foundations of Freedom* (San Francisco: HarperSanFrancisco, 1990).

117. George Steiner, *Nostalgia for the Absolute* (Toronto: Canadian Broadcasting Corporation, 1974), 4.

persons who "mortgage themselves to the world" of secular affairs do so, by and large, unwittingly. Many are simply unconscious of even having a self before God. They have not yet dared to believe in themselves, and have simply submerged themselves in mass society and culture, perhaps believing that their only destiny is to be like all the others anyway. As sad as this state of affairs is, there is still a significant element of hope in it, for this kind of more or less unconscious secularity does not yet disclose the fully self-conscious repudiation of the things of God. The contemporary situation is still redeemable, therefore, for it has not yet become fully demonic. Thus, in spite of the fact that the larger society and culture may well exhibit the marks of the conscious rejection of the LORD and of his anointed one, and in spite of the fact that the individuals who inhabit modern society and culture are indeed egregiously inhibited from finding themselves by modernity's will-to-self-definition, many of these individuals have not yet heard the gospel, and have not yet made their decision with respect to it. The harvest is still plentiful (Matt. 9:37; Luke 10:2). We have not yet arrived at the end of history.

CHAPTER FIVE

Taking Stock of "The Huge Modern Heresy"

Modern man, who has emancipated himself from God's order and usurped the rights of God, has also made for himself the claim: "Behold, I make all things new." Having somehow become omnipotent in his dominion over nature, he thinks himself able to throw overboard all tradition and to create a perfectly new order according to his own design. This new order, however, always carried the stamp of technical rationality. As he overlays nature with his man-made, artificial second nature, by technical civilization, so he also substitutes for already slowly developed culture an artificial, planned civilization, which is ugly and inhuman and destructive of real creativity. . . .

Emil Brunner[1]

The huge modern heresy is to alter the human soul to fit modern social conditions, instead of altering modern social conditions to fit the human soul.

G. K. Chesterton[2]

1. Emil Brunner, *Christianity and Civilization, Part Two: Specific Problems* (New York: Charles Scribner's Sons, 1949), 41.
2. Adapted from G. K. Chesterton, *What's Wrong with the World?* (New York: Sheed & Ward, 1910), 104.

237

The primary purpose of our study thus far has been to identify and to discuss aspects of modern society and culture which render secularity and practical atheism plausible. We have tried to show that secularity is quite literally built into the central institutions of modern society and culture both theoretically and practically, and that this is why modernity has proven to be so corrosive of Christian faith and why it is so resistant to substantive theological criticism. The modern political apparatus, for example, invites something very much like religious adoration and encourages us to locate more and more of our aspirations in the possibilities of immanent political-social change. Modern science continues to disclose the structural secrets of the universe, and modern technology advances from one technical triumph to another, both without any apparent need of the so-called "god hypothesis." The modern economy continues to churn out its revolutionary consequences, transforming the material conditions of our lives, and evidently functioning all the more efficiently and effectively in the absence of substantive religious reflection. And all of these characteristically modern endeavors both presuppose and foster a uniquely anthropocentric self-understanding in which we are encouraged, not simply to discover our own meanings and purposes for ourselves, but, in effect, to create them *ex nihilo*. And so, although the temptation to godlessness is not new, it has been rendered uniquely plausible, attractive, and even imperative under modern, and now presumably "postmodern," conditions. To the extent that worldliness lies in an interpretation of reality that excludes the reality of the living God from the world, the heart of contemporary society and culture must be judged — in spite of its largely Christian origins — to be profoundly worldly. This is the way of the modern world.

Yet from a Christian point of view, the crucial threat that the modern world poses to faith does not actually lie in the denial of God's existence, as much as it lies in the tacit repudiation of divine *authority*. The question modernity raises — even for Christians — is whether or not God possesses any real authority to define our everyday existence. Of course, when the question is stated this way, it begs an affirmative response, for the very notion of "god" presupposes a measure of authority over the world. But even assuming we believe that God exists, do we really understand his existence to have any real bearing on our own practical circumstances here and now? Modern society and culture function in such a way as to discourage us from believing this. Indeed, contemporary social existence is such that we are discouraged from embracing anything beyond the belief that God might somehow be of use within the ongoing construction of private identity: obviously a very far cry from the obedience of faith to which Christians are called (Rom. 1:5). The godlessness of contemporary society and culture may thus be seen to be an evasion, finally, of the lordship of God.[3] As Tage Lindbom observes at the beginning of a powerful essay on modern democracy:

> Who will rule, God or man? This is the great constitutional question of human existence; this is the question that determines everything in mortal life, and especially and most acutely in our social arrangements. . . . The perennial question is always whether we humans are to understand our presence on this earth as a vice-regency or trusteeship under the mandate of heaven and the divine commandments, or whether we must strive to emancipate ourselves from any higher dominion, with human supremacy as our ultimate aim.[4]

Yet the contemporary evasion of the "mandate of heaven," as Lindbom puts it, is not accomplished by the outright rejection of divine authority, though explicit atheism does occasionally surface in modern culture. More commonly it is accomplished simply by way of neglect. Under modern conditions, the question of God is simply irrelevant to so much of what we do on a daily basis that it eventually drops out of mind and heart. God is simply forgotten. Bearing in mind Jesus' enigmatic reply to the question of whether taxes should be paid to Caesar or not, we find that after all those things that belong to modern society and culture have been rendered to them, there simply is not very much left over to render to God, even if we still believe in him.

To say that modern society is profoundly worldly is not to say that it presents a uniformly secular front, however. Indeed, a number of curious ironies float very near the surface of modern culture, and one of them is the striking contemporary coincidence of radical secularity and furious religiosity. The same culture that celebrated the "death of God" and the triumph of an entirely "secular theology" only

---

3. This is the thesis of Klaus Bockmuehl's essay "Secularism and Theology," *Crux* 19 (June 1983):13.

4. Tage Lindbom, *The Myth of Democracy* (Grand Rapids: Eerdmans, 1996), 18.

a generation ago seems prepared to believe virtually anything anyone has to say about the "gods," transcendence, and spirituality today. The recent return to the sacred appears to stem, at least in part, from a loss of secular nerve. Having liberated ourselves from a divinely inspired and therefore inherently meaningful universe, we find that we are now plagued by an acute sense of insecurity and homelessness. We are terrified by the freedom we have grasped, even if we are not willing to let go of it. This appears to explain why contemporary culture exhibits a longing for a *real* God, in spite of the fact that all of the various modern "theologies" tend to leave the modern will-to-self-definition largely intact, thereby repudiating divine authority. Apparently we want the coherence that the *idea* of God was once able to provide for our culture without the inconvenience of actually having to obey the living God.

Contemporary society and culture also exhibit the ironic coincidence of autonomous individuality and oppressive cultural homogeneity. As one recent observer put it rather wryly: "Modernity promised us a culture of unintimidated, curious, rational, self-reliant individuals, and it produced . . . a herd society, a race of anxious, timid, conformist 'sheep,' and a culture of utter banality."[5] And so, while our collective aspirations may well be strikingly Promethean, we are, as individuals, much more hesitant. Indeed, the grand modern project, which has always been humanistically inspired and legitimated, has actually proven to be quite oppressive of real individuality. G. K. Chesterton insisted that this is the huge heresy of the modern world. Whereas social conditions ought to be tailored to the needs of real individuals, Chesterton observed, the individual soul is now altered to fit modern social conditions. It appears that not only have the rational-technical means we have employed in the service of the modern desire for absolute autonomy failed to liberate us spiritually, but our utilization of these means has created a situation in which humanistically inspired modern society and culture have by now assumed a kind of fate-like quality over and against us. While we remain committed to the ideals of rational individuality and to the project of autonomous self-construction, we have also committed ourselves to theoretical paradigms and, even more importantly, to practical schemes

5. Robert Pippen, *Modernism as a Philosophical Problem* (Oxford: Basil Blackwell, 1990), 22.

which permit little, if any, room for genuinely personal existence. The vast market that exists today for elaborate forms of diversion and distraction reflects this irony, just as it illustrates the odd coincidence of deeply personal longing with the utilization of profoundly impersonal methods. Indeed, even as we utilize the inherently impersonal modern industrial economy to produce and distribute multi-million-dollar films, increasingly exotic travel opportunities, computers capable of fabricating "virtual reality" and other clever consumer electronic devices, designer fashions, and a panoply of standardized products designed for mass consumption, we purchase and consume these products in the hopes of realizing authentic individuality. We have apparently become convinced that the alchemy of self-construction must somehow render these impersonal and standardized products individually and personally fulfilling; and the fact that it does not only intensifies our need for more effective forms of diversion and distraction. It is a viciously hollow cycle, and yet we appear to be quite willing to participate in it. Here we are reminded of Kierkegaard's contention, cited in the Introduction, that modernity's characteristic depravity is the contempt for actual individuality. While such contempt emanates most visibly from the institutional realities of modern society and culture, Kierkegaard rightly observed that it is, finally, our own fault. "Fascinated and deceived by a magic witchery," Kierkegaard complained, "no one *wants* to be an individual human being . . . [emphasis added]."6

The most profound ironies that haunt the modern imagination may thus be said to stem from the odd coincidence of secularity and impersonality in modern society and culture. Just as we have managed to throw off the fetters of traditional religion, so we have found ourselves hard-pressed by the "gods" of rational-technical practicality, bureaucratic efficiency, cost effectiveness, productivity, and market conditions, as well as those of self-fulfillment, the immediate experience of well-being, "need," etc. Just as we have become increasingly incapable of apprehending and of having any relation with anything genuinely independent of ourselves, so it seems that we have found it increasingly difficult to get along with each other and to understand ourselves. The ironic and unforeseen consequence of attempting to achieve mastery over the world and over ourselves, in other words, has actually been

6. Søren Kierkegaard, *Concluding Unscientific Postscript*, trans. David F. Swenson and Walter Lowrie (Princeton: Princeton University Press, 1941), 317.

estrangement; estrangement from God, from the world, from each other, and from ourselves — in short, estrangement from *real* life.

John Macmurray contended that it is, after all, our preoccupation with mastery that accounts for "the crisis of the personal" in modern culture.[7] Along this line, Macmurray simply observed that the typically modern endeavor to take control of the world has forced us to subordinate the personal dimensions of life to its functional aspect. The desire for rational control, in other words, required us to focus on how things — as well as people — can be made to function in the service of such worthy goals as the rationalization of political and social order. Of course, the focus on the functional aspect of life was supposed to have been just a temporary measure, necessary only until rational mastery was established. As it turned out, however, the functional orientation has actually become a permanent feature of modern institutional life. Macmurray further observed that the subordination of the personal dimensions of life to merely functional considerations has only accelerated in the absence of religious understanding, and particularly in the absence of Christian theology. The contemporary decline of religion, Macmurray suggested:

> betrays, and in turn intensifies, a growing insensitiveness to the personal aspects of life, and a growing indifference to personal values. Christianity, in particular, is the exponent and the guardian of the personal, and the function of organized Christianity in our history has been to foster and maintain the personal life and to bear continuous witness, in symbol and doctrine, to the ultimacy of personal values. If this influence is removed or ceases to be effective, the awareness of personal issues will tend to be lost, in the pressure of functional preoccupations. . . . The sense of personal dignity as well as of personal unworthiness will atrophy with the decline in habits of self-examination. Ideals of sanctity or holiness will begin to seem incomprehensible or even comical. Success will tend to become the criterion of rightness, and there will spread through society a temper which is extroverted, pragmatic and merely objective, for which all problems are soluble by better organization.[8]

7. John Macmurray, *The Self as Agent* (London: Faber & Faber, 1957), 30.
8. Ibid., 30-31.

Modernity's dogged secularity — and in particular its obdurate repudiation of the Christian God — has thus resulted in the demise of personal existence *as such*. At the same time and for exactly the same reasons that God's existence has become increasingly implausible for us, so it seems that we have found it increasingly difficult to make sense of individuality and of personal existence. Having lost sight of truly personal existence, furthermore, we have unwittingly — though not altogether unwillingly — surrendered ourselves to impersonal institutional realities and have, in effect, consented to the depersonalization of modern society and culture. Such is the dialectic of godlessness or, as Kierkegaard put it, the earnestness of existence. "When God is displaced as the focus and unity of things," Colin Gunton recently noted similarly, "the function he performs does not disappear, but is exercised by some other source of unity — some other universal. This universal is false because it does not encompass the realities of human relations and of our placing in the world, and so operates deceptively or oppressively."[9] Those who worship idols made by the hands of humans, so the Psalmist says, "will be like them, and so will all who trust in them" (Ps. 115:8).

So how, as Christians, do we go about living *in* but not *of* this modern world? This is the question we have been preparing to answer over the course of our study and, although the brief meditations offered at the end of each of the last four chapters were meant to contribute to an answer to this crucial question, we have arrived at the point where we must begin to try to answer it more fully and systematically. Of course, at the most important level our hope is simply that, having now seen how destructive the way of the modern world is of genuine individuality and personality, we would be moved to pray for God's grace, for we have no hope beyond his gracious provision. More specifically, however, what we need to pray for is the grace to apprehend the huge heresy of modernity's secularity and impersonality, to expose and to lament this heresy, and, where possible, to offer resistance to it. Political scientist Glenn Tinder captured this task recently under the heading of Christianity's "prophetic stance."[10]

9. Colin E. Gunton, *The One, the Three and the Many: God, Creation and the Culture of Modernity* (Cambridge: Cambridge University Press, 1993), 31.

10. Glenn Tinder, *The Political Meaning of Christianity: The Prophetic Stance, An Interpretation* (San Francisco: HarperSanFrancisco, 1989).

On the basis of the unconditional love shown to us in Jesus Christ, Tinder reasons, we are as Christians able to appreciate what true love really entails. "We love," the apostle John reminds us (1 John 4:19), "because he first loved us." It has also been revealed to us in Jesus' glorious resurrection from the dead, and in his ascension into heaven, that human destiny far transcends "this-worldly" existence. Indeed, "this-worldly" existence is entirely relativized over and against "the world to come" in Christian understanding. "Do not store up for yourselves treasures on earth, where moth and rust destroy, and where thieves break in and steal," Jesus warns us (Matt. 6:19-20), "[b]ut store up for yourselves treasures in heaven, where moth and rust do not destroy, and where thieves do not break in and steal." Yet because we have also been alerted to the deadly seriousness of sin, we are also, as Christians, aware of the fact that the world at large is absolutely incapable of appreciating either the nature of true love or the matter of eternal life, for both are revealed only by the Spirit of Christ. Indeed, from the perspective of the world, *agape* and the Kingdom of God are simply foolishness.

Taken together, the basic Christian insights about love and sin mean that, as Christians, we will always find ourselves in tension with the world at large. We will, for example, find ourselves in the awkward position of insisting that people be treated with very great care socially, economically, and politically, while refusing to pledge allegiance to any of the ideologies that promise to do just this. Indeed, just as Jesus refused to give himself to the crowd because he "knew what was in a man" (John 2:25), so we must also take human life so seriously that we refuse to simply entrust it to humanly constructed systems of care. Needless to say, the world at large will neither understand nor appreciate this reticence. In short, the "prophetic stance" requires us to take political, economic, and cultural realities seriously for the sake of our neighbor, but it forbids us from taking them with ultimate seriousness for precisely this same reason. As Jacques Ellul contended at the conclusion of his polemic *The New Demons* (1975):

> The fight of faith to which we are committed is not a fight against man. It is not a question of destroying him, of convincing him that he is wrong. It is a fight for his freedom. Reinserted into a sacred, a prisoner of his myths, he is completely alienated in his neoreligions — this brave "modern man." Every religion is both necessary and

alienating. To smash these idols, to desacralize these mysteries, to assert the falseness of these religions is to undertake the one, finally indispensable liberation of the person of our times.[11]

The prophetic stance is complicated today, however, by the fact that Christians — and particularly Protestant Christians — *have* been criticizing modernity for several hundred years already, and not without considerable effect. Indeed, the present existence of many institutions designed to enhance individual existence — the establishment and protection of human rights, public education, hospitals and medical research facilities, programs of public assistance, and the like — is a reflection of past, largely Protestant, attempts to humanize the modern social order. Yet in spite of these notable achievements, the Church's prophetic reparation of modernity has obviously not been able to stem the tide of secularization. Why not? In retrospect, it appears that one of the reasons for this is that, even as our predecessors sought to reform modern society and culture, they mistakenly harbored certain characteristically modern assumptions, assumptions that frustrated the prophetic stance and that have, by now, come back to haunt the Church. Before attempting to outline a Christian theology of personal existence in our final chapter, therefore, we should see if we can determine, briefly, what some of these assumptions may have been and what, if anything, we can learn from our own past.

Mistaken Accommodation of Modernity

Given the close connection between the Christian Church — and particularly the Protestant churches — and the development of modern society and culture, it is hardly surprising that Protestant theologians have repeatedly sought to accommodate modern ideas and assumptions within Christian theology. Along this line, some accommodation has perhaps been inevitable, for the Scriptures do not comprehend all fields of human knowledge, and the biblical tradition is open in principle — by way of its understanding of general revelation — to the possibility of natural wisdom and science. Indeed, Christian theologians have, from

11. Jacques Ellul, *The New Demons* (New York: Seabury Press, 1975), 228.

the very beginning, borrowed ideas and theories from pagan sources, especially for the sake of interpreting the natural world. The problems have arisen, however, when the ideas and assumptions thus borrowed have been elevated to the status of revealed doctrine. As Stephen Toulmin has noted with respect to Christianity and science:

> Twice already, Christian theologians have committed themselves enthusiastically to the detailed ideas of particular systems of scientific theory. This happened, firstly, when the medieval church naturalized Aristotle, and gave his views about nature an authority beyond their true strength: secondly, when, from the 1680s up to the late nineteenth century, Protestant thinkers (especially in Britain) based a new religious cosmology on mechanical ideas about nature borrowed from Descartes and Newton, as interpreted by an edifying reading of the argument from design. In both cases, the results were unfortunate. Having plunged too deep in their original scientific commitments, the theologians concerned failed to foresee the possibility that Aristotle's or Newton's principles might not forever be the last word; and when radical changes took place in the natural sciences, they were unprepared to deal with them.[12]

And so it was that, as Alasdair MacIntyre has suggested, the "God" in whom the eighteenth- and nineteenth-century philosophers disbelieved may really only have been invented in the natural theology of the seventeenth century.[13]

As unfortunate as these scientific commitments may have been, however, the most damaging theological accommodation to modern ideas and assumptions did not lie so much in the acceptance of Cartesian or Newtonian principles, but in the acceptance of the validity of the modern project of attempting to master nature for the sake of human comfort and convenience. Indeed, this is one of the crucial ideas that has animated so much of the process of secularization in recent centu-

12. Stephen Toulmin, "The Historicization of Natural Science: Its Implications for Theology," in *Paradigm Change in Theology*, ed. Hans Küng and David Tracy (New York: Crossroad, 1989), 237.

13. Alasdair MacIntyre and Paul Ricoeur, *The Religious Significance of Atheism* (New York: Columbia University Press, 1969).

ries. As Leszek Kolakowski noted recently in a series of essays entitled *Modernity on Endless Trial* (1990): "The perception of religious sensibility as meaningless resulted neither from science nor from the possible conflict between scientific truth and the content of revelation, but from human preferences and from the priority given, on our scale of values, to those kinds of mental activities that were likely to increase the scope of our domination of nature; science was something to be trusted in terms of verifiable effects; religion could not be trusted in the same sense."[14]

Our study thus far has revealed a number of examples of the distinctively modern "scale of values." The enlightened suggestion that the Christian religion was to be reinterpreted in terms of the practical improvement of the material conditions of life, for example, entailed a kind of reversal of classical Christian priorities and shifted the focus away from eternal life and toward the practical exigencies of life in this world. The much-discussed "Protestant ethic," furthermore, appears itself to have been a kind of amalgamation of Christian and modern assumptions eventually geared exclusively toward this-worldly concerns and purposes. Along this line, Barth's analysis of the inversion of eighteenth-century Protestant priorities in his study *Protestant Theology in the Nineteenth Century* (1972) sheds some helpful light on the early concessions Protestant theologians made to the distinctively modern project.[15]

Barth discusses the problem of Protestant accommodation of modern ideas and assumptions under the heading of "humanization" and notes that, while certain Protestant theologians sought to accommodate political assumptions about the sovereignty of nation-states within the evangelical theology of the eighteenth century, others tried to accommodate bourgeois morality and individuality. Still others sought to accommodate the assumptions of early modern science. Barth contended that it was these eighteenth-century modifications of Protestant theology that set the stage for Protestantism's slide into "liberalism" and eventually into secularity in the nineteenth and twentieth centuries.

14. Leszek Kolakowski, *Modernity on Endless Trial* (Chicago: University of Chicago Press, 1990), 97-98.

15. Karl Barth, *Protestant Theology in the Nineteenth Century: Its Background and History* (London: S.C.M. Press, 1972), 82ff.

Barth insists that, in the end, the "liberal" theological project really only amounted to a kind of absorption of God into the sphere of sovereign human awareness.[16] "From the eighteenth century onward," Barth noted, "Protestant theology . . . acquired that obvious habit of looking round outside, at the circumstances and movements in the Church and the world, before venturing to speak, so as to be able to speak in a timely way, appropriate to reality and to the situation."[17]

Jesuit scholar Michael Buckley elaborated on Barth's insights in a study entitled *At the Origins of Modern Atheism* (1987). Buckley's provocative thesis is that modern Protestant theology has actually been its own worst enemy. Protestant theology has repeatedly produced its own atheistic opposition by means of the apologetic strategies it has adopted to appease modern sensibilities.[18] By attempting to lessen the offense of the gospel, in other words, modern Protestant theologians only exacerbated the problem of modern atheistic opposition to Christianity. In attempting to rescue the Christian faith from the criticism of pure reason, for example, Kant decided to shift theology's focus away from revealed truth and to the practical concerns of living morally in the midst of bourgeois culture. In Kantian theology, then, God was reduced to a postulate of practical moral reasoning, necessary only to guarantee the immortality of the soul and the eventual triumph of good over evil. Schleiermacher subsequently reduced God to a kind of necessary precondition for the possibility of "inwardness" in an attempt to rescue the Christian faith from, among other things, Kantian moralism. Buckley thus suggests that, while both apologetic strategies sought to deliver God from modern skepticism by making human experience the basis of Christian affirmation, they ultimately only elicited the atheistic countermove of Feuerbach. Feuerbach's central contention — that religion in general, and theology in particular, is nothing but the projection of human subjectivity — is simply the inverted mirror image of Kant and Schleiermacher. Far from alleviating the challenge posed to Christian faith by enlightened atheism, then, the apologetic strategies of Kant, Schleiermacher, and other eighteenth- and nineteenth-century Protes-

16. Ibid., 84.

17. Ibid., 139.

18. Michael J. Buckley, *At the Origins of Modern Atheism* (New Haven: Yale University Press, 1987), 332.

tant theologians only served to intensify the problem. In evading the knotty problem of revelation, the strategy of adducing evidence for faith from human experience only reinforced the typically modern suspicion that the Christian religion was simply the product of the human imagination. Thus Buckley concludes after a Barthian fashion:

> Atheism is not the secret of religion, as Feuerbach would have it, but it is the secret contradiction within a religion that denies its own abilities to deal cognitively with what is central to its nature. Atheism is the secret of that religious reflection which justifies the sacred and its access to the sacred primarily through its own transmogrification into another form of human knowledge or practice, as though the only alternative to fideism were such an alienation, as though religion had to become philosophy to remain religion. The unique character of religious knowledge does not survive this reduction. Another discipline cannot be made more fundamental and religion its corollary or its epiphenomenon. Religion, with all of its intersubjectivities, cannot but be destroyed if dissolved into some other human experience in order to justify its most critical cognitive claims. Eventually, such a dissolution will out as atheism.[19]

Or, as Kierkegaard put it earlier and somewhat more poetically:

> When faith begins to feel embarrassed and ashamed, like a young woman for whom her love is no longer sufficient, but who secretly feels ashamed of her lover and must therefore have it established that there is something remarkable about him — when faith thus begins to lose its passion, when faith begins to cease to be faith, then a proof becomes necessary so as to command respect from the side of unbelief.[20]

Of course, by contrast to "liberal" Protestantism, evangelical (conservative) Protestants have prided themselves on their resistance to modern ideas and assumptions and on their preservation of the gospel from "modernist" adulteration. While this is undoubtedly true to some

19. Ibid., 359-60.
20. Kierkegaard, *Concluding Unscientific Postscript*, 31.

extent, especially relative to their "liberal" counterparts, it is important to stress that conservatives have also accommodated typically modern ideas and assumptions within evangelical theology in a number of material ways, and not without profoundly damaging results for evangelical churches. In this connection, it may help to recall our previous discussion of American evangelicalism's unqualified admiration for the methods of modern science and the terrible bind this put them in with respect to the secularization of modern higher education. By assuming the automatic concurrence of natural-scientific and revealed truth, turn-of-the-century evangelical scholars were, in effect, blind-sided by Marxism, Darwinism, Freudianism, and a host of other secular and purportedly "scientific" readings of the human situation.

American evangelical accommodation to modern scientific ideas and assumptions appears to have begun long before the turn of the century, however. Indeed, in his provocative study *The Scandal of the Evangelical Mind* (1994), evangelical historian Mark Noll dates the problem of mistaken accommodation to modernity back at least as far as the turn of the eighteenth century.[21] Along this line, Noll argues that the typically anti-authoritarian and anti-traditional American temper had the effect of biasing early American evangelicals against traditional theological reasoning, and of rendering certain enlightenment principles very attractive to them, particularly those of the so-called Scottish Enlightenment. The Scottish Enlightenment ideal suggested that all human beings are endowed with the innate capacity to grasp the basic principles of nature and morality, and that these principles are best disclosed by means of Baconian science, which was held to be simply an extension of common sense.[22] This "common sense philosophy," as it has been called, provided early American thought with a new *ahistorical* and *anti*-traditional rationale. No longer were any of the traditional props for social order — tradition, divine revelation, history, social hierarchy, inherited government, and the authority of the churches — needed within the American experiment. Instead, the only "principle" that American social order required was that of agreeing to adhere to those natural and moral principles which could be shown to be

21. Mark A. Noll, *The Scandal of the Evangelical Mind* (Grand Rapids, MI: Eerdmans, 1994), 83ff.
22. Ibid., 85.

self-evident by means of "scientific" inquiry. In this connection, we note that, although the American faith in the self-evident nature of these truths has been rather badly shaken of late, American society and culture continue to exhibit a profoundly ahistorical and anti-traditional bias. Yet however dubious "common sense" ideals may now appear, eighteenth-century American evangelical theologians were deeply impressed by them and this, Noll argues, is what accounted for the eventual collusion of evangelical and secular-scientific thought toward the end of the nineteenth century. This, for example, is why the Bible came to be viewed within American fundamentalism as a storehouse of scientifically discoverable facts which could be manipulated and arranged by "scientific" induction to yield the truth on practically any issue or topic.[23] Even faith and conversion would come to be seen in a scientific and mechanical fashion within American evangelicalism. In this connection, one need only recall Charles G. Finney's "new measures" for revival around 1830. And, indeed, the scientistic spirit has surfaced most recently in the manipulative and technical orientation of the so-called "Church Growth movement."[24] Noll thus concludes that it was the accommodation of supposedly "common sense" enlightenment principles, in conjunction with the adoption of republican theories of politics (suspicion of concentrated power), the sensibilities of democratic populism, and the assumptions of classical-liberal economics, that together contributed to twentieth-century evangelicalism's "Christian-American synthesis."[25]

23. Ibid., 98. An important result of this assumption, as Lesslie Newbigin pointed out in *Foolishness to the Greeks: The Gospel and Western Culture* (Grand Rapids, MI: Eerdmans, 1986), p. 46, is that Scripture is encumbered with the burden of a kind of proof that it is not really intended to bear, thus eventually undermining its authority in the minds of all those who take science seriously.

24. See, for example, Lyle Schaller, *Forty-four Ways to Increase Church Attendance* (Nashville: Abingdon, 1988); Norman Shawchuk, Philip Kotler, Bruce Warren, and Gustave Ruth, *Marketing for Congregations* (Nashville: Abingdon, 1971); George Barna, *Marketing the Church* (Colorado Springs: NavPress, 1988); Steven Durkin, *Church Advertising*, Creative Leadership Series, ed. Lyle Schaller (Nashville: Abingdon, 1982); and Larry Hollon, *Promotional Strategies for the Local Church* (Nashville: Broadman Press, 1992). Os Guinness has recently published an insightful critique of the Church Growth movement under the provocative title *Dining with the Devil: The Megachurch Movement Flirts with Modernity* (Grand Rapids, MI: Baker, 1993).

25. Noll, *The Scandal of the Evangelical Mind*, 60.

Two critical assumptions lay behind the American evangelical adoption of the "common sense" outlook. The first was that "common sense" was capable of perceiving both natural and supernatural truths. The second assumption was that, because all truth is ultimately God's truth, the truths revealed by Baconian science must inevitably buttress the revealed truths of Holy Scripture.[26] What eighteenth- and nineteenth-century evangelicals failed to realize, however, is that if unaided "common sense" is able to discern the truths of the human situation, then there is, finally, no real need *for* Holy Scripture. As Marsden has recently noted concerning the revolutionary implications of enlightened moral philosophy:

> By purporting to discover a universal set of rationally based moral principles, the new ["common sense"] ethics was presuming to do for core elements in human experience what the new physics did for the periphery. This audacious yet plausible project seemed entirely complementary to Christianity, since most of the moralists assumed that such a rationally discovered ethic had to originate with the creator, and so could not contradict truly revealed religion. Reinforcing a divinely sanctioned ethic with the authority of universally valid rationality seemed obviously a good thing for civilization. It was hence more difficult to see that this project, at least when it was conducted by pious confessing Christians, also had the potential for making Christian revelation superfluous.[27]

And this project did eventually render biblical religion largely superfluous within American intellectual culture. The process took well over a century but, as Marsden goes on to note, once Christianity had been defined simply in terms of the ethical ideals of freedom, science, and service, it was inevitable that questions would arise as to the relevance of the Christian religion *as such* to the advance of American civilization.[28] Not surprisingly, then, American intellectual culture has, since

26. See Timothy Dwight Bozeman, *Protestants in an Age of Science: The Baconian Ideal and Antebellum American Religious Thought* (Chapel Hill, NC: University of North Carolina Press, 1977).

27. George M. Marsden, *The Soul of the American University: From Protestant Establishment to Established Nonbelief* (New York: Oxford University Press, 1994), 50.

28. Ibid., 177-78.

the early decades of this century, then, become increasingly hostile to, or at the very least embarrassed by, "sectarian" Christianity.

Of course, by conceiving of modern science as simply an extension of "common sense," American evangelicals also failed to realize that science does far more than just discover "facts" about created reality. Rather, science inevitably gives an interpretive account *of* reality. While it is possible for such an account to be in accord with Scriptural truth, it is equally possible, as the emergence of "evolutionary" theory made painfully clear toward the end of the nineteenth century, for the "scientific" account of reality to be atheistic and antithetical to biblical religion. As discussed in our last chapter, evangelical intellectuals did not for the most part recognize this until it was too late to stem the tide of evolutionary science in the universities.

Even more importantly, however, the long-standing American evangelical attachment to "common sense philosophy" betrayed a fundamentally mistaken overestimation of our natural ability to perceive spiritual truth, and the failure to discern that natural human understanding, however much it might be enlightened by "common sense," is still utterly incapable of accepting, as the apostle Paul says, "the things that come from the Spirit of God" (1 Cor. 2:14). Thus while the construction and maintenance of American civilization might well have benefited practically — and might well still benefit — from "common sense" moralism and Baconian science, this should never be taken to mean that American civilization is therefore also necessarily "Christian." Unfortunately, this is precisely what many American evangelicals believed right until the end of the nineteenth century. America was held to be *the* preeminently Christian nation, and the American national task was to civilize and "Christianize" the world by means of the closely interrelated duties of Christian missions, moral instruction, and scientific advance. The only prerequisite for full participation in this glorious project, furthermore, was the surrender of certain "sectarian" doctrines such as that of total depravity. Yet it was precisely this backing away from classical Reformed theology and the optimistic insistence on humankind's presumably natural capacity for supernatural truth which, when combined with their ardent enthusiasm for modern science, left American evangelicals intellectually defenseless against the acids of scientism and the charge of cultural irrelevance. Curiously, just as Sentimentalism and Romanticism appear to have emerged out of an Arminian rejection of strict Calvinism,[29] so the American evangelical adoption of the "common sense philosophy," with its implicit repudiation of the Reformed position on human incapacity, also eventually had largely unforeseen and unintended consequences. One of the few who did foresee these consequences was Jonathan Edwards, perhaps the most perceptive early critic of "enlightened" American Christianity. "It is evident," Edwards wrote in *The Religious Affections* (1746),

> that those gracious influences which the saints are subjects of, and the effects of God's Spirit which they experience, are entirely above nature, altogether of a different kind from anything that men find within themselves by nature, or only in the exercise of natural principles; and are things which no improvement of those qualifications or principles that are natural, no advancing or exalting them to higher degrees, and no kind of composition of them, will ever bring men to; because they not only differ from what is natural, and from everything that natural men experience, in degree and circumstances, but also in kind; and are of a nature vastly more excellent. . . . From hence it follows, that in those gracious exercises and affections which are wrought in the minds of the saints, through the saving influences of the Spirit of God, there is a new inward perception or sensation of their minds, entirely different in its nature and kind from anything that ever their minds were the subjects of before they were sanctified. . . .[30]

The implications for enlightened moral philosophy of such admonitions went largely unnoticed within eighteenth- and nineteenth-century American evangelical culture, however. The optimistic and anti-authoritarian, anti-traditional American disposition, combined with the enormous practical potential of Baconian science, appears to have simply blinded evangelical theologians to the obvious discrepancies between "common sense" moralism and biblical Christianity. Yet we note

29. Recall Colin Campbell's discussion, cited in the last chapter, of the emergence of modern consumerism in *The Romantic Ethic and the Spirit of Modern Consumerism* (Oxford: Basil Blackwell, 1987).

30. Jonathan Edwards, *The Religious Affections* (1746; Edinburgh, UK: The Banner of Truth Trust, 1994), 132-33.

that it was the Pelagian assumption that the "natural man" is capable of genuine spiritual discernment that was, perhaps more than any other single philosophical commitment, responsible for rendering historic Christian orthodoxy — with its emphases upon human inability, sovereign grace, new birth, and conversion — irrelevant and even offensive within modern intellectual culture.

But returning to our consideration of how well or poorly evangelicals have actually been able to resist certain modern ideas and assumptions, it is important to recall that the conservative Protestant strategy for coping with these ideas and assumptions has very often entailed a retreat into private religious experience. North American evangelicals, for example, have repeatedly withdrawn from the larger society and culture in an effort to preserve the purity of the gospel and the freedom of private religiosity. Conservatives have sought to keep the Christian faith safe from modernity, in other words, by sequestering it off the field of battle. While this strategy has apparently met with a great deal of success over the course of the last several centuries, it has been far more costly than conservatives generally recognize. Barth, for example, blamed the secularization of eighteenth-century political life on continental Pietism's pursuit of private religiosity at the expense of active engagement in public political life.[31] The tendency toward privatism has bedeviled evangelical Protestants ever since, for by refusing to engage modernity directly, the conservative strategy of resistance-by-withdrawal only surrenders whole sectors of society and culture to the process of secularization. The strategy of resistance-by-withdrawal also has the ironic effect of rendering the Christian faith somewhat less than real even for those who are trying to preserve it. After all, how solid can the Christian faith really appear to be if it is rendered in such a way as to make it almost completely irrelevant to much of what goes on every day in the workplace, or in political life, or in the production and transmission of the larger culture? It comes as no great surprise to learn, then, that the strategy of resistance-by-retreat has only made the Christian faith all the more vulnerable to the logic of privatization and to the therapeutic subjectivism discussed in the last chapter.

The mistaken accommodation of certain modern ideas and assumptions, then, in combination with the mistaken strategy of trying to

---

31. Barth, *Protestant Theology in the Nineteenth Century*, 90.

preserve the purity of faith by withdrawing from modern public life into private religious experience, helps to explain why twentieth-century Christians — and particularly Protestants — have found it so difficult to assume a truly prophetic stance vis-à-vis modernity and now "post-modernity." These factors also explain why recent Protestant criticism of modern society and culture has not tended to be very effective. The reparation of both of these problems will need to figure into future Protestant attempts at confronting the secularity and impersonality of modern society and culture.

The Gravedigger Dilemma

Yet beyond the mistaken accommodation of certain modern ideas and assumptions, perhaps the most stubborn obstacle standing in the path of our prophetic criticism of modernity is that the Christian religion is so closely bound up with the development of modern society and culture. As our previous discussions have shown, where typically modern ideas and assumptions begin and Christianity leaves off is not at all easy to determine in a number of cases. In fact, Christianity and modern society and culture are so closely intertwined that separating the one from the other, while perhaps not impossible, would probably be inadvisable for much the same reason that the harvesters were advised not to separate the wheat from the tares in Jesus' Parable of the Weeds (Matt. 13:24ff.). To try to completely eradicate all traces of modernity from the life of the contemporary Church would probably do far more damage to the Church than it would be worth. This is an unavoidable aspect of what might be termed the "gravedigger dilemma."

As we have seen, the gravedigger hypothesis suggests that Christianity — and in particular Protestant Christianity — is ultimately (albeit unintentionally) responsible for sowing the seeds of its own destruction within modern secular society and culture. The characteristically Protestant stress upon individual conscience, for example, has become the most elemental of modern civil rights, now guaranteeing the right even to profess atheism and to voice bitter opposition to the Christian religion. Protestantism's "disenchantment" with the world, furthermore, appears to have provided the cosmological foundation for modern science's secular investigations into nature and thus for the secular and anthropocentric manipulation of the natural world. And, of course, the celebrated "Protestant ethic" appears to have contributed quite substantially to the secular spirit of modern capitalism, as well as to the distinctively modern ethos of autonomous individuality. In short, it does appear to be the case that Protestantism educated its own modern gravediggers in a number of significant respects.

Identifying various and sundry Protestant contributions to the development of modern institutional life should not obscure the fact that Protestantism did not in itself invent the social space for secularity within modern society and culture, however. The Church has always conceded a certain separateness and integrity to secular affairs and, although it has struggled with the question of where to place the boundary between the sacred and the secular, it has fairly consistently repudiated the ideal of a totally religious civilization. This essentially pagan ideal has simply been too difficult to square with Jesus' assertion that his kingdom is "not of this world" (John 18:36). And it has been the Christian religion *as such,* and not simply Protestantism, that has fostered genuine individuality within Western civilization, and the prospect of real hope in the possibilities of historical development. Indeed, the Christian religion has given rise to a fundamentally new kind of *self*-consciousness in the West, an exalted self-consciousness which is the fruit of the uniquely Christian conviction that human beings are worthy of having been called into covenantal relationship with the living God. Much of what we value within contemporary culture, and indeed in the Western tradition generally — the conviction that each individual human being is of inestimable value, the belief that the universe is ultimately *humanly* meaningful, that justice and righteousness must eventually prevail, etc. — all these beliefs attest to the decisive impact of the Christian religion upon modern society and culture and betray a uniquely Christian worldview. These are simply not the sorts of convictions and aspirations that emerge naturally out of human experience *as such.* As G. K. Chesterton argued in his brilliant apology for Christian faith, *The Everlasting Man* (1925):

> If anybody says that philosophic maxims preserved through many ages, or mythological temples frequented by many peoples are things of the same class and category as the Church, it is enough to answer quite simply that they are not. . . . The Church Militant is . . . unique

because it is an army marching to effect a universal deliverance. The bondage from which the world is thus to be delivered is something that is very well symbolised by the state of Asia. . . . It is not prejudice but practical experience which says that Asia is full of demons as well as gods. But the evil I mean is in the mind. And it is in the mind wherever the mind has worked for a long time alone. It is what happens when all dreaming and thinking have come to an end in an emptiness that is at once negation and necessity. It sounds like an anarchy, but it is also a slavery. It is what has been called already the wheel of Asia; all those recurrent arguments about cause and effect or things beginning and ending in the mind, which make it impossible for the soul really to strike out and go anywhere or do anything. And the point is that it is not necessarily peculiar to the Asiatics; it would have been true in the end of Europeans — if something had not happened. If the Church Militant had not been a thing marching, all men would have been marking time. . . . What the universal yet fighting faith brought into the world was hope.[32]

The fact that the Church Militant has enabled the Western soul to strike out and go places and do things has been something of a mixed blessing, however. For in creating the possibility of genuine hope, the Christian religion also necessarily created the possibility that hope might be misplaced, and that instead of placing our hope in God we would place it in the world. More specifically, the advent of genuine faith in God created the possibility that a kind of counterfeit faith might be misplaced in disenchanted nature, or in human reason, in social justice, in immanent historical-social change, or in individuality, in short, in the very convictions and aspirations that the Christian religion had itself made possible within the culture in the first place. This is ironic, but it is also inevitable. It is an inescapable aspect of the dialectical relation of the gospel and the world.

Not surprisingly, however, once human reason, or social justice, or history, or individuality, become the objects of worship, they immediately begin to contend with each other for supremacy. Indeed, a great deal of the tension within modern culture may be said to stem from the ongoing

32. G. K. Chesterton, *The Everlasting Man* (Garden City, NY: Image, 1955), 244-45.

conflict between a number of the idols that the Christian religion has made possible within Western society and culture. Christianity's "disenchantment" with the natural world, for example, created the possibility of disciplined scientific inquiry into the nature of things, and the subsequent emergence of modern natural science has been of inestimable benefit to all of us. Yet along with the possibility of disciplined rational inquiry into nature, there emerged also the possibility that science and the natural world disclosed by science might themselves be worshipped. The sadly ironic "death of the soul" is evidence that we have turned this possibility into an actuality within modern culture. Christianity's affirmation of history, furthermore — that is, its affirmation of real movement from the fallen present toward the Kingdom of God — gave rise to the possibility that historical-social change might also become the object of worship. Although the Christian faith unequivocally condemns such idolatrous worship, it seems that once truly Christian faith and hope are lost, they have quite often, under modern conditions, only been transmuted into faith and hope in a humanly constructed future. Indeed, it seems that, just as apostate Christian believers never simply revert to a state of innocent ignorance or to the beliefs they held before they became Christians, so a culture that has once experienced the creative power of the gospel never simply reverts to pre-Christian paganism. This is why faith in secular "progress," either by way of revolutionary social change, by way of technological mastery, or even by way of a kind of mystical renunciation of technology, may be said to be a kind of "bastard offspring of an optimistic anthropology and Christian eschatology."[33]

This list of examples could be lengthened, but the point to stress here is simply that the relation between Christianity and modernity has been and will undoubtedly continue to be a dialectical one. Just as in the Parable of the Seven Spirits (Matt. 12:43-45), the Church — and in particular the Protestant churches — swept much of early modern Western society and culture clean of pagan superstitions and irrationalities. Indeed, Protestantism relentlessly criticized anything — including even the Christian religion itself — which threatened to separate the individual soul from God. The Reformation subsequently led to a

---

33. Brunner, *Christianity and Civilization, Part One: Foundations* (New York: Charles Scribner's Sons, 1948), 55; see also Christopher Dawson, *Progress and Religion: An Historical Inquiry* (1931; Peru, IL: Sherwood Sugden & Co., 1991).

number of remarkable social innovations and cultural achievements. Yet it has been precisely these same innovations and achievements that have, just as we have seen, contributed so substantially to the process of secularization. The relationship between the Church and the world, it seems, is intractably paradoxical. Or, put somewhat differently, the social and cultural possibilities created by the gospel are always double-edged. "Do not suppose that I have come to bring peace to the earth," Jesus warned us (Matt. 10:34); "I did not come to bring peace, but a sword. . . ." Jesus' sword is that of an intensified consciousness which must give rise, either to true faith in God, or to the more completely self-conscious rejection of the things of God. This, again, is the earnestness of existence. And so it is that, just as in Jesus' parable, the final condition of modern secular culture has turned out to be worse than the first. As Helmut Thielicke observed:

> If, then, we live in this world as though there were no god, we do so before God, since the dedivinization of the world has its source in him, and since the world is sustained in this dedivinization only as he is remembered as the normative power in it. If he is not, the world begins to fill itself with gods again. Redivinization begins. . . . This does not mean a return to the vanquished religions. It means post-religious ideologizing. The banished gods return as idols. If the world is not viewed before God, if its upper boundary is eliminated, immanence itself takes on religious and metaphysical proportions and the gods are back. The world is decked out in the attributes of God. . . .[34]

The characteristically modern aspiration to autonomy and self-creation by means of secular technological and/or economic progress, by way of various secular ideological movements of social and political change, and even by means of quasi-religious techniques of individual enlightenment may thus all be said to stem from the impact of the gospel upon modern society and culture. In effect, modern secular culture represents the repudiation of Christianity on the basis of Christian social and cultural achievements. It is this irony that interprets the paradoxical

34. Helmut Thielicke, *The Evangelical Faith, Vol. One: Prolegomena* (Grand Rapids, MI: Eerdmans, 1974), 325-26.

quality of many of the features of modern society and culture. As we mentioned toward the end of the last chapter, we have, in effect, employed the virtues of individual autonomy, of freedom, and of progress — all Christian in origin — to undermine the authority, first of the Christian Church, and now finally even of God himself.

There is clearly an eschatological dimension to this modern situation, for it bears witness to the fact that history is indeed moving toward a culmination in which Christian faith in God will be sharply juxtaposed with the refusal to have faith and the refusal to enter into the Kingdom of God. Of course, this is not to say that the end is necessarily near, for Jesus has told us (Matt. 26:36) that only the Father knows the day and the hour. Still, as Romano Guardini observed: "If we speak here of the nearness of the End, we do not mean nearness in the sense of time, but nearness as it pertains to the essence of the End, for in essence man's existence is now nearing an absolute decision. Each and every consequence of that decision bears within it the greatest potentiality and the most extreme danger."[35] This is both good and bad news for the contemporary Church. The secular quality of modern society and culture is evidence of the ferment on the gospel in the world and affirms that history is moving toward its conclusion in Christ, but it also suggests that the Church's work in the modern or "postmodern" or, more accurately, in the *post-Christian* world will probably only become more, and not less, difficult in the years to come.

Several Things We Can Learn from the Past

A number of conclusions can be drawn from our discussion thus far. The first is that we can expect our efforts to criticize and to reform modern society and culture to be frustrated by the dialectical relation of the gospel and the world. As we just discussed above, modern secularity is intractable because it is *post-Christian*: modern society and culture have, in effect, been inoculated against the transforming impact of the gospel due to the immanentization of Christian truth. This is not to say that the Church

35. Romano Guardini, *The End of the Modern World: A Search for Orientation*, trans. Joseph Theman and Herbert Burke (1956; Chicago: Henry Regnery Company, 1968), 133.

cannot continue to exert a redemptive influence within modern society and culture, or that the possibility of reform does not exist. Rather, it is only to recognize, among other things, that the modern situation is not parallel to that of classical antiquity prior to the arrival of Christianity, and hence that we should probably not expect the future to reduplicate the Church's original regeneration of pagan culture. While our churches will hopefully experience revival, we should probably not expect the Christian faith to become as predominant a social and cultural force as it was in the West prior to the end of the seventeenth century. Rather, we should probably better prepare ourselves for the future by listening to those who have suggested that we are, culturally speaking at least, entering a period of darkness and confusion.

A second conclusion to draw from our discussion thus far is that we cannot resist the secularity of modern society and culture by retreating into the private sphere. While such a retreat does present the path of least resistance, the withdrawal into private life has left the contemporary Church far too vulnerable to subjectivism and to the triumph of therapeutic sensibilities. By rendering the Christian faith so that it appears to be irrelevant to public life, the strategy of resistance-by-withdrawal has also made faith seem somewhat unreal to those who must staff the public sphere on a daily basis. In compensating for the impersonal quality of the modern marketplace, furthermore, private religiosity only increases our tolerance for the barrenness and secularity of modern public life, thereby actually contributing to the ongoing process of secularization.[36]

Thirdly, it should be clear that the protests we lodge against the secularity and impersonality of modern society and culture must be grounded in an effective challenge to therapeutic sensibilities and to the modern will-to-self-definition. Indeed, unless we directly contest the distinctively modern understanding of the *self*, our resistance to modern secular society will probably be construed — and may actually result — either in yet another expression of ideological manipulation, or in yet another eccentric expression of the triumph of the therapeutic.

---

36. Thomas Luckmann, "The Invisible Religion," in *Secularization and the Protestant Prospect*, ed. James F. Childress and David B. Harned (Philadelphia: Westminster, 1970), 91. See also Robert Booth Fowler, *Unconventional Partners: Religion and Liberal Culture in the United States* (Grand Rapids, MI: Eerdmans, 1989).

With respect to the former, we should not presume that the problem of secularization is somehow up to us to solve and, indeed, that the measure of our prophetic effectiveness within modern society and culture lies in the extent to which we have managed to solve it. Far from standing in contrast to the Promethean ethos of modernity, the self-understanding disclosed in this kind of stoic assumption of responsibility is actually very much in harmony with it. Indeed, it is fundamentally worldly. We will return to this point below, but the desire to establish control over the modern situation by "spiritual" means is much more modern, and much less genuinely spiritual, than many contemporary Christians apparently recognize. At the same time, however, unless our prophetic protest against secular society clearly challenges the narcissism that lies at the heart of modern self-understanding, it will likely only be purloined in a therapeutic direction, that is, it will simply be seen as another expression of the private and individual pursuit of the experience of well-being.

Modernity's repeated absorption and neutralization of protest is the subject of Jackson Lears's interesting historical study *No Place of Grace: Antimodernism and the Transformation of American Culture* (1981), in which he examines a number of the protests that were lodged against modernism in America between 1880 and 1920, such as the Arts and Crafts movement, the cult of martial experience, the "vitalist" longing for medieval order, and the attempted revival of Catholic mysticism.[37] His provocative thesis is simply that anti-secular and anti-modern sentiments — Christian and otherwise — have not only failed to slow the process of secularization in recent American history, but have actually only hastened the process by contributing more grist for the modern mill of private self-construction and hence by diverting attention away from the cultural offense of radical secularity. Lears concludes:

> Rooted in reaction against secularizing tendencies, antimodernism helped ease accommodation to new and secular cultural modes. This was an ironic, unintended consequence of the antimodernist efforts to salvage meaning and purpose amid the crumbling Protestant culture of the late nineteenth century. Embracing premodern symbols as

37. T. J. Jackson Lears, *No Place for Grace: Antimodernism and the Transformation of American Culture, 1880-1920* (New York: Pantheon, 1981).

alternatives to the vagueness of liberal Protestantism or the sterility of nineteenth-century positivism, antimodern seekers nevertheless adapted those symbols *for modern ends* [emphasis added]. Craftsmanship became less a path to satisfying communal work than a therapy for tired businessmen. The martial ideal ennobled not a quest for the Grail but a quest for foreign markets. Even Catholic mysticism, art, and ritual were adjusted to secular purposes. They became instruments for promoting intense experience, rather than paths to salvation. By exalting "authentic" experience as an end in itself, antimodern impulses reinforced the shift from a Protestant ethos of salvation through self-denial to a therapeutic ideal of self-fulfillment in *this* world through exuberant health and intense experience. The older morality embodied the "producer culture" of an industrializing, entrepreneurial society; the newer nonmorality embodied the "consumer culture" of a bureaucratic corporate state. Antimodernists were far more than escapists: their quest for authenticity eased their own and others' adjustments to the streamlined culture of consumption.[38]

Thus even when it has arisen out of genuine discontent with modern secularity and impersonality, the protest against modernity has repeatedly been reduced to a kind of insipid quest for individual self-fulfillment. The record of recent protests against modernity should sober us. It seems that we can expect our protests against modern society and culture to be rather readily absorbed into the contemporary culture of narcissism and distraction unless and until we are quite clear in our rejection of the therapeutic view of the self.[39]

A fourth conclusion to draw from the Church's past experience with modernity is that our criticism and resistance to modern society and culture must be genuinely *theological*. The problem of secularization, in other words, is not simply a practical problem calling for organization and the mobilization of resources and constituencies and other activities that contemporary Christians — both liberal and conservative — seem

38. Ibid., xv-xvi.

39. Interestingly, Lears concludes his study by suggesting that, while the recent resurgence of evangelicalism may perhaps prove a genuine source of resistance to the process of secularization, it is more likely that evangelicals will surrender, just as liberal Protestantism did at the turn of the century, to largely therapeutic ideals. Sadly, he appears to have been correct about this.

busily preoccupied with. Rather, the secularity and impersonality of modern society and culture are problems that call for disciplined reasoning and careful analysis. Such analysis must hold more than merely worldly social and cultural ends in view, however. For not only do we do violence to the Christian faith when we "use" it in the service of merely worldly ends — such as in the projection of "influence" within modern political culture, or in the streamlining of enterprise, or even in the conservation of traditional social order — but, as we have seen, the secular cast of modern social life is such as to be able to withstand all but truly substantive theological proscription. Descriptive analysis cannot, in and of itself, generate enough spiritual energy to really challenge the modern *status quo*. As Leszek Kolakowski commented recently:

> [The] intellectuals' awakening to the dangers of secularity does not seem to be a promising avenue for getting out of our present predicament, not because such reflections are false, but because we may suspect that they are born of an inconsistent, manipulative spirit. There is something alarmingly desperate in intellectuals who have no religious attachment, faith or loyalty proper and who insist on the irreplaceable educational and moral role of religion in our world and deplore its fragility, to which they themselves eminently bear witness . . . to spread faith, faith is needed and not an intellectual assertion of the social utility of faith.[40]

Anything short of a genuinely theological critique of modernity, in other words, is simply not up to the task of restraining the intrinsically secular logic of modernity's central institutions. Not only is faith needed to spread faith, but the acids of modernity will quickly corrode even Christian protest that does not demonstrate theological depth and integrity.

In addition, as Protestant theology was in many important respects the midwife to modernity, and as a number of Protestant ideas are already built into modern institutions, those of us who are Protestants will probably need to be prepared — as we should be in any case — to reform our own theological traditions from within. Modernity has al-

---

40. Leszek Kolakowski, *Modernity on Endless Trial* (Chicago: University of Chicago Press, 1990), 9.

ready absorbed a great deal of past Protestant criticism. Simply returning to the classical evangelical orthodoxies of the eighteenth, nineteenth, or early twentieth centuries, then, will probably not by itself make for any real resistance to modern tendencies. We may also need to follow the Christian theological tradition back to the onset of modernity, and perhaps back even farther, to recover theological resources adequate to the task of standing up to the secular logic of contemporary society and culture.[41] One of the most important of these resources, I believe, is the classical theological understanding of the *person*, and it is to this consideration that we will turn in our final chapter.

The Importance of Reflecting on Our Natural Inabilities

We began by suggesting that contemporary society and culture so emphasize human potential and and agency and the immediate practical exigencies of life in this world, that most of us have, in effect, become "practical atheists." We have gotten out of the habit of giving God much thought as we go about our daily business. Our preoccupation with the practical tasks at hand has tempted us to employ practical-rational systems and methods which have tended to undermine personal existence, however. And so we have arrived at the point where it often appears easier to try to adjust our souls to fit the circumstances and requirements of our social system — by means of entertainment and therapy, etc. — than to try to restore the system on the basis of truly human values. This, as we have said, is "the huge modern heresy."

Of course, from a Christian point of view the modern heresy may be said to stem from the Fall from grace, that is, that we too have succumbed to the original temptation "to be like God" and have, therefore, fallen into confusion, bondage, and alienation. Such a reading of

---

41. See Thomas C. Oden, *After Modernity What? Agenda for Theology* (Grand Rapids, MI: Zondervan, 1990). *"The agenda for theology at the end of the twentieth century,"* Oden contends (p. 34), *"following the steady deterioration of a hundred years and the disaster of the last few decades, is to begin to prepare the postmodern Christian community for its third millennium by returning again to the careful study and respectful following of the central tradition of classical [Patristic] Christian exegesis."*

the contemporary situation is obviously true, for modern — and now "postmodern" — aspirations do disclose the *hubris* and desire for godlike autonomy that have always characterized Original Sin. Yet in our haste to interpret the modern predicament in terms of the Fall from grace, it occurs to me that we may fail to grasp an important piece of the puzzle of our culture, which is that Christians have themselves been among the most enthusiastic proponents of modernity and modernization since the seventeenth century. The popularization of "the new philosophy" within English culture, for example, was largely due to Christian enthusiasm for the practical potential of Baconian science. This has been largely true within North American culture as well. Indeed, most North American Christians believed that the advancement of modern scientific civilization was more or less synonymous with the advancement of Christianity right up to the early decades of this century. And, of course, North American evangelical Christians continue to be among the most enthusiastic supporters of republican politics and free enterprise.

Recalling again the "gravedigger hypothesis," how do we explain the curious fact that Christians have participated so enthusiastically in the development of what would almost invariably become completely secularized — that is, practically atheistic — institutions and habits of thought? We discussed a few of the reasons for this earlier. That Christian proponents of scientific methods have often failed to perceive that such methods entail more than simply the extension of "common sense," appears to be one of them. Even more significant appears to have been the assumption, by and large shared by "liberal" and "conservative" Christians alike, that unaided "common sense," or natural reason, is capable of discerning spiritual truth. This assumption has inspired the development of Protestant "liberalism" right up to the present day. It has also inspired the attraction that Protestant "conservatives" have tended to display for modern methods and techniques. The fact that a good many modern Christians appear to have assumed that natural human reason is capable of discerning the truth of the human condition helps to explain the enthusiasm with which these same Christians have been able to participate in the development of modernity. The critical assumption lying at the heart of the gravedigger dilemma, in other words, may well be a kind of overly optimistic assessment of natural human abilities.

By contrast, the Scriptures are not very optimistic about natural human abilities. From the early chapters of Genesis to the prophetic lament, abridged by Paul in his letter to the Roman Christians, that "[t]here is no one who understands; no one who seeks God . . ." (Rom. 3:10ff.), the Scriptures have much more to say about human *inability* than about human ability, particularly when it comes to perceiving spiritual truth. In his letter to the Ephesians, for example, the apostle Paul insists that his readers "must no longer live as the Gentiles do, in the futility of their thinking" (Eph. 1:17ff.). Those whose hearts have not been quickened by the inspiration of the Holy Spirit, Paul continues, are "darkened in their understanding" and "separated from the life of God" (v. 18). Their natural "ignorance," furthermore, interprets the willingness with which they give themselves to sensuality and impurity (v. 19). "The man without the Spirit [of God]," Paul writes elsewhere (1 Cor. 2:14), "does not accept the things that come from the Spirit of God, for they are foolishness to him, and he cannot understand them, because they are spiritually discerned."

In sharp contrast to our natural ignorance, Paul goes on to exhort his readers to "be made new in the attitude of your minds" and "to put on the new self, created to be like God in true righteousness and holiness" (Eph. 4:22ff.). The new life in Christ, Paul suggests, does not simply enhance our natural abilities; nor does it merely augment our natural judgment; rather, the Spirit of Christ *creates* within us the possibilities of loving God and neighbor, of exercising truthful judgment with respect to ourselves, and of becoming truly sensitive to contours of created moral order. "This is what the Sovereign LORD says," the prophet Ezekiel declares concerning God's gracious *restoration* of human ability (Ezek. 36:26-28). "I will give you a new heart and put a new spirit in you; I will remove from you your heart of stone and give you a heart of flesh. And I will put my Spirit in you and move you to follow my decrees and be careful to keep my laws. You will live in the land I gave your forefathers; you will be my people, and I will be your God."

Admittedly, the Scriptures' bleak assessment of natural human abilities runs counter to "common sense," especially in light of the remarkable achievements of modern humanity. It also runs counter to modern therapeutic sensibilities, which are largely optimistic with respect to our innate spiritual capacity. Yet the Scriptures do not say that "the natural man" is incapable of *anything*, rather simply that we are naturally incapable of *righteousness* — that is, of *genuine spirituality* before God. Calvin puts it this way in his commentary on the Ephesians passage cited above:

[E]xperience, so it seems, is openly opposed to [Paul's] opinion; for men are not so blind that they see nothing, nor so vain that they make no judgment. [Yet] . . . as to the Kingdom of God, and all that relates to spiritual life, the light of human reason differs little from darkness; for, before it has shown the way it is extinguished; and its perspicacity is worth no more than blindness, for before it comes to harvest, it is gone. For true principles are like sparks, but these are choked by the depravity of nature before they are put to their true use.[42]

Whatever natural capacity we may still possess for judging correctly with respect to the human situation, in other words, is quickly extinguished by ignorance and/or sensuality. While we may well remain capable of a good many things in the absence of God's grace, we are naturally *in*capable of solving our most pressing problems.

The reason for reflecting for a moment about human inability here at the end of our discussion of "the huge modern heresy" is simply that, even granting the enormous capacity of the human mind attested in the development of modern science and in the development of practical methods and techniques for improving the material conditions of our lives, natural reason is still utterly unable to arrive at a true assessment of the human situation before God. For want of a true assessment of our situation before God, "common sense" is prone to misunderstanding the nature of created moral order, thus inevitably stumbling into sensuality and moral foolishness. Lacking a true assessment of our situation before God, natural reason is also given to misusing the very tools and methods we have developed in order to make life better for ourselves, a problem only exacerbated by the fact that our tools and methods have become increasingly more powerful. As we confront the modern predicament, then, we must continually remind ourselves that we do not necessarily need bigger machines, or better tools, or more effective techniques; and neither do we necessarily need better education, more information, or better theoretical constructions. What we *do* need is a

42. John Calvin, *The Epistles of Paul the Apostle to the Galatians, Ephesians, Philippians and Colossians*, trans. T. H. L. Parker, Calvin's Commentaries Volume 11, eds. David W. Torrance and Thomas F. Torrance (Grand Rapids, MI: Eerdmans, 1965): 186.

fundamentally new disposition of heart, a disposition able to direct our otherwise "natural" abilities toward the works of love and holiness. We must confess that we are simply not able to work this change within our own hearts. If we are ever to enjoy "hearts of flesh," God must create them anew within us. For our cultural prognosis to be truly Christian, then, top priority must always be given to the conversion of souls. There is simply no other way of overcoming our natural inabilities and of arriving at a true assessment of our situation before God.

CHAPTER SIX

Toward a Theology of Personhood

One cannot divide one's life between an actual relationship to God and an inactual I-It relationship to the world — praying to God in truth and utilizing the world. Whoever knows the world as something to be utilized knows God the same way.

Martin Buber[1]

The motive that impels modern reason *to know* must be described as the desire to conquer and to dominate. For the Greek philosophers and the Fathers of the church, knowing meant something different: it meant knowing in wonder. By knowing or perceiving one participates in the life of the other. Here knowing does not transform the counterpart into the property of the knower; the knower does not appropriate what he knows. On the contrary, he is transformed through sympathy, becoming a participant in what he perceives. Knowledge confers fellowship. That is why knowing, perception, only goes as far as love, sympathy and participation reach. Where the theological perception of God and his history is concerned, there will be a modern discovery of Trinitarian thinking when there is at the same time a fundamental change in modern reason — a change from

---

1. Martin Buber, *I and Thou*, trans. Walter Kaufmann (1937; New York: Charles Scribner's Sons, 1970), 156.

lordship to fellowship, from conquest to participation, from production to receptivity.

Jürgen Moltmann[2]

See how the perfection of one person requires the fellowship with another.

Richard of St. Victor[3]

Given the intrinsic secularity and impersonality of modernity's central institutions and the despairing failure of the distinctively modern cult of self-fulfillment to satisfy the soul, the importance of defending genuine individuality and truly personal existence should by now be reasonably clear. Just how we should go about doing this, however, is perhaps not so clear, for as we have seen, the impersonality of modern existence appears to rest upon a larger foundation that was, at least initially, theological in origin. In this connection, we have observed that the impersonal quality of modern social life appears to have emerged, in large measure, out of the impersonal conception of nature exhibited by modern science. Modern science's objectification of persons, furthermore, appears to have been developed from a theological position which, in effect, objectified the natural world. It was theological "nominalism," after all, which first encouraged Western thinkers to conceive of existence in terms of individual, discrete, and separate "things" which could be exhaustively known by means of observation and experiment. Even God came to be understood from within this perspective as *una res,* that is, one thing among all of the other things in existence.[4] Before reviewing the classical Christian doctrine of the person, then, it will be helpful to reconsider some of the problems Christian theologians have had thinking theologically about created nature.

2. Jürgen Moltmann, *The Trinity and the Kingdom of God: The Doctrine of God,* trans. Margaret Kohl (London: S.C.M. Press, 1981), 9.
3. Richard of St. Victor, "On the Trinity: Book III," in *Richard of St. Victor,* ed. G. Zinn, Classics in Western Spirituality (New York: Paulist Press, 1979), 379.
4. Tage Lindbom, *The Myth of Democracy* (Grand Rapids, MI: Eerdmans, 1996).

Of course, the difficulty Protestant theologians have had thinking conceptually and theologically about the natural world has been a recurring theme in our discussions of Protestantism's contribution to the development of modern society and culture. The Reformers, it seems, jettisoned Aristotelian science in their rejection of medieval scholasticism, and although they can hardly be blamed for this, their rejection of the classical (Aristotelian) teleological account of nature appears to have created something of a theological vacuum, a vacuum that was subsequently filled with the completely *anti*-teleological and inherently secular perspective of early modern science. And once nature began to be envisioned "naturalistically" — that is, in terms of efficient causality and more or less mechanical cause and effect — it rather quickly became plausible to view human nature and natural human existence in the world naturalistically as well. The Protestant disenchantment of early modern understanding with respect to the natural world thus accidentally led — at least in part — to disenchantment with human nature *as such,* and it was not long before human existence was subjected to the methods and explanations of the natural, and eventually of the so-called "social," sciences. The Protestant failure to develop an adequate theology of nature thus appears to have contributed substantially — albeit unintentionally — to what is perhaps the most critical aspect of the intellectual secularization of modern times, namely, the emergence of modern secular scientific understanding.

Yet we note that the problem of thinking theologically about nature antedates the Reformation by several centuries at least. As mentioned above, the so-called "nominalist" account of natural order of the late thirteenth and fourteenth centuries, which emphasized the independence of the created order and the virtues of an inductive natural theology, seems already to have portended the emergence of secular natural science. Along this line, Colin Gunton recently suggested that the Western theological tradition has actually been plagued by an inadequate theology of nature for most of its long history, indeed, perhaps even since the time of Augustine. This inadequacy, Gunton argues, stems from its deficient formulation of the doctrine of *creation;* more provocatively, he claims that there is actually a kind of causal relation between the way creation has been expressed in the Western theological tradition and the secular and *anti*-theological bias of modern society and culture.[5] In expressing the doctrine of creation, Western theology placed so much emphasis upon the sovereignty, irresistibility, and inscrutability of God's creative *will* that it all but ensured that there would eventually be a strong counterreaction in the direction of *human* creativity and autonomy.[6] The Western theological tradition's misconstrual of the deep mystery of divine sovereignty, in other words, had the effect of making human decision and human effort seem completely inconsequential. This was bound to evoke a protest, and, indeed, such a protest lies at the very heart of modern intellectual life. Modernity is, as Gunton puts it, a revolt of the many against the One; and the radical secularity of modern intellectual life may be understood as a justifiable — albeit mistaken and destructive — reaction to a theological account of creation which contained little space for human creativity, individuality, and freedom:

> The [early modern] scene is thus set for a contest of wills: between the God who appears to impart particularity only to that which is a function of his will, and therefore to deprive of true particularity; and the human will which appears to achieve independence only in the kind of arbitrary self assertion which appears to be the mark of divinity. The ingredients of the development are a God unitarily conceived,

5. Colin E. Gunton, *The One, the Three and the Many: God, Creation and the Culture of Modernity* (Cambridge: Cambridge University Press, 1993). We note that Christopher Dawson argued an essentially similar thesis in his classic study *Progress and Religion* (1931), particularly with reference to Rousseau. "All the vehemence of religious conviction with which his Calvinist ancestors had affirmed the doctrine of Original Sin and the impotence of the human will," Dawson observed (pp. 193-94), "was turned by Rousseau to the service of the diametrically opposite doctrines of the original goodness of human nature and the perfectibility of society, and so, too, he attacked the actual state as the one cause of all man's evils and sufferings with the same violence that the Calvinists had shown towards the Catholic Church of their time."

6. Of course, Gunton's broad thesis is controversial. As John S. Grabowski recently noted in an article entitled "Person: Substance and Relation," in *Communio: International Catholic Review* 22, no. 34 (Spring 1995): 147: "While not all of Gunton's criticism's are unfounded, it must be noted that: he produces little evidence for such sweeping historical claims, he fails to note that the emphasis on the divine unity was characteristic of all Western patristic theology, and not merely Augustine, his analysis treats only of *De Trinitate* and not the whole of Augustine's thought, and that his reading of Augustine is highly selective and unsparingly unsympathetic."

and largely in terms of will; the divorce of creation and redemption in the concept of divine action . . . and a world whose shape is attributed largely to the (essentially unknown) predestining will of God. There can accordingly be seen to take place a kind of reflex process which takes the form of a human filling of the vacuum left by the irrelevance of the unknown God: a process of self-assertion, in which responsibility for the ordering of the world — personal and non-personal alike — is transferred to the human from the divine will.[7]

We have observed this transfer to the human from the divine will in a number of places already. Indeed, it cuts to the very heart of our definition of worldliness as an interpretation of reality that overemphasizes human agency at God's expense. Yet the fact that this transfer may initially have been motivated, not simply by human pride, but by legitimate disaffection with Christian theology — both Protestant and Roman Catholic — should give us pause. For it does indeed appear to be the case that the Western theological tradition has had trouble representing God in such a way as not to preclude the possibility of genuine human individuality and creativity. Perhaps the most important

7. Gunton, *The One, The Three and the Many*, 58. See also Steven Seidman, *Liberalism and the Origins of European Social Theory* (Berkeley: University of California Press, 1983). The Enlightenment critique, Seidman argues, was not simply directed at Christianity, but against all systems of thought which implied limits to human individuality and creativity. "Underlying the critique of closed systems," Seidman observes (p. 38), "is the idea that their dogmatic character reflects cosmological presuppositions. To the extent that the world is viewed as an ordered cosmos, fully accessible to reason or revelation, to that extent there evolve completely closed and dogmatic systems. In this regard, we can see that implicit in the structure of Enlightenment criticism of closed systems is an attack upon cosmological presuppositions, i.e., external fixity, finiteness, hierarchy, and teleology. In the place of cosmological presuppositions, the philosophes sought an alternative configuration of presuppositions or a world-view that coincided with their commitment to liberal values. These world-defining presuppositions I call secularism. . . . The notion of a secular order is the antithesis of the idea of a cosmic order. . . . Secularism refers to a set of assumptions about the world. In contrast to cosmological presuppositions, a secular order projects a universe that places all entities on the same level of being, and is changing, infinite, and governed by efficient, nonteleological causality. Translated into sociocultural terms, secularism reveals a pronounced drift toward liberal values and orientations: progress, tolerance, egalitarianism, and empiricism."

conclusion we need to draw from the Church's past experience with modernity, then, is that if we are to cut to the heart of the problem of modern secularity we are going to need to give a better theological account of individuality, freedom, and personality than we have managed to give for quite some time.

Of course, our desperate need today for an adequate account of individuality, freedom, and personality is not simply due to the failure of modern theology to make the Church's classical positions on these matters clear, but to the spectacular failure of modernity to make good on its various and sundry promises of liberated individuality. Even against the intellectual backdrop of the purportedly "enlightened" defense of individuality, it seems that we have actually been only too ready to submit, both theoretically and practically, to systems and programs which are far more repressive of individuality and personality than the Christian tradition was at its very worst. As Romano Guardini observed:

> No man truly aware of his own human nature will admit that he can discover himself in the theories of modern anthropology — be they biological, psychological, sociological or any other. Only the accidents of man — his attributes, his relations, his forms — make up these theories; they never take man simply as he is. They speak about man, but they never really see man. They approach him, but they never truly find him. They handle him, but they never grip him as he actually is. . . . Mechanical, biological, psychological or sociological abstractions are all variations of a basic urge to make man one with "nature," even if it be a "nature of the spirit." But a vital reality escapes this type of mind; namely, man's very act of being which constitutes a man in the primitive, absolute sense, which makes man a man at the very core of his self, which makes him a finite person existing. This is what the existing man is even when he does not want to be, even when he denies his own nature.[8]

8. Romano Guardini, *The End of the Modern World: A Search for Orientation*, trans. Joseph Theman and Herbert Burke (1956; Chicago: Henry Regnery Company, 1968), 99-100. In this connection we note that the failure to develop an adequate account of personality is singularly evident in the so-called "postmodern" (genealogical) theories of social construction, which stress absolute human freedom even at the expense of personal responsibility and the continuity of personality over time. As Alasdair

The profound paradox of the modern secular condition is thus that our "liberation" from the supposedly repressive Christian God has only resulted in our subjection to other, far less merciful "deities."[9]

Given the secularity of the modern condition, and particularly in light of Protestantism's substantial contribution to the development of modern institutions, it is perhaps not surprising that a number of recent scholars have advocated rediscovering medieval theology, and particularly Aristotelian teleology as it was developed within late medieval scholasticism. Alasdair MacIntyre, for example, recommended recovering a kind of modified Aristotelianism in his influential study *After Virtue* (1984).[10] Similarly, John Milbank has recently suggested refitting Aristotelianism within the larger *mythos* of Augustine's "city of God."[11] Canadian social philosopher George Grant contended for a rediscovery of a kind of medieval "natural theology" in which we are again enabled to admire and appreciate the creation and createdness.[12] R. H. Tawney argued for a return to medievalism by means of the recovery of an understanding of society as "social organism."[13] Yet while all of these proposals are worth considering in detail, it is somewhat distressing that they all appear to require a return to a kind of medieval understanding of theological and social authority. All of them seem to imply the

---

MacIntyre notes, however, in *Three Rival Versions of Moral Inquiry: Encyclopedia, Genealogy, and Tradition* (Notre Dame, IN: University of Notre Dame, 1990), 210: "We can enquire whether in telling the tale of how he or she came to advance those claims, the genealogist does not have to fall back into a mode of speech in which the use of personal pronouns presupposes just that metaphysical conception of accountability which genealogy disowns. Or to put this question another way: can the genealogist legitimately include the self out of which he speaks in explaining himself within his or her genealogical narrative? Is the genealogist not self-indulgently engaged in exempting his or her utterances from the treatment to which everyone else's is subjected?"

9. Gunton, *The One, the Three and the Many*, 34.

10. See Alasdair MacIntyre, *After Virtue: A Study in Moral Theory*, 2nd edition (Notre Dame: University of Notre Dame Press, 1984); in particular chapter 18, "Nietzsche or Aristotle, Trotsky and St. Benedict," 256ff.

11. See John Milbank, *Theology and Social Theory: Beyond Secular Reason* (Oxford: Basil Blackwell, 1990).

12. See Grant, "In Defense of North America," in *Technology and Empire: Perspectives on North America* (Toronto: Anansi, 1969).

13. R. H. Tawney, *Religion and the Rise of Capitalism: A Historical Study* (1926; New York: Harcourt, Brace & Company, 1952).

necessity of some sort of theological magisterium that would somehow possess the authority to determine the substance of the relationships within the social/spiritual organism. The Protestant distinctives of *sola Scriptura, sola gratia, sola fides,* the priesthood of all believers, etc., although they are not condemned or even explicitly addressed in many of these recent proposals, tend to be implicitly repudiated by them to the extent that the medieval social order is held up as the model of Christian social order. Here again, it is not difficult to see why the burden of modernity has become such a particularly heavy one for modern Protestants. For if Protestantism was, at least in part, responsible for catalyzing the secularization of modern life, so it would seem that the most obvious "solution" to the problem of modern secularity would be to try to "undo" the Reformation by attempting to reintroduce the authoritative social order of Christendom, or at least something like it, to the modern situation. Indeed, we note that there has often been a kind of anti-Protestant (anti-bourgeois) bias even in the most thoroughly secular proposals for resolving the problems of the modern condition.

It is important to stress, however, that, quite apart from the actual impossibility of turning the clock back, the attempt to repristinate the medieval social order would not be a very good idea for a number of other reasons. In the first place, Aristotelian science is simply not believable any more.[14] Even more significantly, attempting to revitalize Aristotelian teleology by way of Aquinas would not really solve the crucial problem of human individuality and creativity. Whatever the Aristotelian "god" is, it is *not* personal, and the Aristotelian system does

14. Leo Strauss, *Natural Right and History* (Chicago: University of Chicago Press, 1950). Strauss rightly argues that the teleological view of the universe, in which natural beings are understood anthropomorphically and in terms of final causality, was destroyed by modern natural science, and therefore that we have been left to conclude either that the nonteleological conception of the universe must be completed with a nonteleological conception of human life (the "naturalistic" solution), or that a nonteleological natural science and a teleological science of human beings could somehow be held together (the dualistic solution). It is the dualistic position, Strauss writes (p. 8), "which the modern followers of Thomas Aquinas, among others, are forced to take, a position which presupposes a break with the comprehensive view of Aristotle as well as that of Thomas Aquinas himself. The fundamental dilemma, in whose grip we are, is caused by the victory of modern natural science. An adequate solution to the problem of natural right cannot be found before this basic problem has been solved."

not permit any real space for human freedom and creativity. Indeed, even modern scientific nominalism allows more latitude for personal agency than medieval (Aristotelian) science did.[15] We also note that the Aristotelian suggestion that each being contains its own natural *telos* within itself is very much at odds with the essentially dialectical quality of truly personal existence that we began to develop in our fourth chapter with reference to Kierkegaard's understanding of despair. Personhood is not a kind of faculty we possess, like intellect or memory; it is not simply an aspect of our nature which we can develop given only the proper instruction. Rather, we *become* persons only *in relation* to other persons. As Greek Orthodox theologian John Zizioulas has noted:

> Man's personhood should not be understood in terms of 'personality,' i.e., of a complex of natural, psychological or moral qualities which are in some sense 'possessed' by or 'contained' in the human *individuum*. On the contrary, being a person is basically different from being an individual or 'personality' in that the person can not be conceived in itself as a static entity, but only as it *relates to*. Thus personhood implies the 'openness of being,' and even more than that, the *ek-stasis* of being, i.e., a movement toward communion which leads to a transcendence of the boundaries of the 'self' and thus to *freedom*.[16]

Ultimately, we only become persons when this "*ek-stasis* of being" moves us toward communion with God. Again, this was one of Kierkegaard's central contentions, that is, that the others to whom we relate

---

15. As Jesse De Boer put it: "As for the breakdown of Aristotle and Stoic natural law . . . this I've learned not to feel sorry for. I think that Augustine — apart from his constant leaning on the Platonists — was the discoverer of personality and he also saw that the person as an agent in history *makes* himself and affects other folk and so helps create a culture. Forget about nature's apparent hierarchy. We must *choose* what to do, remember who we are, look ahead, choose our aim, and act *now*! This is human historical existence. . . . This outlook — and it *is* being worked out by the rejection of Aristotle — is closer to biblical thinking than the Scholastic theme." De Boer, cited in Diogenes Allen, *Philosophy for Understanding Theology* (Atlanta: John Knox Press, 1985), 165.

16. John D. Zizioulas, "Human Capacity and Human Incapacity: A Theological Exploration of Personhood," *Scottish Journal of Philosophy* 28 (1975): 407-8.

determine the degree of self-consciousness it will be possible for us to achieve, and hence that we are only enabled to achieve full and authentic selfhood in relation to the Person of God. That such a possibility even exists for us, furthermore, is wholly due to God's gracious *call* to us in Jesus Christ. Emil Brunner insightfully emphasized this crucial point a number of years ago in a work aptly entitled *Truth as Encounter* (1938):

> The being of man as person depends not on his thought but on his responsibility, upon the fact that a supreme Self calls to him and communicates Himself to him. It depends on what is called . . . "responsive actuality," the claim of the Self who is Lord that is at the same time the assurance of the graciously creating and justifying Self, as it is perceived in faith. Only in this double relation, not in his rationality, has man as person his origin and fundamental being. His deepest nature consists in this "answerability," i.e., in this existence in the Word of the Creator.[17]

Christianly understood, then, personal existence is the creative act of the personal God who graciously calls us into relationship with himself. Indeed, the Gospel of Jesus Christ is, finally, a call to the reconciliation of deeply *personal* relationships through which the possibility of genuinely personal existence is opened up for us. "*I* am the way and the truth and the life," Jesus tells us (John 14:6). Jesus Christ is himself the truth that will make us free if we love him and give ourselves over to his lordship (John 8:32).

Unfortunately, in our concern to protect the doctrinal integrity of the Christian faith, we Christians have shown a tendency to forget what doctrine itself was (and is) designed to protect: namely, the possibility of entering into a relationship with the living God in and through Christ by the power of the Spirit. North American evangelicals, for example, have tended to become so preoccupied with a strictly "propositional" conception of Christian truth that they have often lost sight of the essentially relational *telos* of all Christian propositions. Yet this oversight has led to confusion on the question of how the dignity of persons ought to be

17. Emil Brunner, *Truth as Encounter*, trans. Amandus W. Loos and David Cairns (1938; London: S.C.M. Press, 1964), 19.

derived and expressed theologically, and this confusion has contributed — albeit passively and unintentionally — to the devaluation of persons in the modern rationalized context. In addition, we note that defending the Christian faith solely in terms of "values," "principles," and "ideas" abstracts away from the relational *telos* of Christian faith as well. What is needed in the contemporary situation, then — in the context of evangelical theology just as much as in the modern context generally — is the recovery and reassertion of a truly Christian theology of personhood.

Divine and Human Persons

We have said that we are only enabled to become persons by virtue of our having been called into a relationship with God, and only as we respond to his call in a certain way. Just how such a relationship is possible, then, and just what the appropriate response to God's call is, become critical anthropological questions. The way that we answer these questions will determine how we think about the nature and possibilities of human existence in general and how we think about ourselves in particular. And yet we have no way of answering these questions without first knowing something about the nature of the God who has called us into relationship with himself. Our anthropology is entirely dependent upon our theology. We cannot know who we are, in other words, without first knowing who God is. This is a simple but particularly important point to stress today, for the subjective and anthropocentric bias of modern thought has encouraged us to imagine that our conception of God is necessarily only a kind of logical extension of our own self-understanding. The reverse is actually the case. Our understanding of ourselves is necessarily only a kind of logical extension of our understanding of God. Or, put differently, our understanding of the nature and possibilities of human existence does not precede but rather *proceeds* more or less directly out of our conception of the nature and possibilities of ultimate reality. If our conception of ultimate reality — our "onto-theology," as it has been called — is impersonal, or if it is one in which the personality of the "gods" is affirmed only weakly or ambiguously, then we will either deny the possibility of individual human personality altogether, or we will only affirm this possibility weakly and ambiguously. Once again, anthropology is logically and existentially dependent upon theology; our understanding of what it means to be a human being will necessarily emerge out of our understanding — or lack thereof — of who or what "god" finally is.

It has been noted, for example, that the affirmation of the possibility of individual personality was either wholly missing from ancient pagan cultures or, if it was not entirely absent, that it was somewhat feckless by modern Western standards. This appears to have been because it was not clear to the ancients that the ultimate nature of reality really was personal. Indeed, the ultimate principle of unity in the universe seemed to most of them to transcend individuality and personality. This is why pagan cultures did not as a rule — and still do not — place a very high value upon the individual. Rather, the cultural tendency within pagan culture was (and is) to absorb particularity, including individual human personality, into some presumably larger principle of unity — into Nature, into *dharma*, the tribe, fate, the eternal Forms, the irresistible Will of the Absolute, etc. — that is, into some principle of unity which is usually religiously defined. Curiously, this same tendency is evident in modern *post-Christian* society and culture as well. Indeed, as we have seen, the collapse of individual personality into a kind of stultifying social and cultural homogeneity for the sake of such things as technical efficiency, or progress, or the good of the Nation, etc., has become a kind of hallmark of contemporary civilization, in spite of modernity's liberal emphasis on the importance of individuals. Again, as Kierkegaard observed so incisively, the characteristic depravity of the modern age is "not pleasure or indulgence or sensuality, but rather a dissolute pantheistic contempt for the individual man."[18]

In contrast to ancient pagan, and now to modern post-Christian, ambiguity with respect to the possibility of individuality and personality, the Christian religion affirms that the ultimate nature of reality is actually personal, and indeed that God's essential being consists in the absolutely personal communion of Father, Son, and Holy Spirit. Christianity further affirms that the world that God has created does not simply reflect dimly the personal and relational quality of his being, but that the world was created and is destined to participate in the divine nature and to share in personal communion with the Father, through

18. Søren Kierkegaard, *Concluding Unscientific Postscript*, trans. David F. Swenson and Walter Lowrie (1846; Princeton: Princeton University Press, 1941), 317.

the Son, and in the power of the Holy Spirit eternally. Here we must stress that no other religion, ancient or modern, has ever dared to place as much emphasis upon the person as Christianity. Indeed, personal existence is Christianity's distinctive glory; and to the extent that our culture still appreciates such things as the rights of conscience, individual responsibility, and the dignity of persons, this is largely the legacy of Christian theology. Both the idea and the actual experience of personhood in Western society and culture are the fruit of Christianity's trinitarian onto-theology.[19] As John Grabowski has noted:

> The roots of the notion of "person" are closely interwoven with those of Christian theology. Historical study has demonstrated that the ancient world, whether in biblical or classical sources, did not have an equivalent concept, even though both provide important linguistic and conceptual antecedents to its development. It is only as the Church sought to articulate its faith concerning the unity of humanity and divinity in Christ or to express the idea of plurality within the unity of the divine essence that this concept emerged and began to take shape. In this sense it is correct to assert that the notion of person is a uniquely Christian theological insight and contribution to the broader intellectual history of humanity.[20]

Yet to say that the Church discovered the meaning of personhood as it sought to articulate the unity of humanity and divinity in Christ, or to express the idea of plurality within the unity of the divine essence, is perhaps to put the matter too abstractly, as though the concept was simply the product of speculative theology. Nothing could be farther from the truth. While theologians did develop a sophisticated language in an attempt to articulate the Church's experience, the experience itself came through the Church's *encounter* with the person of Jesus of Nazareth, the man who was born of Mary, was crucified under Pilate, and was buried by his friends and followers. It was *this* Jesus whom God raised to life again. It was *this* Jesus who was declared to be both Lord and Christ by the apostles (Acts 2:32ff.). And it is *this* Christ in whom our lives are now

19. See Cardinal Joseph Ratzinger, "Concerning the Notion of Person in Theology," *Communio: International Catholic Review* 17 (Fall 1990): 439-54.

20. Grabowski, "Person: Substance and Relation," 139-40.

hidden (Col. 3:3). As Martin Luther emphasized, God has opened his heart to us in the person of Christ. "See his friendly heart," Luther stressed, "so full of love for you, which compels him to bear the heavy burden of your conscience and guilt. After that ascend through Christ's heart to God's heart and see that Christ could not have shown this love to you if God, whom Christ obeys, had not willed it in eternal love."[21] And so it is that Jesus Christ was, and is, and will ever be the One in whom the meaning of personhood is revealed to the Church.

We note that the offense of the gospel is closely related to Christianity's stress upon personal responsibility, however. For while God's call to us in Christ opens up the possibility of truly personal existence, it also calls for our decision and so leaves open the possibility that we might refuse the invitation, indeed, that we might go our own way and try to establish ourselves in some other fashion. In fact, variations on the theme of refusing to respond to God's call in faith, hope, and love — on the theme of *despair*, as Kierkegaard put it — actually define the modern post-Christian condition.

And so it is not particularly surprising to find that the Christian understanding of God's personal self-revelation in Christ — particularly as expressed in the doctrine of the Trinity — has proven offensive to modern post-Christian sensibilities. After all, Christian understanding intensifies what Kierkegaard termed "the earnestness of existence" by quite clearly placing us in a position of having to respond to God's call. We would much rather not have been placed in this position, and in an attempt to evade our "response-ability," modern post-Christian thought has sought to debunk the suggestion that God could possibly have gotten so close to us as to be able to call us into personal relation with himself. The traditional Christian notions of Revelation and of Incarnation have thus been deemed to be absurd within modern thought; the doctrine of the Trinity has been dismissed as an illogical impossibility; and Christianity has been reduced to the status of a "high" religion — perhaps even the "highest" — of deep moral insight.[22]

21. Martin Luther, cited in Paul Althaus, *The Theology of Martin Luther*, trans. Robert C. Schultz (Philadelphia: Fortress Press, 1966), 183-84, n. 14.

22. "Men have confused Christianity in many ways," Kierkegaard noted in *Works of Love: Some Christian Reflections in the Form of Discourse*, trans. Howard and Edna Hong (New York: Harper & Row, 1962), 70, "but among them is this way of calling it the highest, the deepest, and thereby making it appear that the purely human was

"Whatever or whoever 'god' is," modern thinkers have said in effect, "he must possess more self-respect than to want to be as intimately related to us as traditional Christianity has suggested so vulgarly." Such sentiment is often taken to be an indication of deep reverence for "the divine," but it is really only an evasive maneuver, for what is most often left unsaid is that we would much rather be left alone to create ourselves by ourselves anyway.

Having been left to its own devices, modern post-Christian thought has not been able to articulate an adequate basis for individuality and personality, however. Nor will it ever be able to do so, for it is committed, almost by definition, to rejecting the traditional Christian answers to the questions of who God is and of who we are before him. This, intellectually speaking, is the way of the modern world, and it comes as no great surprise. What does come as something of a disturbing surprise, however, is the extent to which trinitarian theology has been forgotten within our churches of late. For all of our orthodox profession of faith in the Trinity, we are very often "unitarian" in practice, simply imagining God to be a source of power, as some*thing* to be utilized, and thus failing to cultivate any genuinely personal relationship with him. As Karl Rahner lamented: "One might almost dare to affirm that if the doctrine of the Trinity were to be erased as false, most religious literature could be preserved almost unchanged throughout the process."[23] But what does this suggest except that we may ourselves have forgotten just Whom it is that we bear witness to in the Church? If this is in fact the case, furthermore, how can we expect our churches to offer any real resistance to the secularity and impersonality of modern society and culture? How can we expect to be able to restrain the secular and impersonal drift of modern institutional life? The answer, of course, is that we cannot, for unless we are equipped with the appropriate *theology*, with the truth of God's Self-revelation and hence with the truth of who we are in relation to him, we have no real alternative to offer in lieu of modernity's tragically less than personal anthropologies. In discerning

---

related to Christianity as the high or the higher to the highest or supremely highest. But this is a deceptive way of speaking which untruthfully and improperly lets Christianity in a meddlesome way try to ingratiate itself with human curiosity and craving for knowledge."

23. Rahner, cited in Kallistos Ware, "The Human Person as an Icon of the Trinity," *Sobernost* 8 (1986): 6.

just what it means for us to be *in* but not *of* the modern world, in other words, we must begin by reconsidering the essentially personal nature of God. In this connection, while modern post-Christian thought retains a vague awareness of the importance of individuality and personality, its refusal to ground these notions in God's Self-revelation means that it can have no real consciousness of the relational essence that forms the absolute ground of each one of us, an absolute ground which transcends social achievement and psychological and/or cultural advantage.[24] Bearing witness to the infinite personal God, then, and hence the possibility of genuinely personal existence in him, is precisely to be "salt and light" in the contemporary situation. As T. F. Torrance recently noted:

> Far from crushing our creaturely nature or damaging our personal existence, the indwelling presence of God through Jesus Christ and in the Holy Spirit has the effect of healing and restoring and deepening human personal being . . . it is through Christ and in the Spirit that we are granted personalising communion with the ever-living God in the perfection of his triune personal being.[25]

Although the Scriptures instruct us that the divine nature is revealed already in the creation, and indeed in our own created nature, we are also told that sin prevents us from benefiting from creation's testimony and that our thinking has become foolish and useless (Rom. 1:20-21). If we find that we are able now to speak about the triune and personal nature of God, then this knowledge must somehow have been made known to us apart from nature, and in such a way that we have been enabled to understand it. This knowledge, in short, must have been *revealed* to us.

Of course, in actual fact God's revelation of himself as triune and personal has a long history which began with his gracious call to Abram, and eventually to Israel, to go out from among the nations and to live in covenantal relation with him. God's call to the nation of Israel had the effect of placing *spiritual* agency and *personal* will at

---

24. Guardini, *The End of the Modern World*, 121.
25. T. F. Torrance, *The Trinitarian Faith: The Evangelical Theology of the Ancient Catholic Church* (Edinburgh: T. & T. Clark, 1993), 230-31.

the center of existence in the place of the impersonal forces of nature and fate. It thus reopened the possibility of truly human existence. Indeed, ancient Israel's exodus from Egypt was far more than simply a demographic relocation. It represented an escape from an ancient religious consciousness that had long sought to dissolve the human into the merely natural. It was in ancient Israel, then, and on the basis of God's gracious call, that human existence first emerged clearly as a kind of existence that transcends nature, possessing a quality of being which, while obviously still related to the natural, is also truly spiritual and capable of genuine conversation with God. This is the kind of being that is celebrated in the eighth Psalm as having been created "a little lower than the heavenly beings" and as having been given dominion over the other merely natural works of God's hands. This new humanity which was called into existence by God was not simply an unarticulated mass or species, furthermore, but a family of individuals, each capable of consciously responding to God's call in freedom. In this connection, social historian Eric Voegelin insisted that the impact of God's revelation of himself to Israel was such as to have given rise to a fundamentally new kind of human consciousness or, as he termed it, a "leap in being." "The leap in being, the experience of divine being as world transcendent," Voegelin noted, "is inseparable from the understanding of man as human. The personal soul as the sensorium of transcendence must develop parallel with the understanding of a transcendent God."[26]

The Hebraic conception of the human person thus emerged as something qualitatively different from the very limited conception permitted within pagan consciousness. Strictly speaking, few if any individuals within ancient pagan culture appear to have been accorded the status of what today we would call "persons," that is, few if any were considered capable of the exercise of real personal will. While the king may have been deemed capable of the exercise of freedom, or the priests, or the ruling caste, most were not and were instead simply held to be mindless representatives or "archetypes" of natural and/or cosmic processes. "What is new in the eleventh and tenth centuries of Israelite history," Voegelin observed:

26. Eric Voegelin, *Order and History*, Vol. 1, *Israel and Revelation* (Louisiana State University Press, 1956), 235.

is the application of . . . psychological knowledge to the understanding of personalities who, as individuals, have become the carriers of a spiritual force on the scene of pragmatic history. No such character portraits [as those found on page after page in the Old Testament] were ever drawn of Babylonian, Assyrian, or Egyptian rulers, whose personalities . . . disappear behind their function as the representatives and preservers of cosmic order in society.[27]

It is in this connection that we note that it was precisely because human existence was so closely identified with nature in archaic cosmology that this cosmology was so vehemently repudiated by Moses and the Prophets. In effect, pagan understanding prevented individuals from communicating *as persons* with the transcendent personal God. It absolved individuals of real "response-ability" before God. As long as the "gods" could be experienced indirectly through natural and/or cosmic processes, or through the mediation of human representatives of these processes, the personal love of God simply could not become the "ordering center of the soul."[28]

Describing ancient Israel's experience of God as "personal" is somewhat anachronistic, however, for this specific term would only come into use as the Christian Church struggled to develop a language adequate to its experience of God's self-revelation in Jesus Christ. Along this line, in his detailed study *The Triune Identity* (1982), Robert Jensen stresses that one of the distinguishing characteristics of the entire biblical tradition is its impassioned insistence upon precision with respect to the divine *name*.[29] Thus, whereas in classical thought the word "god" registered a rather vague sentiment of "deity-in-general" — either indistinguishable from the larger cosmic order or captive within this order — in the Old Testament the tetragrammaton YHWH denoted the specific God of Abraham, Isaac, and Jacob: the God who, while sovereign over his creation, had nevertheless spoken specifically to Israel and had acted expressly on Israel's behalf, bringing one particular nation out of the land of bondage and into the land of the promise. It was this

27. Ibid., 223.
28. Ibid., 240.
29. Robert W. Jensen, *The Triune Identity: God According to the Gospel* (Philadelphia: Fortress, 1982).

particular God who would be true to his promises, and *his* was, therefore, the name that the people were forbidden to misuse.

Jensen went on to observe that the Christian Church inherited this emphasis upon precision with respect to the divine name, but that instead of continuing to use the tetragrammaton, the early Church arrived instead at the formulation "Father, Son, and Holy Spirit" to describe the God of the gospel. This was the name that best described the Church's primal experience of redemption in Christ.[30] The Church arrived at the formulation "Father, Son, and Holy Spirit" after having struggled to come to terms with three crucial questions: Who *is* Jesus? Who *is* the Father who sent his Son into the world? and Who *is* the Comforter who is sent by the Father at the request of the Son to lead the Church into all truth? The early Church concluded that the answer to all three of these questions must be "God" *without qualification. God* created the world and the Church; *God* was in Christ reconciling the world to himself; and *God* is in the Church enabling the Church to recognize his Christ and thus enabling the Church to be reconciled with God. And yet the "God" who does all of these things, while One in spirit and intention and power, is obviously neither monolithic nor monochromatic. Rather, he is manifold and varied, necessarily describable in terms of a *tri-unity* of Father, Son, and Holy Spirit.

The Church then borrowed the term "person" *(prosopon)* from the Greek, a term of relatively little consequence in either classical Greek or Hebrew thought, to describe the nature and quality of the relations between the Father, the Son, and the Holy Spirit in the unity of the Godhead.[31] The term was used to denote divine individuality. Each divine "person" was held to possess genuine individuality vis-à-vis the other two. Yet the individuality of each of the divine persons was not revealed to be such as to result in a kind of tri-theism, for the individuality of each one is clearly realized only *in relation* to the other two. "Don't you believe that I am in the Father, and that the Father is in me?" Jesus asks his Church (John 14:10); "The words I say to you are

---

30. Ibid., 21.

31. In addition to Jensen, see also Ratzinger, "Concerning the Notion of Person in Theology"; John D. Zizioulas, *Being as Communion: Studies in Personhood and the Church* (Crestwood, NY: St. Vladimir's Seminary Press, 1985); and Thomas F. Torrance, "The Trinitarian Structure of Reality," in *Reality and Scientific Theology* (Edinburgh: Scottish Academic Press, 1985).

not just my own. Rather, it is the Father, living in me, who is doing his work." The early Church was thus able to recognize that God the Father is the eternal source of the Son's and the Spirit's Godhead; God the Son is the eternal recipient of the Father's Godhead; and God the Spirit is the eternal Spirit of the Son's possession of the Father's Godhead.[32] The divine persons are, in short, mutually constituting, eternally maintaining each other's existence in love. "The unity of God," St. Basil wrote (c. 370), "lies in the communion [*koinonia*] of the Godhead."[33] This is why the apostle John's statement that "God is love" (1 John 4:8, 16) must be understood as an ontological assertion and not simply as modifying God's character, as if simply to say that God is loving. Love is not simply something that God creates. It is the essence of his existence. It is the quality of the relation that eternally unites the Father, the Son and the Holy Spirit. It is thus the essence of all existence.

Zizioulas recently coined the term "being in communion" to describe the early Church's understanding of God's triune identity. The critical implication stemming from this understanding is that because God's essential being is personal and communal, personal relationality must be the ground of creaturely existence as well. Put somewhat differently, because God can only be truly known through the personal actions of faith, hope, and love, this must also be true of the world he has created. We should not therefore be surprised to find that, as Michael Polanyi and others have pointed out, even the inanimate creation is really only genuinely known through personal commitment and communion.[34] "Being means life," Zizioulas comments, "and life means communion."[35]

It is this conception of God as "being in communion" that has formed the theological foundation of the Church's understanding of the nature and possibilities of human existence. Indeed, it is only in the ongoing encounter with the Father, through the Son, and in the power of the Holy Spirit, that the Church is enabled to know and to say what truly human existence really is. Because we continually wit-

32. Jensen, *The Triune Identity*, 106.
33. Basil, cited in Ware, "The Human Person as an Icon of the Trinity," 8.
34. See Michael Polanyi, *Personal Knowledge* (New York: Harper Torchbooks, 1964).
35. Zizioulas, *Being in Communion*, 16.

ness the quality of the Father's love for the Church in the gift of his only begotten Son, and because we celebrate the Son's willingness to lay down his life for the sake of the Church, and because we confess the Father's and the Son's gift of the Comforter to guide the Church into all truth, we have been enabled to know what love really is. It is on the basis of what the Church has *seen and heard,* in other words, that we have been enabled to know that, although we must each give evidence of genuine individuality and we must each act in real freedom, we only truly become ourselves as we freely give ourselves away to others in love. "We love," the Apostle recognizes, "because he first loved us" (1 John 4:19).

Thus it was that the early Church came to understand that the essence of personal existence is self-transcendence, for it was the self-transcendent love shown to the Church by the Father, the Son, and the Holy Spirit in their eternal "being in communion" that bore witness to the foundation upon which all genuine human individuality, personality, and relatedness must be developed. This is how "the image and likeness of God," emphasized in the account of our creation (Gen. 1:26-27), is therefore to be understood, and it is to the renewal of the possibility of genuine mutuality and love that we are called in Christ by grace through faith (Col. 3:10).

Of those who subsequently elaborated upon the early Church's theology of personhood, the twelfth-century Victorine mystic, Richard of St. Victor (d. 1173), has been one of the most creative and helpful. Richard started from the New Testament's assertion that "God is love" (1 John 4:8, 16), but then sought to qualify this assertion by considering our own experience of love. Richard reasoned that because we know, even in the imperfection of human relationships, that self-love is not yet true love, divine love must entail genuine mutuality. For divine love to entail genuine mutuality, furthermore, there must be a plurality of persons within the Godhead, persons capable of real freedom. Finally, if the divine love is to be truly copious and abounding, the plurality within the Godhead must extend beyond the simple mutuality of two persons to include a third. "It is necessary," Richard argued, "that each of those loved supremely and loving supremely should search with equal desire for someone who would be mutually loved and with equal concord willingly possess him. . . . Thus you see how the perfection of charity requires a Trinity of persons, without which it is wholly unable to subsist in the integrity of its fullness. . . . And so a sharing of love cannot exist among any less than three persons."[36] As Kallistos Ware has noted with respect to Richard's insights: "it is mutual love that provides, within our human experience, the least imperfect analogue of divine life."[37] Interestingly, Richard of St. Victor's discussion of interpersonal relations and his observation that true love must be genuinely self-transcendent anticipate the insights of twentieth-century personalism, both philosophical and theological.[38]

It is because the ground of genuinely human existence is inescapably relational that we find our awareness of ourselves to be indirect and reflexive.[39] Indeed, we find that we are only really able to see ourselves as reflected in our relations with others, with the world, and ultimately with God. If these relations are whole and true, we will find that we will experience real freedom. If, on the other hand, our relations are distorted — as they invariably are in our fallen situation because of our sinful hearts — then our experience of ourselves will be distorted as well, and we will find ourselves entrapped and enslaved in various ways. In this connection, we are never actually able to construct ourselves by ourselves, as typically modern anthropologies suggest, and we do not ever really stand alone, as modern liberal ideology has so doggedly insisted. Rather, we always stand *in relation* to others, and it is the quality of these relations — and most especially the quality of our relation to God in Christ — that determines the quality of our own existence. With the measure we use, it has been truly said, so it will also be measured to us (Luke 6:38). Or, to put this more bluntly, *we become what we love*. Such is the glory of having been created in the image and likeness of God. Yet this capacity for mutuality is also our greatest burden, for we have been left free to determine the quality of the relations we will have with God, with others, and to the world. This freedom is a reflection of the quality of the relation that God has freely chosen to have with us.

Although it is possible for us to run from our freedom by denying

36. Richard of St. Victor, "On the Trinity: Book III," 385, 88.

37. Ware, "The Human Person as an Icon of the Trinity," 15.

38. See Ewert Cousins, "A Theology of Interpersonal Relations," *Thought* 45, no. 1 (1970): 56.

39. Alister I. McFadyen, *The Call the Personhood: A Christian Theory of the Individual in Social Relationships* (Cambridge: Cambridge University Press, 1990), 22.

that we possess it, or by surrendering it to others, this evasion itself amounts to a decision to be related to others and to the world — and ultimately to God — in a certain way. The quality of this chosen relation, furthermore, will determine the quality and possibilities of our own existence. This, as we have said on a number of occasions, is the earnestness of existence. For although the relational quality of human life can be seriously damaged and distorted, it can never — not even in the case of severe autism — be entirely obliterated. We always remain "response-able" at some level, however debased we may have become relative to our created potential. If we do not choose to enter into relation with God and with each other in a fully human — which is to say a loving, self-transcending — fashion, then this only means that we will instead relate to these others in a subhuman fashion, and that we will ourselves become something less than fully human in the process, though still responsible before God for the choices we have made. Such, after all, is the nature of the idolatry that characterizes the fallen human condition in sin (Rom. 1:25). As the Psalmist observed:

> The idols of the nations are silver and gold, made by the hands
> of men.
> They have mouths, but cannot speak, eyes, but they cannot see;
> they have ears, but cannot hear, nor is there breath in their
> mouths.
> Those who make them will be like them, and so will all who trust
> in them. (Ps. 135:15-18)

Put somewhat differently, the reflexive nature of our existence ensures that we will become whatever it is that we worship. If we worship "nature," then our self-understanding — if it can even be called that — will be imprisoned within the fateful confines of naturalism and determinism. If we worship technological "making," and if we view the world and others as "devices" to be constructed and manipulated in the service of technical-rational ends, then we will view the quality and possibilities of our own existence in the same fashion.[40] If, finally, we worship ourselves, foreclosing on the possibility of self-transcendence

---

40. See Arnold Gehlen, *Man in the Age of Technology*, trans. Patricia Lipscomb (New York: Columbia University Press, 1980), 13ff.

and undermining our ability to be truly related to God and to our neighbor, then we will in the end become incapable of experiencing our selves at all.[41] And so we can see that when Jesus tells us that "whoever finds his life will lose it, and whoever loses his life for my sake will find it" (Matt. 10:39), he is not simply speaking of the rule of Christian religious devotion, but of the rule of existence itself. We *must* lose ourselves to Christ and others if we are ever truly to find ourselves.

Yet losing ourselves to Christ necessarily entails suffering. The "loss" of self Jesus speaks of in the above passage, or his insistence (Matt. 16:24) that "if anyone would come after me, he must deny himself and take up his cross and follow me . . . ," are not simply metaphorical expressions. Rather, this loss, and this denial of self, are quite painfully real and run entirely counter to our fallen nature. This is the final and perhaps most weighty point to make in trying to understand personal existence after the likeness of the divine "being in communion." The quality of the love shared eternally by the Father, the Son, and the Holy Spirit is *kenotic;* it is a suffering love. Kallistos Ware described it very beautifully:

> Here, then, is a further corollary of the Trinitarian image. To be human, after the image and likeness of God the Holy Trinity, means to love others with a love that is costly and self-sacrificing. If God the Father so loved us that he gave his only-begotten Son to die for us on the Cross, if God the Son so loved us that he descended into hell on our behalf, then we shall only be truly in the image and likeness of the Trinity if we also lay down our lives for each other. Without *kenosis* and cross-bearing, without the exchange of substituted love and all the voluntary suffering which this involves, there can be no genuine likeness to the Trinity. 'Let us love one another,' we proclaim in the Liturgy, 'that with one mind we may confess Father, Son and Holy Spirit, the Trinity consubstantial and undivided.' Without mutual love there is no true confession of faith in the Trinity. But 'love one another' means 'lay down your lives for one another.'[42]

Thankfully, we have not been left to our own devices in trying to muster the courage to lay down our lives for the sake of Christ and for each

41. McFadyen, *The Call to Personhood,* 26-27.
42. Ware, "The Human Person as an Icon of the Trinity," 20.

other. Rather, our ability to suffer with and for each other, and for the sake of the Kingdom of God, and indeed our ability to rejoice in our sufferings, is itself a reflection of the fact that, as the apostle Paul writes (Rom. 5:5), "God has poured out his love into our hearts by the Holy Spirit." God supplies everything that we lack, in other words, and it is entirely on the basis of his gracious provision that we are enabled to become truly ourselves in relation to him.

This uniquely Christian theology of personhood provides the only truly adequate basis for evaluating and for prophetically resisting the secularity and impersonality of so much of modern society and culture. T. F. Torrance put this well when he wrote:

> I submit that it is only through a divine Trinity who admits us to communion with himself in his own transcendence that we can be consistently and persistently personal, with the kind of freedom, openness and transcendent reference which we need both to develop our own personal and social culture and our scientific exploration of the universe. I believe that it is in a radical renewing of our personal and inter-personal structures that comes from communion with God, that we are to look for a healing of the deep splits which have opened up in our modern civilisation. But this means that what we need is the recovery of spiritual being, being that is open to personal reality and not imprisoned in its own self-centredness.[43]

Of course, one of the deepest splits that has opened up within our modern civilization has been between our need for genuinely personal relatedness and the dreary impersonality of so much of modern institutional life, a split that has been helpfully characterized as a kind of "overgrowth of objective culture" at the expense of truly human subjectivity.[44] This overgrowth of objectivity is evident in the "managed" quality of modern political life; in modern science's "objectification" of the world and in the utilitarian spirit of modern technology; and in the modern economy's "leveling" of all quality by means of merely quantitative monetary abstraction. Indeed, the overgrowth of objective culture

---

43. Thomas F. Torrance, *Reality and Scientific Theology*, 196.

44. Georg Simmel, "The Metropolis and Mental Life," in *The Sociology of Georg Simmel*, trans. and ed. Kurt H. Wolff (Glencoe, IL: The Free Press, 1950), 421-22.

is even evident in the so-called private sphere of subjective autonomy, for it appears that self-constructing individuals quite often envision and treat even themselves largely as manipulable objects. If we are to assume a prophetic stance over and against the secularity and impersonality of modern, and now "postmodern," society and culture, then, we will need to examine the reasons for this "overgrowth of objective culture." We will also need to evaluate carefully the quality of relatedness — to God, to others, and to the world — that such an overgrowth of objectivity discloses. Our previous discussions have hopefully provided a kind of introduction to the former consideration. We still stand to learn a great deal with respect to the latter from Martin Buber's remarkable little book *I and Thou* (1922).

"I-Thou" versus "I-It"

By the time Buber wrote *I and Thou* in the early 1920s, many had already observed that the impersonality of modern society and culture seemed somehow related to the growth of "objectivity" in modern science and technology, in political affairs, and in modern economic life. Buber's concern in *I and Thou*, then, was to explain this development at the deepest level. He began by observing that the human attitude toward the world is basically two-sided. The world may be viewed as an "object," in effect, ontologically inferior to the knowing subject, in which case it will be experienced in terms of the juxtaposition of "I" and "it." Or the world may be beheld as a genuine "other," that is, on an ontological par with us as we behold it. In this latter case, the world will be experienced personally as in the relation between an "I" and a "Thou." To the extent that we desire to achieve control over the world, Buber continued, we will be attracted by the utility of rendering it "objectively," for rendering the world in terms of potentially manipulable objects is far easier and much more conducive to effective management than contemplating the world, admiring it, entering into genuine dialogue with it, and caring for it. Along this line, Buber observed that the "objectification" of the world has become, just as we have seen, a hallmark of modern civilization.

Buber then went on to observe that the *self-understanding* emerging out of the "I-It" conjunction is fundamentally different from that which is made possible in the "I-Thou" relation, and this is the heart of his argument. The act of objectification, Buber observed, does not really require one's whole self, but rather discloses a kind of one-sided relation in which there is really only one active voice. The "I-it" conjunction does not really expose the self, therefore, to the possibility of relational mutuality. It does not require or foster self-transcendence. As Alister McFadyen noted more recently in a study entitled *The Call to Personhood* (1990):

> Intending someone or something as an object is to intend the relation as a monologue. For an object is intended and perceived as having no independent meaning or existence apart from this relation. It cannot offer a point of moral resistance because it is not perceived as ethically transcendent. The relation can only be exploitative and manipulative. . . . The I of an I-It relation has an unbounded sense of its proper claims, seeking from the other only that which is a confirmatory repetition of itself. In seeking oneself from the other, one is engaged in a one-way communication open only to oneself. . . .[45]

Of course, while this "one-way communication open only to oneself" may enhance our ability to control the world in certain respects, it also inhibits our ability to enter into an "I-Thou" relation with the world, with other people, and ultimately with God, and so is extremely costly in personal terms. In the first instance, the objective attitude essentially prevents us from apprehending such things as beauty, for anything that is appreciated only as a "resource" — that is, as something to be utilized — cannot really be apprehended as beautiful.[46] The objective spirit is also quite obviously destructive of any number of relationships that it is possible to have with other persons. While the objective utilization of others may be of some benefit to instrumental relationality and may improve our ability to "get things done" in the world, it is not at all conducive to such things as family, friendship, camaraderie, and fellowship. It is obviously not conducive to worship either. Indeed, the objective attitude is largely

---

45. McFadyen, *The Call to Personhood*, 122-23.
46. George Grant, *Technology and Justice* (Toronto: Anansi, 1986), 51.

atheistic, even if only tacitly and practically so, for the possibility of truly spiritual relationality simply does not survive the process of objectification. While the various idols do not seem to mind being treated as objects, in other words, the living God does not allow himself to be known "objectively," that is, as an object of human manipulation. If we seek to know him in this fashion, he quite quickly retreats from our view. As Buber noted in a collection of essays entitled *The Eclipse of God* (1952):

> It has become necessary to proclaim that God is "dead." Actually, this proclamation means only that man has become incapable of apprehending a reality absolutely independent of himself and of having a relation with it — incapable, moreover, of imaginatively perceiving this reality and representing it in images, since it eludes direct contemplation. For the great images of God fashioned by mankind are born not of imagination but of real encounters with real divine power and glory. Man's capacity to apprehend the divine in images is lamed in the same measure as is his capacity to experience a reality independent of himself.[47]

It is precisely our modern preoccupation with control, in other words, that has led to the widespread impression that God is distant and/or disinterested.[48] Preoccupied with establishing mastery over the world, over others, and even over the self, the modern and now "postmodern" mind assumes that God must be preoccupied with the same things and in much the same way. Yet this modern "theology" only exacerbates the apparent conflict, mentioned earlier, between divine sovereignty and human creativity, and only strengthens the typically modern presumption that we can only really achieve genuine independence by displacing God from the world altogether. "The unbelieving marrow of the capricious man," Buber observed, "cannot perceive anything but unbelief and caprice, positing ends and devising means. His world is devoid of sacrifice and grace, encounter and presence, but shot

---

47. Martin Buber, *The Eclipse of God: Studies in the Relation between Religion and Philosophy* (New York: Harper & Row, 1952), 14.

48. James M. Houston, "Do the Works of Men Secularise the Service of Christ?" *Interchange* 45 (1989): 62.

through with ends and means."[49] And so it is that our knowledge and experience of God are quite directly related to our ability to sustain "I-Thou" relations and, indeed, to our capacity to apprehend "otherness" in general.

It is, of course, not terribly surprising to find that the overgrowth of objectivity in modern society and culture has yielded the fruit of loneliness. Unable to truly apprehend others, the self that is possessed by the spirit of objectification is itself reduced to an object incapable of

49. Buber, *I and Thou*, 110. Interestingly, this is why Buber is suspicious of those who would use the language of "idolatry" to describe the modern problem. He comments (pp. 153-55): "A modern philosopher [apparently Max Scheler] supposes that every man believes of necessity either in God or in 'idols' — which is to say, some finite good, such as his nation, his art, power, knowledge, the acquisition of money, the 'ever-repeated triumph with women' — some good that has become an absolute value for him, taking its place between him and God; and if only one proves to a man the conditionality of this good, thus 'smashing' the idol, then the diverted religious act would all by itself return to its proper object. . . . This view presupposes that man's relation to the finite goods that he 'idolizes' is essentially the same as his relationship to God, as if only the object were different: only in that case could the mere substitution of the proper object for the wrong one save the man who has gone wrong. But a man's relation to the 'particular something' that arrogates the supreme throne of his life's values, pushing eternity aside, is always directed toward the experience and use of an It, a thing, an object of enjoyment. For only this kind of relation can bar the view to God, by interposing the impenetrable It-world; the relationship that says You always opens it up again. Whoever is dominated by the idol whom he wants to acquire, have, and hold, possessed by his desire to possess, can find a way to God only by returning, which involves a change not only of the goal but also of the kind of movement. One can heal the possessed only by awakening and educating him to association, not by directing his possession toward God. . . . It is blasphemy when a man whose idol has fallen down behind the altar desires to offer to God the unholy sacrifice that is piled up on the desecrated altar. . . . If one serves a people in a fire kindled by immeasurable fate — if one is willing to devote oneself to it, one means God. But if the nation is for him an idol to which he desires to subjugate everything because in its image he extols his own — do you fancy that you only have to spoil the nation for him and he will then see the truth? And what is it supposed to mean that a man treats money, which is un-being incarnate, 'as if it were God'? What does the voluptuous delight of rapacity and hoarding have in common with the joy over the presence of that which is present? Can mammon's slave say You to money? And what could God be to him if he does not know how to say You? He cannot serve two masters — not even one after the other; he must first learn to serve differently. . . . Whoever has been converted by substitution, now 'has' a phantom that he calls God. God, however, the eternal presence, cannot be had. Woe unto the possessed who fancy that they possess God!"

truly personal existence. The cost of establishing control over the world by means of technical-rational objectification, in other words, has been nothing short of personal existence, and we have established a measure of control over our world only to discover that the self-understanding responsible for initiating the process — which seemed at first to be so confident in its position in the universe — has by now vanished into "postmodern" nothingness. This is perhaps the supreme irony of the modern intellectual condition. The immensely painful and perplexing nature of this condition, furthermore, which might otherwise be such as to call the whole project of objectification into question, is assuaged by the distractions and diversions of consumer culture, so that even the experience of the "death of the soul" has been reduced to a kind of manipulable — and marketable — factor within the modern equation.

Of course, this is not to suggest that we must somehow forsake all desire for control for the sake of personal existence. After all, genuine individuality presupposes freedom, and freedom would be meaningless in the absence of all control. Rather than renouncing all aspirations to control, then, the critical matter, just as Buber suggested, has to do with the self-understanding disclosed by the relative ordering of "I-it" and "I-Thou" relations. If personal relations are eclipsed by or subordinated to merely impersonal ones, what else does this say about us except that we must imagine ourselves to be independent and, finally, self-existent. Love, on the other hand, requires us to be genuinely open to others, and indeed to the possibility of "otherness" even in nature, in which case objective and impersonal relations will always be understood to be in the service of personal ones.

The difficult problem we face today, as we have seen, is that the manipulative "objectivity" required within modernity's central institutions encourages us to adopt a manipulative attitude toward the rest of our lives. After all, "I-It" relationality promises faster results with less effort. Objectification and *not* contemplation, we are told in effect, is the surest route to mastery and so to the alleviation of our anxieties. To the extent that we believe this typically modern lie, however, we are drawn into a kind of endless regress, for objectification actually only has the effect of intensifying our anxiety because it further erodes the possibility of genuinely personal existence. Under modern conditions, this erosion only makes objectification seem all the more necessary, and so forth. Indeed, we are told that we really have no other choice today *but* to pursue control over the world by means of an "I-It" relationality. Buber concludes:

> In sick ages it happens that the It-world, no longer irrigated and fertilized by the living currents of the You-world, severed and stagnant, becomes a gigantic swamp phantom and overpowers man. As he accommodates himself to a world of objects that no longer achieve any presence for him, he succumbs to it. Then common causality grows into an oppressive and crushing doom.[50]

Healing the sickness of our age will thus require us, at the very least, to swim against the modern current of objectification for the sake of control.

On Being in But Not of the Modern World

The gospel of Jesus Christ has always been a "stumbling block to Jews and foolishness to Gentiles" (1 Cor. 1:23) for a variety of reasons, and it will undoubtedly continue to give offense until the end of history. Yet the contemporary situation is such that even before the gospel manages to give offense, it is quite often discarded as irrelevant. This is one of the measures of the novelty of modern, and now of purportedly "postmodern," times. The age-old questions of truth and error, of orthodoxy and heresy, and even those of salvation and perdition, appear to be simply uninteresting from the contemporary point of view. There are, as we have seen, any number of reasons for this, but perhaps the most basic is that such questions inevitably point to a reality outside and independent of our own social construction of reality. Yet we no longer believe that such a reality exists. Our collective sense of responsibility for the world has become so grossly inflated, and our relation to the world so thoroughly objectified, that the whole world now simply appears to us to be grist for the mill of self-construction. As we have become increasingly incapable of truly apprehending "otherness," however, we have essentially been inoculated against the possibility of experiencing truly personal existence. Secular self-definition has thus

50. Buber, *I and Thou*, 102-3.

come at the cost of meaninglessness and impersonality. Such is the way of the modern world.

Here it is important to stress that many of those wholly committed to the project of secular self-definition are not any happier with modernity's meaninglessness and impersonality than those of us who attribute these problems to modernity's secularity. In this connection, we need to recognize that we face something of a fork in the road at present with respect to the matter of self-transcendence, with the followers of Nietzsche pointing in one direction and with Jesus Christ pointing in quite a different direction. The "postmodern" followers of Nietzsche would have us reach beyond the meaninglessness and impersonality of contemporary society and culture by sheer acts of will. From this point of view, it is precisely the autonomous will-to-self-definition, the will to power, that is authentically human, and it is believed that it will be through the exertion of our will to power that we will somehow "transcend" our present circumstances. Needless to say, the potential for brutality and death in this Nietzschean "spirituality" is very great. In sharp contrast to this "postmodern" Nietzscheanism, Jesus Christ exhorts us to heroic self-transcendence by means of love understood in terms of servanthood. "The kings of the Gentiles lord it over them," Jesus reminded his disciples (Luke 22:25-26), "and those who exercise authority over them call themselves Benefactors. But you are not to be like that. Instead, the greatest among you should be like the youngest, and the one who rules like the one who serves." From a Christian point of view, then, the path of genuine self-transcendence, of authentic spirituality, lies in giving one's self away for the sake of Christ and for the sake of one's neighbor. Again, it is the way of the cross.

In sum, we might say that the key to living *in* but not *of* the modern world lies in the recovery of the possibility of genuinely personal relationality, and thus in the recovery of our capacity for relating to the world, to others, and ultimately to God in such a way as not simply to reduce them all to objects potentially subject to our control. Such a rediscovery of truly personal relationality would pose an elementary yet profound challenge to the will-to-self-definition which, as we have seen, holds much of the modern world together. Of course, this is far more easily said than done, especially under modern conditions. For we must begin by conceding that we cannot manage this recovery all by ourselves. Indeed, as the nature of personal existence is dialogical and dialectical, we must begin by confessing that we must be invited — indeed, *called* — into personal relation with each other and with God *by God himself*, and that our response to this call — which is itself a gift of grace — must be to surrender ourselves to God and to our neighbor in love. Such a confession will not come at all naturally in the context of our culture of narcissism. Yet apart from surrendering ourselves to others — and ultimately to God in Christ — in love and trust, the only other possibility is for us to remain stuck in the state of self-enclosure that Kierkegaard labeled "despair."

Happily, and as we have already seen, the Church exists to bear witness to the fact that we have been graciously invited into a personal relationship with the living God. Indeed, the Church witnesses to the possibility of sharing eternally in the personal communion of the Father, the Son, and the Holy Spirit. This is the life of the world to come over and against which this-worldly existence pales into insignificance and worthlessness. This is also the essence of the Kingdom of God that Christians already mysteriously bear within themselves. In terms of our analysis above, the Church bears witness to the possibility of experiencing God's infinitely loving and gracious *Otherness* and thus to finding genuinely personal existence in and through him.

How does the Church bear witness to the possibility of entering into fellowship with the living God? Certainly not by mimicking the falsely "objective" spirit of the age and by trying to demonstrate the "cash value" of Christian faith with respect to those tasks that the world has set for "religion." Nor can it by surrendering to the therapeutic sensibilities of contemporary culture, which, as we have seen, ultimately deny this possibility in their advocacy of autonomous self-construction. Both of these apologetic strategies are attractive today because they appear to demonstrate the relevance of Christian faith within contemporary culture. Indeed, both strategies are presently employed by churches of both "liberal" and "conservative" theological persuasions. But it should be amply clear by now that, to the extent that the Christian faith is made to appear attractive from the worldly point of view, this probably means that faith has somehow been emptied of the possibility of any real encounter with the living God, and so has really ceased to be faith at all. We speak most prophetically today, then, simply by bearing witness to the possibility of knowing a *living* God. This is the relation that Christian doctrine has been designed to protect. It is also the one possibility that our secular and impersonal modern world has almost completely lost sight of, in spite of its largely Christian origins.

Prayer is perhaps the Church's single most important witness to the living God — at least so long as prayer is not itself surrendered to the therapeutic or to the logic of technique — for real prayer is a dialogue. It discloses a genuinely personal relation. Jesus has called us to pray to the Father, not because the Father does not already know what we need (Matt. 6:8), but because he desires to see us enter into a *living* relation with the Father. He wants us to entrust ourselves to the Father on the sure basis of his completed work and by the empowering presence of the Holy Spirit. In this connection, the apostle Paul tells us that we are saved "by grace through faith" (Eph. 2:8). We are saved *by grace* because the invitation to enter into dialogue with the living God is, and can only be, issued by God himself. The invitation, as Paul says, is "the gift of God." We are saved *through faith*, furthermore, because our faith indicates that we have indeed chosen to enter into a living conversation with God. Faith moves us to read the Scriptures because we believe that the living God is speaking to us in and through them, and faith also leads us to pray because we believe that the living God answers prayer. Conversely, if we do not read, and if we do not pray, what else can this mean except that we have lost confidence in God's willingness — and perhaps even in his ability — to keep the conversation going?

The spiritual disciplines of *waiting* and *watching* for God need to be mentioned in connection with prayer, however, for God's answers to our prayers are rarely obvious, and his presence in the world is always ambiguous and somewhat hidden. Indeed, God's presence and work in the world is always such as to call for our interpretation. Along this line, we might say that his presence is such as to uphold belief, but it is also rather easily "explained away" by unbelief. With respect to the latter, it is precisely God's "hiddenness" and the ambiguity of his presence and work in the world that tempt many to doubt that he cares for us, and perhaps even to doubt that he exists at all. Yet it is important to stress that the kind of "proof" that unbelieving humanity demands of God's existence effectively obviates the need for faith and so denies the heart of the gospel, which is "by faith from first to last" (Rom. 1:17). In fact, under modern conditions the demand for "proof" most often discloses only the attempt to objectify our relation with God and to confine him within an "I-it" conjunction. But, here again, God does not allow himself to be known in this way. While he constantly confirms and demonstrates his gracious presence to those who place their trust in him, he refuses to adhere to merely human criteria for demonstrability. As Klaus Bockmuehl observed: "Demonstrability has man as its subject; man controls what is demonstrable. But demonstration has God as its subject; it thus confirms the freedom of God and the absence of human control."[51]

From the perspective of faith, then, God's "hiddenness" and the ambiguity of his work in the world bespeak his graciousness toward us. After all, it is ultimately for our sakes and not for his own that God has chosen to reveal himself only to those who earnestly seek him (Heb. 11:6), for it is only through earnest faith that we are enabled to enter into life, that is, into truly personal communion with the Father, the Son, and the Holy Spirit. It is for this reason that it would be pointless — and even counterproductive — for God to reveal himself too unambiguously at present. The interests of genuine faith and trust would simply not be served in the provocation of grudging submission. Of course, Scripture does speak of a time when God will reveal himself incontrovertibly, and that, indeed, on that day *every* knee will bow before God and *every* tongue will swear by him (Isa. 45:23; Rom. 14:11). Yet this unanimous confession of God's sovereign presence in the world waits for the end of history; it waits for the day of judgment, when the time for coming to faith shall have passed. At present we must wait and watch for God in faith, hope, and love. This is often difficult, but we should take heart in this necessity, for it means that there is still time to repent and to be forgiven for our sins. Besides, if we wait and watch for God, we will see him. As Christoph Blumhardt observed: "If one is watchful, one is always able to say something about the works of God. They happen all around us, in our hearts, and in our neighbors. If one is not watchful, though, one does not see anything."[52]

That the presence and work of God are disclosed only to those

---

51. Klaus Bockmuehl, *The Unreal God of Modern Theology: Bultmann, Barth, and the Theology of Atheism, A Call to Recovering the Truth of God's Reality* (Colorado Springs: Helmers & Howard, 1988), 152.

52. Blumhardt, cited in Karl Barth, *Action in Waiting for the Kingdom of God*, trans. the Hutterian Society of Brothers (Norfolk, CT: Deer Spring Press, 1979), 24.

who wait and watch for him raises rather serious questions about the presumptive activism which characterizes the life of the contemporary North American church. In fact, the contemporary preoccupation with such things as planning, with the organization and mobilization of resources, with "programming," with the projection of the Church's influence within the culture, etc., may actually be quite destructive of real faith. For not only does activism precipitate the phenomenon of ministry "burnout," but even more significantly it diverts our attention — and that of the watching world — away from God's agency and toward our own. Yet, as we have seen, this is the very definition of modern worldliness. And so, although Christian activism is very much in step with the manipulative spirit of modernity, it appears to be profoundly out of step with the Spirit of Christ. Indeed, it would seem to be a rather sure route to practical atheism. To paraphrase Martin Buber's comments cited at the beginning of this chapter, whoever knows the Church as something to be utilized — even presumably in the service of the Kingdom of God — must know God in the same way. Because God does not actually allow himself to be known in this way, however, Christian activism ends only in disillusionment and perhaps even in godlessness. And so we must continually remind ourselves that, just as Martin Luther confessed: "It is not we who can sustain the church, nor was it those who came before us, nor will it be those who come after us. It was, and is, and will be, the one who says: 'I am with you always, even to the end of time.'"[53]

In addition to prayer and to the spiritual disciplines of waiting and watching for God, the quality of our actual relation to God must be demonstrated in discipleship and obedience to his Word. Perhaps it is unnecessary even to say this, but the human condition in sin is such that knowledge is often detached from love, and our words are often disconnected from the habits of our hearts. Thus, although we are surrounded by a great deal of talk about religious experience today, and even by talk about God's presence in the world, we must insist that all such talk comes to naught as a genuine witness to God's Otherness — that is, it comes to naught as a witness to the possibility of really knowing the *living* God — unless it is accompanied by *holiness*. After all, religious

---

53. Luther, cited in Alister McGrath, *Luther's Theology of the Cross* (Oxford: Basil Blackwell, 1985), 181.

experience *as such* may not actually dislodge the autonomous self from its position at the center of its own universe, and the deceitfulness of the human heart is such that the failure of religious experience to "de-center" the self is not always *self*-evident.[54] As Kierkegaard observed, 'it is the very nature of despair to mask its existence as despair. It is only in the ethical claims of righteousness, then, that the self encounters Otherness in such a way as to limit its selfish desire to define itself; and it is often only in the act of submitting to the discipline of righteousness that we are given an indication that we are indeed participating in a living, two-sided conversation with God. This is why Jesus said (John 15:10): "If you obey my commands, you will remain in my love, just as I have obeyed my Father's commands and remain in his love." This is also why James writes that we are justified by what we do, and not by faith alone (James 2:24), for in the fallen context our deeds must confirm — even to ourselves! — that our faithful speech has indeed issued from a regenerate heart.

Unfortunately, many of our churches today attempt to mitigate the offense the gospel so often gives to modern sensibilities by failing to stress that faith must issue in obedience. Instead of conveying that our lives in Christ must rest upon the foundation of repentance and holiness, the gospel is often presented today as a kind of reflection of the depth of one's own innate spirituality. While perhaps of fleeting utility in capturing the world's attention, such a strategy only encourages the self-centered self to remain so, perhaps forever. Yet how could this possibly be construed as good news? By evading the matter of righteousness, such a truncated "gospel" sidesteps — albeit largely unintentionally — the issue of Otherness, and effectively forecloses on the possibility of truly personal existence. This is tragic. For from what other source can the gospel of the possibility of really *knowing* God and of participating in his eternal "being in communion" be expected to come if not from the Christian Church? To the extent that we fail to preach this gospel, then, we have, especially under modern conditions, become tasteless salt that deserves only to be trampled underfoot (Matt. 5:13). As James Hitchcock observed:

54. See Merold Westphal, "Religious Experience as Self-Transcendence and Self-Deception," *Faith and Philosophy* 9 (April 1992): 168-93.

If all religious "revelation" is treated as an expression of the ongoing spiritual search either of individuals or peoples, then it holds no ultimate authority over the self, is indeed merely an emanation of that self. . . . But one of the purposes of authentic Christianity is to take people out of themselves, to provide them with the means to overcome self-centredness and distorted self-love.[55]

We only overcome self-centeredness and distorted self-love, furthermore, in the obedience that comes from faith. "If you love me," Jesus tells us (John 14:15-17), "you will obey what I command. And I will ask the Father, and he will give you another Counselor to be with you forever — the Spirit of truth. The world cannot accept him, because it neither sees him nor knows him. But you know him, for he lives with you and will be in you." This is genuinely good news, for we are hereby assured that we will be upheld by the gracious presence of God the Holy Spirit, as we obey the commands of God the Son, to the glory of God the Father. It is thus ultimately by the grace of the Lord Jesus Christ, and the love of God, and the fellowship of the Holy Spirit that the Church is enabled to live in, but not of, the modern world.

A Concluding Meditation on the Christian Virtue of Patience

At the outset we asserted that modernity is characterized by the three interrelated themes of *control, secularity,* and *anxiety.* We suggested that the unusual secularity of modern society and culture is the result of modern aspirations to technical-rational control over the world that leave very little room for any kind of "god" within modern culture save that of the self-defining self. We also observed that the assumption of godlike responsibilities has turned out to be a heavy burden and that we have become increasingly anxious beneath the weight of this burden. This anxiety, in turn, discloses what is possibly the master theme of modernity, and now of "postmodernity": that of *impatience.*

55. James Hitchcock, "Self, Jesus, and God: The Roots of Religious Secularization," in *Summons to Faith and Renewal: Christian Renewal in a Post-Christian World,* ed. Peter S. Williamson and Kevin Perotta (Ann Arbor, MI: Servant, 1983), 34-35.

The modern project, it seems, was inaugurated with the more or less deliberate decision to forswear theological anticipation of the Kingdom of God for the sake of trying to establish peace and prosperity *here and now* by means of science and technology. Indeed, in spite of whatever other differences of opinion they may have had, what united the likes of Machiavelli, Descartes, Bacon, Hobbes, Locke, Rousseau, and other modern thinkers was their repudiation of the classical philosophical and biblical affirmations of natural, created, and eschatological limits to human freedom.[56] This repudiation was based upon their belief that human beings could construct a much more peaceful and prosperous social and political order *more quickly* if left unencumbered by arcane philosophical disputation about "the Good" and invidious theological wrangling about "the Kingdom of God." Representatives of the classical philosophical tradition, for example, had stressed that nature was a "Good" wholly independent of human willing, for which one must be willing to patiently seek, and to which one must acquiesce if one is to find happiness. Representatives of the biblical tradition, furthermore, had stressed that the Kingdom of God is something for which one must be willing to sacrifice earthly happiness, and for which one must be willing to wait. In sharp contrast to both of these traditions, modern, and now "postmodern," philosophers insist that human happiness is something human beings must construct for themselves and by themselves more or less autonomously *now.* We cannot realize the best society of which we are presently capable, so the modern argument runs, if we insist upon wasting our time dreaming about utopian futures and arguing about such things as "the will of God." Machiavelli stands at the head of this development with his insistence that the modern prince must dispense with theological disputation about what *ought* to be if he would make the best of his *actual* circumstances here and now. "Criticism of religion," as Marx was to put this same point several centuries later, "is the premise of all criticism."[57] As we have seen, this impatient repudiation of theological reasoning has, by now, been literally "built into" the central institutional features of modern society and culture.

56. See Leo Strauss, "The Three Waves of Modernity," in *Introduction to Political Philosophy: Ten Essays,* ed. Hilail Gildin (Detroit: Wayne State University Press, 1989).

57. Karl Marx, "A Contribution to the Critique of Hegel's Philosophy of Law: Introduction," in *Karl Marx: Early Writings,* trans. Rodney Livingstone and Gregor Benton (1844; Harmondsworth, UK: Penguin, 1975), 342.

Modernity thus began in a kind of impatient disaffection with the philosophical and theological conviction that we must penetrate behind immediate human experience to the true meaning of things. The various thinkers who launched the modern project recognized that this entailed a certain lowering of our sights, as it were, but it was hoped that the material payoff would more than adequately compensate us for the loss of religion's sacred canopy of meaning. "After all," the moderns and now postmoderns reply in effect, "meaning is in the eye of the beholder; it lies only in what we choose to make meaningful." Putting this in biblical perspective, we might say that the modern project is founded upon a kind of impatient rejoinder to Jesus' assertion that humans do not live by bread alone. "On the contrary," modern thinkers retort, "man lives quite well by bread alone so long as he can be distracted — by means of entertainment and therapy — from asking imponderable religious questions."

Of course, anxious impatience is evident in virtually all aspects of modern social and cultural existence, and not least in the increasingly frantic pace with which so much of life is carried on today. It is largely by reason of impatient frustration, after all, that we have been persuaded to try to perform the functions of the hidden — and, indeed, seemingly absent — God. "God is either unwilling or incapable of helping us," we say in effect, "therefore we have no choice but to help ourselves, to take matters into our own hands, and to try to engineer a habitable environment for ourselves." Ironically, it is this same anxious impatience that has consequently moved us to surrender ourselves so naively to the dehumanizing techniques of the modern world. Indeed, it is anxious haste that has incited us to mortgage ourselves to technical rationality for the sake of its promise of control. "After we have taken control of the world," so we tell ourselves, implying that taking control of the world must somehow enable us to take control of *ourselves*, "*then* we will discover how to be human persons again." But the horizon keeps receding, and we always seem to be waiting for the promised control to be established. The longer we are forced to wait, however, the more anxious we become; and the more anxious we become, the more prone we are to placing what little hope we have left into the possibility of technical-rational control, and thus to giving ourselves over to dehumanizing modern systems; and so forth. It is an unfortunately vicious cycle.

Modern secular society is thus a culture of anxious impatience, a culture in which so much stress has been placed upon human abilities and human agency that the modern mind has effectively lost the ability to trust anything, or more importantly *anyone,* else. And yet the modern, and now "postmodern," mind appears to know itself just well enough to suspect that this just might not be the best of news. To be sure, "enlightened" apologies for secularity are still occasionally made in the name of "liberation" from purportedly repressive religious traditions, but more often than not these days the "postmodern" mind simply submits to the ways of the modern world because it just doesn't seem that we have any other choice. Returning to nature, though attractive, is not really an option any more, for the modern mind has become, as Descartes had hoped that it would, the master and possessor of nature. Yet this mastery and possession of nature has so inflated our self-confidence that we have all but lost sight of the possibility of trusting the One who created us to have a certain dominion within his creation. We have, in effect, and just as the apostle Paul stated in his summary of the human condition (Rom. 1:23), "exchanged the glory of the immortal God" for humanly constructed idols and images. And so the modern mind appears to be caught in the undertow of its own reigning assumptions and, even more importantly, of its own most distinguished accomplishments. In trying to encourage the modern, and now "postmodern," mind to break free from itself, we would do well to recall the Christian virtue of patience.

The fruit of the Spirit of God, Paul reminds us (Gal. 5:22-23), is love, joy, peace, patience, kindness, goodness, faithfulness, gentleness, and self-control. Against such things, Paul observes, there is no law, for these are goods that even the natural person recognizes as valuable, even if he cannot recognize their source. Perhaps in keeping with the double commandment of love, some of these virtues appear to qualify our relation to God, and others to qualify our relation to our neighbor. We are, then, by the power of the Spirit, to live joyfully and peacefully before God, expressing our love for him by faithfully observing his commandments in the Spirit of self-control; and we are, by this same Spirit, to deal kindly and gently with our neighbor, loving him or her patiently and in good faith. Yet perhaps dividing the Apostle's list of virtues up in this fashion does not quite do justice to the unity of the Spirit to which they all bear witness. Keeping the peace is an obvious kindness to our neighbor, and a joyful spirit cannot help but encourage him or her. There is also a great deal to be said for being kind, gentle, and, above all, for being patient *with* God.

In classical usage the term for "patience" *(hypomeno)* meant "to stay behind" and carried the fateful military connotation of standing one's ground and remaining steadfast in the face of the enemy, even in the face of certain defeat.[58] The Hebrew equivalent to the Greek, "await" *(qawah)*, carried a similarly military connotation, except that the virtue of staying patiently behind and remaining steadfast in the face of the enemy was conjoined with confidence in God's promised deliverance. There was, in other words, no hint of Stoic resignation in Israel's attitude. Rather, it reached up toward the living God and drew its strength from his covenantal promises. Whereas in classical usage the object of patience was limited to the somewhat abstract maintenance of honor, the object of patience in the Old Testament is the God of Abraham, Isaac, and Jacob, the God who has been and will be true to his promises. It is in this sense, then, that the word "patience" is used in the New Testament. Of course, the term is used to describe how we are to bear with one another in love (1 Cor. 13:7); but it is used interpersonally in the much larger sense of being patient also with God. Being patient with God means to "hold fast" to the apostles' teaching (Rom. 2:7); to "endure" sufferings for the gospel's sake, and ultimately to "wait" patiently for Jesus to return (Matt. 24:9ff.). When he was asked about the signs of the end of the world (Luke 21:7ff.), for example, Jesus described the numerous trials his disciples would face and said (v. 19), "By standing firm you will gain life." Conversely, the failure of patience is described in the New Testament in terms of "growing cold" (Matt. 24:9ff.), of "falling away" (Heb. 3:7-11), of "unfruitfulness" (Luke 8:15), and ultimately of "losing eternal life." "If we endure," Paul writes in 2 Tim. 2:12, "we shall also reign with him; if we deny him, he also will deny us. . . ." The Christian virtue of patience, in sum, discloses an eschatological horizon in which the living God guarantees our eventual deliverance. By way of contrast, impatience is a sure indication of loss of heart,

---

58. The etymological material on "patience" here is taken from U. Falkenroth and C. Brown, "Patience," in Colin Brown (ed.), *Dictionary of New Testament Theology*, vol. 2 (Grand Rapids, MI: Zondervan, 1986), 772ff.

that we no longer really believe that God is willing, and perhaps even that he is able, to deliver us.

The relevance of the Christian understanding of patience cannot be overemphasized in the midst of our culture of anxious impatience. If the potential of human agency has been vastly overestimated in modern society and culture, and if this exaggeration has precipitated a kind of restless movement back and forth between the attempt to establish technical-rational control over the world, on the one hand, and ever deepening despair over the dehumanizing consequences of this attempt, on the other, then this destructive oscillation may be said to stem ultimately from the fact that modern society and culture have grown impatient with God. Indeed, as we have seen, the fundamental dilemma of post-Christian culture is that it has been so decisively shaped by the Christian hope, but can no longer place this hope in the Christian God, and so is left only to place hope in human abilities and agencies. And, as remarkable as human accomplishments in recent centuries have been, we appear to have reached the point now where we realize that placing hope in human abilities and agencies is a profoundly uncertain proposition. Such is the way of the modern — and increasingly post-modern — world.

Living in but not of the modern world, then, must mean, at the very least, living patiently and expectantly before the living God, refusing to surrender ourselves and our churches to the various schemes that are finally only expressions of modernity's, and now postmodernity's, godless impatience. This will not be easy, but our Lord has promised to uphold his Church in the midst of every trial, even those of today's secular world. "In this world you will have trouble," Jesus says (John 16:33); "but take heart! I have overcome the world."

Maranatha! Come, Lord Jesus!

Selected Bibliography

Allen, Diogenes. "The End of the Modern World." *Christian Scholar's Review* 22 (April 1993): 339-47.

Arendt, Hannah. *The Human Condition*. Chicago: University of Chicago Press, 1958.

Balthasar, Hans Urs von. "On the Concept of Person." *Communio: International Catholic Review* 13 (Spring 1986): 18-26.

Barbour, Ian. *Ethics in an Age of Technology: The Gifford Lectures 1989-1991, Volume Two*. San Francisco: HarperSanFrancisco, 1993.

Barrett, William. *The Death of the Soul: From Descartes to the Computer*. New York: Anchor, 1986.

Barth, Karl. *Protestant Theology in the Nineteenth Century: Its Background and History*. Translated by Brian Cozens and John Bowden. London: S.C.M. Press, 1972.

————. *Action in Waiting for the Kingdom of God*. Norfolk, CT: Deer Spring Press, 1979.

Baumer, Franklin L. *Religion and the Rise of Skepticism*. New York: Harcourt, Brace & World, 1960.

Bebbington, David. "Evangelical Christianity and Romanticism." *Crux* 26, no. 1 (1990): 9-15.

————. "The Secularization of British Universities since the Mid-Nineteenth Century." In *The Secularization of the Academy*, ed. George M. Marsden and Bradley J. Longfield, 259-77. Oxford: Oxford University Press, 1992.

Becker, Carl L. *The Heavenly City of the Eighteenth Century Philosophers*. New Haven, CT: Yale University Press, 1932.

Becker, Ernest. *The Denial of Death*. New York: The Free Press, 1973.

Bell, Daniel. *The Cultural Contradictions of Capitalism*. New York: Basic Books, 1976.

————. "The Return of the Sacred?: The Argument on the Future of Religion." *British Journal of Sociology* 28, no. 4 (1977): 419-49.

Bellah, Robert N. "Civil Religion in America." *Daedalus* 96 (Winter 1967): 1-21.

————. "The Historical Background of Unbelief." In *The Culture of Unbelief*, ed. Rocco Caporale and Antonio Grumelli, 39-52. Berkeley: University of California, 1971.

Beniger, James R. *The Control Revolution: Technological and Economic Origins of the Information Society.* Cambridge, MA: Harvard University Press, 1986.

Bercovitch, Sacvan. *The Puritan Origins of the American Self.* New Haven: Yale University Press, 1975.

Berdyaev, Nicholas. *The Fate of Man in the Modern World.* Ann Arbor, MI: University of Michigan Press, 1935.

Berger, Peter L. "A Sociological View of the Secularization of Theology." *Journal for the Scientific Study of Religion* 6 (Spring 1967): 3-16.

———. *The Sacred Canopy: Elements of a Sociological Theory of Religion.* Garden City, NY: Anchor, 1969.

———. "A Call for Authority in the Christian Community." *Princeton Seminary Bulletin* 64 (December 1971): 14-24.

———. *Pyramids of Sacrifice: Political Ethics and Social Change.* Garden City, NY: Anchor, 1976.

———. *Facing Up to Modernity: Excursions into Society, Politics, and Religion.* New York: Basic Books, 1977.

———. "Ethics and the Present Class Struggle." *Worldview* (April 1978): 6-11.

———. *The Heretical Imperative: Contemporary Possibilities of Religious Affirmation.* Garden City, NY: Anchor, 1980.

———. "From Secularity to World Religions." *The Christian Century* 97 (January 16 1980): 41-45.

———. "Secularity West and East." *This World* 4 (Winter 1983): 49-62.

———. "From the Crisis of Religion to the Crisis of Secularity." In *Religion and America: Spirituality in a Secular Age,* ed. Mary Douglas and Stephen M. Tipton, 14-24. Boston: Beacon, 1983.

———. "Western Individuality: Liberation and Loneliness." *Partisan Review* 52 (1985): 323-36.

———. *The Capitalist Revolution: Fifty Propositions about Prosperity, Equality, & Liberty.* New York: Basic Books, 1986.

Berger, Peter L., and Brigitte Berger. *The War over the Family: Capturing the Middle Ground.* Garden City, NY: Anchor, 1983.

Berger, Peter L., Brigitte Berger, and Hansfried Kellner. *The Homeless Mind: Modernization and Consciousness.* New York: Vintage Books, 1973.

Berger, Peter L., and Thomas Luckmann. "Secularization and Pluralism." *International Yearbook for the Sociology of Religion* 1 (1966): 73-84.

———. *The Social Construction of Reality: A Treatise in the Sociology of Knowledge.* New York: Penguin, 1966.

Berman, Marshall. *All That Is Solid Melts into Air: The Experience of Modernity.* New York: Simon & Schuster, 1982.

Bibby, Reginald W. "Religion and Modernity: The Canadian Case." *Journal for the Scientific Study of Religion* 18, no. 1 (1979): 1-17.

———. "Searching for Invisible Thread: Meaning Systems in Contemporary Canada." *Journal for the Scientific Study of Religion* 22 (1983): 101-19.

————. *Mosaic Madness: The Poverty and Potential of Life in Canada*. Toronto: Stoddart, 1990.

Bockmuehl, Klaus. "Secularism and Theology." *Crux* 19 (June 1983): 6-14.

————. "Recovering Vocation Today." *Crux* 24 (September 1988): 25-35.

————. "Secularization and Secularism: Some Christian Considerations." In *Christian Faith and Practice in the Modern World: Theology from an Evangelical Point of View*, ed. Mark A. Noll and David F. Wells, 263-84. Grand Rapids, MI: Eerdmans, 1988.

————. *The Unreal God of Modern Theology: Bultmann, Barth, and the Theology of Atheism: A Call to Recovering the Truth of God's Reality*. Colorado Springs: Helmers & Howard, 1988.

Borgman, Albert. *Technology and the Character of Contemporary Life: A Philosophical Inquiry*. Chicago: University of Chicago Press, 1984.

Bozeman, Timothy Dwight. *Protestants in an Age of Science: The Baconian Ideal and Antebellum American Religious Thought*. Chapel Hill, NC: University of North Carolina Press, 1977.

Brown, Callum G. "A Revisionist Approach to Religious Change." In *Religion and Modernization: Sociologists and Historians Debate the Secularization Thesis*, ed. Steve Bruce, 31-58. Oxford: Clarendon Press, 1992.

Bruce, Steve. "Modernity and Fundamentalism: The New Christian Right in America." *British Journal of Sociology* 41 (December 1990): 477-96.

————. *A House Divided: Protestantism, Schism, and Secularization*. New York: Routledge, 1990.

————. "Pluralism and Religious Vitality." In *Religion and Modernization: Sociologists and Historians Debate the Secularization Thesis*, ed. Steve Bruce, 170-94. Oxford: Clarendon Press, 1992.

Brunner, Emil. *Truth as Encounter*. 1938. London: S.C.M. Press, 1964.

Buber, Martin. *The Eclipse of God: Studies in the Relation between Religion and Philosophy*. New York: Harper & Row, 1952.

————. *I and Thou*. 1924. Translated by Walter Kaufmann. New York: Charles Scribner's Sons, 1970.

Buckley, Michael J. *At the Origins of Modern Atheism*. New Haven: Yale University Press, 1987.

Bultmann, Rudolf. "Science and Existence." 1955. In *New Testament and Mythology and Other Basic Writings*, ed. Schubert M. Ogden, 131-44. Philadelphia: Fortress, 1984.

Burtchaell, James Tunstead. "The Decline and Fall of the Christian College, Part 1." *First Things* (April 1991): 16-29.

————. "The Decline and Fall of the Christian College, Part 2." *First Things* (May 1991): 30-38.

Butterfield, Herbert. *The Origins of Modern Science: 1300-1800*. London: G. Bell & Sons, 1958.

Campbell, Colin. *Towards a Sociology of Irreligion*. London: Macmillan, 1971.

————. "The Cult, the Cultic Milieu and Secularization." In *A Sociological Yearbook for Religion in Britain*, ed. Michael Hill, 119-36. London: S.C.M. Press, 1972.

————. "The Secret Religion of the Educated Classes." *Sociological Analysis* 39 (1978): 146-56.

————. "Romanticism and the Consumer Ethic: Intimations of a Weber-style Thesis." *Sociological Analysis* 44 (Winter 1983): 279-96.

Campbell, Douglas F., and Dennis W. Magill. "Religious Involvement and Intellectuality among University Students." *Sociological Analysis* 29 (1968): 79-93.

Carruthers, Bruce G., and Wendy Nelson Espeland. "Accounting for Rationality: Double-Entry Bookkeeping and the Rhetoric of Economic Rationality." *American Journal of Sociology* 97 (July 1991): 31-69.

Chadwick, Owen. *The Secularization of the European Mind in the Nineteenth Century.* Cambridge: Cambridge University Press, 1975.

Chesterton, G. K. *What's Wrong with the World?* New York: Sheed & Ward, 1910.

Childress, James F., and David B. Harned. "Introduction: Secularization and Protestant Faith." In *Secularization and the Protestant Prospect*, ed. James F. Childress and David B. Harned, 13-29. Philadelphia: Westminster, 1970.

Cohen, Patricia Cline. *A Calculating People: The Spread of Numeracy in Early America.* Chicago: University of Chicago Press, 1982.

Cohen, Erik. "Radical Secularization and the Destructuration of the Universe of Knowledge in Late Modernity." *Knowledge and Society* 7 (1988): 203-24.

Cohen, H. Floris. *The Scientific Revolution: A Historiographical Inquiry.* Chicago: University of Chicago Press, 1994.

Cousins, Ewert. "A Theology of Interpersonal Relations." *Thought* 45, no. 1 (1970): 56-82.

Cox, Harvey. *The Secular City: Secularization and Urbanization in Theological Perspective.* New York: Macmillan, 1965.

————. "The Secular City Twenty-five Years Later." *Christian Century* 107 (November 7, 1990): 1025-29.

Crippen, Timothy. "Old and New Gods in the Modern World: Toward a Theory of Religious Transformation." *Social Forces* 67 (December 1988): 316-36.

Croce, Paul Jerome. "Erosion of Mass Culture." *Society* 30 (July/August 1993): 11-16.

Crowley, J. E. *This Sheba, Self: The Conceptualization of Economic Life in Eighteenth-Century America.* Baltimore: Johns Hopkins University Press, 1974.

Cuddihy, John Murray. *The Ordeal of Civility: Freud, Marx, Lévi-Strauss, and the Jewish Struggle with Modernity.* New York: Basic Books, 1974.

————. *No Offense: Civil Religion and Protestant Taste.* New York: Seabury, 1978.

Dawson, Christopher. *The Modern Dilemma: The Problem of European Unity.* London: Sheed & Ward, 1933.

————. *Progress and Religion: An Historical Inquiry.* 1931. Peru, IL: Sherwood Sugden & Co., 1991.

————. *Religion and the Rise of Western Culture.* 1950. New York: Image Books, 1991.

De Lubac, Henri. *The Drama of Atheist Humanism.* 1950. New York: World Publishing Company, 1963.

Deason, Gary B. "Reformation Theology and the Mechanistic Conception of Nature." In *God and Nature: Historical Essays on the Encounter between Christianity and Science*, ed. David C. Lindberg and Ronald L. Numbers. Berkeley: University of California Press, 1986.

Despland, Michel. "Christian Religion under the Conditions of Modernity: Aspects of the Nineteenth-Century Quest for Redemption." *Studies in Religion* 13 (1984): 151-65.

DiMaggio, Paul J., and Walter W. Powell. "The Iron Cage Revisited: Institutional Isomorphism and Collective Rationality in Organizational Fields." *American Sociological Review* 48 (April 1983): 147-60.

Dobbelaere, Karel. "Secularization: A Multi-Dimensional Concept." *Current Sociology* 29 (1981): 1-216.

———. "Secularization Theories and Sociological Paradigms: Convergences and Divergences." *Social Compass* 31 (1984): 199-219.

———. "Secularization Theories and Sociological Paradigms: A Reformulation of the Private-Public Dichotomy and the Problem of Societal Integration." *Sociological Analysis* 46, no. 4 (1985): 377-87.

———. "Some Trends in European Sociology of Religion: The Secularization Debate." *Sociological Analysis* 48, no. 2 (1987): 107-37.

———. "The Secularization of Society? Some Methodological Suggestions." In *Secularization and Fundamentalism Reconsidered: Religion and the Political Order*, ed. Jeffrey K. Hadden and Anson Shupe, 27-44. New York: Paragon, 1989.

Dobbelaere, K., J. Billiet, and R. Creyf. "Secularization and Pillarization: A Social Problem Approach." *Annual Review of the Social Sciences of Religion* 2 (1978): 97-124.

Doede, Robert. "The Decline of Anthropomorphic Explanation: From Animism to Deconstructionism." Unpublished paper presented to Regent faculty, 1992.

Dooyeweerd, Herman. *The Secularization of Science.* Memphis, TN: Christian Studies Center, 1954.

Dupré, Louis. "The Closed World of the Modern Mind." *Religion and Intellectual Life* 1 (Summer 1984): 19-29.

Eisenstadt, S. N. "The Protestant Ethic Thesis in an Analytical and Comparative Framework." In *The Protestant Ethic and Modernization: A Comparative View*, ed. S. N. Eisenstadt, 3-45. New York: Basic Books, 1968.

Eisenstein, Elizabeth. *The Printing Revolution in Early Modern Europe.* Cambridge: Cambridge University Press, 1983.

Ellul, Jacques. *The Technological Society.* New York: Vintage, 1964.

———.*The New Demons.* New York: Seabury Press, 1975.

———. *The Technological Bluff.* Grand Rapids, MI: Eerdmans, 1990.

Fenn, Richard K. "The Secularization of Values: An Analytical Framework for the Study of Secularization." *Journal for the Scientific Study of Religion* 8 (Spring 1969): 112-34.

———. "Max Weber on the Secular: A Typology." *Review of Religious Research* 10 (Spring 1969): 159-69.

————. "The Process of Secularization: A Post-Parsonian View." *Journal for the Scientific Study of Religion* 9 (Summer 1970): 117-36.

————. *Toward a Theory of Secularization.* Society for the Scientific Study of Religion Monograph Series, ed. William M. Newman. Storrs, CT: Society for the Scientific Study of Religion, 1978.

————. "Secular Constraints on Religious Language." *The Annual Review of the Social Sciences of Religion* 4 (1980): 61-83.

————. *Liturgies and Trials: The Secularization of Religious Language.* Oxford: Basil Blackwell, 1982.

————. *The Dream of the Perfect Act: An Inquiry into the Fate of Religion in a Secular World.* New York: Tavistock, 1987.

————. "The Secularization of Dread and Despair: Demand for a Day of Reckoning." In *Religion and the Social Order,* Vol. 1: New Developments in Theory and Research, ed. David G. Bromley. Greenwich, CT: JAI Press, 1991.

————. *The Secularization of Sin.* Philadelphia: Westminster Press, 1992.

Finke, Roger. "An Unsecular America." In *Religion and Modernization: Sociologists and Historians Debate the Secularization Thesis,* ed. Steve Bruce, 145-69. Oxford: Clarendon Press, 1992.

Fischoff, Ephraim. "The Protestant Ethic and the Spirit of Capitalism: The History of a Controversy." In *The Protestant Ethic and Modernization: A Comparative View,* ed. S. N. Eisenstadt, 67-86. New York: Basic Books, 1968.

Fukuyama, Francis. "The End of History?" *The National Interest* (Summer 1989): 3-18.

Funkenstein, Amos. *Theology and the Scientific Imagination from the Middle Ages to the Seventeenth Century.* Princeton, NJ: Princeton University Press, 1986.

Gehlen, Arnold. *Man in the Age of Technology.* New York: Columbia University Press, 1980.

George, Charles and Katherine. "Protestantism and Capitalism in Pre-Revolutionary England." In *The Protestant Ethic and Modernization: A Comparative View,* ed. S. N. Eisenstadt, 155-76. New York: Basic Books, 1968.

Gergen, Kenneth J. *The Saturated Self: Dilemmas of Identity in Contemporary Life.* New York: Basic Books, 1991.

Gerharz, George P. "Secularization as Loss of Social Control: Toward a New Theory." *Sociological Analysis* 31 (January 1970): 1-11.

Giddens, Anthony. *The Consequences of Modernity.* Stanford, CA: Stanford University Press, 1990.

————. *Modernity and Self-Identity: Self and Society in the Late Modern Age.* Stanford, CA: Stanford University Press, 1991.

Gilbert, Alan D. *The Making of Post-Christian Britain: A History of the Secularization of Modern Society.* London: Longman, 1980.

Gill, Robin. "Secularization and Census Data." In *Religion and Modernization: Sociologists and Historians Debate the Secularization Thesis,* ed. Steve Bruce, 90-117. Oxford: Clarendon Press, 1992.

Glasner, Peter E. *The Sociology of Secularization: A Critique of the Concept.* London: Routledge & Kegan Paul, 1977.

Goodridge, R. Martin. "Relative Secularization and Religious Practice." *Sociological Analysis* 29 (March 1968): 122-35.

Grabowski, John S. "Person: Substance and Relation." *Communio: International Catholic Review* 22 (Spring 1995): 139-63.

Grant, George P. *Philosophy in the Mass Age.* Toronto: Copp Clark, 1966.

———. "How Deception Lurks in the Secular City." *The Observer* (July 1, 1966): 16-17, 26.

———. *Technology and Justice.* Toronto: Anansi, 1986.

———. *Lament for a Nation: The Defeat of Canadian Nationalism.* 1965; Ottowa: Carleton University Press, 1989.

———. *Technology and Empire: Perspectives on North America.* Toronto: Anansi, 1969.

Greeley, Andrew M. "Religion in a Secular Society." Social Research 41 (February 1974): 226-40.

Guardini, Romano. *The End of the Modern World: A Search for Orientation.* 1956; Chicago: Henry Regnery Company, 1968.

———. "The End of the Modern World." *Communio: International Catholic Review* 17 (1990): 281-93.

———. *Letters from Lake Como: Explorations in Technology and the Human Race.* 1923; Grand Rapids, MI: Eerdmans, 1994.

Guinness, Os. "Mission in the Face of Modernity: Nine Checkpoints on Mission without Worldliness in the Modern World." In *Faith and Modernity,* ed. Philip Sampson, Vinay Samuel, and Chris Sugden. Oxford: Regnum/Lynx, 1994.

———. *Dining with the Devil: The Megachurch Movement Flirts with Modernity.* Grand Rapids, MI: Baker, 1993.

———. *Fit Bodies, Fat Minds: Why Evangelicals Don't Think and What to Do about It.* Grand Rapids, MI: Baker, 1994.

Gumelli, Antonio. "Secularization: Between Belief and Unbelief." In *The Culture of Unbelief,* ed. Rocco Caporale and Antonio Gumelli, 77-90. Berkeley: University of California Press, 1971.

Gunton, Colin E. *The Promise of Trinitarian Theology.* Edinburgh: T. & T. Clark, 1991.

———. *The One, the Three and the Many: God, Creation and the Culture of Modernity.* Cambridge: Cambridge University Press, 1993.

Hadden, Jeffrey K. "Desacralizing Secularization Theory." In *Secularization and Fundamentalism Reconsidered: Religion and the Political Order,* ed. Jeffrey K. Hadden and Anson Shupe, 3-26. New York: Paragon, 1989.

Hammond, Phillip E., and James Davison Hunter. "On Maintaining Plausibility: The Worldview of Evangelical College Students." *Journal for the Scientific Study of Religion* 23 (1984): 221-38.

Hart, D. G. "The Troubled Soul of the Academy: American Learning and the Problem of Religious Studies." *Religion and American Life: A Journal of Interpretation* 2 (Winter 1992): 49-77.

———. "Faith and Learning in the Age of the University: The Academic Ministry of Daniel Coit Gilman." In *The Secularization of the Academy,* ed. George M. Marsden and Bradley J. Longfield, 107-45. Oxford: Oxford University Press, 1992.

————. "Christianity and the University in America: A Bibliographic Essay." In *The Secularization of the Academy*, ed. George M. Marsden and Bradley J. Longfield, 303-9. Oxford: Oxford University Press, 1992.

Hartt, Julian N. "Secularity and the Transcendence of God." In *Secularization and the Protestant Prospect*, ed. James F. Childress and David B. Harned, 151-73. Philadelphia: Westminster, 1970.

Harvey, Van A. "On the Intellectual Marginality of American Theology." In *Religion and Twentieth-Century American Intellectual Life*, ed. Michael J. Lacey, 172-92. New York: Cambridge University Press, 1989.

Hatch, Nathan O. *The Democratization of American Christianity*. New Haven: Yale University Press, 1989.

Hedwig, Klaus. "The Philosophical Presuppositions of Postmodernity." *Communio: International Catholic Review* 17 (Summer 1990): 167-80.

Heidegger, Martin. "The Question concerning Technology." In *The Question concerning Technology and Other Essays*, trans. William Lovitt, 3-35. New York: Harper & Row, 1977.

Heller, Agnes. "The Dissatisfied Society." *Praxis International* 2 (January 1983): 359-70.

Henry, Carl F. H. "Natural Law and a Nihilistic Culture." *First Things* (January 1995): 54-60.

Herberg, Will. "Religion in a Secularized Society (Part 1)." *Review of Religious Research* 3 (1962): 145-58.

————. "Religion in a Secularized Society (Part 2)." *Review of Religious Research* 4 (1962): 33-45.

Hitchcock, James. "Self, Jesus, and God: The Roots of Religious Secularization." In *Summons to Faith and Renewal: Christian Renewal in a Post-Christian World*, ed. Peter S. Williamson and Kevin Perotta, 23-35. Ann Arbor, MI: Servant, 1983.

Hoge, Dean R. "Changes in College Students' Value Patterns in the 1950s, 1960s, and 1970s." *Sociology of Education* 49 (1976): 155-63.

Hoge, Dean R., and Larry G. Keeter. "Determinants of College Teachers' Religious Beliefs and Participation." *Journal for the Scientific Study of Religion* 15 (1976): 221-35.

Holl, Karl. "The History of the Word Vocation (Beruf)." *Review and Expositor* 55 (April 1958): 126-54.

Hollinger, David A. "Justification by Verification: The Scientific Challenge to the Moral Authority of Christianity in Modern America." In *Religion and Twentieth-Century American Intellectual Life*, ed. Michael J. Lacey, 116-35. New York: Cambridge University Press, 1989.

Hooykaas, R. "Science and Reformation." In *The Protestant Ethic and Modernization: A Comparative View*, ed. S. N. Eisenstadt, 211-39. New York: Basic Books, 1968.

————. *Religion and the Rise of Modern Science*. Grand Rapids: Eerdmans, 1972.

Hornsby-Smith, Michael P. "Recent Transformations in English Catholicism: Evidence of Secularization?" In *Religion and Modernization: Sociologists and Historians Debate the Secularization Thesis*, ed. Steve Bruce, 118-44. Oxford: Clarendon, 1992.

Horowitz, Gad, and George Grant. "A Conversation on Technology and Man." *Journal of Canadian Studies* 4 (August 1969): 3-6.

Houston, James M. "Do the Works of Men Secularise the Service of Christ?" *Interchange* 45 (1990): 54-64.

Hunsberger, Bruce E. "Religiosity and College Students' Stability and Change over Years at University." *Journal for the Scientific Study of Religion* 17 (1978): 159-64.

Hunter, James Davison. "Subjectivization and the New Evangelical Theodicy." *Journal for the Scientific Study of Religion* 20, no. 1 (1982): 39-47.

———. "Conservative Protestantism." In *The Sacred in a Secular Age,* ed. Phillip E. Hammond, 150-66. Berkeley: University of California Press, 1985.

———. "'America's Fourth Faith': A Sociological Perspective on Secular Humanism." *This World* 19 (Fall 1987): 101-10.

———. *Culture Wars: The Struggle to Define America.* New York: Basic Books, 1991.

Jacobs, Jerry. "From Sacred to Secular: The Rationalization of Christian Theology." *Journal for the Scientific Study of Religion* 10 (Spring 1971): 1-9.

Jaki, Stanley L. *The Road of Science and the Ways to God.* Chicago: University of Chicago Press, 1978.

Jensen, Robert W. *The Triune Identity: God according to the Gospel.* Philadelphia: Fortress, 1982.

Johnson, Phillip E. "Nihilism and the End of Law." *First Things* (March 1993): 19-25.

———. *Reason in the Balance: The Case against Naturalism in Science, Law and Education.* Downers Grove, IL: InterVarsity Press, 1995.

Kaiser, Christopher. *Creation and the History of Science.* The History of Christian Theology Series, ed. Paul Avis. Grand Rapids, MI: Eerdmans, 1991.

Kalberg, Stephen. "Max Weber's Types of Rationality: Cornerstones for the Analysis of Rationalization Processes in History." *American Journal of Sociology* 85, no. 5 (1980): 1145-79.

Kierkegaard, Søren. *Concluding Unscientific Postscript.* 1846. Translated by David F. Swenson and Walter Lowrie. Princeton: Princeton University Press, 1941.

———. *The Present Age & Of the Difference between a Genius and an Apostle.* 1846. Translated by Alexander Dru. New York: Harper & Row, 1962.

———. *The Sickness unto Death: A Christian Psychological Exposition for Upbuilding and Awakening.* 1849. Translated by Howard V. Hong and Edna H. Hong. Princeton: Princeton University Press, 1980.

King, William McGuire. "An Enthusiasm for Humanity: The Social Emphasis in Religion and Its Accommodation in Protestant Theology." In *Religion and Twentieth-Century American Intellectual Life,* ed. Michael J. Lacey, 49-77. New York: Cambridge University Press, 1989.

Kolakowski, Leszek. *Modernity on Endless Trial.* Chicago: University of Chicago Press, 1990.

Koyré, Alexandre. *From the Classical World to the Infinite Universe.* New York: Harper Torchbooks, 1957.

Kuklick, Bruce. "John Dewey, American Theology, and Scientific Politics." In *Religion and Twentieth-Century American Intellectual Life*, ed. Michael J. Lacey, 78-93. New York: Cambridge University Press, 1989.

Kuyper, Abraham. *Lectures on Calvinism*. Grand Rapids, MI: Eerdmans, 1931.

Lacey, Michael J. "Introduction: The Academic Revolution and American Religious Thought." In *Religion and Twentieth-Century American Intellectual Life*, ed. Michael J. Lacey, 1-11. New York: Cambridge University Press, 1989.

Laermans, Rudi. "Learning to Consume: Early Department Stores and the Shaping of the Modern Consumer Culture (1860-1914)." *Theory, Culture and Society* 10 (November 1993): 79-102.

Laeuchli, Samuel. "Epilogue: Theology in a New Key." In *Secularization and the Protestant Prospect*, ed. James F. Childress and David B. Harned, 174-205. Philadelphia: Westminster, 1970.

Lampe, G. W. H. "Secularization in the New Testament and the Early Church." *Theology* 71 (April 1968): 163-75.

Lapsley, I. N. "Personhood in a Technological World." *Princeton Seminary Bulletin* 61 (Summer 1968): 36-41.

Lasch, Christopher. *The Culture of Narcissism: American Life in an Age of Diminishing Expectations*. New York: Warner Books, 1979.

Laski, Harold J. *The Rise of European Liberalism: An Essay in Interpretation*. 1936; London: Unwin Books, 1962.

Lears, T. J. Jackson. *No Place for Grace: Antimodernism and the Transformation of American Culture, 1880-1920*. New York: Pantheon, 1981.

Leites, E. "Autonomy and the Rationalization of Moral Discourse." *Sociological Analysis* 35 (Summer 1974): 95-101.

Lerner, Daniel. *The Passing of Traditional Society: Modernizing the Middle East*. New York: The Free Press, 1958.

Levine, Donald N. "Rationality and Freedom: Weber and Beyond." *Sociological Inquiry* 51 (1981): 5-25.

Lewis, C. S. *The Abolition of Man*. 1943; Glasgow: Collins, 1984.

Lidz, Victor M. "Secularization, Ethical Life, and Religion in Modern Societies." *Sociological Inquiry* 49 (1979): 191-217.

Lindbom, Tage. *The Myth of Democracy*. Grand Rapids, MI: Eerdmans, 1996.

Little, David. "Calvinism and Law." In *The Protestant Ethic and Modernization: A Comparative View*, ed. S. N. Eisenstadt, 177-83. New York: Basic Books, 1968.

———. "Religion, Morality, and Secularization." In *Secularization and the Protestant Prospect*, ed. James F. Childress and David B. Harned, 135-50. Philadelphia: Westminster, 1970.

Longfield, Bradley J. "From Evangelicalism to Liberalism: Public Midwestern Universities in Nineteenth-Century America." In *The Secularization of the Academy*, ed. George M. Marsden and Bradley J. Longfield, 46-73. Oxford: Oxford University Press, 1992.

———. "'For God, for Country, and for Yale': Yale, Religion, and Higher Education between the World Wars." In *The Secularization of the Academy*, ed. George M.

Marsden and Bradley J. Longfield, 146-69. Oxford: Oxford University Press, 1992.

Lossky, Vladimir. *The Mystical Theology of the Eastern Church.* 1944; London: James Clarke & Co., 1957.

Löwith, Karl. *Meaning in History.* Chicago: University of Chicago Press, 1949.

———. "Weber's Interpretation of the Bourgeois-Capitalistic World in Terms of the Guiding Principle of 'Rationalization.'" In *Max Weber,* ed. Dennis Wrong, 101-22. Englewood Cliffs, NJ: Prentice Hall, 1970.

Luckmann, Thomas. "On Religion in Modern Society: Individual Consciousness, World View, Institution." *Journal for the Scientific Study of Religion* 2 (Spring 1963): 147-62.

———. "The Invisible Religion." In *Secularization and the Protestant Prospect,* ed. James F. Childress and David B. Harned, 71-92. Philadelphia: Westminster, 1970.

———. "Belief, Unbelief, and Religion." In *The Culture of Unbelief,* ed. Rocco Caporale and Antonio Grumelli, 21-37. Berkeley: University of California Press, 1971.

———. "Theories of Religion and Social Change." *The Annual Review of the Social Science of Religion* 4 (1980): 1-27.

Lundin, Roger. *The Culture of Interpretation: Christian Faith and the Postmodern World.* Grand Rapids, MI: Eerdmans, 1993.

Lynn, Robert Wood. "'The Survival of Recognizably Protestant Colleges': Reflections on Old-Line Protestantism, 1950-1990." In *The Secularization of the Academy,* ed. George M. Marsden and Bradley J. Longfield, 170-94. Oxford: Oxford University Press, 1992.

Lyon, David. "Secularization and Sociology: The History of an Idea." *Fides et Historia* 13 (Spring 1981): 38-52.

———. "Secularization: The Fate of Faith in Modern Society." *Themelios* 10 (September 1984): 14-22.

———. "Rethinking Secularization: Retrospect and Prospect." *Review of Religious Research* 26 (March 1985): 228-43.

———. *The Steeple's Shadow: On the Myths and Realities of Secularization.* Grand Rapids, MI: Eerdmans, 1985.

———. "New Technology and the Information Society: Whose Vision?" *Transformation* (October/December 1992): 11-16.

———. *Postmodernity.* Concepts in Social Thought, ed. Frank Parkin. Minneapolis: University of Minnesota Press, 1994.

MacIntyre, Alasdair. *Secularization and Moral Change.* London: Oxford University Press, 1967.

———. *Three Rival Versions of Moral Inquiry: Encyclopedia, Genealogy, and Tradition.* Notre Dame, IN: University of Notre Dame, 1990.

MacMurray, John. *Reason and Emotion.* London: Faber & Faber, 1935.

———. *The Boundaries of Science: A Study in the Philosophy of Psychology.* London: Faber & Faber, 1939.

———. *The Self as Agent.* London: Faber & Faber, 1957.

———. *Religion, Art & Science: A Study of the Reflective Activities in Man.* Toronto: John MacMurray Society, 1961.

———. *Persons in Relation.* London: Faber & Faber, 1961.

Mantzarides, George. "The Phenomenon of Secularization." *Greek Orthodox Theological Review* 25 (Spring 1980): 1-9.

Marcel, Gabriel. "The Sacred in the Technological Age." *Theology Today* 19 (1962): 27-38.

Marsden, George M. "The Collapse of American Evangelical Education." In *Faith and Rationality: Reason and Belief in God,* ed. Alvin Plantinga and Nicholas Wolterstorff, 219-64. Notre Dame: University of Notre Dame, 1983.

———. "Evangelicals and the Scientific Culture: An Overview." In *Religion and Twentieth-Century American Intellectual Life,* ed. Michael J. Lacey, 23-48. New York: Cambridge University Press, 1989.

———. "The Soul of the American University: A Historical Overview." In *The Secularization of the Academy,* ed. George M. Marsden and Bradley J. Longfield, 9-45. Oxford: Oxford University Press, 1992.

———. "God and Man at Yale (1800)." *First Things* (April 1994): 39-42.

———. *The Soul of the American University: From Protestant Establishment to Established Nonbelief.* New York: Oxford University Press, 1994.

Martin, David. "Towards Eliminating the Concept of Secularization." In *Penguin Survey of the Social Sciences,* ed. Julius Gould, 169-82. London: Penguin, 1965.

———. *The Religious and the Secular: Studies in Secularization.* London: Routledge & Kegan Paul, 1969.

———. *A General Theory of Secularization.* New York: Harper Colophon, 1978.

———. "General Tendencies and Historical Filters." *The Annual Review of the Social Sciences of Religion* 3 (1979): 1-16.

———. "The Clergy, Secularization, and Politics." *This World* 6 (Fall 1983): 131-42.

Marty, Martin E. *Varieties of Unbelief.* New York: Doubleday, 1964.

———. *The Modern Schism: Three Paths to the Secular.* London: S.C.M., 1969.

———. "The Sacred and Secular in American History." In *Transforming Faith: The Sacred and the Secular in Modern American History,* ed. M. L. Bradbury and James B. Gilbert, 1-10. New York: Greenwood Press, 1989.

Mascall, E. L. *The Secularization of Christianity: An Analysis and Critique.* New York: Holt, Rinehart & Winston, 1965.

Mathisen, James A. "Twenty Years After Bellah: Whatever Happened to American Civil Religion?" *Sociological Analysis* 50, no. 2 (1989): 129-46.

May, Henry. *The Enlightenment in America.* New York: Oxford University Press, 1976.

McFadyen, Alistair I. *The Call to Personhood: A Christian Theory of the Individual in Social Relationships.* Cambridge: Cambridge University Press, 1990.

McGrath, Alister E. *Luther's Theology of the Cross: Martin Luther's Theological Breakthrough.* Oxford: Basil Blackwell, 1985.

———. *The Intellectual Origins of the European Reformation.* Oxford: Blackwell, 1987.

McLeod, Hugh. "The Age of Religious Polarisation." *The Annual Review of the Social Sciences of Religion* 6 (1982): 1-22.

————. "Secular Cities?: Berlin, London, and New York in the Later Nineteenth and Early Twentieth Centuries." In *Religion and Modernization: Sociologists and Historians Debate the Secularization Thesis*, ed. Steve Bruce, 59-89. Oxford: Clarendon Press, 1992.

Meland, Bernard Eugene. *The Secularization of Modern Cultures*. New York: Oxford University Press, 1966.

Merton, Robert K. *Science, Technology and Society in Seventeenth-Century England*. New York: Harper & Row, 1970.

————. "Motive Forces of the New Science." In *Puritanism and the Rise of Modern Science: The Merton Thesis*, ed. I. Bernard Cohen, 112-31. New Brunswick, NJ: Rutgers University Press, 1990.

Michaelsen, Robert S. "Changes in the Puritan Concept of Calling or Vocation." *New England Quarterly* 26 (1953): 315-36.

Milbank, John. *Theology and Social Theory: Beyond Secular Reason*. Oxford: Basil Blackwell, 1990.

Miller, Samuel H. *The Dilemma of Modern Belief*. New York: Harper & Row, 1963.

Miller, Donald E. "Sectarianism and Secularization: The Work of Bryan Wilson." *Religious Studies Review* 5 (July 1979): 161-74.

Miller, John T., Jr. "Private Faith and Public Religion: S. T. Coleridge's Confrontation with Secularism." In *The Secular Mind: Transformations of Faith in Modern Europe*, ed. W. Warren Wager, 70-82. New York: Holmes & Meier, 1982.

Mol, J. J. "Secularization and Cohesion." *Review of Religious Research* 11 (March 1970): 183-91.

Molnar, Thomas. *Twin Powers: Politics and the Sacred*. Grand Rapids, MI: Eerdmans, 1988.

Mommsen, Wolfgang. *The Age of Bureaucracy: Perspectives on the Political Sociology of Max Weber*. Oxford: Basil Blackwell, 1974.

Moore, R. Laurence. "Secularization: Religion and the Social Sciences." In *Between the Times: The Travail of the Protestant Establishment in America 1900-1960*, ed. William R. Hutchison, 233-52. Cambridge: Cambridge University Press, 1989.

————. "Religion, Secularization, and the Shaping of the Culture Industry in Antebellum America." *American Quarterly* 41 (June 1989): 216-42.

Mueller, Gert. "The Notion of Rationality in the Work of Max Weber." *Archives Européennes de Sociologie* 20 (1979): 149-71.

Muggeridge, Malcolm. *Christ and the Media*. Grand Rapids, MI: Eerdmans, 1977.

Mumford, Lewis. *Technics and Civilization*. London: Routledge & Sons, 1934.

Murphey, Murray G. "On the Scientific Study of Religion in the United States, 1870-1980." In *Religion and Twentieth-Century American Intellectual Life*, ed. Michael J. Lacey, 136-71. New York: Cambridge University Press, 1989.

Murphy, H. R. "The Ethical Revolt against Christian Orthodoxy in Early Victorian England." *American Historical Review* 60 (1955).

Nelson, Benjamin. "Conscience and the Making of Early Modern Cultures: The Protestant Ethic beyond Max Weber." *Social Research* 36 (Spring 1969): 4-21.

Neuhaus, Richard John. *The Naked Public Square: Religion and Democracy in America.* Grand Rapids, MI: Eerdmans, 1984.

Newbigin, Lesslie. *Honest Religion for Secular Man.* Philadelphia: Westminster, 1966.

———. *Foolishness to the Greeks: The Gospel and Western Culture.* Grand Rapids, MI: Eerdmans, 1986.

———. "Can the West Be Converted?" *International Bulletin of Missionary Research* 11 (January 1987): 2-7.

———. *The Gospel in a Pluralist Society.* Grand Rapids, MI: Eerdmans, 1989.

———. "Truth and Authority in Modernity." In *Faith and Modernity,* ed. Philip Sampson, Vinay Samuel, and Chris Sugden. Oxford: Regnum/Lynx, 1994.

Niebuhr, Reinhold. "The Christian Church in a Secular Age." In *The Essential Reinhold Niebuhr: Selected Essays and Addresses,* ed. Robert McAffee Brown, 79-92. New Haven: Yale University Press, 1986.

Nisbet, Robert A. *The Sociological Tradition.* New York: Basic Books, 1966.

Noll, Mark A. "Christian Thinking and the Rise of the American University." *Christian Scholar's Review* 9 (1979): 3-16.

———. *The Scandal of the Evangelical Mind.* Grand Rapids, MI: Eerdmans, 1994.

Oakeshott, Michael. *Rationalism in Politics and Other Essays.* Indianapolis, IN: Liberty Press, 1962.

Oberman, Heiko. *The Harvest of Medieval Theology: Gabriel Biel and Late Medieval Nominalism.* 1963; Grand Rapids, MI: Eerdmans, 1967.

———. *Masters of the Reformation: The Emergence of a New Intellectual Climate in Europe.* Cambridge: Cambridge University Press, 1981.

Oddie, William. "Introduction." In *After the Deluge: Essays Towards the Desecularization of the Church,* ed. William Oddie, 1-38. London: S.P.C.K., 1987.

Oden, Thomas C. *After Modernity What?: Agenda for Theology.* Grand Rapids, MI: Zondervan, 1990.

Ortega y Gasset, José. *The Revolt of the Masses.* New York: Mentor, 1932.

Packer, J. I. "Christian Morality Adrift." In *A Society in Peril,* ed. Kevin Perotta and John C. Blattner. Ann Arbor, MI: Servant, 1989.

Pannenberg, Wolfhart. *Christianity in a Secularized World.* New York: Crossroad, 1989.

Parsons, Talcott. "Religion in a Modern Pluralistic Society." *Review of Religious Research* 7 (Spring 1966): 125-46.

———. "Christianity and Modern Industrial Society." In *Secularization and the Protestant Prospect,* ed. James F. Childress and David B. Harned, 43-70. Philadelphia: Westminster, 1970.

———. "Religion in Postindustrial America: The Problem of Secularization." *Social Research* 41 (1974): 193-225.

Paulson, Steven K. "Printed Advertisements as Indicators of Christian Institutional Secularization." *Review of Religious Research* 19 (Fall 1977): 77-83.

Pfautz, Harold W. "The Sociology of Secularization: Religious Groups." *American Journal of Sociology* 61 (1955): 121-28.

Pieper, Josef. *On Hope.* Translated by Sister Mary Frances McCarthy. San Francisco: Ignatius, 1986.

Postman, Neil. *Technopoly: The Surrender of Culture to Technology.* New York: Vintage, 1993.

Potter, David. *People of Plenty: Economic Abundance and the American Character.* Chicago: University of Chicago Press, 1968.

Pratt, Vernon. *Religion and Secularization.* New Studies in the Philosophy of Religion Series, ed. W. D. Hudson. London: Macmillan, 1970.

Ratzinger, Cardinal Joseph. "Concerning the Notion of Person in Theology." *Communio: International Catholic Review* 17 (Fall 1990): 439-54.

Rawlyk, G. A. "Protestant Colleges in Canada: Past and Future." In *The Secularization of the Academy,* ed. George M. Marsden and Bradley J. Longfield, 278-302. Oxford: Oxford University Press, 1992.

Richey, Russell E. "Methodism and Providence: A Study in Secularization." In *Protestant Evangelicalism: Britain, Ireland, Germany, and America c. 1750–c. 1950,* ed. Keith Robbins, 51-77. Oxford: Basil Blackwell, 1990.

Rieff, Philip. *The Triumph of the Therapeutic: Uses of Faith after Freud.* London: Chatto & Windus, 1966.

Riesman, David. *The Lonely Crowd: A Study of Changing American Character.* Garden City, NY: Anchor, 1956.

Ritzer, George. *The McDonaldization of Society.* Newbury Park, CA: Pine Forge, 1993.

Robertson, Roland. "A New Perspective on Religion and Secularization in the Global Context." In *Secularization and Fundamentalism Reconsidered: Religion and the Political Order,* ed. Jeffrey K. Hadden and Anson Shupe, 63-77. New York: Paragon, 1989.

Roth, Guenther. "Religion and Revolutionary Beliefs: Sociological and Historical Dimensions in Max Weber's Work — In Memory of Ivan Vallier (1927-1974)." *Social Forces* 2 (December 1976): 257-72.

Runia, Klaas. "The Challenge of the Modern World to the Church." *The European Journal of Theology* 2 (1993): 147-61.

Sandel, Michael. "The Procedural Republic and the Unencumbered Self." *Political Theory* 12 (1984): 81-96.

Satinover, Jeffrey Burke. "Psychology and the Abolition of Meaning." *First Things* (February 1994): 14-18.

Schall, James V. *The Distinctiveness of Christianity.* San Francisco: Ignatius, 1982.

Schiffhorst, Gerald J. "Some Prolegomena for the Study of Patience, 1480-1680." In *The Triumph of Patience: Renaissance Studies,* ed. Gerald J. Schiffhorst, 1-64. Orlando, FL: University Presses of Florida, 1978.

Schillebeeckx, Edward. "Silence and Speaking about God." *Theology* 71 (1968): 256-67.

Schluchter, Wolfgang. *The Rise of Western Rationalism: Max Weber's Developmental History.* Berkeley, CA: University of California Press, 1981.

Schmitz, Kenneth L. "Postmodern or Modern-Plus?" *Communio: International Catholic Review* 17 (Summer 1990): 152-66.

Seidman, Steven. *Liberalism and the Origins of European Social Theory.* Berkeley: University of California Press, 1983.

———. "Modernity, Meaning, and Cultural Pessimism in Max Weber." *Sociological Analysis* 44, no. 4 (1983): 267-78.

———. "Modernity and the Problem of Meaning: The Durkheimian Tradition." *Sociological Analysis* 46, no. 2 (1985): 109-30.

Shenk, Robert. "Robert Frost and the Early Puritan Idea of Vocation." *Christian Scholar's Review* 10, no. 3 (1981): 229-37.

Shils, Edward. *The Intellectuals and the Powers.* Chicago: University of Chicago Press, 1972.

Shiner, Larry. *The Secularization of History: An Introduction to the Theology of Friedrich Gogarten.* New York: Abingdon, 1966.

———. "The Meanings of Secularization." In *Secularization and the Protestant Prospect,* ed. James F. Childress and David B. Harned, 30-42. Philadelphia: Westminster, 1970.

Simmel, Georg. "The Metropolis and Mental Life." In *The Sociology of Georg Simmel,* ed. Kurt H. Wolff, 409-24. Glencoe, IL: The Free Press, 1950.

———. *The Philosophy of Money.* London: Routledge & Kegan Paul, 1978.

Slesinski, Robert. "Postmodernity and the Resources of the Christian East." *Communio: International Catholic Review* 17 (Summer 1990): 220-37.

Smith, Gary Scott. "The Great Secularization Debate." *The Reformed Journal* 35, no. 7 (1985): 15-19.

———. *The Seeds of Secularization: Calvinism, Culture, and Pluralism in America 1870-1915.* Grand Rapids, MI: Eerdmans, 1988.

Sommerville, John. "The Destruction of Religious Culture in Pre-Industrial England." *The Journal of Religious History* 15 (June 1988): 76-93.

———. *The Secularization of Early Modern England: From Religious Culture to Religious Faith.* New York: Oxford University Press, 1992.

Spadafora, David. "Secularization in British Thought, 1730-1789: Some Landmarks." In *The Secular Mind: Transformations of Faith in Modern Europe,* ed. W. Warren Wager, 35-56. New York: Holmes & Meier, 1982.

Stackhouse, Max L. "Godly Cooking? Theological Ethics and Technological Society." *First Things* (May 1991): 22-29.

Stark, Rodney. "On the Incompatibility of Religion and Science: A Survey of American Graduate Students." *Journal for the Scientific Study of Religion* 3 (1963): 3-20.

Stark, Rodney, and William Sims Bainbridge. "Secularization, Revival, and Cult Formation." *Annual Review of the Social Science of Religion* 4 (1980): 85-119.

———. "Secularization and Cult Formation in the Jazz Age." *Journal for the Scientific Study of Religion* 20, no. 4 (1981): 360-73.

———. *The Future of Religion: Secularization, Revival, and Cult Formation.* Berkeley: University of California Press, 1985.

Steiner, George. *Nostalgia for the Absolute.* Massey Lectures, Fourteenth Series. Toronto: Canadian Broadcasting Corporation, 1974.

———. *Real Presences.* Chicago: University of Chicago, 1989.

Stout, Harry S. "Puritanism Considered as a Profane Movement." *Christian Scholars Review* 10 (1980): 3-19.

Strauss, Leo. *Natural Right and History*. Chicago: University of Chicago Press, 1950.

———. "Comment on the Weber Thesis Reexamined." *Church History* 30 (1961): 100-102.

———. "The Crisis of Our Time." In *The Predicament of Modern Politics*, ed. Harold J. Spaeth, 41-54. Detroit: University of Detroit Free Press, 1964.

———. "The Crisis of Political Philosophy." In *The Predicament of Modern Politics*, ed. Harold J. Spaeth, 91-103. Detroit: University of Detroit Free Press, 1964.

———. "Niccolo Machiavelli." In *History of Political Philosophy*, ed. Leo Strauss and Joseph Cropsey, 296-317. Chicago: University of Chicago Press, 3rd edition, 1987.

———. *The Rebirth of Classical Political Rationalism: An Introduction to the Thought of Leo Strauss*. Introduced by Thomas L. Pangle. Chicago: University of Chicago Press, 1989.

———. "The Three Waves of Modernity." In *Introduction to Political Philosophy: Ten Essays*, ed. Hilail Gildin. Detroit: Wayne State University Press, 1989.

St. Victor, Richard of. "On the Trinity, Book III." In *Richard of St. Victor. Classics in Western Spirituality*. Edited by G. Zinn. New York: Paulist Press, 1979.

Sumithra, Sunand. "Syncretism, Secularization and Renewal." In *The Church in the Bible and the World*, ed. D. A. Carson. Grand Rapids, MI: Baker, 1987.

Swatos, William H., Jr. "Beyond Denominationalism?: Community and Culture in American Religion." *Journal for the Scientific Study of Religion* 20 (1981): 217-27.

———. "Enchantment and Disenchantment in Modernity: The Significance of 'Religion' as a Sociological Category." *Sociological Analysis* 44 (1983): 321-38.

Swidler, Ann. "The Concept of Rationality in the Work of Max Weber." *Sociological Inquiry* 43 (January 1973): 35-42.

Tawney, R. H. *The Acquisitive Society*. Rahway, NJ: Quinn & Boden, 1920.

———. *Religion and the Rise of Capitalism: A Historical Study*. 1926; New York: Harcourt, Brace & Company, 1952.

Taylor, Charles. *Sources of the Self: The Making of the Modern Identity*. Cambridge, MA: Harvard University Press, 1989.

———. "Inwardness and the Culture of Modernity." In *Zwischenbetrachtungen: Im Process der Aufklärung*, ed. Axel Honneth, Thomas McCarthy, Claus Offe, and Albrecht Wellmer, 601-23. Frankfurt am Main: Suhrkamp Verlag, 1989.

———. *The Malaise of Modernity*. Concord, Ontario: Anansi, 1991.

———. "The Politics of Recognition." In *Multiculturalism and "The Politics of Recognition,"* ed. Amy Gutman, 25-73. Princeton: Princeton University Press, 1992.

———. *The Ethics of Authenticity*. Cambridge, MA: Harvard University Press, 1993.

Thalheimer, Fred. "Religiosity and Secularization in the Academic Professions." *Sociology of Education* 46 (Spring 1973): 183-202.

Thomas, Keith. *Religion and the Decline of Magic*. New York: Charles Scribner's Sons, 1971.

Tinder, Glenn. *Against Fate: An Essay on Personal Dignity*. Loyola Lecture Series in Political Analysis, ed. Richard Shelley Hartigan. Notre Dame, IN: University of Notre Dame Press, 1981.

————. *The Political Meaning of Christianity: The Prophetic Stance, An Interpretation.* San Francisco: HarperSanFrancisco, 1989.

Tocqueville, Alexis de. *Democracy in America.* Translated by George Lawrence. Garden City, NY: Doubleday & Co./Anchor, 1969.

Torrance, Thomas F. *Reality and Scientific Theology.* Edinburgh: Scottish Academic Press, 1985.

————. *The Trinitarian Faith: The Evangelical Theology of the Ancient Catholic Church.* Edinburgh: T. & T. Clark, 1993.

Toulmin, Stephen. "The Historicization of Natural Science: Its Implications for Theology." In *Paradigm Change in Theology,* ed. Hans Küng and David Tracy. New York: Crossroad, 1989.

————. *Cosmopolis: The Hidden Agenda of Modernity.* Chicago: University of Chicago Press, 1990.

Trillling, Lionel. *Sincerity and Authenticity.* Cambridge, MA: Harvard University Press, 1971.

Troeltsch, Ernst. "The Ideas of Natural Law and Humanity in World Politics." In *Natural Law and the Theory of Society,* ed. Otto Giercke. Cambridge: Cambridge University Press, 1934.

————. *Protestantism and Progress: The Significance of Protestantism for the Rise of the Modern World.* Philadelphia: Fortress, 1986.

Trudinger, L. Paul. "The Gospel Meaning of the Secular: Reflections on Hebrews 13:10-13." *Evangelical Quarterly* 54 (October 1982): 235-37.

Tschannen, Olivier. "The Secularization Paradigm: A Systematization." *Journal for the Scientific Study of Religion* 30 (1991): 395-415.

Turner, Frank M., and Jeffrey Von Arx. "Victorian Ethics of Belief: A Reconsideration." In *The Secular Mind: Transformations of Faith in Modern Europe,* ed. W. Warren Wager, 83-101. New York: Holmes & Meier, 1982.

Turner, James. "Secularization and Sacralization: Speculations on Some Religious Origins of the Secular Humanities Curriculum, 1850-1900." In *The Secularization of the Academy,* ed. George M. Marsden and Bradley J. Longfield, 74-106. Oxford: Oxford University Press, 1992.

Van der Vloet, Johan. "Faith and the Postmodern Challenge." *Communio: International Catholic Review* 17 (Summer 1990): 132-40.

van Peursen, C. A. "Towards a Post-Secular Era: A First-World Contribution." *The Ecumenical Review* 41 (January 1989): 36-40.

Voegelin, Eric. *The New Science of Politics: An Introduction.* Chicago: University of Chicago Press, 1952.

————. "Liberalism and Its History." *Review of Politics* 37 (1974): 504-20.

Wager, W. Warren. "Introduction." In *The Secular Mind: Transformations of Faith in Modern Europe,* ed. W. Warren Wager, 1-14. New York: Holmes & Meier, 1982.

————. "World's End: Secular Eschatologies in Modern Fiction." In *The Secular Mind: Transformations of Faith in Modern Europe,* ed. W. Warren Wager, 239-64. New York: Holmes & Meier, 1982.

Wallace, Walter. "Rationality, Human Nature, and Society in Weber's Theory." *Theory and Society* 19 (1990): 199-223.

Wallis, Roy, and Steve Bruce. "Secularization: The Orthodox Model." In *Religion and Modernization: Sociologists and Historians Debate the Secularization Thesis*, ed. Steve Bruce, 8-30. Oxford: Clarendon Press, 1992.

Walsh, David. *After Ideology: Recovering the Spiritual Foundations of Freedom.* San Francisco: HarperCollins, 1990.

Walsh, Thomas. "Religion, Politics, and Life Worlds: Jürgen Habermas and Richard John Neuhaus." In *Secularization and Fundamentalism Reconsidered*, ed. Jeffrey K. Hadden and Anson Shupe, 91-106. New York: Paragon, 1989.

Walzer, Michael. "Puritanism as a Revolutionary Ideology." In *The Protestant Ethic and Modernization: A Comparative View*, ed. S. N. Eisenstadt, 109-34. New York: Basic Books, 1968.

Ware, Kallistos. "The Human Person as an Icon of the Trinity." *Sobornost* 8 (1986): 6-23.

Weber, Max. *The Protestant Ethic and the Spirit of Capitalism.* New York: Charles Scribner's Sons, 1958.

Webster, Charles. *The Great Instauration: Science, Medicine, and Reform 1626-1670.* New York: Holmes & Meier, 1976.

————. *From Paracelsus to Newton: Magic and the Making of Modern Science.* New York: Cambridge University Press, 1982.

Weigert, Andrew J. "Whose Invisible Religion? Luckmann Revisited." *Sociological Analysis* 35 (1974): 181-88.

Weizenbaum, Joseph. *Computer Power and Human Reason: From Judgment to Calculation.* San Francisco: W. H. Freeman, 1976.

Wells, David F. *No Place for Truth: or, Whatever Happened to Evangelical Theology?* Grand Rapids, MI: Eerdmans, 1993.

————. *God in the Wasteland: The Reality of Truth in a World of Fading Dreams.* Grand Rapids, MI: Eerdmans, 1994.

Wentworth, William M. "A Dialectical Conception of Religion and Religious Movements in Modern Society." In *Secularization and Fundamentalism Reconsidered*, ed. Jeffrey K. Hadden and Anson Shupe, 45-60. New York: Paragon, 1989.

West, Charles. "Community — Christian and Secular." In *Secularization and the Protestant Prospect*, ed. James F. Childress and David B. Harned, 117-34. Philadelphia: Westminster, 1970.

Westfall, Richard S. "Isaac Newton's *Theologiae Gentilis Origines Philosophicae*." In *The Secular Mind: Transformations of Faith in Modern Europe*, ed. W. Warren Wager, 15-34. New York: Holmes & Meier, 1982.

————. "The Rise of Science and the Decline of Orthodox Christianity: A Study of Kepler, Descartes, and Newton." In *God and Nature*, ed. David C. Lindberg and Ronald L. Numbers, 218-37. Berkeley: University of California Press, 1986.

Westoff, C. F., and E. E. Jones. "The Secularization of Birth Control Practice." *Family Planning Perspectives* 9 (1977).

Westphal, Merold. "Religious Experience as Self-Transcendence and Self-Deception." *Faith and Philosophy* 9 (April 1992): 168-93.

Whitehead, Alfred N. *Science and the Modern World*. London: Pelican, 1926.

Wiener, Norbert. *The Human Use of Human Beings: Cybernetics and Society*. London: Free Association Books, 2nd edition, 1954.

Wilson, Bryan R. "The Debate over Secularization: Religion, Society and Faith." *Encounter* 45 (1975): 77-84.

————. "Aspects of Secularization in the West." *Japanese Journal of Religious Studies* 3 (1976): 259-76.

————. *Contemporary Transformations of Religion*. Oxford: Oxford University Press, 1976.

————. "The Return of the Sacred." *Journal for the Scientific Study of Religion* 18 (September 1979): 268-80.

————. "Morality and the Modern Social System." In *Acts 16th Conference for the Sociology of Religion: Religion, Values, and Daily Life*, 339-60. Paris: C.I.S.R., 1981.

————. *Religion in Sociological Perspective*. New York: Oxford University Press, 1982.

————. "Secularization: The Inherited Model." In *The Sacred in a Secular Age*, ed. Philip E. Hammond, 9-20. Berkeley: University of California Press, 1985.

————. "Reflections on a Many Sided Controversy." In *Religion and Modernization: Sociologists and Historians Debate the Secularization Thesis*, ed. Steve Bruce, 195-210. Oxford: Clarendon Press, 1992.

Witten, Marsha G. *All Is Forgiven: The Secular Message in American Protestantism*. Princeton: Princeton University Press, 1993.

Wood, Douglas K. "The Twentieth Century Revolt against Time: Belief and Becoming in the Thought of Berdyaev, Eliot, Huxley, and Jung." In *The Secular Mind: Transformations of Faith in Modern Europe*, ed. W. Warren Wager, 197-219. New York: Holmes and Meier, 1982.

Wuthnow, Robert. "Recent Patterns of Secularization: A Problem of Generations?" *American Sociological Review* 41 (October 1976): 850-67.

————. "Science and the Sacred." In *The Sacred in a Secular Age*, ed. Philip E. Hammond, 187-203. Berkeley: University of California Press, 1985.

————. *The Restructuring of American Religion: Society and Faith since World War II*. Princeton: Princeton University Press, 1990.

————. *Rediscovering the Sacred: Perspectives on Religion in Contemporary Society*. Grand Rapids, MI: Eerdmans, 1992.

Yinger, J. Milton. "Pluralism, Religion, and Secularism." *Journal for the Scientific Study of Religion* 1 (1967): 17-28.

Zalen, Joseph. "Religious Apostasy, Higher Education, and Occupational Choice." *Sociology of Education* 41 (1968): 370-79.

Zizioulas, John D. "Human Capacity and Human Incapacity: A Theological Exploration of Personhood." *Scottish Journal of Philosophy* 28 (1975): 401-48.

————. *Being as Communion: Studies in Personhood and the Church*. Crestwood, NY: St. Vladimir's Seminary Press, 1985.

————. "On Being a Person: Towards an Ontology of Personhood." In *Persons Divine and Human: King's College Essays in Theological Anthropology*. Edited by Christoph Schwöebel and Colin E. Gunton, 33-46. Edinburgh: T. & T. Clark, 1991.

Index